International Joint Venture Performance in
South East Asia

NEW HORIZONS IN INTERNATIONAL BUSINESS

Series Editor: Peter J. Buckley
Centre for International Business,
University of Leeds (CIBUL), UK

The New Horizons in International Business series has established itself as the world's leading forum for the presentation of new ideas in international business research. It offers pre-eminent contributions in the areas of multinational enterprise – including foreign direct investment, business strategy and corporate alliances, global competitive strategies, and entrepreneurship. In short, this series constitutes essential reading for academics, business strategists and policy makers alike.

Titles in the series include:

Multinational Enterprises, Innovative Strategies and Systems of Innovation
Edited by John Cantwell and José Molero

Multinational Firms' Location and the New Economic Geography
Edited by Jean-Louis Mucchielli and Thierry Mayer

Free Trade in the Americas
Economic and Political Issues for Governments and Firms
Edited by Sidney Weintraub, Alan M. Rugman and Gavin Boyd

Economic Integration and Multinational Investment Behaviour
European and East Asian Experiences
Edited by Pierre-Bruno Ruffini

Strategic Business Alliances
An Examination of the Core Dimensions
Keith W. Glaister, Rumy Husan and Peter J. Buckley

Investment Strategies in Emerging Markets
Edited by Saul Estrin and Klaus E. Meyer

Multinationals and Industrial Competitiveness
A New Agenda
John H. Dunning and Rajneesh Narula

Foreign Direct Investment
Six Country Case Studies
Edited by Yingqi Annie Wei and V.N. Balasubramanyam

Japanese Multinationals in Europe
A Comparison of the Automobile and Pharmaceutical Industries
Ken-ichi Ando

International Joint Venture Performance in South East Asia
Craig C. Julian

Governance, Multinationals and Growth
Edited by Lorraine Eden and Wendy Dobson

European–American Trade and Financial Alliances
Edited by Gavin Boyd, Alan M. Rugman and Pier Carlo Padoan

International Joint Venture Performance in South East Asia

Dr Craig C. Julian

School of Commerce,
University of Adelaide,
South Australia

NEW HORIZONS IN INTERNATIONAL BUSINESS

Edward Elgar
Cheltenham, UK • Northampton, MA, USA

Published by
Edward Elgar Publishing Limited
Glensanda House
Montpellier Parade
Cheltenham
Glos GL50 1UA
UK

Edward Elgar Publishing, Inc.
136 West Street
Suite 202
Northampton
Massachusetts 01060
USA

A catalogue record for this book
is available from the British Library

ISBN 1 84376 094 0

Printed and bound in Great Britain by MPG Books Ltd, Bodmin, Cornwall

DEDICATION

I dedicate this book to my beautiful daughter Chloe, forever and always loved.

Contents

List of Tables and Figures   viii

1. Introduction   1
2. Trends and Characteristics of International Joint Ventures   20
3. Performance of International Joint Ventures   43
4. Market Characteristics and Performance   70
5. Conflict   87
6. Commitment and Performance   100
7. Product Characteristics   113
8. Marketing Orientation   126
9. Control   137
10. Trust   153
11. Partners' Contributions   165
12. Partners' Needs   180
13. Top Management Teams of International Joint Ventures   191
14. Equity Joint Ventures and the Theory of the Multinational
    Enterprise   214
15. Investing in Thailand via Joint Ventures   229
16. Legal Implications of Investing in Thailand   243
17. A Guide for Managers of International Joint Ventures   263
18. Future Research Agenda for International Joint Ventures in
    South East Asia   277

References   290
Index   351

List of Tables and Figures

TABLES

1.1	Country of Origin of Principal Foreign Partner	14
1.2	IJV Marketing Performance in Thailand	18
2.1	Equity Percentage of Principal Foreign Partner	41
2.2	Year in which IJV was Established	42
3.1	IJV Marketing Performance (using the composite measure)	62
3.2	IJV Marketing Performance (using the single-item measure)	65
3.3	IJV Marketing Performance via Country of Origin, Equity Structure, Industry Structure and IJV Sales Volume	66
4.1	Summary of Exploratory Factor Analysis	76
4.2	Exploratory Factor Analysis: Final Statistics	79
4.3	Mean Factor Scores	81
4.4	Multiple Regression Analysis	82
4.5	Summary of Univariate ANOVAs for the Discriminant Analysis	84
4.6	Classification of Results using the Discriminant Function	85
5.1	Canonical Discriminant Function Coefficients	97
5.2	Structure Matrix: Pooled Within-Groups Correlations Between Discriminating Variables and Canonical Discriminating Functions	98
5.3	Summary Table of Discriminant Analysis	98
10.1	Path Regression Results	162
13.1	Correlations of Variables	206
13.2	Path Regression Results	207
15.1	Year of IJV Formation	234
15.2	Industry Classification of IJV Formation	236
15.3	Country of Origin of the IJV's Principal Foreign Partner	237
15.4	A Summary of the IJV's Principal Foreign Partner by Country of Origin and by Year of Formation	237
15.5	Equity Percentage of the Principal Foreign Partner	240

FIGURES

13.1	Path Model	201

1. Introduction

Although the literature on international joint ventures (IJVs) is already sizeable and steadily growing, there is a paucity of studies on at least four critical issues relating to the growth of IJVs in the South East Asian economies. Firstly, the salient factors influencing the marketing performance of IJVs; secondly, the relative importance of the factors; thirdly, the measurement of the marketing performance of IJVs as opposed to overall business performance; and finally, the importance of marketing orientation to the overall marketing performance of IJVs. This book seeks to fill part of the gap in the existing literature. More specifically, it examines the antecedents of international joint venture marketing performance in South East Asia; investing in South East Asia, specifically Thailand, via IJVs; the legal implications of doing so; a guide for managers of IJVs for successful IJVs in South East Asia; and a suggested future research agenda for IJVs in South East Asia.

In general, an IJV is an equity sharing arrangement in which a foreign corporation and a local firm (either private or government owned) pool their resources, sharing risks and operational control to operate an independent business unit on a continuous basis for profit and/or to attain some strategic objectives (Geringer and Hebert, 1991). A 'factor' is a source variable that affects the outcome e.g., economic performance, stability, durability, interpartner relations, and level of conflict in the joint venture process. IJV performance is a measure of effectiveness of an IJV unit in attaining the relevant objectives or meeting the basic expectations of its parents.

1.1. Major Objectives

The major objectives of this study are (1) to examine the trends of IJVs in South East Asia, (2) to assess the marketing performance of IJVs in South East Asia (3) to identify the key factors influencing the marketing performance of IJVs in South East Asia, and (4) to evaluate the relative importance of the identified factors. Based on the IJV experiences of

1

foreign/based corporations (i.e. corporations based in Japan, North America, Australia, Europe and a number of developing countries) and host companies based in South East Asia (i.e. Singapore, Malaysia, Thailand, Indonesia, the Philippines etc.), firstly, this book examines the marketing performance of IJVs in South East Asia by taking into consideration both strategic and economic measures of performance. Secondly, it examines a range of salient factors influencing the marketing performance of IJVs in South East Asia. Finally, by taking into consideration several background characteristics of the firms being studied, it proceeds to evaluate the relative importance of the identified factors. In examining the factors influencing the marketing performance of IJVs in South East Asia this book focuses on the importance of marketing orientation as a significant factor influencing performance.

In the international business literature there are many studies that identify important determinants of IJV performance in general (Beamish, 1984, 1993; Chowdhury, 1989; Cullen *et al.*, 1995; Johnson *et al.*, 1993; Lee and Beamish, 1995; Luo and Chen, 1995; Madhok, 1995; Makino and Beamish, 1995). However, the literature does not adequately cover the issues relating to the marketing performance of IJVs. In the international business literature, studies on marketing performance are largely confined to those firms involved in direct or indirect exporting (Cavusgil and Zou, 1994; Cavusgil *et al.*, 1993; Chetty and Hamilton, 1993; Dominguez and Sequeira, 1993; Koh, 1991; Madsen, 1989; Namiki, 1989) with very little empirical evidence on the marketing performance of IJVs.

Schaan (1983) studied the relationship between parent control and IJV success based on a small sample of IJVs located in Mexico. As a useful avenue of future research he suggested: 'More research is needed to identify other factors which may be important in explaining JV success' (p. 344). Given that successful marketing performance is critical to overall successful business performance (Crocombe, 1991), and the deficiency in the level of empirical evidence on the marketing performance of IJVs, it was decided to focus on marketing performance in order to enhance the already significant body of IJV literature.

The marketing performance of an IJV defined as the degree to which the IJV's marketing objectives, both economic and strategic, with respect to a product/service are achieved in a foreign market (that foreign market being a South East Asian Country market) through the planning and implementation of a specific marketing plan. An IJV usually has a number of marketing objectives, which can be economic (i.e. profits, sales, return on investment, cost leadership and return on assets) and/or strategic (market expansion, access to raw materials, technology transfer, economies of scale, gaining a foothold in a foreign market and erecting entry barriers). Subsequent to the formulation and implementation of its marketing plan, some of the IJV's marketing objectives can be achieved fully, some only marginally, and others not at all. The extent to which an IJV's strategic and marketing objectives are achieved will therefore be a measure of its marketing performance.

There appears to be no uniform definition of marketing performance in the literature. There have been a variety of marketing performance measures adopted by previous researchers. These include sales growth (Cooper and Kleinschmidt, 1985; Kirpalani and Mckintosh, 1980; Madsen, 1989), market share and profitability (Anderson, 1990; Geringer and Hebert, 1991; Venkatraman and Ramanujam, 1986), technology transfer, durability, organisational learning and access to markets (Cullen *et al.*, 1995; Johnson *et al.*, 1993; Venkatraman and Ramanujam, 1986) and others. The most frequently used marketing performance measures appear to be economic in nature. However, as an IJV is a hybrid formed from two separate organisations, that may have different marketing objectives for the IJV and different time frames in which to achieve those objectives, this book includes both economic and strategic measures of marketing performance.

1.2. Scope of the Study

As a mode of ownership or participation, the IJV has been studied in the past from two different perspectives: from the point of view of the foreign parent; and from the point of view of the domestic parent (local partner, government, and host society). As IJVs are hybrids formed from two distinctly separate organisations, these organisations may have different objectives for the IJV entity and may evaluate the performance of the IJV differently. For example, one partner, the domestic partner, may rate the IJV as performing successfully because it is achieving its stated objectives of profitability and return on investment whilst the other partner, the foreign partner, may rate the IJV's performance as being unsatisfactory because it is refusing to use the raw materials of the foreign partner. Therefore, in order to assess the marketing performance of the IJV accurately it should be considered as a stand-alone entity (Julian, 1998). This supports the research findings of Anderson (1990) who argued that an IJV should be evaluated as a stand-alone entity.

As a result, this book examines the marketing performance of the IJVs being studied by considering only the perceptions of marketing performance of the most senior executive within the IJV entity itself. Arguably the most senior executive within the IJV entity itself is likely to be the best judge of how the IJV entity is actually performing. Therefore, only the IJV's most senior executive's perception of marketing performance will be considered.

An IJV by definition is a partnership arrangement between a foreign corporation and a local firm. The organisational form (i.e. the joint/structure involving sharing of equity ownership and control) itself tends to give rise to certain unique difficulties and problems (e.g., conflict of interest in the marketing channel) that can undermine its marketing performance and stability. As a matter of focus, this book concentrates on those unique difficulties and problems in addition to the positive influences that are likely to have the greatest influence on the marketing performance of the IJV.

The marketing performance of an IJV can be influenced by environmental issues both internal and external to the organisation. Environmental factors that are largely external to the IJV that can influence its marketing performance include adverse government policies (e.g., an institution or legislation that restricts or liberalises foreign ownership); market conditions such as a new entrant in the industry or increased price competition; economic conditions, in and outside the host country, such as a recession in the local and/or world economy, or a slump in the industry. Internal environmental issues may include inopportune timing of entry, limitations of product/service mix, lack of marketing channels to service consumers or users and the level of product and promotion adaptation required in an international market. Any organisation is susceptible to these factors regardless of whether it is wholly owned by a single firm or jointly owned and operated by more than one independent firm.

There are differences in national propensity to undertake IJVs, per se, and to undertake IJVs in different economic regions. In general, Japanese and European firms show a greater propensity to enter into IJVs in the developing regions (Beamish, 1984; Makino and Beamish, 1995). Hence, it is anticipated that Japanese and European firms together with North American firms will provide the majority of the foreign parents in IJV relationships in South East Asia. Accordingly, it is expected that the Japanese, Europeans and North Americans will provide the majority of Managing Directors for the IJVs under review. However, it is also anticipated that a large number of foreign parents will be from developing countries (Connolly, 1984), given the nature of this study.

1.3. Key Variables, Definitions and Terms

The literature has defined JVs and IJVs in a variety of ways so that many loosely defined international strategic alliances could be identified as being a JV as such. An analysis of the literature on international management, business law, political science, and accounting indicates that there is no unanimity regarding the definition of JVs. At times they are defined very broadly, including all types of cooperation between companies.

Bivens and Lovell (1966) defined a JV as pooled research and development, or joint purchasing or marketing or a whole host of cartel activities. In other words, all situations in which two or more persons or independent firms join forces to achieve some common goal. Gullander (1976) goes one step further and describes a JV as essentially an equity sharing arrangement between two or more independent firms. A more specific definition is offered by Young and Bradford (1977, p. 11) who defined a JV as:

> 'An enterprise, corporation or partnership, formed by two or more companies, individuals, or organisations, at least one of which is an operating entity which wishes to broaden its activities, for the purpose of conducting a new, profit-motivated business of permanent duration. In general, the ownership is shared by the participants with more or less equal equity distribution and without absolute dominance by one party.'

The more specific definitions emphasise the joint control over the venture (Liebman, 1975; Zaphiriou, 1978) by parent firms. Young and Bradford (1977) pointed out that different terms are used to describe parties who own and control IJVs: such as 'co-owners', 'co-venturers', 'partners', and 'parents'. From among these the term 'parents' is preferable as it emphasises both the independence of the JV as a separate legal entity as well as its partial dependence on those parties for raw materials, know-how, capital, trademarks, resources, markets, political support and/or personnel. The term also emphasises that the parties are economically independent of each other (Bernstein, 1965; Byrne, 1978; Spinks, 1978) and that a JV is a separate legal and organisational entity (Boyle, 1968; Dobkin *et al.,* 1986; Joelson and Griffin, 1975; King, 1969; Pfeffer and Knowack, 1976).

Evan (1978) defined an IJV as a multipartite structure, owned (and often managed) by at least two parent firms (typically one foreign and one host). This structure depends on cooperation among at least three different entities: the foreign firm, the host firm, and the IJV itself, each having its own organisation set. Shenkar and Zeira (1987, p. 547) also offer a definition that:

> 'An IJV is a separate legal organisational entity representing the partial holdings of two or more parent firms, in which the headquarters of at least one is located outside the country of operation of the JV.

This entity is subject to the joint control of its parent firms, each of which is economically and legally independent of the other.'

This view was supported by Harrigan (1988a) who identified JVs as business agreements whereby two or more owners create a separate entity. The JV can be a partnership or a corporation, or can issue corporate securities; however, no matter what the relationship there is some form of equity agreement between the partners. Kogut (1988) offered a similar definition of a JV, defining it as where at least two companies pool their resources to create a new, separate organisation. Koot (1988, p. 347) provided further support for this definition defining an IJV as a:

'Subsidiary company that is established by a corporation together with a partner company in a foreign country, the normal case being the multinational company from an industrialised economy having a share of some 20 percent or more in the equity of a company outside its home country, with the remainder of the equity being in possession of a company located in the country where the joint venture is to be established.'

Koot's definition of an IJV received support from Anderson (1990) and Gomes-Casseres (1989, p. 17) who defined an IJV 'as any affiliate of a MNC where the equity is partly owned by another firm, usually one from the host country'. Gomes-Casseres' definition excluded non-equity cooperative ventures, such as licensing. Hennart (1988, p. 361) also differentiated between equity and non-equity joint ventures, identifying equity JVs as:

'Whenever two or more sponsors bring given assets to an independent legal entity and are paid for some or all of their contribution from the profits earned by the entity, or when a firm acquires partial ownership of another firm. The term "non-equity JV" describes a wide array of contractual arrangements, such as licensing, distribution, and supply agreements, or technical assistance and management contracts.'

Therefore, based on the previous definitions of JVs and IJVs in the literature, for the purpose of this book the following definitions of joint ventures (JVs) and international joint ventures (IJVs) will be applied. Firstly, with regards to JVs, JVs will involve two or more legally distinct organisations (the parents), each of which shares in the decision-making activities of the jointly owned entity and each of which has a minimum of 5 percent equity and a maximum of 95 percent equity in the jointly owned entity. Although there is no consensus on a cut-off point that should be used to distinguish a JV from a wholly owned subsidiary (Horaguchi, 1992), the international business literature has used 95 percent as a cut-off point to differentiate a JV and a wholly owned subsidiary. For example, major studies that have used the 95 percent cut-off point include Anderson and Gatignon (1986), Franko (1971), Gomes-Casseres (1989), Hennart (1991) and Stopford and Wells (1972). Therefore, this study follows the above convention and uses a 95 percent cut-off point. It will be considered to be an IJV when at least one parent is headquartered outside the venture's country of operation, or if the IJV has a significant level of operations in more than one country (Geringer and Hebert, 1989, 1991).

As authors in international marketing and international business have not agreed upon a uniform set of terminologies, definitions of some of the key terms used in this research are given below.

Foreign corporation is used synonymously with multinational corporation, international corporation, and multinational firm and is defined as any firm, large, medium or small, with headquarters outside the host country.

A wholly owned subsidiary (WOS) or company is defined as an enterprise that is more than 95 percent owned by the foreign parent. Although there is no consensus on a cut-off point that should be used to distinguish a JV from a wholly owned subsidiary (Horaguchi, 1992), the international business literature has used 95 percent or less as a cut-off point to differentiate a JV from a wholly owned subsidiary. Therefore, this study follows the above convention and uses a 95 percent cut-off point.

A joint venture (JV) is where an organisation is made up of two or more legally distinct organisations (the parents), each of which shares in the decision-making activities of the jointly owned entity, and each of which has a minimum of 5 percent equity ownership of the jointly owned entity and 95 percent or less equity of the jointly owned entity (Anderson and Gatignon, 1986; Franko, 1971; Gomes-Casseres, 1989; Hennart, 1991; Stopford and Wells, 1972).

An international joint venture (IJV) is when at least one parent is headquartered outside the venture's country of operation (Geringer and Hebert, 1989, 1991).

International joint venture (IJV) marketing performance is defined as the degree to which the IJV's marketing objectives, both economic and strategic, with respect to a product/service are achieved in a foreign market through the planning and implementation of a specific marketing plan. An IJV usually has a number of marketing objectives, which can be either economic (i.e. profit, sales, return on investment, production costs or return on assets) and/or strategic (market expansion, access to raw materials, technology transfer, economies of scale, gaining a foothold in a foreign market or erecting barriers to entry). The extent to which the IJV's strategic and economic objectives are achieved will be the measure used to determine the marketing performance of the IJV.

Other key variables in this research include the effect of the key IJV antecedents on performance, those key antecedents being market characteristics, conflict, commitment, product characteristics, marketing orientation, control, trust, partner's contributions and partner's needs (Julian, 1998).

Following a series of pilot survey interviews conducted in Bangkok, Thailand, the potential impact of these variables upon marketing performance emerged. In the subsequent focus on these variables, trust, partner's needs and partner's contributions were not included in any further analysis because the constructs used to measure these phenomena had low reliabilities. They have still been included as antecedents of performance in this research because of their acknowledged impact on performance from previous research (Beamish, 1988; Fey, 1995; Fey and Beamish, 2000; Madhok, 1995; Sohn, 1994). Market characteristics were assessed based on the adequacy of the supply of capital resources, the adequacy of supply of certain raw materials (Beamish and Banks, 1987), the availability of distribution channels (Jacque, 1986), the knowledge of local business practices by at least one of the foreign partners (Blodgett, 1991a), the transference of much needed new technology (Lecraw, 1984), the influence of host country government intervention (Beamish, 1984) and the influence of industry price competition (Christensen *et al.,* 1987). Conflict was assessed based on the conflict between the partners over the roles and functions to be performed by each of the partners, the conflict between the partners over the staffing policies for the IJV and the conflict between the partners over the terms and conditions of the IJV contract (Habib, 1987). Commitment was assessed based on the commitment to the IJV by the foreign parent, the IJV partners' capital and resource contributions and the specific human resource contributions made by the IJV partners (Lee and Beamish, 1995). Product characteristics were assessed based on the stage of the product life cycle the products/services were in, the level of product/service adaptation required for the local market, consumer familiarity with the IJV's products/services, standardisation of the promotional campaign and the culture-specificity of the product/service

(Cavusgil and Zou, 1994). Firm-specific characteristics were assessed based on the unit value of the IJV's products/services, the uniqueness of the IJVs products/services (Cavusgil and Zou, 1994) and relating customer expectations as a measure against which the IJV evaluates its performance (Pitt and Jeantrout, 1994). Marketing orientation was assessed based on how regularly senior management contacts customers to determine their needs and to better understand their business, how frequently the IJV conducts research among its customers in order to find out what they expect of its products/services, and how regularly the IJV attempts to assess the impact that the prices of its products/services have on customer expectations (Pitt and Jeantrout, 1994). Control was divided between organisational control and managerial control. Organisational control was assessed based on transferring a large proportion of the IJV's outputs (e.g., profits or components for a future production process) to a parent company and the sourcing of much of the input needs of the IJV from a parent company (Dymsza, 1988). Managerial control was assessed based on one parent's overall managerial control of the IJV entity (Dymsza, 1988). Finally, one statement was included to assess adapting to foreign market needs. This assessed the extent to which the foreign parents were willing to adapt the IJVs products/services to meet the needs of the local market (Beamish, 1988).

The dependent variable – joint venture marketing performance – was assessed based on the respondent's level of satisfaction with the achievement of certain strategic objectives for which the IJV was set up to achieve. Using the literature and the pre-tests of the research instrument, strategic objectives were pre-set in the research instrument that corresponded with each of the measures of marketing performance. Towards the end of the research instrument, respondents were asked to indicate the relative importance attached to each objective by allocating a constant-sum (100 points) to the individual objectives proportional to their importance. Joint venture marketing performance was calculated by computing the extent to which each of the strategic objectives was achieved by multiplying the level of satisfaction associated with the achievement of each strategic objective by the points allocated to the importance of the same strategic objective. The combined scores for each of the strategic objectives were then added together to give a composite score for each IJV for measuring IJV marketing performance.

The research also investigated the impact of a number of independent variables (e.g., equity participation, industry etc.) considered important by researchers examining joint venture performance primarily in developed countries. Investigation of their effect upon performance represents a replication of the work of other researchers, to some extent, although on what was considered to be a different population of joint ventures – joint ventures in the developing countries of South East Asia.

1.4. Methodology

Data were gathered by Julian (1998) in four stages on a total of 161 joint ventures located in Thailand. Within the first stage, which consisted of personal interviews with ten Managing Directors of IJVs located in Thailand on four separate occasions, emphasis was placed on establishing content validity of the research instrument. At stage two, questionnaires were administered to the Managing Director of the IJV entity of 831 IJVs located in Thailand. After a telephone follow-up encouraging all those who hadn't responded to do so a second-round mailing was implemented resulting in 161 useable questionnaires accounting for an effective response rate of 19.38 percent. This attempt to assess IJV marketing performance using a subjective performance measure and only assessing the IJV's perception of performance represents a major point of departure from many previous works on joint venture performance. In this research, the interest was to obtain the most accurate perception and evaluation of overall IJV marketing performance, as the principal objective was to identify those factors that had the greatest influence on IJV marketing performance. Therefore, this research adopted Anderson's (1990) viewpoint and sought only the IJV entity's perception of marketing performance as it was the position taken in this research that the IJV should be evaluated as a stand-alone entity in order to identify the most accurate perception of marketing performance. Also, Dess and Robinson (1984) and Geringer and Hebert (1991) identified that there was a strong positive relationship between how one of the IJV partners viewed IJV performance and how the senior executive within the IJV entity viewed performance.

The primary setting for the research was Thailand, where the subject of IJV marketing performance was explored through an empirical investigation of those foreign corporations in IJV relationships with Thai companies in the Republic of Thailand. The IJVs studied came from a wide cross-section of industries, including agriculture; mining; light industries such as gems, jewellery and textiles; machinery and transport equipment; electrical and electronic industries; chemical industries; and services. The firms comprising the sample were provided by the Thai Board of Investment (BOI, 1996).

The major steps followed to accomplish the research objectives can be outlined as follows. First, on the basis of an extensive review of prior literature, a wide range of potentially important variables that were likely to influence the performance of IJVs in Thailand were identified. Second, from the initial list, those variables that were specifically related to marketing performance were identified and isolated. For the purpose of a mailed questionnaire survey, the list of marketing performance variables was far too inclusive. The number of variables was, therefore, systematically reduced to a smaller subset of the original list of variables based on the importance of the respective variable as identified in the literature review.

Third, the variables were then incorporated into a preliminary questionnaire and pre-tested through a medium of personal interviews with the Managing Directors of ten foreign/Thai IJVs located in Thailand on four separate occasions. Input from the pre-tests was used for two purposes: to further cut down the number of variables and to refine the questionnaire. On the basis of the pre-tests a final, more condensed and specific list of variables was identified to examine IJV marketing performance.

Pre-tests of the draft questionnaire were conducted to see how the questionnaire would perform under actual conditions of data collection. As the questionnaire was a new research instrument, without any previous history of being able to provide the desired information, it was considered essential that the questionnaire be pre-tested. Also, the questionnaire pre-tests would provide the real test of the questionnaire's level of acceptability and the mode of administration (Churchill, 1987).

The pre-tests of the questionnaire were used to assess both individual questions and their sequencing. On each of the four separate occasions the Managing Directors of ten IJVs were interviewed to see if the respondent was able to access the information requested, to see if any of the questions asked seemed confusing, and to see if any of the questions produced respondent resistance or hesitancy for one reason or another, e.g., confidentiality of financial details requested. On each occasion, the personal interview pre-tests revealed some questions in which the wording needed to be improved and in which the sequence of words needed to be changed. However, the changes were only minor.

Finally, the ultimate questionnaire was mailed to a sample of 831 IJVs in Thailand provided by the Thai Board of Investment (BOI, 1996). The ultimate questionnaire was forwarded by mail from Australia to the Managing Director of the IJV in Thailand. It was expected that for small or medium-sized companies the Managing Director is likely to be the person responsible for most or all of the marketing functions and therefore, the person most knowledgeable about the organisation's marketing performance. Many small or medium-sized companies in Thailand could not afford the appointment of middle management and a marketing manager. It was also expected that many Thai IJVs would be classified as medium to small given the nature of the industry classifications. For larger companies, where the Managing Director was not directly responsible for the organisation's marketing function it was expected that the Managing Director, as Chief Executive Officer, would re-direct the questionnaire to the appropriate executive within the organisation.

Included in the direct mail package to the respondents were instructions requesting the respondent to forward the completed questionnaire in the stamped self-addressed envelope provided to a Professor at Bangkok University who had agreed to coordinate the data collection. This was arranged to ensure that the best possible response rate would be achieved. It was felt that the response rate would be improved if the respondents were able to return the questionnaires to a well-known and well-respected Thai institution as opposed to an Australian institution that they knew nothing about.

Having finalised the questionnaire, the method of data collection was that of a self-administered mail survey, consisting of both scaled response and open-ended questions, directed to the Managing Director of the IJV entity. The self-administered mail survey consisted of a questionnaire with a covering letter mailed to the respondent from Australia and the return by mail of the completed questionnaire in the stamped self-addressed envelope provided to a Professor at Bangkok University. As soon as the last remaining questionnaires had been returned the available questionnaires were collected from Bangkok University. The covering letter together with each instruction and corresponding statement of the questionnaire had both an English and Thai translation.

After the pre-tests it became obvious that it was necessary to provide both an English and Thai translation of each statement as some of the respondents proved to be Thai nationals and felt more comfortable answering in Thai. Some respondents that were also Thai nationals could not speak any English whatsoever and still other respondents proved to be expatriates that felt more comfortable responding in English. Therefore, in order to accommodate both types of respondents it was deemed necessary to provide both an English and Thai translation of each statement. Once the statements were translated into Thai they were then translated back into English to ensure the Thai translation was conveying to the respondent the meaning that was intended.

The sample of joint ventures was not a random sample of joint ventures in the region. A census sample of joint ventures between foreign and local Thai firms, in one country (Thailand), was used. However, this was not considered to be an issue as Thailand was central to all South East Asian nations, its foreign investment policies, especially in relation to the IJV, were similar to that of Singapore, Malaysia, Indonesia, the Philippines and other South East Asian nations and its economic growth rate was equal to or better than all other South East Asian nations at the time. Therefore, the sample of IJVs provided by the Thai Board of Investment (BOI, 1996) for Thailand as a form of foreign direct investment (FDI) should be representative of other South East Asian nations. Furthermore, the sample of IJVs provided by the Thai Board of Investment (BOI, 1996) was by far the largest one available from all South East Asian nations and demonstrated a wide diversity of foreign partners consistent with their trends in FDI (Julian, 2001). The sampling frame provided by the Thai Board of Investment (BOI) was a recent publication, published in February 1996, of the list of IJVs in Thailand between foreign companies and Thai companies. It should be considered a reliable source of IJVs in Thailand as the BOI is a government organisation operating from the Office of the Prime Minister and is the principal government agency responsible for providing investment incentives to stimulate investment in Thailand. The Thai Board of Investment (BOI, 1996) provided a list of over 2,000 companies that detailed whether or not the company concerned was in an IJV relationship with a foreign company. The total number of companies that were identified as being in an IJV relationship from the initial list of 2,000 companies was 831 and that was the sample size used for this study.

The companies could be involved in any industry, from manufacturing to agriculture to services. No restriction was placed on the type of industry to which the participating companies in the IJV can be involved with. The only restrictions that were placed on the participating companies in the IJVs being studied were, firstly, no one partner can have greater than 95 percent equity participation in the IJV. Secondly, each partner must have a minimum of 5 percent equity participation in the IJV.

In examining the composition of the sample, the research focuses on the country of origin of the principal foreign partner, equity participation of the principal foreign partner, IJV formation by year, nationality of the respondent, position of the respondent within the organisation, industry classification of the IJV and sales volume of the sample of joint ventures. As far as the country of origin of the principal foreign partner (see Table 1.1) was concerned, knowledge of the country of origin of the principal foreign partner helps understand the nature and structure of IJV formation. In this sample of 161 Thai IJVs, the three largest contributors of IJV formation by far were Japan (providing the principal foreign partner in 49.6 percent of cases), Western Europe (providing the principal foreign partner in 19.9 percent of cases), and the newly industrialised economy (NIE) of Taiwan (providing the principal foreign partner in 12 percent of cases). Between them Japan, Western Europe and Taiwan provided the principal foreign partner in 80.6 percent of cases for the Julian (1998) study. This is an important contribution, especially in the case of Japan, which provided almost half of the principal foreign IJV partners for the Julian study.

Table 1.1 Country of Origin of Principal Foreign Partner

ID	Europe	North America	Japan	Taiwan	Korea	ASEAN	Hong Kong	Tot
(%)	19.9	6.4	49.6	12.0	5.0	5.7	1.4	100

Equity Percentage of Principal Foreign Partner

Equity (%)	5-9	10-19	20-29	30-39	40-49	50-59	60-69	70-95	Tot
(%)	2.2	7.9	9.3	9.3	35.3	13.0	5.0	18.0	100

IJV Formation By Year

Year	1960-1970	1971-1980	1981-1985	1986-1990	1991-1995	Tot.
(%)	5.4	8.7	10.7	53.7	21.5	100

Nationality of the Respondent

ID	Europe	North America	India	Japan	China	Korea	Thailand	Tot
(%)	10.1	4.7	0.7	8.1	5.4	0.7	70.3	100

Position of the Respondent Within the Organisation

ID	MD	Mktg. Mgr	Off. Mgr	Acct.	Sen. Exec	Clerical	Tot
(%)	56.2	6.8	3.4	1.4	29.5	2.7	100

Industry Classification of the IJV

ID	Agric	Min	Light	Metal	Elect	Chem	Serv	Tot
(%)	24.1	4.2	10.3	20.7	16.6	19.3	4.8	100

Sales Volume of IJVs in Thailand

$US million	Below 5	5- 10	10- 25	25- 50	50- 75	75- 100	Over 100	Tot
(%)	18.1	27.1	22.2	13.2	4.8	4.2	10.4	100

As far as equity participation of the principal foreign partner was concerned, much has been written about equity participation of the foreign partner (Beamish, 1988; Sohn, 1994). Many researchers claim for an IJV to perform successfully the foreign partner must maintain control over the local partner and the IJV relationship (Al-Aali, 1987; Killing, 1983; Phatak and Chowdhury, 1991) and one of the best ways to achieve that is through majority equity participation in the IJV. However, in many developing countries this is becoming increasingly difficult to do. Host country governments through government legislation, especially in the developing countries of South East Asia, are restricting foreign companies to minority equity participation in industries which are not considered essential to national security, and in industries where they already have access to the latest technology.

There are also other researchers who believe there are better ways for a foreign corporation to control a local partner than through majority equity participation (Sohn, 1994). There are still other researchers that have shown where foreign companies have been prepared to take a minority share in the IJV and make a commitment to a developing-country market, minority equity participation has been a major factor in successful business performance (Beamish, 1988; Cullen *et al.,* 1995).

Knowledge of equity participation by foreign corporations in IJV relationships helps academics and policy makers alike to understand the IJV climate and structure (see Table 1.1). As with previous studies (Higginbottom, 1980), the sample of 161 Thai/foreign IJVs in the Julian (1998) study revealed a similar trend with 64.0 percent of the sample showing the principal foreign partner as having equity participation of 49 percent or less. In real terms this represents 89 firms where the foreign partner had 49 percent or less equity participation. This continuing trend of minority equity participation by the principal foreign partner demonstrates that it is likely to be commonplace for the principal foreign partner to have minority equity participation in IJVs in Thailand and other South East Asian nations. This is in part due to the Alien Business Law (1972) that restricted majority equity participation by foreign firms in certain industries, and is an important finding as it may influence how IJV marketing performance was perceived, especially by the foreign partner or non-Thai respondents.

As far as IJV formation by year was concerned, from Table 1.1 it was possible to identify two periods during which IJV formation exhibited distinctly different trends in the Julian (1998) study. (1) Between 1960 and 1985 out of a sample of 161 companies IJV formation was relatively low with only 24.8 percent of IJVs in the sample being formed during this period. This represents a very small percentage of the total. This is especially the case when you consider that this period represents nearly three-quarters (71 percent) of the total period (35 years) being examined. (2) Between 1986 and 1995 the growth rate of IJV formation in Thailand showed outstanding growth, growing threefold over the previous 25-year period. During this ten-year period 75.2 percent of all IJVs in the Julian (1998) sample were formed. This is quite a remarkable achievement considering there was a slowing in economic growth during this period from 9.7 percent in 1986 to 8.6 percent in 1995 (Far Eastern Economic Review, 1995), a slowing in total FDI (Economic and Social Commission for Asia and the Pacific, 1995), and three changes of government.

As far as the nationality of the respondent and the position of the respondent within the organisation were concerned, it was evident that the principal respondents in the Julian (1998) study were Thai nationals and Managing Directors or senior executives of their respective companies. Table 1.1 indicates that 70.3 percent of respondents in the Julian study were Thai nationals, identifying the importance of having the research instrument translated into Thai. A further 14.2 percent of respondents were of North Asian origin (i.e. Japanese, Chinese and Korean). This meant that a very large percentage of the respondents (84.5 percent) were of Asian origin, an important finding in itself as it may have an influence on how IJV marketing performance was perceived.

Table 1.1 also indicates that a very large percentage of the respondents were senior executives within their organisations and as such have an adequate level of knowledge on how the IJV was actually performing. This is evidenced by the data with 56.2 percent of respondents being classified as Managing Directors of their respective organisations and a further 29.5 percent of respondents being classified as senior executives within their respective organisations, indicating that 85.7 percent of respondents were senior executives within their organisations. Those respondents that were classified as senior executives were further identified as Directors, Vice-Presidents, Presidents, General Managers, Production Managers and Factory Managers, indicating that the sample respondent had an adequate level of knowledge on how the IJV was actually performing in relation to the dimensions of this research.

As far as industry classification of the IJV was concerned, from Table 1.1 it was evident that there had been an even spread of IJV activity across four industry groupings. Those industry groupings being agriculture (with 24.1 percent of IJV activity); metal working industries (with 20.7 percent of IJV activity); chemical industries (with 19.3 percent of IJV activity); and electrical industries (with 16.6 percent of IJV activity). Together the industry groupings of agriculture, metal working, chemical and electrical accounted for 80.7 percent of IJV activity in the Julian (1998) study. The remaining industry groupings of mining, light industries and service industries were surprising in their limited IJV activity, light industries and service industries especially. The light industries classification incorporated many of the smaller firms, and having such a broad classification, it was expected that many of the IJVs would come from this classification. As far as the service industries were concerned, as Thailand moves rapidly towards developed-country status it was expected there would be many more IJVs formed in the service industries classification, especially in the industries of transportation, hospitality, and finance. However, jointly the industry groupings of mining, light industries and service industries only accounted for 19.3 percent of IJV activity and that is very small considering the nature of these industries.

Finally, as far as the sales volume of the IJV's products/services were concerned, the important issue here was one regarding company size. Firstly, 80.6 percent of the Julian (1998) sample companies had sales volumes less than US$50 million with 45.2 percent of the sample having sales volumes less than US$10 million. This means that these companies could be classified as small and medium-sized organisations. Finally, the reasonably small percentage (10.4 percent) of companies having sales volumes in excess of US$100 million indicates that these companies could be classified as reasonably large organisations. The important finding here is that the companies in this sample are predominantly small and medium-sized organisations and the results of the study should only be applied to small and medium sized organisations. If the sample was made up of predominantly large organisations there could have been a different result.

The basis for the measure of IJV marketing performance used in this study assessed the achievement of specific research objectives. Using the literature and the pre-tests of the research instrument, strategic objectives were pre-set in the research instrument that corresponded with each of the measures of marketing performance. Towards the end of the research instrument, respondents were asked to indicate the relative importance attached to each objective by allocating a constant-sum (100 points) to the individual objectives proportional to their importance. This measure of marketing performance computed the extent to which each of the strategic objectives was achieved by multiplying the level of satisfaction associated with the achievement of each strategic objective by the points allocated to the importance of the same strategic objective. The combined scores for each of the strategic objectives were then added together to give a composite score for each IJV for measuring IJV marketing performance. The findings are summarised in Table 1.2.

Table 1.2 IJV Marketing Performance in Thailand

Marketing Performance Score	Frequency	Percent	Cumulative Percent
100 – 400 (Low Performers)	41	27.7	27.7
401 – 500 (Med Performers)	55	37.1	64.8
501 – 700 (High Performers)	52	35.2	100.0
Total	148	100.0	

As indicated, this measure of marketing performance computed the extent to which each of the strategic objectives was achieved by multiplying the level of satisfaction associated with the achievement of each strategic objective by the points allocated to the importance of each strategic objective. The level of satisfaction associated with the achievement of each strategic objective was measured from 1 to 7 on a seven-point Likert Scale, with 1 being identified as extremely dissatisfied and 7 being identified as extremely satisfied. Thus, the weighted score of marketing performance for an IJV will fall between 100 and 700 points.

As the mid-point of the seven-point Likert Scale was identified as being 4 (or 400 using this measure of marketing performance), IJVs were classified as being low marketing performers if they had a marketing performance score of 400 or below; they were classified as being medium marketing performers if they had a marketing performance score of between 401 and 500; and they were classified as being high marketing performers if they had a marketing performance score of above 500.

Marketing performance scores ranged from a minimum of 128 to a maximum of 700 with a mean score of 419, a median score of 457, and a standard deviation of 162. This indicates that overall the majority of companies (72.3 percent of companies) were identified as having medium or high marketing performance. It was also evident after analysing Table 1.2 that the dispersion of marketing performance scores identifying whether the IJV was a low marketing performer, medium marketing performer or high marketing performer were evenly spread across the sample. From Table 1.2 it was apparent that 27.7 percent of the sample or 41 IJVs were identified as low marketing performers; 37.1 percent of the sample or 55 IJVs were identified as medium marketing performers; and 35.2 percent of the sample or 52 IJVs were identified as high marketing performers. This indicates that the IJVs in this sample were well represented at each level of marketing performance.

2.   Trends and Characteristics of International Joint Ventures

Viewed broadly, the IJV phenomenon represents two opposing trends. First, judged by the number of entries, it is becoming increasingly popular as a strategic mode of overseas market entry and expansion (Beamish and Delios, 1997a; Makino and Beamish, 1998; Vanhonacker and Pan, 1997). In recent years an increasing number of global corporations have become involved in IJVs at home and overseas. The composition of firms adopting the IJV entry mode covers many sectors, industries and product groups (Beamish, 1984; Beamish and Inkpen, 1995; Dymsza, 1988; Griffith *et al.,* 2001; Harrigan, 1987; Julian, 1998; Lee and Beamish, 1995; Makino and Beamish, 1995; Tybejee, 1988).

Secondly, IJVs have been shown to be a fragile entity, where it has been repeatedly argued that the failure rate of IJVs is above 30 percent, and it is often markedly higher compared to other alternative forms of market entry and operation (Gomes-Casseres, 1988a; Hennart *et al.,* 1998; Hambrick *et al.,* 2001; Kogut, 1988; Makino and Beamish, 1998; Park and Russo, 1996; Park and Ungson, 1997). The significance of a robust growth trend is somewhat overshadowed by the high incidence of failure (Killing, 1983; Lane and Beamish, 1990; Makino and Beamish, 1998; Yan, 1998) and JV failure is often costly and extremely frustrating for both partners (Cullen *et al.,* 1995). Gomes-Casseres (1989) offers two explanations for reasons of instability in any JV, including that the partners simply made a mistake in forming a JV when it may not have been the best thing to do, or they joined up with the wrong partner. Also, their initial decision could have been right, but conditions changed so that the JV was no longer useful.

2.1. Growth of International Joint Ventures

As far as the increased popularity of the IJV as a strategic mode of overseas market entry is concerned, since the early 1960s, researchers have claimed that the use of JVs, especially by MNCs (multinational corporations), had been increasing (Beamish, 1984; Beamish and Delios, 1997a; Gomes-Casseres, 1988a; Hergert and Morris, 1988; Hladik, 1988; Julian, 1998; Koot, 1988; Lee and Beamish, 1995; Madhok, 1995; Makino and Beamish, 1998; Oman, 1988). With significant fluctuations, the yearly share of JVs in new manufacturing subsidiaries grew about 10 percent in the first decade of the last century to over 50 percent in the early 1960s. Just as striking as this rising trend was a sharp decline in JV use during most of the 1960s. The yearly share of JVs in new subsidiaries fell continuously from 55 percent in 1961 to 31 percent in 1968 (Gomes-Casseres, 1988a; Harrigan, 1988a).

A closer look at the post-war period revealed other surprising trends. There appear to have been two and a half cycles in MNC's use of JVs at entry. From 1946 to 1951, the yearly share of JVs in new entries rose from 15 percent to over 50 percent; after that, it fell to 28 percent in 1955. Then came another rise to the 55 percent peak in 1961, followed by the decline to 31 percent. A third increase began in 1969, with the share of JVs reaching 41 percent in 1975. These JV entry trends appear to be closely correlated to trends in ownership changes after entry. On average over the 1945-75 period, 21 percent of JVs were eventually reorganised into wholly owned subsidiaries (Gomes-Casseres, 1988a).

One explanation for the rise in IJVs in some periods might be that the foreign corporations were diversifying as they went abroad. The number of new subsidiaries that were outside each MNC's main product line increased sharply in the late 1940s and then fell gradually after the late 1950s (Gomes-Casseres, 1985, p. 431). Previous studies have also shown that this factor sometimes encouraged IJVs (Beamish, 1984; Beamish and Inkpen, 1995; Gomes-Casseres, 1987; Harrigan, 1988a; Lee and Beamish, 1995). This trend might also explain increases in IJV use in the late 1940s and the late 1950s.

The size distribution of the parent firms of new subsidiaries also seemed to have influenced aggregate ownership patterns. The proportion of subsidiaries of relatively small parent firms rose at the end of the 1940s and fell in the early 1950s, perhaps contributing to the first peak in JV formation around 1952. But after that, the patterns in the size distribution of MNCs do not correspond to those in JV activity (Gomes-Casseres, 1988).

One country factor that partly accounted for the fluctuation of MNC ownership strategies in the 1960s and 1970s was the impact of host government restrictions. As has been shown elsewhere, such restrictions influenced MNC's ownership choices even though the firms could often bargain successfully for exemptions to the regulations (Beamish, 1984, 1993; Fagre and Wells, 1982; Gomes-Casseres, 1985; Hladik, 1988; Lecraw, 1984).

Host government restrictions play an important role in the structure and establishment of IJVs in developing countries. Most developing countries in the ASEAN region will only allow wholly owned operations where the industries attracted are considered of prime national importance or where the technology is highly developed (Ahn, 1980; Higginbottom, 1980).

Host country government policies offer only a partial explanation for the cyclical patterns in IJV formation. Clearly, other factors must have also been at work. Cross-sectional tests have shown that industry factors too can affect ownership strategies. For example, subsidiaries in marketing-intensive industries were less likely to be IJVs than others, because global marketing strategies often conflicted with the interests of local partners. Similarly, the R&D intensity of subsidiaries' industries and the extent to which subsidiaries depended on local inputs of natural resources could also influence ownership choices (Beamish, 1984, 1993; Beamish and Inkpen, 1995; Dymsza, 1988; Koot, 1988; Gomes-Casseres, 1987; Hladik, 1988; Stopford and Wells, 1972).

According to Anderson (1990), Blodgett (1991a), Gomes-Casseres (1989), Geringer and Hebert (1991) and Koot (1988) there have been more JVs and other collaborative ventures announced since 1981 than in all the previous years combined. This finding is supported by Julian's (1998) work where he found that 75.2 percent of all international joint ventures (IJVs) formed in Thailand in the 35-year period between 1960 and 1995 were formed in the period 1986 to 1995. Previously, IJVs have been used to exploit peripheral markets or technologies. However, now JVs are being seen as critical elements of a business unit's network and as strategic weapons for competing within a firm's core markets and technologies.

Datta (1988) described the reason for the increase in the number of IJVs in the 1980s as partially attributed to changes that have taken place in the global business environment since the early 1970s. These changes include, firstly, significant erosion in the bargaining power of MNCs, especially in terms of technical know-how. As a result, many host governments now insist that foreign companies form partnerships with local companies before being given permission to set up operations in their country (Ahn, 1980; Beamish, 1984, 1993; Connolly, 1984; Higginbottom, 1980; Millin, 1984). For example, India required a minimum of 60 percent local participation in any venture (Sethi *et al.*, 1990) and similar restrictions have been imposed by governments in many other countries (Ahn, 1980; Baker and McKenzie, 1993; Higginbottom, 1980).

Secondly, foreign corporations have begun to recognise that local firms can make a significant contribution to a venture through their intimate knowledge of what is often a complex and volatile local business environment (Beamish and Inkpen, 1995; Hall, 1984; Lee and Beamish, 1995; Madhok, 1995).

Finally, the recent increase in overall JV activity has probably been the outgrowth of a growing awareness among organisations in developed countries that the continuing globalisation of their markets requires them to be more cost effective and efficient if they are to succeed in the global marketplace (Jain, 1989, 1994; Levitt, 1983; Shanks, 1985). This, in turn, might require that operations be set up in other countries that provide cheaper raw materials and/or lower processing costs.

Several studies have also indicated that the increased use of the IJV as a market entry mode is likely to continue well into the 21st century (Anderson, 1990; Beamish, 1984, 1993; Beamish and Delios, 1997a; Beamish and Inkpen, 1995; Deloitte *et al.,* 1989; Fey, 1995; Julian, 1998; Lee and Beamish, 1995; Makino and Beamish, 1995, 1998). Business leaders and researchers cite five main reasons for the rising popularity of IJVs:

- The governments of many countries with attractive domestic markets - including China, Thailand and South Korea - try to restrict foreign ownership (Baker and McKenzie, 1993; Beamish, 1993; Beamish and Delios, 1997a; Julian, 1998; Kim, 1995; Lee and Beamish, 1995; Pilafidis, 1995a).

- Many firms have found that host country partners could help them enter new markets quickly by providing management expertise and local connections (Goldenberg, 1987).

- This help is particularly important because of intensifying global competition in many industries. Competitors are often willing to settle for IJVs in host countries where previously foreign corporations have insisted on wholly owned subsidiaries (Beamish, 1984; Franko, 1987; Oman, 1988).

- Foreign firms, especially from Europe and Japan, have become more attractive IJV partners as their technological capabilities and market presence have grown (Beamish, 1993; Datta, 1988; Dymsza, 1988; Koot, 1988; Luo and Chen, 1995; Makino and Beamish, 1995).

• In many industries global scale is becoming a distinct advantage in R&D and production, leading all but the largest firms to consider IJVs as a way to achieve economies of scale and share risks (Beamish, 1993; Hladik, 1988; Gomes-Casseres, 1989).

2.2. High Failure Rates

As far as the disconcerting trend, relating to the high fragility of IJV arrangements was concerned, from 1974 to 1982, the number of newly formed IJVs increased except for a slight drop during 1981-82 (Hladik, 1985). As of 1979, roughly 40 percent of the largest US industrial firms were engaged in one or more IJVs (Janger, 1980). It also appears that the failure rate was quite high during this period (Holton, 1981). Empirical studies suggest that anywhere between one-third and two-thirds of IJVs eventually break up (Beamish, 1985; Bleeke and Ernst, 1991; Gomes-Casseres, 1989; Killing, 1983; Kogut, 1988; Makino and Beamish, 1998; Park and Ungson, 1997). Vaupel and Curhan (1969) studied 1,812 manufacturing IJVs and found that 464 were subsequently taken over by the multinational parent. Of the 1,100 IJVs Franko (1971, 1974) studied, 182 became wholly owned subsidiaries of the American parent, 84 were dissolved and 48 changed control. This high failure rate may result from the difficulty and complexity in managing IJVs. Drucker (1974) noted that IJVs are the most difficult and demanding but the least understood of all the tools of diversification. Young and Bradford (1977, p. 9) also suggest that IJVs contain 'built-in, self destruct devices' since parents see them as provisional compromises rather than desirable permanent arrangements (Arni, 1982; Friedmann and Beguin, 1971; Janger, 1980; Kobayashi, 1967a).

Although compelling, the empirical evidence supporting the premise of poor JV performance might be challenged on several grounds (see Delios and Beamish, 2004) as Delios and Beamish found that two-partner IJVs perform no worse than wholly owned subsidiaries. First, countervailing evidence about JV performance exists in data compiled as part of the Harvard Multinational Enterprises (HMNE) project (Curhan *et al.,* 1977). Using the HMNE data, Chowdhury (1992, p. 130) found that for 8,741 US manufacturing foreign entries, the exit rates for JVs and wholly owned subsidiaries were nearly identical.

A second reason is that statements of IJV performance are often made independent of comparisons to other modes, even though the difficulty of moving operations across borders imparts a high exit rate, as compared to domestic expansions (Pennings *et al.,* 1994). In studies that have compared performance across entry modes the evidence is mixed (Delios and Beamish, 2004). A few studies (Hennart *et al.,* 1998; Li, 1995; Pennings *et al.,* 1994), found that JVs had lower survival rates than wholly owned subsidiaries, while others found no substantial differences in survival rates (Chowdhury, 1992).

A third reason is that research has tended to focus on survival or stability, without looking at how a JV performs financially or in terms of satisfying partner objectives (Julian, 1998; Julian and O'Cass, 2002a; Yan and Zeng, 1999). Multiple indicators of performance can lead to different inferences about the success of a JV, that can also vary across host country contexts (Beamish and Delios, 1997b; Julian and O'Cass, 2004a). Studies using financial performance measures have shown that wholly owned subsidiaries tended to have higher perceived financial performance than IJVs, for subsidiaries established in Western Europe (Nitsch *et al.,* 1996) and North America (Woodcock *et al.,* 1994). Yet, in South East Asia, the order is reversed: JVs have a better perceived financial performance than wholly owned subsidiaries (Makino and Beamish, 1998), and higher success rates in developing economies (Newman, 1992; Yan, 1993). Reviews of JV performance point to the differential performance of JVs formed in developed and developing countries, with JVs established in developing economies exhibiting higher performance (Beamish and Delios, 1997b, 110).

Furthermore, using a longitudinal sample of nearly 28,000 Japanese foreign investments, Delios and Beamish (2004) found that JVs had a perceived financial performance and survival rate no worse than wholly owned subsidiaries. This finding does not support the prevailing view that JVs are poorly performing. Using Li's (1995) study as a base, Delios and Beamish (2004) identified that conclusions about JV performance could have been different if other measures of performance, such as financial performance, were utilised, or if the research considered the role of contextual factors, such as JV management capabilities, JV ownership structure and host country influences that moderate entry mode and performance relationships.

Delios and Beamish found evidence that JVs formed in Asia had moderately better performance than those formed in North America and Europe. They found strong evidence that a firm can develop JV management capabilities that decrease JV exit rates, and these capabilities extend from prior experience of managing successful overseas JVs. An implication of this is that research on JV performance should consider the differential alliance management capabilities of the firms involved in the JV (Delios and Beamish, 2004). They also found that JV financial performance levels and exit rates differed by JV ownership types. JVs with a moderate ownership split or co-ownership, had a higher performance than wholly owned subsidiaries and better performance than JVs in which ownership was highly skewed towards a majority for one partner. Meanwhile, Japanese-majority JVs had the highest survival rates among all JVs, and a survival rate equal to that of wholly owned subsidiaries. These results point to the importance of distinguishing among JV types when evaluating JV performance (Delios and Beamish, 2004). JVs in which a Japanese firm held a low-equity position, less than 50 percent of the subsidiary's equity, had higher exit rates than other forms of JVs (Delios and Beamish, 2004).

This latter result could be related to the ease of divestment of a JV in which one partner had a low equity stake (Hennart *et al.,* 1998). Although this would account for the poor survival rates of JVs in which a local partner had a high equity share, it would not explain why Japanese firms would willingly exit a JV type that has a comparatively high perceived financial performance.

JVs are clearly not all the same. Research (Makino and Beamish, 1998) has developed analytical frameworks for distinguishing among the performance outcomes of different types of JVs. The Delios and Beamish (2004) work makes a more simple distinction that shows that JVs with different divisions of equity ownership have different levels of performance. This complements the findings of Hennart *et al.* (1998) who showed that dissolution and dissolving rates differ by ownership category type. As such, when developing arguments and empirical analyses about JVs and entry mode performance and stability, consideration should be given to equity ownership divisions, where the difference between sole and shared ownership is just one such type of differentiation.

Furthermore, in the longitudinal study conducted by Delios and Beamish (2004) on Japanese subsidiaries around the world, differences emerged in the findings about performance along the survival and financial performance dimensions. JVs in which no partner held more than 80 percent of the JVs equity were superior along the financial performance dimension compared to wholly owned subsidiaries. The same finding was not observed in the exit analysis, thereby, suggesting that research that builds exclusively from the exit perspective might be missing part of the overall picture of performance, and subsequently drawing inaccurate conclusions about the poor performance of JVs. This also implies a greater need to use measures other than survival, or multiple measures of performance (Delios and Beamish, 2004; Julian, 1998; Julian and O'Cass, 2002a, 2004a).

However, as duly noted by the authors, the Delios and Beamish (2004) findings were limited to the foreign investments of Japanese firms. As such, the generalisability of their findings needs to be exerted with due caution and explored further using the foreign investments of firms from other nations. Second, the Delios and Beamish measure of subsidiary exit was an undifferentiated one. It did not capture the motivation for exit, nor did it differentiate between exit by dissolution or sale of the subsidiary. Third, they concentrated on only two performance measures when analysing JV performance. For their findings to be generalisable, future research should explore if the same implications are derived using other measures.

Yet the Delios and Beamish work is a revelation in that they present new evidence that challenges conventional notions about JV performance. The Delios and Beamish findings suggest that JVs do not really perform poorly when compared to alternative market entry modes. JVs have marginally lower survival rates than wholly owned subsidiaries, with two-partner JVs having survival rates equal to that of wholly owned subsidiaries. Further, their findings suggest that JVs have a perceived financial performance equal to that of wholly owned subsidiaries. They suggest several contextual factors need to be considered when evaluating the comparative performance of JVs against other market entry modes. If these factors are not considered, and the analytical focus is limited to just the survival measure of performance, the conclusion can be incorrectly drawn that JVs perform poorly. Additionally, they suggest that JVs do not perform worse than other entry modes. As such, the academic community should re-evaluate its perceptions about JVs as being an entry mode that has poorer performance than wholly owned subsidiaries. However, before that can occur greater research is required to confirm the generalisability of the Delios and Beamish (2004) findings to foreign investments from firms in countries other than Japan.

2.3. Venture Creation Rationales

There are a number of overriding economic and political reasons for the rise in the popularity of IJVs. A number of researchers (Beamish, 1984, 1988, 1993; Beamish and Inkpen, 1995; Datta, 1988; Dymsza, 1988; Gullander, 1976; Harrigan, 1987; Hladik, 1988; Koot, 1988) have identified a variety of reasons behind MNC's decisions to enter into IJV agreements. These include:

- Entering new and potentially profitable markets.
- Sharing heightened economic and political risks in new business ventures.
- Satisfying nationalistic demands and reducing risks of expropriation.
- Government suasion.
- Economies of scale.
- Pooling organisational know-how to realise synergistic benefits.

As far as entering new and potentially profitable markets is concerned, given the fixed costs of innovation, the larger the market, the higher the JV's expected rate of return on investment. A number of studies have shown, in fact, that JV investment is positively influenced by the expected domestic and international sales of the product (Harrigan, 1988a; Higginbottom, 1980). Immediate access to a large market can be especially important in industries where product lifetimes are short (Cavusgil and Zou, 1994). Expected sales are dependent on both market size and the length of time over which the product is sold in these markets. As the time factor grows shorter, market access can become critical to long-term product viability.

From a foreign corporation's perspective, an IJV offers the opportunity of entering promising new markets where other forms of market entry (e.g., as a wholly owned subsidiary) may be barred. Other country markets may be characterised by less formal barriers to entry. Still, foreign firms may find it difficult to penetrate these markets without local marketing expertise. A JV partner may provide the know-how or established local distribution channels through which to market the new product. Foreign partners have also been of critical value in markets where important customers have been state-owned enterprises or governments that favour national suppliers. Whilst many foreign firms have looked to foreign partners as a means of entering the host-country market alone it has become increasingly important to ensure access to international markets as well and foreign partners have been useful in this respect also.

As far as sharing heightened economic and political risks in new business ventures are concerned, the use of the IJV as a foreign market entry mode has helped in reducing the significant political and economic risks generally associated with foreign projects. These political and economic risks can be due to a variety of factors, including unstable local governments, fluctuating currencies, and perennially strained communications and transportation infrastructures in host countries (The Economist, 1986, p. 19).

By reducing the amount of capital resources required in a given project, JVs help foreign corporations reduce the element of financial risk. Moreover, rising economic nationalism has resulted in many host countries imposing formal and/or informal restrictions on foreign companies doing business in their countries. In this context, JVs with local firms can be one of the few ways in which foreign corporations can satisfy host governments' requirements for local participation and ownership in the management of enterprises within their boundaries (Ajami and Khambata, 1991; Beamish, 1984; Berlew, 1984; Dymsza, 1988; Kedia and Chokar, 1986; Koot, 1988).

Further insights identify that IJVs offer certain advantages, whether or not they are necessary in a given situation. Hladik (1988, p. 187) provided insight into the benefits of JV research and development identifying that:

> 'There are several reasons why joint venture R&D can be an attractive strategy for some firms. The benefits of R&D joint ventures are based on the pooling of complementary resources provided by the different partners. While one partner may contribute certain critical resources, such as technological skills and assets, another partner may be helpful in providing financing, complementary technical know-how, or access to the large domestic or international markets for the product of the joint R&D effort. The contributions of each partner are determined by both the assets at its disposal and its comparative advantage in different inputs. In some cases, the contributions are clear-cut. Each partner may possess one set of key resources and be deficient in others. In other joint ventures, there may be an overlap of skills and resources.'

JVs, whether international or not, tend to spread risks (and rewards) in projects, and provide cross-access to scarce resources.

As far as satisfying nationalistic demands and reducing risks of expropriation is concerned, there are many considerations required of developing countries when viewing relations with a foreign firm, including the amount of local employment, the supply and price of goods, access to marketing systems and foreign exchange earnings potential. However, two considerations increasingly dominate: developing countries are determined to retain control of economic decisions in order to ensure that these decisions are compatible with national objectives; and they acknowledge the importance of acquiring a sufficient quantity and quality of high-level skills to make effective control possible. Developing countries seek to minimise the surrender of control to foreigners, while at the same time maximising skills acquisition.

In order to achieve these objectives, developing countries around the world are increasingly resorting to the IJV as the only form of foreign investment that will be permitted in certain industries, and are increasingly insisting upon local capital participation in foreign corporate ventures. Discriminatory taxation, selective foreign exchange restrictions, selective bureaucratic delays and foreign employment restrictions are also being sought (Wright and Russel, 1975). Independence, national sovereignty and a more representative and sophisticated national leadership have made such measures feasible. Developing countries in South East Asia are increasingly in control of the natural resources and markets sought by MNCs. Therefore, IJVs have proliferated for the reason that they have been one of only a few ways for foreign corporations to satisfy host-country governments' requirements for local participation in ownership and management of enterprises within their boundaries (Beamish, 1984; 1993; Blodgett, 1991a; Higginbottom, 1980; Wright and Russel, 1975).

As far as government suasion is concerned, governments may not actually require JV participation by MNCs, but government pressure for local participation usually exists in some form. Government suasion is identified here as the direct or indirect imposition of restrictions on foreign investors by a host-country government (Blodgett, 1991a). Beamish (1985) found that 57 percent of JVs between US MNCs and entities in developing countries were formed because of government suasion, while only 17 percent of the JVs of US MNCs and firms in other developed countries were formed for that reason. Third world indigenisation programmes, by injecting a political factor into the bargaining power of a local entity, have had an important impact on how the developed world MNCs operate overseas and MNCs have formed IJVs in order to maintain good relations with host country governments.

If the government is an active partner to the IJV, which is the case with many developing countries, e.g., China and Thailand, it means an important diminution of bargaining power for the MNC, since the government that owns equity in the IJV also has the power to regulate the venture's activities. In addition, when import substitution policies are pursued, the host-country government can be expected to have a strong motivation to increase control over the venture once operations are going smoothly. Even when the local partner is a private enterprise, the host country government can exert control as a shadow partner by imposing and enforcing regulations that interfere with the venture's operations, e.g., the choice of suppliers, the choice of markets, the repatriation of profit, the employment of locals etc.

As a bargaining resource, the implicit or explicit role of the host-country government as a gatekeeper to the investment process resides in the country's right of sovereignty. Therefore, government suasion is an enduring asset and is not readily appropriated by international law. Current nationalistic feeling dictates that few countries will tolerate uncontrolled foreign investment by foreign enterprises and they often erect barriers against certain types of foreign investment. Beamish (1985), Contractor (1985) and Gomes-Casseres (1987) found that the most crucial factor in relative bargaining power is government-imposed restrictions. The IJV, especially where the host-country government is an active partner, is a means of reducing the effect of government-imposed restrictions and developing good relations with host-country governments, and is often used as a market entry mode for that reason.

As far as economies of scale are concerned, in many industries advantages connected with the size of operations exist. One such advantage results from economies of scale. A decreasing unit cost is linked to an increasing level of activity per time period. Economies of scale pertain not only to manufacturing but to some other functions as well, notably R&D and sales (Ganitsky *et al.,* 1991; Hladik, 1988; Luo and Chen, 1995). A JV with another firm allows a company to benefit from these economies of scale in a way not possible if it remained completely independent (Anazawa, 1994; Aswicahyono and Hill, 1995; Datta, 1988; Dunning, 1993; Dymsza, 1988; Franko, 1971; Gullander, 1976; Hladik, 1988; Stopford and Wells, 1972).

Through a JV firms can also benefit from the 'experience curve' effect. The experience curve shows how the unit cost decreases as the total product volume produced by the firm over the product's entire existence increases (Jain, 1989, 1994a). The reason for this is to be found in the successive improvements in efficiency that normally takes place in companies as they gain more experience in the production of a particular product/service.

As far as pooling organisational know-how to realise synergistic benefits is concerned, technological linkages with other firms who may be suppliers, customers and/or other firms at the same production stage can enable a company to benefit by cooperating through JVs with these firms. In concentrated industries with strong competition, firms may also experience a high dependence on other firms. A JV between competitors may then improve the conditions for the joining companies, although antitrust regulations may cause difficulties (Dymsza, 1988; Gullander, 1976; Hladik, 1988; Koot, 1988).

Certain resources in the economy are not always available through free markets. Technology and distribution networks are not always available for sale, and in such cases the need for access to these resources can only be satisfied through a JV. A typical case occurs when a foreign firm possesses a product which it wants to market abroad. A JV with local partners can then offer access to an efficient distribution network together with knowledge of local business practices and institutions. In such a case there is a high degree of complementarity between the partners. Generally, complementarity is found in many JVs, encompassing not only functional complementarity, as in the case mentioned, but also technological complementarity. For example, the development of a new product that requires technical know-how not available in a single company (Beamish and Inkpen, 1995; Blodgett, 1991a; Calof and Beamish, 1995; Dymsza, 1988; Fey, 1995; Harrigan, 1987; Hladik, 1988).

The local partner, on the other hand, usually enters the JV with a different set of objectives. For example, such a venture might be attractive because it provides access to technology that would otherwise be difficult to develop or buy (Berlew, 1984). In fact, transfer of technology probably constitutes the single most important reason why firms in developing countries seek JVs with organisations in technologically advanced countries (Beamish, 1984, 1988, 1993; Blodgett, 1991a; Connolly, 1984; Datta, 1988; Wright and Russel, 1975).

JVs, therefore, offer a unique opportunity of combining the distinctive competences and the complementary resources of participating firms. Such combinations provide a wide range of benefits, benefits that neither participant might be able to attain on its own. These include, among others, economic benefits in the form of reductions in factor costs, transportation costs, overheads and taxes. Therefore, JVs can be a particularly desirable alternative in situations and industries where the 'critical mass' (the input activity level that has to be surpassed to obtain any significant output or result) is very high (Hall, 1984).

Along with those mentioned above, there are also a number of other benefits associated with JVs. For example, JV arrangements permit the foreign firm to specialise in the sale of commodities in which its greatest comparative advantage lies: technical know-how and management skill. Equity risk is also lower. In brief, the JV form may be the only effective means of simultaneously fulfilling the needs of both the foreign firm and the host country. By planning for more effective skills transfer and for eventual transfer of control, and by viewing their long-run involvement in the fully dimensioned JV space, the foreign firm will help to ensure its continued participation in high-growth markets such as Thailand and other South East Asian country markets. Therefore, there are significant benefits associated with entering into an IJV relationship. These benefits, to a large extent, explain the reason for the significant increase in IJV formation since the early 1980s (Beamish, 1984; Beamish and Delios, 1997a; Dymsza, 1988; Gomes-Casseres, 1989; Hladik, 1988; Julian, 1998; Julian and Ramaseshan, 2001).

2.4. Instability

The benefits associated with IJVs are counterbalanced by a wide range of problems. The failure rate of IJVs, in general, is high (Beamish, 1985; Bleeke and Ernst, 1991; Dymsza, 1988; Gomes-Casseres, 1989; Hladik, 1985, 1988; Killing, 1983; Kogut, 1988; Makino and Beamish, 1998; Park and Ungson, 1997). The problems are heightened when the partners are of different nationalities and cultures, and when collaboration occurs at the base of each firm's competitive advantage. This section describes some of the major causes of instability associated with IJVs. Some IJVs have successfully resolved these problems. Others have led to failure: either failure to establish the IJV in the first place or failure leading to the eventual dissolving of the agreement (Hladik, 1988).

Managers and staff specialists of examined companies confirm the image of the JV as a cumbersome form of organisation. An overview of the main causes of instability in an IJV identifies a few critical issues. That the JV is hard to direct, in its goals; it requires a formation period with hardship; and it is difficult to manage even when it starts operating (Anderson, 1990; Beamish, 1984; Dymsza, 1988; Hladik, 1988; Geringer and Hebert, 1989; 1991; Gomes-Casseres, 1989; Koot, 1988). More specifically, some of the main causes of instability include:

- Significant differences in the major goals of the parties.
- Risks of sharing proprietary technology.
- Desire for control.
- The foreign corporation's global integration and the local partner's national orientation.
- Perception of unequal benefits and costs.
- Details of the joint venture contract.
- Conflict over decision-making, managerial processes and style.
- Differences between the partners concerning marketing.
- Transfer pricing conflicts.
- Royalties, management fees and headquarters' charges.

The foreign corporation and the local partner in an IJV may have significant differences in their goals with respect to that business. These significant differences could be due to the size and type of companies involved; their particular business, industry and products; their international and other experience; and many other factors (Beamish and Inkpen, 1995; Douglas and Craig, 1989; Dymsza, 1988; Hladik, 1988; Parkhe, 1991; Schaan and Beamish, 1988). A foreign corporation may desire to enter into a viable operation through an IJV that will yield a target rate of return on investment in the medium and long term. Therefore, it strives to reinvest a substantial portion of earnings in the venture in order to expand the operation and increase its return over this time horizon. The local partner, on the other hand, often enters into the IJV to earn a good immediate rate of return on its investment. Therefore, it strives for maximum pay-out of dividends. The situation, of course, can also be the reverse. The foreign corporation may have the goal of a quick payback on its investment of capital, technology and management. The local partner may strive to develop a growing, profitable business yielding satisfactory profits over the medium to long term. As a result, the partners may experience a stalemate that could interfere with the successful management of the business (Anderson, 1990; Beamish, 1984; Beamish and Banks, 1987; Chowdhury, 1989; Datta, 1988; Dymsza, 1988; Hladik, 1988; Killing, 1983).

Therefore, managers of some parent companies perceive the JV as a vague and risky business. The dependence on a partner does make the disposition and commitment of future financial resources insecure or rather less secure than it seems to be without a partner. There is a fair chance that short-term and long-term objectives of partners are misunderstood so that the combined direction of the venture may not be clearly visible to anyone (Roberts, 1980), except perhaps to the JV general manager.

In terms of finance and know-how, JV partners have to balance internally their own projections of what is to be expected from the venture. Thus, the amount of investment in fixed assets and product development is to be balanced against the profitability objectives and self-financing goals of each parent company. For each of the parent companies, one major goal is to make a certain profit after a period of start-up investments. But how big the return on investment should be and how long a realistic payback period would be, are questions that even the most stringent policy statement cannot solve. Different goals cannot be that precise. Business interests may actually diverge drastically among partners in such a way that sooner or later, a shared concern about the venture leads to a lack of unity in company policy for the venture, with a heightened chance of failure.

Another cause of instability in IJVs involves the risks associated with the sharing of proprietary technology. One of the biggest concerns in most IJV relationships is the reluctance by the foreign partner to share proprietary technology outside of the firm, even with an IJV partner (Ajami and Khambata, 1991; Beamish, 1993; Blodgett, 1991a; Ganitsky *et al.,* 1991; Hladik, 1988; Julian, 1998; Julian and O'Cass, 2002a; Prahalad and Hamel, 1989; Stuckey, 1983). A foreign corporation may well possess the technology and resources that would make an IJV a profitable venture. It may hesitate, however, before sharing this know-how with a subsidiary or partner that is only partially under its control. The risk is heightened by the possibility that, if the IJV dissolves, the firm providing valuable technology to its partner may well have been training a future competitor (Hladik, 1985, 1988).

Another cause of concern for IJV participants involves control of the IJV (Beamish, 1985; Beamish and Inkpen, 1995; Delios and Beamish, 2004; Dymsza, 1988; Geringer and Hebert, 1989; Hladik, 1988; Julian, 1998; Julian and O'Cass, 2002a, 2004a; Julian and Ramaseshan, 2004; Kobrin, 1988; Lee and Beamish, 1995; Sohn, 1994). This is particularly true if the IJV is involved in the development of new products for world markets. In many high-technology industries, strategic flexibility and the desire to remove bureaucratic interference have favoured majority control over 50:50 partnerships (Dymsza, 1988; Geringer and Hebert, 1989; Hladik, 1988; Kobrin, 1988).

At the strategic level, a firm attempting to coordinate its operations in a global market may seek to ensure that the IJV fits in with these other activities. Without majority control of the venture, this may cause problems. At the personal level, human nature can also be an important factor in the creation and success of IJV efforts. Where ownership control of the IJV is concerned, personal and corporate pride and nationalistic feelings can block involvement in important new ventures where the firm does not have majority control.

A further cause of instability in IJVs involves the foreign corporation's global integration and the local partner's national orientation. A number of IJVs fail because the foreign corporation strives for global integration of their business, while the local partner is emphasising the operations within their country (Datta, 1988; Dymsza, 1988; Koot, 1988; Wright and Russel, 1975). Many foreign corporations aim to maximise their profits or earn a target rate of return on their investments globally, rather than maximise their business in a particular country, including those in which they have IJVs. Accordingly, foreign corporations strive to integrate their IJV affiliates with their system of enterprises around the world in production, finance, marketing and management. Furthermore, since IJV affiliates in developing countries are generally a small part of the total international business of most foreign corporations, they may not grant high priority to them in resource allocation, management and technological effort. On the other hand, an IJV involved in any sort of manufacturing commonly represents a major business involvement for the local partner. Thus, the national partner commits major capital and management effort to the IJV affiliate and expects comparable commitment from the foreign corporation in order to have a highly successful business. Serious conflicts can emerge when the local partner finds that the foreign corporation does not grant high priority to the IJV and does not commit sufficient resources and effort. These conflicts can become deeper, causing the IJV to fail (Datta, 1988; Dymsza, 1988).

Another issue in the IJV relationship could involve the perception of unequal benefits and costs by one or all of the parties to the relationship. A perception by the foreign corporation or the national partner that it is not obtaining sufficient benefit from the IJV in return for its contribution of resources leads to the failure of some ventures (Ahn, 1980; Datta, 1988; Dymsza, 1988; Koot, 1988; Kobrin, 1988; Wright and Russel, 1975). Of importance is not only the actual contribution made by each party but what the partners perceive over the life of the operation. In some instances, the foreign corporation perceives that it is not obtaining an adequate return for its contribution of manufacturing and product technology, management, technical training, trademarks and business expertise. In other instances, the national partner believes that its contribution of existing factories and facilities, management, local capital, sales organisation and contacts with the government are excessive in relation to its share of ownership, the responsibilities it has in the venture and the profit it earns. These perceptions of benefits obtained in relation to contributions made can change over the years. When one or both partners perceive an unsatisfactory ratio between benefits and costs from the venture, serious conflicts develop, which often can lead to the failure of the venture.

A further cause of concern that has led to instability in some IJVs involves the joint venture agreement or contract. The long period between the first steps abroad and the rounding up of JV negotiations usually requires much attention from top managers and their staff (Berg and Friedmann, 1980; Calof and Beamish, 1995; Otterbeck, 1981; Schaan and Beamish, 1988). The composition and functioning of the JV's board and management, the informal and formal lines of communication, recruitment and compensation of key staff and adaptation to political forces at hand all form potential built-in difficulties for the interacting companies (Cullen *et al.,* 1995; Geringer and Hebert, 1989, 1991; Johnson *et al.,* 1993; Killing, 1983; Madhok, 1995; Porter and Fuller, 1986). When the IJV agreement does not clearly specify the goals of each party, the resources contributed by the partners, their major responsibilities and obligations, their rights, the character of the business, their share of profits and mode of distribution, ways of resolving disputes, and other key aspects of the venture, disagreements can take place and disrupt the venture (Beamish, 1988; Dymsza, 1988; Geringer, 1988; Geringer and Hebert, 1989; Pan, 1996).

The next issue with the IJV organisation structure involves conflicts over decision-making, managerial processes and style. The strife between a foreign corporation and a local partner to control major policies and decisions constitutes a major reason for the failure of certain IJVs (Blodgett, 1991a; Dymsza, 1988; Ganitsky *et al.,* 1991; Geringer and Hebert, 1989; Schaan and Beamish, 1988). The foreign corporation may strive to control major policies of the venture through the appointment of a majority of the board of directors, including outside, allegedly neutral directors, who are favourable to it. The role of the board of directors of joint venture affiliates varies a great deal. Some boards determine major policies of the venture, select the chief and top executives, and monitor the overall management and operations of the enterprise, but many boards primarily grant advice to the Chief Executive and perform rather perfunctory responsibilities. Other boards assume a legal function to meet the requirements of law, e.g., Malaysia (Ahn, 1980; Baker and McKenzie, 1993; Dymsza, 1988).

Foreign corporations control the management of joint venture affiliates in other ways. They obtain authority to appoint the Chief Executive and key managers; they establish the managerial and control processes and have the right to veto major decisions. The continuing control by the foreign corporation of combinations of manufacturing, marketing, finance and other decisions in the venture often leads to major conflicts with the national partners and the host governments. These conflicts can lead to the failure of IJVs (Dymsza, 1988).

Major differences with respect to management processes, style of management and corporate culture between the foreign corporation and the local partner can lead to serious conflicts which contribute to the failure of IJVs (Dymsza, 1988; Lane and Beamish, 1990; Schaan and Beamish, 1988; Zhu and Dowling, 1995). For example, a foreign corporation may seek to impose its process of strategic and operational planning, an information and control system, budgeting and accounting on the JV affiliate. The local partner may not have any experience with these processes and consider them inappropriate. A foreign corporation may emphasise a more participatory style of management, delegation of responsibility to subordinates, profit centres and periodic evaluation of performance. The local partner, that is often a family-owned business in the developing countries of South East Asia, may have a more authoritarian style of management, with no delegation of responsibility to subordinates and very little formal planning and control. Although such differences in management processes and style can sometimes be harmonised through a learning process in the JV, they can often disrupt the venture, leading to its demise (Dymsza, 1988; Schaan and Beamish, 1988).

Another related cause of concern for the IJV and its participants involves the differences between the partners over marketing-related issues. A JV between a marketing-oriented foreign corporation and a local firm can fail because of major differences between the parties about marketing policies and procedures. Many highly marketing oriented foreign corporations try to avoid IJVs, but when they do enter into them because of the requirements of host governments, strive to adopt their own marketing systems, based upon product differentiation, aggressive promotion and advertising, selling and emphasis upon trademarks and brand names (Aaby and Slater, 1989; Cavusgil and Zou, 1994; Douglas and Craig, 1989; Stopford and Wells, 1972). Some foreign corporations work for standardisation of their marketing mixes globally, but they do adapt some aspects of marketing to the national environment and institutional setting (Cavusgil and Zou, 1994; Douglas and Craig, 1989). They consider control of the key elements in the marketing mix in a JV crucial in their type of business. Having a dissimilar experience in their own country, the local partner may strive to adopt different marketing programmes and procedures with less emphasis on product differentiation, promotion, aggressive selling and trademarks. The foreign corporation and the national partner may also differ on pricing practices, market segmentation, introduction of new products and marketing expenditures. As a result, the partners may encounter serious conflicts in marketing management that result in stalemates in decision-making and, ultimately, failure of the IJV (Blodgett, 1991a; Dymsza, 1988).

Also, objectives of both partners in terms of marketing and technical development efforts may change unnoticeably over time, no matter how formalised the proposed policy for the JV is (Franko, 1971; Stopford and Wells, 1972). The supposed risks of a JV go together with a tempered publicity: partners are reticent (Berg and Friedmann, 1980), JVs are often not registered, and the annual reports may quote their proceeds as 'other income'

(Anderson, 1990; Geringer and Hebert, 1989, 1991; Johnson *et al.*, 1993; Koot, 1988; Venkatraman and Ramanujam, 1986). This can contribute to a somewhat volatile relationship and the eventual failure of the IJV.

A further cause of concern for the IJV participants involves the issue of transfer pricing. Major conflicts can erupt between partners in IJVs with respect to purchase of raw materials, intermediates and components of the affiliate from the foreign partner, and issues of transfer pricing. Some foreign corporations strive to have the JV affiliate purchase intermediate goods or components from it on the grounds that it assures required quality standards and meets delivery requirements, and that competitive alternative sources are not readily available. Local partners, on the other hand, want to explore alternative sources in order to obtain the materials from the lowest-cost supplier. The local partner may believe that the foreign partner is charging excessive prices and aims to earn additional income from selling the necessary materials to the affiliate. If the foreign partner aggressively presses for continued sales of these materials to the affiliate, despite the fact that the local partner finds alternative suppliers at a lower cost, serious conflicts could arise between the partners of the IJV which can disrupt their relationship and contribute to the failure of the venture (Blodgett, 1991a; Dymsza, 1988; Harrigan, 1988a).

Finally, instability in IJVs has been known to arise over the payment of royalties, management fees and headquarters charges. Allocation of headquarters administrative costs, royalties on licensing agreements, technical fees and management fees in supplementary agreements negotiated by the foreign corporation in IJV agreements can lead to serious conflicts with the local partner and in some cases host governments. Even though IJV contracts may provide for such payments to the foreign partner, the local partner may scrutinise such charges in order to avoid excessive or unnecessary charges to the business. For example, the partner or the government may find royalties on licensing agreements excessive when the foreign partner contributes no new technology. Management fees may be considered unjustified if national managers are not trained to take over management positions in the process. A specific grievance with many local firms in IJV relationships occurs when headquarters allocates a share of its administrative costs to a JV affiliate. The local partner in an IJV relationship often wants to revise licensing agreements, management contracts and other agreements when they perceive the foreign partner is not providing the technological, managerial, technical and training inputs to justify the continued payments of royalties, management and technical fees, and other charges. As a result, serious conflicts can arise between the foreign and local partner leading to the eventual failure of the IJV (Blodgett, 1991a; Contractor and Lorange, 1988c; Dymsza, 1988; Schaan and Beamish, 1988).

Therefore, the causes of instability associated with IJV formation, management and evaluation are quite significant and contribute substantially to the frequent demise of the venture.

2.5. Ownership

Much has been written in the IJV literature about the equity participation of the principal foreign partner (Beamish, 1988; Beamish and Inkpen, 1995; Lee and Beamish, 1995; Sohn, 1994). Many authors claim that for an IJV to perform successfully the foreign partner must maintain control over the local partner and the IJV relationship (Al-Aali, 1987; Killing, 1983; Phatak and Chowdhury, 1991), and one of the best ways to achieve that is through majority equity participation in the IJV. However, in many developing countries this is becoming increasingly difficult to do. Host governments through government legislation, especially in developing countries like Thailand and other South East Asian nations, are restricting foreign companies to minority equity participation in industries which are not considered essential to national security and in industries where they already have access to the latest technology (Ahn, 1980; Higginbottom, 1980).

There are also researchers who believe that there are better ways for a foreign corporation to control a local partner other than through majority equity participation, e.g., through social knowledge (Sohn, 1994). There are still other researchers that have shown where foreign companies have been prepared to take a minority share in the IJV and make a commitment to a developing country market, the minority equity participation has been a major factor of successful business performance (Beamish, 1988; Beamish and Inkpen, 1995; Cullen *et al.*, 1995; Lee and Beamish, 1995). Therefore, through changing host country government legislation restricting most foreign companies in developing country markets to minority equity participation and the successful performance of many IJVs with minority equity participation, arguably minority equity participation is going to be the norm, not the exception.

In the Higginbottom (1980) study of IJVs in the ASEAN group of countries, minority equity participation by the foreign partner was commonplace in Malaysia, Thailand, Singapore, Indonesia and the Philippines. Higginbottom found that on average in more than 50 percent of the IJVs studied the principal foreign partner had 49 percent or less equity in the IJV. In the case of Thailand the number of IJVs where the principal foreign partner had 49 percent or less equity participation was above average with 60 percent of the IJVs studied. The reason cited by the foreign corporations for minority equity participation, in most cases, was host country government legislation (Higginbottom, 1980).

Although the level of equity participation by the foreign corporation is not a dimension of primary concern in this research, knowledge of equity participation by foreign corporations in IJV relationships in Thailand and other South East Asian nations helps academics and policy makers alike to understand the IJV climate and structure of IJVs in these countries. As was the case with the Higginbottom (1980) study, in a study of 1,047 BOI-promoted companies (BOI, 1996) in IJV relationships in Thailand the findings revealed a very high percentage of foreign corporations having minority equity participation in the IJV in which they were involved. In that study (BOI, 1996), 74.8 percent of the IJVs studied showed the principal foreign partner with 49 percent or less equity participation (see Table 2.1). In real terms, that represents 783 IJVs where the principal foreign partner had 49 percent or less equity participation. This is a significant number and cannot be overlooked in any analysis on IJVs in Thailand and other South East Asian nations.

Table 2.1 Equity Percentage of Principal Foreign Partner

Equity	Frequency	%	Cumulative %
5% to 9%	51	4.9	4.9
10% to 19%	101	9.6	14.5
20% to 29%	114	10.9	25.4
30% to 39%	151	14.4	39.8
40% to 49%	366	35.0	74.8
50% to 59%	48	4.6	79.4
60% to 69%	45	4.3	83.7
70% to 79%	62	5.9	89.6
80% to 89%	63	6.0	95.6
90% to 95%	46	4.4	100.0
TOTAL	1,047	100.0	

The Alien Business Law came into effect in 1972 (Baker and McKenzie, 1993), which is government legislation preventing majority equity participation in many industries by foreign corporations. If this is taken into consideration together with the knowledge that 85.5 percent of the IJVs studied in Thailand (BOI, 1996) were formed after 1980 (see Table 2.2) the likely cause of this high minority equity participation is host-country government legislation.

Table 2.2 Year in which IJV was Established

Year	Frequency	%	Cumulative %
Before 1960	1	0.1	0.1
1961–65	23	2.2	2.3
1966–70	32	3.0	5.3
1971–75	50	4.8	10.1
1976–80	46	4.4	14.5
1981–85	114	10.9	25.4
1986–90	484	46.2	71.6
1991–96	297	28.4	100.0
TOTAL	1,047	100.0	

Another factor likely to contribute to the high minority equity participation by foreign corporations in this sample is that they are all BOI-promoted companies. IJVs that are not BOI-promoted may have, on average, higher equity participation by the foreign partner, and only specific industries qualify to be promoted by the Thai BOI. Nevertheless, this sample has a very high percentage of minority equity participation by foreign corporations and this could have a major effect on how the IJVs marketing performance is viewed by senior executives.

3. Performance of International Joint Ventures

3.1. Developed versus Developing Countries

Prior to World War II, the main thrust of private international corporate activity in the developing nations was toward commodity trade and/or foreign direct investment involving full ownership. In the post-war years, three factors have been significant in modifying this concentration on export and foreign direct investment. The first has been the rising tide of nationalism with the most pervasive goal being that of rapid and sustained economic growth and development aimed at achieving economic independence. The foreign direct investment of MNCs has increasingly been perceived by less developed countries (LDCs) as a less than satisfactory contribution to this goal (Ahn, 1980; Ali and Sim, 1995; Beamish, 1984, 1993; Connolly, 1984; Wright and Russel, 1975; Zhao and Culpepper, 1995). A second factor has been the explicit recognition that in order to achieve their ambitious growth and development goals, developing countries require a massive purposeful inflow of technical, managerial and entrepreneurial skills. The final factor affecting the emergence of new forms of corporate involvement has been the increasing technical complexity of much of the capital equipment exported to developing countries. Technology, telecommunications and basic production equipment are all required desperately by these nations as a development base.

Developing countries have responded to these factors by attempting to modify foreign corporations' involvement in their country. This has been achieved by:

- More effective integration of economic activity under national development plans.
- Maintaining full sovereignty and satisfying nationalistic sentiments.

- Controlling the transfer of resources specifically required for development.
- Minimising the time over which foreign exchange is spent on importing corporate skills.
- Minimising the time in which control of the operations lies with the foreign corporations.

There are many considerations required of developing countries when viewing relations with a foreign firm, including the amount of local employment, the supply and price of goods, access to marketing systems and foreign exchange earnings. However, two considerations increasingly dominate: developing countries are determined to retain or regain control of economic decisions in order to ensure that these decisions are compatible with national objectives; and they acknowledge the importance of acquiring a sufficient quantity and quality of high-level skills to make effective control possible (Beamish, 1984; Blodgett, 1991a; Dymsza, 1988; Ganitsky *et al.,* 1991; Wright and Russel, 1975). Developing countries seek to minimise the surrender of control to foreigners, while at the same time maximising skills acquisition.

In order to achieve these objectives, developing countries are increasingly resorting to such measures as nationalisation of foreign enterprise, exclusion of all foreign investment from certain fields, insistence on local capital participation in foreign corporate ventures, discriminatory taxation, selective foreign exchange restrictions, selective bureaucratic delays and foreign employment restrictions. Independence, national sovereignty and a more representative and sophisticated national leadership have made such measures feasible.

Developing countries are increasingly in control of the natural resources and markets sought by foreign corporations, and the balance of power between the negotiating parties appears to be swinging towards the host nation. Previous researchers (Beamish, 1984, 1993; Beamish and Inkpen, 1995; Connolly, 1984; Fey, 1995; Koot, 1988; Lee and Beamish, 1995; Makino and Beamish, 1995; Wright and Russel, 1975) have identified additional factors that have contributed to the change in the relative bargaining power of foreign corporations and host governments. These include, firstly, that the East/West stalemate has imposed upon the industrial states a new code of conduct toward the 'poor' countries, and has sharply limited the responsiveness of their foreign policy to private business interests. Secondly, the ubiquity and competition among the industrialised countries often permits the 'host' country to play one foreign investor off against another to secure terms most advantageous to itself. Finally, the growth in developing countries of local entrepreneurship, both public and private, in areas once the domain of capital, confronts the foreign investor with this dilemma: his very success in the host country promotes the growth of local capabilities that threaten his continued presence.

Basic factors such as return on investment and commercial risk are of fundamental concern to any firm. However, in the developing world, effective control of operations and the risk of compounding earnings or seizing assets commands particular attention in the present environmental circumstances. In the international scene, there are as many differences in conception of faithfulness and moral duty as there are interpretations of profitability. Experience in developing countries reveals that foreign partners grant themselves the authority as well as the moral right to alter contractual statements unilaterally without any consultation (Hodgetts and Luthans, 1994; Kogut and Singh, 1988; Koot, 1988).

Traditionally, maintenance of effective control has been perceived by the firm as a fundamental prerequisite to ensure overall corporate success (Anderson and Gatignon, 1986; Geringer and Hebert, 1989; Hill *et al.,* 1990; Jaeger, 1983; Sohn, 1994). Partners in developing countries can be doomed to become silent or even fake partners who after a few years have no effect on the performance or management of the venture's business (Connolly, 1984; Koot, 1988; Sethi *et al.,* 1990; Wright and Russel, 1975). Control has many facets: profitability is controlled through operating decisions that ensure efficiency and effectiveness of the purchasing, production and marketing effort. Growth is controlled through investment and dividend policy and basic marketing strategy, including territory allocation for export marketing (Cavusgil and Zou, 1994). The foreign corporation could once achieve and maintain control of its overseas operation with relative ease. The operations of the parent company can be exported in a ready-made form in such a way that no adaptation in manufacture or sales methods is allowed, keeping product quality and brand name in tact. Many of the biggest multinationals, particularly in capital-intensive or high-precision product industries, try to transmit the exact design of managing the new operations to the newborn stepchild company.

If the venture is to keep the standards and procedures of the parents and negotiate on any adaptations, the parent can be said to mould the venture. In many developing country ventures with a dominant partner, this seems to be the case as well (Koot, 1988). Today, control objectives set for the IJV by either one or both of its parents are often on a collision course with those of the host nation, and the accustomed degree of control becomes increasingly difficult to achieve. The risk element also traditionally has been a fundamental consideration of the firm. But in the past, risk was viewed primarily in terms of normal commercial risk. The new risk of impairment of earning power or seizure of assets is increasingly real and of prime concern for the foreign corporation. Based on these realities, a new form of corporate involvement in the developing countries has continued to gain acceptance, that form being the IJV.

Historically, the trend of foreign investments in developing countries has been marked by a continuous worldwide decline of 100 percent direct investments, while the share of foreign minority holdings in JVs has been increasing at the expense of majority participations (Beamish, 1984, 1993; Beamish and Delios, 1997a; Delios and Beamish, 2004; Gomes-Casseres, 1989; Higginbottom, 1980; Julian, 1998; Julian and Ramaseshan, 2001; Makino and Beamish, 1995, 1998; Millin, 1984; Sohn, 1994). This trend is also evident in the ASEAN countries where they pursue the 'indigenisation policy' with great consistency. Therefore, it can be predicted that in the future foreign minority holdings will be the rule rather than the exception (Ahn, 1980; Baker and McKenzie, 1993; Higginbottom, 1980; Julian, 1998; Julian and Ramaseshan, 2001).

Apart from a few exceptions, foreign investors in all ASEAN countries are obligated to carry out their investment activities through the medium of JVs with indigenous partners. JVs between foreign and indigenous entrepreneurs are a special form of foreign investment and may arise from:

- The establishment of a new enterprise in the legal form of a separate entity.
- The participation of local partners in an existing foreign enterprise.
- The participation of foreign partners in an existing indigenous enterprise.

The governments of the ASEAN countries do not as a rule welcome the third variant and therefore sanction it only in rare cases (Ahn, 1980; Higginbottom, 1980). In essence, the ASEAN countries are opposed to the authorisation of foreign investments in any other form than through JVs. JVs are held to have positive importance as an instrument of investment policy that may be hoped to improve the effectiveness of foreign investments.

It is assumed that nationalistic feelings in developing countries may induce the state to keep foreign investments under strict control. The local public thinks of a foreign direct investment without indigenous participation as foreign, while a JV is frequently held to be a national firm. When it comes to the final decision a JV is less at risk than a direct investment. As all ASEAN countries are pursuing a 'fading-out' strategy, involving the successive reduction of foreign interest in implemented projects, this can also be an added incentive for foreign investors to engage in JVs from the outset (Beamish, 1993).

3.2. Performance

When using the broad-based definition that a JV is at least two companies pooling resources to create a new, separate organisation (Geringer and Hebert, 1989) it raises the difficult question: How is the performance of a JV to be evaluated? At first glance the answer seems quite clear: Evaluate the JV just like a division of the parent. But which parent? And what if the JV does well, but at the expense of a parent's interests? To further complicate the picture, JVs are likely to be used in risky, uncertain settings (Anderson, 1990; Beamish, 1984; Harrigan, 1988a; Johnson *et al.,* 1993) with profitability sometime in the future.

JVs, while offering the promise of economic and other benefits, often entail significant costs in their implementation. Shared decision-making makes them much more difficult to manage and evaluate and, therefore, JVs tend to be fragile relationships with a high failure rate; above 30 percent according to some studies (Beamish, 1985; Bleeke and Ernst, 1991; Gomes-Casseres, 1989; Killing, 1983; Kogut, 1988; Makino and Beamish, 1998; Park and Ungson, 1997). Typically, a variety of behavioural, cultural and administrative impediments makes the effective management of a JV quite a demanding task in terms of the executive time and effort. Examples of the effect of cultural differences on JV performance have been well documented by Peterson and Shimada (1978), Simiar (1983) and Tybejee (1988) in their research on JVs in Iran and Japan. They found that cultural differences frequently led to failure on the part of parent company managers to 'understand' or communicate with one another. The resultant breakdown of communications generally had significant negative consequences, sometimes leading to the eventual dismemberment of the venture (Gullander, 1976; Killing, 1983; Koot, 1988; Lane and Beamish, 1990).

Geringer and Hebert (1991) also identify the possibility that agreement on IJV performance among a venture's participants may be influenced by cultural similarity among them. Several authors have shown or hypothesised that different national cultures embody different attitudes, values and beliefs that find their materialisation in distinct business cultures, styles and practices (Davidson, 1982; Deal and Kennedy, 1982; England, 1975; Geringer and Hebert, 1989; Hofstede, 1980; Jain, 1994a; Jain and Tucker, 1995; Kogut and Singh, 1988; Lane and Beamish, 1990; Schneider, 1988; Tayeb, 1995). For example, Ouchi (1981) examined the US and Japanese business cultures and described them as mostly incompatible. The presence of dissimilarities between parent firms' national cultures may be more likely to lead to differences in parent firms' objectives for an IJV, as well as in their approaches to coordination, operating methods and strategy implementation (Brown *et al.,* 1989; Geringer, 1988; Root, 1988a; Sullivan and Peterson, 1982). These dissimilarities may also lead to differences in the partners' perceptions of each other and the IJV, and result in a lower degree of agreement regarding IJV performance. Conversely, the opposite will apply. In IJVs where parents are from the same national culture, a tendency toward greater agreement among the parents and the IJV regarding the venture's performance is expected (Kotabe, 1990; Ouchi, 1980). As shown by Anderson and Weitz (1989), cultural similarity promotes communication among business partners. Better communication among JV partners will result in better perceived performance and satisfaction from all partners.

Along with behavioural and cultural factors, various administrative factors play an important role in determining the extent to which performance expectations in a venture can eventually be realised. For example, incompatible administrative systems of the parent companies can prove to be a serious impediment to the effective implementation of the venture. Problems in the management of the JV also stem from incompatible organisational policies and strategies. The parent companies might have very different notions on the appropriate advertising/sales ratio, the nature of the markets served, the right distribution channels, the quality control standards to be adopted, or the hiring and firing policy, all of which might generate potentially dysfunctional and damaging conflicts (Datta, 1988; Killing, 1983; Schaan and Beamish, 1988).

Effective management of a JV also requires that well-defined reporting relationships and communication channels be established as early as possible. However, it may not be an easy task in JVs, as there is generally no one 'best' organisational structure and the IJV parents themselves may have adopted different organisational structures and may each be wanting to adopt the structure of their parent organisation, thereby leading to conflict between the parents. Most successful ventures, therefore, use a mix of organisational and other managerial devices for promoting unified planning, partner participation and control.

In such an environment, any business is difficult to evaluate because profit is a long-term proposition and because there are no performance baselines for comparison. Additionally, many JVs are not intended to fill standard business objectives (such as making a profit) (Anderson, 1990; Venkatraman and Ramanujam, 1986). Instead, they are created to learn a technology, open a market, 'keep open a window' on an opportunity, or block a competitor (Geringer and Hebert, 1989; Harrigan, 1988a; Johnson *et al.,* 1993; Kogut, 1988). It is not easy to assess how well a JV meets qualitative objectives such as these (Anderson, 1990; Beamish, 1984; Beamish and Inkpen, 1995; Cullen *et al.,* 1995; Geringer and Hebert, 1989, 1991; Johnson *et al.,* 1993; Kogut, 1988; Lee and Beamish, 1995; Venkatraman and Ramanujam, 1986).

There is very little information on how firms monitor and weigh their JV's performance. Whilst many researchers have suggested a variety of ways to measure JV performance (Anderson, 1990; Beamish, 1984; Delios and Beamish, 2004; Geringer and Hebert, 1991; Inkpen, 1992; Makino and Beamish, 1995; Schaan, 1983), the most comprehensive data comes from a survey of 28,000 Japanese subsidiaries around the world where in the sample each partner had 5 percent or more equity ownership (Delios and Beamish, 2004). Delios and Beamish evaluate performance using financial performance and subsidiary survival rates. Using financial performance and subsidiary survival rates to assess JV performance is more than acceptable, but using such narrow indicators of performance it is unlikely to produce accurate assessments of JV performance as some JVs, for example, may be set up for a restricted duration, e.g., turnkey contracts, or set up to conduct joint research and development (Hladik, 1988). Even in their research Delios and Beamish (2004) acknowledge that they concentrated on only two performance measures when analysing JV and entry mode performance. They further acknowledge that these measures capture only a part of the multidimensional aspects of JV performance, suggesting future work should explore if the same implications are derived using other measures, such as a managerial satisfaction measure. Additionally, they recommend taking into consideration the role of contextual factors, such as JV management capabilities, that moderate JV performance. Finally, they advocate the need to use measures other than survival or multiple measures of performance that characterized much of the early JV literature (See Julian, 1998; Julian and O'Cass, 2002a, 2004a).

Most JVs should not be evaluated using the standard operating procedures that corporate headquarters uses to evaluate wholly owned divisions with conventional business objectives. One important reason is that the interests of the JV and the parents are often in conflict. For example, a venture may enjoy excellent market acceptance and provide a high return on investment, which is good performance from one parent's viewpoint. Yet another of the parents may be unhappy because the venture refuses to use one of its divisions as a supplier. From one parent's perspective, then, the JV is performing poorly. Indeed, the same venture may be rated very differently depending on the viewpoint adopted. Parents that evaluate performance strictly in accordance with their own interests, as they do with subsidiaries, risk alienating their partners. Performance evaluation requires incorporating multiple viewpoints, if only to forecast the partners' reactions and future behaviour.

JVs are different from wholly owned divisions in another important way: their organisational politics are much more complicated. Because JVs have multiple parents, they may be viewed as 'outsiders' by parent personnel, who question their commitment to the corporation. Thus, JVs are more likely to become scapegoats and 'political footballs', especially when the parent itself has performance problems. Divisions of the parent may find it easy to blame the JV for their own shortcomings. Hence, JVs are particularly vulnerable players in the game of corporate politics (Anderson, 1990; Beamish, 1984; Geringer and Hebert, 1991; Harrigan, 1987).

Why not use profitability indicators as a method of evaluating JV performance? Profitability is an excellent index of performance. What makes JVs so different? The answer lies in the JVs' setting. While they may be used for many purposes, JVs are especially popular in risky, uncertain situations, for it is there that firms are most likely to concede some control if that will spread risk and expand expertise. But when risk and uncertainty are high, profitability by itself is a poor measure of the JV's value. For start-up, in high-risk businesses, profits if any are in the future, and high costs are in the present (Anderson, 1990; Cullen *et al.,* 1995; Johnson *et al.,* 1993; Venkatraman and Ramanujam, 1986).

The standard way to allow for this when evaluating performance is to use discounted cash flow (DCF) analysis. But DCF analysis is seriously flawed in risky, uncertain settings, and it is in these types of settings that the IJV form of market entry is extremely popular. There are four main problems in using the DCF analysis to assess IJV performance (Myers, 1984). The first is that while subjective estimates of operating results (such as revenue) may be feasible, converting these estimates into cash flows is extremely difficult, especially for later years in the projection. Second, period-by-period long-run forecasts are so difficult that they often end up being mechanical extrapolations of short-term trends. These estimates have the specificity needed for the DCF analysis, but they overlook strategic concerns, such as technological changes. Third, uncertainties are very difficult to incorporate. A standard response is to raise the discount rate, but this penalises uncertain projects exponentially into the future, thereby biasing against significant risk-taking. Finally, and most importantly, many JVs are really options. They allow a firm to maintain a doorway into a market or a technology. If the opportunity eventually looks promising, the firm can exercise its option to enter. Otherwise, the firm may decide not to enter altogether or even defer its entry to a later date. Unfortunately, DCF analysis does not adequately account for the value of an option, nor, for that matter, does any other analytical technique (Anderson, 1990; Cullen *et al.,* 1995; Johnson *et al.,* 1993; Venktraman and Ramanujam, 1986).

In more general terms, many, if not most, JVs operate in settings where current financial results are bound to suggest poor performance. Yet the venture may be making satisfactory progress to longer-term goals, or meeting current goals that are not financial in nature. Standard operating procedure, then, will misstate the venture's performance. When then are financial criteria appropriate, and what other measures should be used when evaluating JV performance?

Several researchers have noted the problems in evaluating the performance of IJVs (Anderson, 1990; Geringer and Hebert, 1991) with a number of researchers arguing that the package approach is the correct way to evaluate a business, even though it is cumbersome and difficult (Johnson *et al.,* 1993; Venkatraman and Ramanujam, 1986). An obviously intuitive approach is the 'financials'. However, as Geringer and Hebert (1991) point out, the numbers are often included in and confounded with parent company performance reports, or not reported at all. Furthermore, even if available, financial data may not be appropriate or even interpretable, thereby invalidating financial performance indicators as the sole measure of performance. Empirical support is provided by a study that finds traditional accounting figures, including profitability measures, are statistically not enough to distinguish excellent firms from ordinary firms (Chakravarthy, 1986).

Excellent firms are also distinguished by their operating characteristics and methods, suggesting the need to view performance as a combination of many factors. In support of this position, a conference board survey of top executives finds strong sentiment that financial measures assess only one facet of performance and that a number of other factors, many of them qualitative, must also be considered (Anderson, 1990; Delios and Beamish, 2004; Beamish, 1984; Geringer and Hebert, 1989, 1991; Johnson *et al.,* 1993; Julian, 1998; Lee and Beamish, 1995; Venkatraman and Ramanujam, 1986).

How do business people view performance? Firms that executives rate as 'most admired' are characterised by a combination of high growth, profit, high (but not necessarily the highest) return on stockholders' equity, consistent avoidance of losses, consistently positive earnings, occasional improvements in operating results, good bond ratings and stable management (Cameron, 1986). It is interesting to note that whilst most of these factors are financial and clearly results oriented, others (such as stable management) are non-financial and related to long-term performance. In short, executives seem to rank organisational performance by considering a package of measures, weighed over time (Anderson, 1990; Beamish, 1984; Geringer and Hebert, 1991; Johnson *et al.,* 1993; Venkatraman and Ramanujam, 1986).

Johnson *et al.* (1993) measured partner satisfaction with the IJV as opposed to direct financial performance. The Johnson *et al.* (1993) study was broad-based and included financial performance given that it is 'highly unlikely that a manager would feel satisfied in an IJV relationship that does not maintain at least some minimum level of economic performance' (Johnson *et al.,* 1993, 33). The Johnson *et al.* study encompassed such IJV goals as technology transfer, access to markets, sharing of risks and equitable division of rewards. Their satisfaction measure focused on the broad-based evaluation of the IJV and the IJV relationship rather than performance.

Killing (1983), Schaan (1983), Beamish (1984), Ding (1997), Beamish and Delios (1997b) and Julian (1998) also used a perceptual measure of a parent's satisfaction with an IJV's performance (e.g., 'To what extent has the IJV met the expectations of your firm?'). The main advantage of this type of measure is its ability to provide this type of information regarding the extent to which the IJV has achieved its overall objectives. Additionally, these authors, as well as Janger (1980), utilised subjective performance measures for each of a limited number of individual dimensions of the IJV. Nevertheless, these types of measures remain subjective and are thus exposed to serious limitations and biases. Many research methods, such as those based on archival or other secondary data sources, do not generally permit collection of these types of data, instead requiring the use of objective performance measures. Furthermore, the consistency between subjective and objective measures of IJV performance is relatively unknown and, while often assumed, has not been formally tested. However, Dess and Robinson's (1984) finding that subjective and objective measures were correlated for traditional organisational forms suggests that this relationship may be found for IJVs as well. Geringer and Hebert (1991) and later Julian (1998) provided empirical support for the Dess and Robinson (1984) finding that subjective and objective measures of organisational performance were significantly correlated for the IJV organisation form.

Support for the package approach when evaluating IJV performance is also provided by Venkatraman and Ramanujam (1986) who argue 'business performance' that reflects the perspective of strategic management, is a subset of the overall concept of organisational effectiveness. According to Venkatraman and Ramanujam, the narrowest conception of business performance centres on the use of simple outcome-based financial indicators that are assumed to reflect the fulfilment of the economic goals of the firm. Venkatraman and Ramanujam refer to this concept as financial performance, which has been the dominant model in empirical research (Hofer, 1983). Hofer (1983, p. 44) is quoted as saying: 'it seems clear that different fields of study will and should use different measures of organisation performance because of the differences in their research questions'. Typical of this approach would be to examine such indicators as sales growth, profitability (reflected by such ratios as ROI, return on sales, return on equity and return on assets) and earnings per share.

A broader conceptualisation of business performance would include emphasis on indicators of operational performance (i.e. non-financial) in addition to indicators of financial performance. According to Anderson (1990), Johnson *et al.* (1993), Julian (1998) and Venkatraman and Ramanujam (1986), under this framework it would be logical to treat such measures as market share, new product introduction, product quality, marketing effectiveness, manufacturing value-added, and other measures of technological efficiency within the domain of business performance as performance measures. Other objective measures of IJV performance would include duration of the IJV, instability, ownership, and re-negotiation of the JV contract (Beamish, 1984, 1993; Beamish and Inkpen, 1995; Fey, 1995; Geringer and Hebert, 1989; Johnson *et al.,* 1993; Madhok, 1995; Makino and Beamish, 1995; Lee and Beamish, 1995). Similarly, market-share position, widely believed to be a determinant of profitability (Buzzell *et al.,* 1975) would be a meaningful indicator of performance within this perspective.

Financial indicators may also not identify the extent to which the IJV has achieved its objectives (Anderson, 1990; Artisien and Buckley, 1985; Beamish, 1984; Blodgett, 1987; Julian, 1998; Julian and O'Cass, 2002a, 2004a; Killing, 1983; Lee and Beamish, 1995). IJVs may be formed for a variety of objectives, e.g., technology transfer, joint research, materials access, new markets or economies of scale (Beamish, 1984; Beamish and Banks, 1987; Contractor and Lorange, 1988c; Harrigan, 1988a; Hladik, 1988;

Porter and Fuller, 1986). Many IJVs also operate in contexts where measures of short-term financial performance might suggest the venture is performing poorly. For example, IJVs formed to develop radical new technologies or penetrate new markets are not likely to generate a financial profit for many years, if at all. In such situations, a financial or objective measure is unlikely to accurately capture an IJV's relative performance versus objectives. As Anderson (1990), Delios and Beamish (2004), Geringer and Hebert (1991) and Venkatraman and Ramanujam (1986) noted, financial measures evaluate only one dimension of performance.

Other factors, including qualitative ones, must also be examined in order to adequately evaluate IJV performance. Thus, despite poor financial results, liquidation or instability, an IJV may have been meeting or exceeding its parents' objectives and thus be considered successful by one or all of the parents. Conversely, an IJV may be viewed as unsuccessful despite good financial results or continued stability.

Therefore, for this research, IJV marketing performance was measured by both financial and operational indicators. The operational indicators used to measure IJV performance included: level of technology transfer, economies of scale, organisational learning, access to markets, access to raw materials and a low-cost labour force, sharing of risks, product quality, price competitiveness, customer satisfaction and erecting barriers to entry. The financial indicators used to measure IJV performance included profitability, return on investment, market share, sales and cost effectiveness.

The most basic issue in JV performance evaluation is the question of whose performance to assess. Parents have their own objectives in creating JVs, and obviously to measure a venture's performance against these objectives is relevant. But it is not the only basis for measuring results. Anderson (1990) argued JVs should be measured primarily as stand-alone entities seeking to maximise their own performance, not the parents'. This perspective frees the venture from parent politics and parochial viewpoints. Further, encouraging the venture to stand alone promotes harmony among the parents. Most JVs face a steep climb to begin with, as their high rates of dissolution show (Beamish, 1985; Bleeke and Ernst, 1991; Gomes-Casseres, 1989; Killing, 1983; Kogut, 1988; Makino and Beamish, 1998; Park and Ungson, 1997). Giving the JV the opportunity to find its own way increases the chances of survival and prosperity. Additionally, giving the JV autonomy facilitates learning and innovation, which are primary reasons to enter a venture.

Other researchers argue that using only the IJV entity to assess IJV performance represents an incomplete method of assessing IJV performance (Beamish, 1993; Beamish and Banks, 1987; Dymsza, 1988; Harrigan, 1988a). Since IJVs are jointly owned, it is reasonable to examine whether both parties (local and foreign) are satisfied with performance. Because one partner is a local firm and one partner is a foreign firm, one could expect differences in how performance may be assessed especially when the partners are from different cultures (Beamish, 1984; Beamish and Banks, 1987; Beamish and Inkpen, 1995; Datta, 1988; Dymsza, 1988; Harrigan, 1988a; Schaan and Beamish, 1988).

A number of researchers (Beamish, 1984, 1993; Beamish and Banks, 1987; Beamish and Inkpen, 1995; Cullen *et al.,* 1995; Datta, 1988; Dymsza, 1988; Geringer and Hebert, 1991; Harrigan, 1988a; Schaan and Beamish, 1988) further argue that more than one perspective on JV performance is required to increase confidence in the findings. This is because IJV parents use different criteria to assess performance, and the objectives of the parents can be significantly different. Therefore, based on whether or not the individual IJV parent's objectives have been achieved is how each individual parent will assess IJV performance, and given firms enter IJV arrangements for quite distinctly different reasons each individual parent's perception of overall IJV performance could be significantly different (Anderson, 1990; Beamish, 1984; Geringer and Hebert, 1989). There has also been argument to suggest that for an IJV to be considered as being successful it needs to be rated as being successful by more than one partner (Beamish, 1984, 1988).

As a result, there is no accepted formula for assessing IJV performance, and to a large extent this depends on whose perception of IJV performance the study is interested in (Lee and Beamish, 1995). Given that IJVs are established for a variety of reasons to achieve a diverse range of objectives, even if all parties' perceptions of performance are obtained it is still possible to obtain different outcomes, making the assessment of IJV performance a most difficult task.

In this research, the interest is to obtain the most accurate perception and evaluation of overall IJV marketing performance, as one of the principal objectives of the research was to identify those factors that have the greatest influence on IJV marketing performance. Therefore, this research adopts Anderson's (1990) viewpoint and only seeks the IJV entity's perception of marketing performance, as it is the position taken in this research that the IJV should be evaluated as a stand-alone entity in order to identify the most accurate perception of marketing performance. That is why a composite measure of IJV marketing performance was developed to provide the most accurate perception of IJV marketing performance possible. All possible objectives (financial and strategic) for establishing an IJV were incorporated into a composite measure of IJV marketing performance, and IJVs were rated as being low, medium or high marketing performers based on the key respondent's level of satisfaction with the achievement of those strategic objectives. Furthermore, Dess and Robinson (1984) and Geringer and Hebert (1991) have already identified that there is a strong positive relationship between how one of the IJV partners view IJV performance and how the senior executive within the IJV entity views performance, providing support for taking only the IJV entity's view of marketing performance. Finally, the measure of IJV marketing performance used in this research adopts the recommendations of the Delios and Beamish (2004) work and incorporates multiple measures of performance that characterized much of the early JV literature.

3.3. Marketing Performance

Since the early 1980s, research on IJVs and IJV performance has been considerable. However, limited empirical research has been conducted on IJV marketing performance. With the exception of Berg (1991), Blodgett (1991a), Ganitsky *et al.* (1991) and some others, most studies on marketing strategy and performance are applied to indirect/direct export firms. With the globalization of markets and competition, foreign markets have become increasingly viable and natural opportunities for growth-oriented domestic firms. Considering the growth in IJVs as a form of market entry it is therefore of practical, as well as of theoretical importance, to address the issue of 'What are the factors that contribute to the success or failure of IJVs' (Julian, 1998, p. 45).

Three distinctive features should be noted at the outset. First, the unit of analysis was an individual IJV between, at least, one foreign firm and a local Thai firm, with the IJV under review involved in the marketing of specific products/services in Thailand. Second, incorporated in the proposed framework was a theoretical conceptualisation that marketing performance was determined by the coalignment between the marketing mix variables and the internal and the external environments of the firm. Furthermore, marketing performance was conceived as the accomplishment of strategic as well as economic objectives. Finally, data were collected based on responses to a self-administered mail survey from a senior executive within the IJV entity itself.

Some of the key success factors highlighted from previous studies on the marketing performance of direct/indirect export firms include marketing strategy; management attitudes; and other firm, industry, product and market factors (Cavusgil and Zou, 1994; Cavusgil *et al.,* 1993; Christensen *et al.,* 1987; Diamantopoulos and Schlegelmilch, 1994; Dominguez and Sequeira, 1993; Julian, 2003; Julian and O'Cass, 2002b; Lages, 2000; Madsen, 1989; O'Cass and Julian, 2003a, 2003b). In their review article, Aaby and Slater (1989) suggest that marketing performance is directly influenced by a firm's business strategy. Using factor analysis, Cavusgil (1983) demonstrated that marketing decision variables influencing successful export marketing performance can be reduced to (1) basic company offering, (2) contractual link with foreign distributors/agents, (3) promotion, and (4) pricing.

Previous research into the key success factors of direct/indirect exporting firms in foreign markets identifies a link between marketing strategy and performance (Cavusgil and Zou, 1994; Julian and O'Cass, 2004a). A similar linkage between marketing strategy and performance is also evident when evaluating the marketing performance of IJVs (Blodgett, 1991a; Ganitsky *et al.,* 1991). However, there are several issues that undermine the strength and nature of this relationship. The first is the level of analysis. With few exceptions, previous studies have either been conducted at the foreign partner level or the local partner level or both (Beamish and Inkpen, 1995; Datta, 1988; Lee and Beamish, 1995). As a result, performance success factors were conceptualised as firm-specific characteristics. An underlying theoretical justification for firm-level studies is the theory of internalisation (Buckley and Casson, 1985; Rugman, 1981), which states that, in an imperfect market, firms should internalise the firm-specific advantages, both tangible and intangible, to extract maximum economic rent. Because firm-specific advantages are derived not only from the development and marketing of a particular product but also from the total learning process of the firm, it is possible to investigate marketing performance at the firm level.

Though previous studies contributed to our knowledge of factors influencing export marketing performance and overall JV performance, there are notable limitations associated with firm-level investigations of IJV marketing performance. Considerable variations in marketing strategy and performance often exist across various product-market ventures depending on the foreign market and the structure established for the IJV. It is also unrealistic to expect that the same structure in all foreign markets will lead to the same marketing performance results.

The second issue is the failure of previous studies to incorporate strategic considerations in the performance of IJVs. Previous studies have viewed marketing performance simply as a means of realising the economic goals of the firm. Marketing performance has been measured in terms of sales or profits, with no deliberate attempt to relate it to a firm's strategic or economic objectives, such as gaining a foothold in a foreign market, collaborative R&D, and erecting barriers to entry. The problems associated with using solely financial measures to measure the performance of an IJV have already been addressed. Short-term profit motives are not the sole reason for establishing IJVs and by using solely economic measures a JV may be rated as performing poorly when actually it is achieving the objectives of the parents for which it was established. Therefore, this study will consider both economic and strategic measures of performance in determining the marketing performance of the IJVs being studied.

The need for strategic considerations in marketing theory has also been emphasised by Cavusgil and Zou (1994), Julian (1998, 2003) and Lages (2000). Increasingly, firms have treated international markets as strategic as well as economic opportunities. Given intense international competition, it is believed that international marketing research can be enriched if marketing performance enquiries incorporate strategic as well as economic considerations into the marketing performance of IJVs. This implies that marketing performance measurement in an IJV should be viewed as the IJV entity's strategic response to the interplay of internal and external forces and its ability to achieve set objectives by the parents, both economic and strategic.

The final issue relates to the diversity of conceptualisation and measurement of marketing performance and the simplistic nature of research approaches employed in previous studies. Both Madsen (1987) and Aaby and Slater (1989) observe that marketing performance has been conceptualised and operationalised in many different ways by different researchers. They point out that researchers previously have made little effort to identify measurement difficulties, sampling, validity or particular technical problems. Data collection methods have ranged from unstructured personal discussions to structured mail surveys to in-depth interviews, and analytical approaches have ranged from simple frequencies to sophisticated multivariate techniques. As a result, confusing and even contradictory findings have surfaced in the literature (e.g., the effect of firm size on marketing performance). These discrepant findings hinder not only practice, but also theory development of marketing performance measures. Hence, there is a need for an integrated approach to marketing performance enquiry. Such an approach must deal with the measurement as well as the conceptualisation of marketing performance and factors internal and external to the firm.

The conceptual framework postulated here is that the marketing performance of an IJV is determined by internal forces such as product characteristics and firm-specific characteristics, and external forces such as market characteristics (Cavusgil and Zou, 1994; Cavusgil *et al.,* 1993; Dominguez and Sequeira, 1993). For various environments the IJV operates in, as defined by product, firm-specific and market characteristics, certain marketing strategies adopted by the IJV must be adapted to enable positive marketing performance to be achieved.

The proposed framework incorporates three key features. Firstly, the unit of analysis is that the IJV can be a single- or multi-product venture. The objective is not to determine the performance of certain products or product lines but to determine the overall marketing performance of the IJV. Secondly, the framework posits that marketing performance involves both economic and strategic considerations. Finally, the framework is presented in general terms, with marketing performance being determined by internal and external forces and represented by broad categories of variables. This is due to the existing marketing performance literature being not very helpful in terms of suggesting specific constructs or measures for the proposed conceptualisation.

There is no uniform definition of marketing performance in the literature. A variety of marketing performance measures have been adopted by previous researchers. These performance measures include sales (Bello and Williamson, 1985; Bilkey, 1985; Cavusgil, 1984b; Cooper and Kleinschmidt, 1985; Madsen, 1989; Sood and Adams, 1984); sales growth (Cooper and Kleinschmidt, 1985; Kirpalani and Mckintosh, 1980; Madsen, 1989); market share and profitability (Anderson, 1990; Geringer and Hebert, 1991; Venkatraman and Ramanujam, 1986); technology transfer (Blodgett, 1991a; Dymsza, 1988; Hladik, 1988; Johnson *et al.,* 1993; Kogut, 1988); durability (Beamish and Inkpen, 1995; Makino and Beamish, 1995); survival (Delios and Beamish, 2004); organisational learning (Johnson *et al.,* 1993; Kim, 1995); and access to markets (Johnson *et al.,* 1993; Schaan and Beamish, 1988; Venkatraman and Ramanujam, 1986). However, the most frequently used performance measures appear to be economic in nature. As an IJV is a hybrid formed from two separate organisations, which may have completely different marketing objectives for the IJV, the intention in this study was to use both economic and strategic measures of marketing performance and incorporate them into a single comprehensive composite measure of IJV marketing performance.

For the purpose of this research, marketing performance was defined as the extent to which the IJV's objectives, both economic and strategic, with respect to marketing a product/service in Thailand was achieved through the planning and execution of a specific marketing strategy. An IJV usually has a number of objectives set by the individual partners, which can be economic (i.e. profits, sales, or costs) and/or strategic (i.e. market expansion, access to raw materials, technology transfer, economies of scale, gaining a foothold in a foreign market and erecting barriers to entry). The extent to which the IJV's strategic and economic objectives were achieved was therefore a measure of its marketing performance.

In an international market an IJV's marketing strategy was the means by which the IJV responds to the environmental forces to meet the set objectives of the IJV. It involves all aspects of the conventional marketing plan, namely, product, price, promotion and distribution. In international marketing, the key consideration is whether the marketing strategy should be standardised or adapted to the conditions of the foreign market (Douglas and Wind, 1987; Jain, 1989; 1994). The degree of marketing adaptation versus standardisation is a function of product, market, organisation and environmental characteristics (Buzzell, 1968; Cavusgil *et al.,* 1993; Jain, 1989, 1994a; Walters, 1986). Therefore, the marketing performance of IJVs in Thailand will be evaluated along that continuum incorporating firm-specific characteristics, product characteristics and market characteristics.

Firstly, consider the influence of a firm's characteristics on its marketing performance; a firm's capabilities and constraints profoundly influences its ability to implement a specific marketing plan and to execute a chosen strategy (Aaker, 1988; Porter, 1980). Key assets and skills of a firm constitute its sources of sustainable competitive advantage (Day and Wensley, 1988; Porter, 1985). In international marketing, the relevant assets and skills of a firm include size advantages (Reid, 1982), international experience (Douglas and Craig, 1989), extent of international business involvement, and resources available for the development of export markets (Terpstra, 1987). Possession of such assets and skills enables an international marketer to identify the opportunities available in international markets, develop the appropriate marketing strategy to take advantage of the opportunities, and implement them effectively. Therefore, firm-specific characteristics will affect marketing strategy and performance.

Secondly, consider the influence of product characteristics on marketing performance. The specific marketing strategy adopted in any foreign market venture is influenced by product characteristics (Cavusgil *et al.*, 1993; Cooper and Kleinschmidt, 1985; McGuiness and Little, 1981). Product attributes can affect the positional competitive advantage (Day and Wensley, 1988), which influences the choice of a defensive or offensive strategy (Cook, 1983). Relevant product characteristics that can influence marketing strategy and performance include culture-specificity of the product, strength of the patent, unit value, uniqueness and age of the product, and service/maintenance requirements of the product (Cavusgil and Zou, 1994).

Finally, when considering market characteristics, the intensity of market entry activity and the nature of marketing strategy vary considerably across markets and industries. This is largely a result of the varying nature of industries in different markets (Porter, 1980). Industry structure has been considered a key determinant of a firm's strategy in the domestic market context (Ganitsky *et al.*, 1991; Kerin *et al.*, 1990; Porter, 1980). In international marketing, analysis of the relationship between certain market characteristics and marketing strategy must incorporate the significant variations in the market systems, government interventions, and presence of foreign competitors across markets. In addition, technology intensity and intensity of price competition in the industry also must be considered as the relevant correlates of the adaptation of marketing strategy that will have a significant influence on marketing performance (Cavusgil and Zou, 1994; Blodgett, 1991a; Ganitsky *et al.*, 1991).

Conditions in international markets pose both opportunities and threats for international marketers. Marketing strategy in international markets must be formulated in such a way as to match a firm's strengths with market opportunities and neutralise the firm's strategic weaknesses, or to overcome market threats (Aaker, 1988; Terpstra, 1987). Therefore, the marketing strategy adopted by international firms in foreign markets tends to be conditioned by market characteristics in that foreign market (Blodgett, 1991b; Cavusgil *et al.*, 1993; Cooper and Kleinschmidt, 1985; Ganitsky *et al.*, 1991; Rosson and Ford, 1982). The key characteristics of an international market that can affect the choice of marketing strategy and have the greatest influence on marketing performance include accessibility to suitable distribution channels (Cavusgil, 1983), access to capital resources (Terpstra, 1987), intensity of price competition (Christensen *et al.*, 1987), and government intervention (Beamish, 1988).

On the basis of this review, a set of product-related, firm-related and market-related characteristics have been selected to examine the influence they have on the marketing performance of IJVs in Thailand. These variables or measures, together with other variables or measures identified in the literature as having a significant influence on IJV performance, broadly categorised under control, conflict, trust, commitment, needs, partners' contributions and marketing orientation, will be used to examine the factors influencing the marketing performance of IJVs in Thailand.

This chapter next evaluates IJV marketing performance by analysing the results generated using the composite measure and a single-item measure of IJV marketing performance (see Julian, 1998).

3.3.1. Composite Measure of IJV Marketing Performance

Using the literature and the pre-tests of the research instrument, 16 strategic objectives were pre-set in the research instrument that corresponded with each of the measures of marketing performance. Towards the end of the research instrument, respondents were asked to indicate the relative importance attached to each objective by allocating a constant-sum (100 points) to the individual objectives proportional to their importance. The composite measure computed the extent to which each of the strategic objectives were achieved by multiplying the level of satisfaction associated with the achievement of each strategic objective by the points allocated to the importance of the same strategic objective. The combined scores for each of the 16 strategic objectives were then added together to give a composite score for each IJV for measuring IJV marketing performance. The results of the composite measure of IJV marketing performance are summarised in Table 3.1.

Table 3.1 IJV Marketing Performance (using the composite measure)

Marketing Performance Score	Frequency	Percent	Cumulative Percent
100-400 (Low Performers)	41	27.7	27.7
401-500 (Medium Performers)	55	37.1	64.8
501-700 (High Performers)	52	35.2	100.0
Total	148	100.0	

As indicated, the composite measure computed the extent to which each of the strategic objectives was achieved by multiplying the level of satisfaction associated with the achievement of each strategic objective by the points allocated (a constant-sum of 100 points) to the importance of each strategic objective. The level of satisfaction associated with the achievement of each strategic objective was measured from 1 to 7 on a seven-point Likert Scale, with 1 being identified as extremely dissatisfied and 7 being identified as extremely satisfied. Thus, the weighted score of marketing performance for an IJV will fall between 100 and 700.

As the mid-point of the seven-point Likert Scale was identified as being 4 (or 400 using the composite index), IJVs were classified as being low marketing performers if they had a composite marketing performance score of 400 or below; they were classified as being medium marketing performers if they had a composite marketing performance score of between 401 and 500; and they were classified as being high marketing performers if they had a composite marketing performance score of above 500.

Marketing performance scores in the composite measure ranged from a minimum of 128 to a maximum of 700 with a mean score of 419, a median score of 457, and a standard deviation of 162. This indicates that overall the majority of companies (72.3 percent of companies) were identified as having medium or high marketing performance. It was also evident after analysing Table 3.1 that the dispersion of marketing performance scores identifying whether the IJV was a low marketing performer, medium marketing performer or high marketing performer were evenly spread across the sample. From Table 3.1 it is apparent that 27.7 percent of the sample or 41 IJVs were identified as low marketing performers; 37.1 percent of the sample or 55 IJVs were identified as medium marketing performers; and 35.2 percent of the sample or 52 IJVs were identified as high marketing performers. This indicates that the IJVs in this sample were well represented at each level of marketing performance.

3.3.2. Single-Item Measure of IJV Marketing Performance

A single-item measure of IJV marketing performance was also included as a subjective measure to determine the respondent's overall perception of IJV marketing performance. This was done to make a comparison with the results achieved using the composite measure, as the composite measure was a completely new measure of IJV marketing performance designed by the author and never previously tested. Similar results for IJV marketing performance were found using either measure. This finding supports Dess and Robinson's (1984) finding that subjective and objective measures were correlated for traditional organisational forms, and it supports Geringer and Hebert's (1991) finding that subjective and objective measures were correlated for the IJV organisational form.

Killing (1983), Schaan (1983), Beamish (1984), Ding (1997), Beamish and Delios (1997b) and Julian (1998) also used a perceptual measure of a parent's satisfaction with an IJV's performance (e.g. 'To what extent has the IJV met the expectations of your firm?'). The main advantage of this type of measure is its ability to provide this type of information regarding the extent to which the IJV has achieved its overall objectives. Additionally, these authors, as well as Janger (1980), utilised subjective performance measures for each of a limited number of individual dimensions of the IJV. Nevertheless, these types of measures remain subjective and are thus exposed to serious limitations and biases. Many research methods, such as those based on archival or other secondary data sources, do not generally permit collection of these types of data, instead requiring the use of objective performance measures. Furthermore, with the exception of Geringer and Hebert (1991), the consistency between subjective and objective measures of IJV performance is relatively unknown and requires further empirical testing. Therefore, a further objective of the study was to test the finding that subjective and objective measures of IJV marketing performance were correlated for the IJV organisation form. The findings from this study suggest that subjective and objective measures of IJV marketing performance are correlated, as the percentage of respondents falling into different categories of marketing performance were almost the same when the respondents were classified using the single-item measure (subjective measure) and the composite measure (objective measure) of performance (see Tables 3.1 and 3.2).

A seven-point Likert Scale was used and respondents were asked to rate their satisfaction with the marketing performance of their IJV on a scale of 1 to 7 with 1 being unsuccessful and 7 being successful. The results of this measure of marketing performance are reported in Table 3.2.

Table 3.2 IJV Marketing Performance (using the single-item measure)

Marketing Performance Score	Frequency	Percent	Cumulative Percent
1-4	52	32.3	32.3
(Low Performers)			
5	56	34.8	67.1
(Medium Performers)			
6-7	53	32.9	100.0
(High Performers)			
Total	161	100.0	

As indicated, this single-item measure identified the respondent's overall satisfaction with IJV marketing performance. Again the mid-point of this seven-point Likert Scale was identified as being 4. Therefore, IJVs were classified as being low marketing performers if they had a single-item score of 4 or below; they were classified as being medium marketing performers if they had a single-item score of above 4 but below 6, i.e. 5; and they were classified as being high marketing performers if they had a single-item score of 6 or 7. In this measure of IJV marketing performance the score of 4 was used as a cut-off point to differentiate between low marketing performers and medium marketing performers. Respondents who rated their satisfaction with IJV marketing performance as 4 are likely to exhibit a fair degree of uncertainty with satisfaction to IJV marketing performance, indicating a reasonable amount of dissatisfaction with IJV marketing performance and thus low IJV marketing performance.

The results generated using the single-item measure of IJV marketing performance were comparable with the results generated using the composite measure. The inconsistency in the IJV marketing performer categories (i.e., low, medium or high) between the single-item measure and the composite measure can be explained by the number of responses. Only 148 responses were received using the composite measure while there were 161 responses received for the single-item measure. It is quite possible that because of the complex nature of the questions associated with the composite measure, some respondents did not understand how to complete the questions. However, there was very little difference in the percentages for each IJV marketing performer category using either measure.

After evaluating Table 3.2 it was evident that 32.3 percent of the sample or 52 IJVs could be identified as low marketing performers (a marketing performance score of 4 or less); 34.8 percent of the sample or 56 IJVs could be identified as medium marketing performers (marketing performance score of 5); and 32.9 percent of the sample or 53 IJVs could be identified as high marketing performers (a marketing performance score of 6 or 7).

This chapter next uses the single-item index of IJV marketing performance to compare IJV marketing performance across the country of origin of the principal foreign partner, equity structures of the principal foreign partner, industry structure, and IJV sales volume (see Table 3.3).

Table 3.3 IJV Marketing Performance via Country of Origin, Equity Structure, Industry Structure and IJV Sales Volume

Country of Origin of the Principal Foreign Partner

Marketing Performance	Europe (%)	North America (%)	Japan (%)	Taiwan (%)	Korea (%)	ASEAN (%)
Low	21.4	66.7	31.4	29.4	57.1	37.5
Medium	39.3	11.1	37.1	29.4	28.6	0.0
High	39.3	22.2	31.5	41.2	14.3	62.5
Total	100.0	100.0	100.0	100.0	100.0	100.0

Equity Structure of the Principal Foreign Partner

Marketing Performance	5-9 (%)	10-19 (%)	20-29 (%)	30-39 (%)	40-49 (%)	50-59 (%)	60-95 (%)
Low	66.7	45.4	53.8	23.1	30.6	16.7	22.2
Medium	0.0	27.3	15.4	46.2	38.8	44.4	41.5
High	33.3	27.3	30.8	30.7	30.6	38.9	36.3
Total	100.0	100.0	100.0	100.0	100.0	100.0	100.0

IJV Industry Structure

Marketing Performance	Agric (%)	Mining (%)	Light (%)	Metal (%)	Elect. (%)	Chem. (%)	Serv. (%)
Low	48.6	33.3	33.4	36.7	20.8	21.4	28.5
Medium	20.0	33.3	53.3	40.0	29.2	35.7	28.6
High	31.4	33.4	13.3	23.3	50.0	42.9	42.9
Total	100.0	100.0	100.0	100.0	100.0	100.0	100.0

IJV Sales Volume (US$ million)

Marketing Performance (%)	Below 5 (%)	5-10 (%)	10-25 (%)	25-50 (%)	50-75 (%)	75-100 (%)	Over 100 (%)
Low	65.4	35.9	15.6	31.6	14.3	33.3	20.0
Medium	19.2	35.9	37.5	36.8	14.3	33.3	33.3
High	15.4	28.2	46.9	31.6	71.4	33.4	46.7
Total	100.0	100.0	100.0	100.0	100.0	100.0	100.0

Firstly, regarding the country of origin of the principal foreign partner, in evaluating Table 3.3 it was apparent that the most significant result concerning the country of origin of the principal foreign partner was that 66.7 percent of the North American/Thai IJVs in the sample were evaluated as being low marketing performers. This might in part be explained by the cultural distance between Thailand and North America and the small number of North American/Thai IJVs in the sample. There were only nine IJVs in the sample (6.4 percent of the sample) whose principal foreign partner was from North America.

Concerning culture distance of the respondent, Geringer and Hebert (1991) identify the possibility that agreement on IJV performance among a venture's participants may be influenced by cultural similarity among them. Several authors have shown or hypothesised that different national cultures embody different attitudes, values and beliefs that find their materialisation in distinct business cultures, styles and practices (England, 1975; Geringer and Hebert, 1989; Kogut and Singh, 1988). For example, Ouchi (1981) examined the US and Japanese business cultures and described them as mostly incompatible. The presence of dissimilarities between parent firms' national cultures may be more likely to lead to differences in parent firms' objectives for an IJV, as well as in their approaches to coordination, operating methods and strategy implementation (Brown *et al.,* 1989). These dissimilarities may also lead to differences in the partners' perceptions of each other and the IJV, and result in a lower degree of agreement regarding JV performance.

Conversely, the opposite will apply. In IJVs where parents are from the same national culture, a tendency toward greater agreement among the parents and the IJV regarding the venture's performance is expected (Kotabe, 1990). As shown by Anderson and Weitz (1989), cultural similarity promotes communication among business partners. Better communication among JV partners will result in better perceived performance and satisfaction from all partners. This could, in part, also explain the high marketing performers, as that was the other significant result to come from the analysis of the country of origin of the principal foreign partner. It was apparent that 62.5 percent of the sample of ASEAN/Thai IJVs rated their IJVs as high marketing performers and 41.2 percent of the sample of Taiwanese/Thai IJVs rated their IJVs as high marketing performers. The cultural distance between the ASEAN countries, Taiwan and Thailand is very small as they are all in close proximity to one another, and this could explain why they rated their IJVs as high marketing performers. The other significant results to come from the analysis of the country of origin of the principal foreign partner were that 78.6 percent of the sample of European/Thai IJVs and 68.6 percent of the sample of Japanese/Thai IJVs rated their IJV's marketing performance as medium-to-high.

Secondly, regarding the equity structure of the principal foreign partner, in evaluating Table 3.3 it was apparent that, generally, the smaller the percentage of equity held by the principal foreign partner the lower the perceived marketing performance. That is, when evaluating the equity percentage held by the principal foreign partner it was evident that a higher percentage of the sample evaluated their IJV marketing performance as low when they had less than 50 percent equity participation as compared to those IJVs whose principal foreign partner had an equity participation of greater than 50 percent. Furthermore, those IJVs whose principal foreign partner had greater than 50 percent equity in the venture were perceived as having a higher marketing performance than those IJVs whose principal foreign partner had less than 50 percent equity in the venture. This finding supports the findings of Al-Aali (1987), Killing (1983) and Phatak and Chowdhury (1991) who identify that domination by the foreign parent in the overall management of the IJV was found to be most effective. Those IJVs whose principal foreign partner had between 5 and 9 percent equity participation were identified as having the largest percentage (66.7 percent) of the sample that identified their IJV marketing performance as low.

Thirdly, regarding IJV industry structure, the industry in which IJV marketing performance was rated the lowest was agriculture, where 48.6 percent of the sample of IJVs involved in agriculture rated their IJV marketing performance as low. The industries in which IJV marketing performance was rated the highest were electrical, chemical, and service industries respectively where 50.0 percent, 42.9 percent and 42.9 percent of the sample of IJVs involved in those industries rated their IJV marketing performance as high.

Finally, regarding the sales volume of the venture, in evaluating Table 3.3 it was apparent that generally, the lower the IJV sales volume the lower the perceived marketing performance. This is much as expected, as sales volume is a predictor of economic performance. The more sales a firm or IJV generates the better the economic performance and the more satisfied the parents and senior management are with its performance.

4. Market Characteristics and Performance

Some of the principal market characteristics likely to influence the marketing performance of a venture in a foreign market include: access to capital resources and low-cost raw materials (Beamish, 1993; Beamish and Banks, 1987); the policies of host-country governments (Blodgett, 1991a; Griffith *et al.,* 2001; Makino and Delios, 1996; Yan, 1998); technology transfer (Beamish, 1988, 1993; Beamish and Delios, 1997a; Blodgett, 1991b; Inkpen and Beamish, 1997; Yan, 1998); the availability of suitable distribution and communication channels (Beamish, 1993; Blodgett, 1991b; Makino and Delios, 1996; Yan, 1998); knowledge of local business practices (Ahn, 1980; Blodgett, 1991b; Ganitsky *et al.,* 1991; Johnson *et al.,* 2001; Simonin, 1999), and industry competition (Cavusgil and Zou, 1994; Christensen *et al.,* 1987; Douglas and Craig, 1989).

4.1. Access to Capital Resources and Low-Cost Raw Materials

One of the major reasons for using the equity joint venture organisation form is a need for the attributes or assets of the other partner. Assets include such things as cash, capital resources and raw material sources (Beamish, 1993, Beamish and Banks, 1987). The understanding that access to capital resources and low-cost raw material access is one of the major reasons the JV form of organisation structure has been used is built around the theory of internalisation (Beamish and Banks, 1987). The internalisation theory posits that due to the transaction costs that must be borne as a result of conducting business in imperfect markets, it is more efficient (less expensive) for the firm to use internal structures rather than market intermediaries to serve a foreign market. According to Williamson's (1975) reasoning these market imperfections arise from two environmental conditions: uncertainty and a small number of market agents. When these conditions coexist with two sets of human factors, opportunism and bounded rationality, he argues that the costs of writing, executing and enforcing arm's-length complex contingent claims contracts with market intermediaries are greater than the costs of internalising the market (Beamish and Banks, 1987).

4.2. Policies of Host Country Governments

As far as the policies of host-country governments are concerned, this is one of the principal market characteristics likely to influence the marketing performance of IJVs in developing countries (Blodgett, 1991b; Ganitsky *et al.*, 1991; Yan, 1998). Changes in the power, roles and policies of host-country governments are the most crucial of all the uncontrollable forces affecting the future success of IJVs. In the borderless world of the 1990s and beyond (Ohmae, 1989a), IJVs will encounter more opportunities to deal with the diminished power and roles of individual governments, but will be challenged to understand and respond promptly and adequately to their emerging new structures and coordinated cross-national policies (Ganitsky *et al.*, 1991).

Indeed, the influence of host-country governments on IJV performance has been the focus of many studies (e.g., Beamish, 1984; Blodgett, 1991b; Contractor, 1990; Fagre and Wells, 1982; Franko, 1987; Ganitsky *et al.*, 1991; Gomes-Casseres, 1988b; 1988c; Griffith *et al.*, 2001; Kim, 1988; Lecraw, 1984; Makino and Delios, 1996; Poynter, 1982; Root, 1988a; Yan, 1998). On the one hand, frequently when a developing country is involved, government pressure may lead a foreign corporation to take on a local partner. The host-country government also may exercise influence over the choice of suppliers and over marketing, once the venture is established. Or it may impose exchange controls, which can have an important impact on an IJV's reinvestment, financing and repatriation decisions. On the other hand, frequently when developed countries are involved, tariffs, quotas or non-tariff barriers may make it imperative for a foreign firm to rely more on local production than on exporting. In both cases, laws or pressure from the government can play a significant role in the marketing performance of the IJV.

Restrictions imposed on foreign corporations in IJV relationships by host-country governments have been identified by many researchers as being a significant factor influencing the performance of those IJVs (Beamish, 1984; Blodgett, 1991b; Dymsza, 1988; Gomes-Casseres, 1989; Griffith *et al.*, 2001; Vanhonacker and Pan, 1997). Host-country governments may not actually require JV participation by foreign corporations, but government pressure usually exists in some form. Beamish (1985) found that 57 percent of JVs between US MNCs and entities in developing countries were formed because of some form of government pressure, while only 17 percent of JVs of US MNCs and other firms in developed countries were formed for that reason. Third world indigenisation programmes, by injecting a political factor into the bargaining power of a local entity, have had an important impact on how the developed world MNCs operate overseas.

If the government is an active partner in the JV (which is the case with many developing countries, especially those countries of the Asia-Pacific region e.g., Myanmar, Cambodia, Indonesia, Malaysia, South Korea, Thailand and Vietnam), it means an important diminution of bargaining power to the foreign corporation, since the government that owns equity in the venture also has the power to regulate the venture's activities. Beamish (1985), Contractor (1985) and Gomes-Casseres (1987) found that the most crucial factor in relative bargaining power that influences performance is host-country government restrictions. In addition, when import substitution policies are pursued, the host-country government can be expected to have strong motivation to increase control over the venture once operations have commenced. But even when the local partner is a private enterprise, the host-country government exerts control as a shadow partner by imposing and enforcing regulations that interfere with the venture's operations e.g., the choice of suppliers, the choice of markets, the repatriation of profit, duty paid on certain products/industries, and the percent of local labour content required. Therefore, interference by host-country governments is likely to have a significant influence on the marketing performance of the IJV.

4.3. Technology Transfer

Apart from host-country government reasons, the transfer of modern and innovative technology is one of the principal reasons why local firms and foreign partners enter into JV arrangements (Beamish, 1988, 1993; Beamish and Delios, 1997a; Blodgett, 1991b; Inkpen and Beamish, 1997; Yan, 1998). In fact, access to modern and up-to-date technology is widely recognised as the principal reason why local firms in developing countries enter into JV arrangements with foreign corporations from developed countries (Beamish, 1993; Beamish and Inkpen, 1995; Blodgett, 1991b; Lee and Beamish, 1995). Failure to deliver to the IJV the technology initially promised by the foreign partner(s) when entering into the IJV agreement could cause conflict between the foreign and local partners, and this conflict together with the lack of the required technology could have a negative influence on the marketing performance of the IJV.

When it has not had a chance to become standardised in widely available machinery, technical knowledge has strong tacit content. It resides predominantly in the development staff rather than in the machinery itself. Against such an asset, particularly if it is protected by continuous innovation, it is difficult to make competitive inroads and those firms that have access to such technology have a significant competitive advantage over those that do not. Such a competitive advantage is likely to make a significant contribution to marketing performance. Kogut (1977) and Fagre and Wells (1982) placed it highest in potential dominance among resources that might be provided by a JV partner. Reich and Mankin (1986) believed that the biggest competitive gains in a partnership come from mastery of the manufacturing processes. Lecraw (1984) ranked technology high because technology, as a proprietary asset, gives a firm control through possession of asymmetric information. Gomes-Casseres (1988b) demonstrated that a MNC can draw considerable leverage in JV bargaining when it possesses technology that the host-country governments need, because host-country governments usually seek technology transfer above all the other resources that a MNC can provide. Relatedly, Paliwoda and Liebrenz (1984) pointed out that Western firms with zero-equity positions in JVs in Eastern Bloc countries still can dominate a JV as long as they control advanced technology (Blodgett, 1991b; Ganitsky *et al.*, 1991; Gomes-Casseres, 1987).

Therefore, technology transfer, particularly when it is characterised by rapid innovation, may be considered a highly dominant contribution to the JV. Technology transfer is what most local firms from developing countries seek when entering a JV agreement with a foreign firm from a developed country. Failure of the foreign corporation to deliver the promised technology is likely to have a negative influence on IJV marketing performance (Julian, 1998).

4.4. Channels of Distribution

As far as the availability of certain distribution and communication channels is concerned, the importance of access to suitable distribution channels as a motive for both international and domestic JVs is apparent from even a cursory reading of the literature (Beamish, 1993; Blodgett, 1991b; Hamel *et al.*, 1989; Ganitsky *et al.*, 1991; Jacque, 1986; Kogut and Singh, 1985; Makino and Delios, 1996; Yan, 1998). Kogut and Singh's (1985) database shows that 42 percent of the JVs entered by foreigners in the US over the 1971/83 period were for marketing and distribution, while Jacque (1986) found that close to 60 percent of US joint ventures in Japan were of that type.

A global company expanding across national boundaries often finds itself in the position of entering new markets. Obtaining distribution can be a major obstacle to establishing a position in a new market (Keegan, 1995). This obstacle is often encountered when a company enters a competitive market where brands and supply relationships are already established. There is little incentive for an independent channel agent to take on a new product when established names are accepted in the market and are satisfying current demands (Keegan, 1995). The global company seeking to enter such a market must either provide some incentive to channel agents, establish its own direct distribution system, or enter into a strategic alliance (e.g., an IJV) with a local firm that has a comprehensive distribution network. The provision of incentives to independent channel agents and the establishment of a direct distribution system as channel strategies have several disadvantages. Firstly, the provision of special incentives to independent channel agents can be extremely expensive. The company might offer outright payments as either direct cash bonuses or contest awards for sales performance. In competitive markets with sufficiently high prices, incentives could take the form of gross margin guarantees. Both incentive payments and margin guarantees are expensive. The incentive payments are directly expensive. The margin guarantees can be indirectly expensive because they affect the price to the consumer and the price competitiveness of a manufacturer's product.

Secondly, the alternative of establishing a direct distribution system in a new market also has the disadvantage of being expensive. Sales representatives and sales managers must be hired and trained. The sales organisation will inevitably be a heavy loser in its early stage of operation in a new market because it will not have sufficient volume to cover its overhead costs. Therefore, any company contemplating the establishment of a direct sales force, even one assigned to distributors, should be prepared to underwrite losses for this sales force for a reasonable period of time.

4.5. Knowledge of Local Business Practices

The alternative of entering into a strategic alliance or some form of IJV with a local firm with a comprehensive distribution network gives the global company access to a suitable distribution network and knowledge of the local business environment. At the same time it reduces the risk associated with entering the new market and is less expensive than the other channel strategies. Therefore, this strategy has significant appeal to a global company and is often cited as one of the principal reasons why foreign firms enter into IJVs in developing countries (Julian, 1998; Connolly, 1984).

Knowledge of the local business environment is an asset often avidly sought by a global company that is establishing a position in a foreign market, especially for the first time. This knowledge has economic value and can take several forms. It usually involves familiarity with economic, political and business conditions, e.g., marketing channel availability that managers of a global firm may be unaware of. The country may be burdened with inadequate infrastructure, a large public sector, an ambivalently regarded colonial history, and intransigent ethnic hostilities. Political connections play a part also. Having a local partner may ease relations between the global company and a suspicious host-country government, which may perceive a joint venture as less threatening than a wholly owned subsidiary of a foreign firm (Connolly, 1984). The public relations benefit often extends to local labour relations and to worker morale as well. In concrete terms, a local partner may provide advantages in obtaining contracts, access to favourable tax treatment, a chance to avoid various non-tariff barriers, and a means of entry into relationships with local businesses and officials. Such connections with the local environment are often an essential precondition to a venture's success. Related areas of expertise that may be placed in this category are distribution channels and marketing skill (Blodgett, 1991b).

Foreign firms may also find it difficult to penetrate international markets without local marketing expertise. A joint venture partner may provide the know-how or established local distribution channels through which to market the product that may not have been available without the local JV partner. As industries evolve, their distribution and communication channels must improve to provide closer and more efficient contacts between suppliers and customers. This long-term imperative may require considerable short-term investments. Though foreign partners might favour such investments, the local partner(s) will oppose such an investment if the change in channel arrangements clashes with their traditional concepts, limited resources, bargaining power base and/or short-term expectations. The greater the divergence in the IJV partners' objectives and time-frame to achieve those objectives, the greater the difficulty for an IJV to take advantage of opportunities and cope with challenges created by changes in its industry's channels, and the greater their need to compromise, given the local partner's reluctance to change, which is a short-term view. As a consequence, IJV partners need to address the eventual changes in the IJV's roles and relationships with the marketing channels, as these changes and the availability of suitable marketing channels not controlled by one or several of its competitors can have a significant influence on the marketing performance of the IJV (Ahn, 1980; Datta, 1988; Ganitsky *et al.,* 1991; Killing, 1983; Makino and Delios, 1996; Yan, 1998).

4.6. Industry Competition

The other market characteristic identified in previous studies as having an influence on marketing performance is competitive pricing strategies (Cavusgil and Zou, 1994). Competitive pricing strategies have been described as one of the strategies by which firms adapt to or fit the idiosyncracies of the foreign market (Douglas and Craig, 1989). Some empirical evidence also supports the positive relationship between marketing performance and competitive pricing (Christensen *et al.*, 1987; Kirpalani and Mckintosh, 1980).

Therefore, the importance to IJV marketing performance of certain market characteristics like access to capital resources and low-cost raw materials, host-country government policies, technology transfer, access to suitable marketing channels, knowledge of local business practices and industry competition should not be underestimated.

4.7. Market Characteristics and Marketing Performance

From the Julian (1998) study that examined the factors influencing IJV marketing performance in Thailand, seven factors and two statements were identified from the initial exploratory factor analysis, market characteristics being one of those initial factors. All items loaded as intended. The data were considered suitable for factor analysis as the Bartlett Test of Sphericity was significant (2083.2278; 0.00000) and the Keyser-Meyer-Olkin (KMO) measure of sampling adequacy (0.75873) was greater than 0.60 (Coakes and Steed, 1997).

Table 4.1 Summary of Exploratory Factor Analysis

Factor Name	Cronbach's Alpha	Dominant Statements	Factor Loadings
FACTOR 1	0.82	Inaccessibility to distribution channels.	0.73
Market		Shortage of the necessary capital resources.	0.71
Characteristics		Shortage in the supply of raw materials.	0.70
		A lack of knowledge of Thai business practices by a foreign partner.	0.65
		Intensity of price competition.	0.62
		Inadequate transference of up-to-date technology from any of the parent companies.	0.58
		Thai Government intervention into the operation of the IJV.	0.56

Table 4.1 Summary of Exploratory Factor Analysis (Continued)

Factor Name	Cronbach's Alpha	Dominant Statements	Factor Loadings
FACTOR 2 Conflict	0.87	Disagreements between the partners regarding interpreting the terms of the IJV contract.	0.88
		Disagreements over a partner's attempt to make changes in the terms of the IJV contract.	0.86
		Disagreements between the partners over the hiring policies for the IJV.	0.78
		Disagreements regarding the roles and functions to be performed by each partner.	0.75
		At least one of the parents of the IJV considered the IJV arrangement unfair because of contractual provisions.	0.73
FACTOR 3 Commitment	0.82	The parents of the IJV were willing to commit key senior management people to the IJV.	0.80
		The foreign parents of the IJV were willing to find special skills required by the venture in the foreign parent firm.	0.79
		The foreign parents of the IJV were willing to regularly visit the IJV and offer assistance as and when required.	0.78
		The parents of the IJV were willing to furnish additional equity or loan capital as and when needed.	0.76
		The foreign parents of the IJV were committed to the IJV.	0.54

Table 4.1 Summary of Exploratory Factor Analysis (Continued)

Factor Name	Cronbach's Alpha	Dominant Statements	Factor Loadings
FACTOR 4 Product Characteristics	0.70	Level of product/service adaptation required for the local Thai market.	0.70
		Lack of familiarity by consumers to the products/services of the IJV.	0.65
		Level of promotion adaptation required due to factors specific to the local Thai market.	0.57
		Factors relating to the culture-specificity of the product/service.	0.53
		Age of the products/services.	0.52
FACTOR 5 Firm-Specific Characteristics	0.61	Unit value of the products/services.	0.79
		Degree of uniqueness of the IJV's products/services compared to that of its competitors.	0.65
		Customer expectations are a measure against which the IJV evaluates its performance.	0.56
FACTOR 6 Marketing Orientation	0.62	The IJV frequently conducts research among its customers in order to find out what they expect of its products/services.	0.79
		The IJV regularly contacts customers to determine their needs and to better understand their business.	0.58
		The IJV regularly assesses the impact that the prices of its products/services have on customer expectations.	0.48
FACTOR 7 Organisational Control	0.67	Transference of a large proportion of the IJV's outputs to a parent company.	0.67
		The sourcing of much of the input needs of the IJV from a parent company.	0.53
Statement 1 Managerial Control		Lack of effective control over the IJV by any of the parents.	0.75
Statement 2 Adapting to Foreign Market Needs		The foreign parents of the IJV were willing to adapt the products/services of the IJV to meet the needs of the local Thai market.	0.69

The results of the exploratory factor analysis are summarised in Table 4.1. The seven factors and two statements explained 64.7 percent of respondent variation on issues about IJV marketing performance in Thailand. The first four factors were the dominant factors, all with eigenvalues greater than 1.5, and explaining 46.3 percent of respondent variation on issues about IJV marketing performance in Thailand. The remaining three factors and two statements accounted for only 18.4 percent of respondent variation. Therefore, the first four factors were the dominant factors in this analysis, with the remaining three factors and two statements making a minimal contribution.

In this seven-factor model the factor of market characteristics (Factor 1) emerged as the single strongest factor, explaining 19.2 percent of respondent variation on issues about IJV marketing performance in Thailand (see Table 4.2). Cronbach's Alpha for this measure of market characteristics was 0.82, indicating a strong level of reliability. The measures of market characteristics identified in this study support the findings of Beamish (1988), Beamish and Banks (1987), Blodgett (1991a), Christensen *et al.* (1987), Jacque (1986) and Lecraw (1984).

Table 4.2 Exploratory Factor Analysis: Final Statistics

Factor/Statement	Eigenvalue	% of Variance	Cumulative %
(1) Market Characteristics	6.13459	19.2	19.2
(2) Conflict	4.55179	14.2	33.4
(3) Commitment	2.48185	7.8	41.2
(4) Product Characteristics	1.61636	5.1	46.3
(5) Firm-Specific Characteristics	1.29254	4.0	50.3
(6) Marketing Orientation	1.24390	3.9	54.2
(7) Organisational Control	1.21944	3.8	58.0
(8) Managerial Control	1.07879	3.4	61.4
(9) Adapting to Foreign Market Needs	1.05056	3.3	64.7

Beamish and Banks (1987) identified the importance to IJV performance of access to an adequate supply of capital resources and low-cost raw materials. The understanding that access to capital resources and low-cost raw material access is one of the major reasons the JV form of organisation structure has been used, is built around the theory of internalisation (Beamish and Banks, 1987). The internalisation theory posits that due to the transaction costs that must be borne as a result of conducting business in imperfect markets, it is more efficient (less expensive) for the firm to use internal structures rather than market intermediaries to serve a foreign market. The Julian (1998) study also found support for the importance of access to capital resources and low-cost raw materials being components of the factor of market characteristics.

Furthermore, this study also found support for Jacque's (1986) and Kogut and Singh's (1985) findings about the importance of channels of distribution to IJV performance. The importance of access to suitable distribution channels as a motive for both international and domestic JVs is evident from Kogut and Singh's (1985) database which shows that 42 percent of the JVs entered by foreigners in the US over the 1971/83 period were for marketing and distribution, and close to 60 percent of US joint ventures in Japan were for marketing and distribution (Jacque, 1986).

The importance of the transfer of up-to-date technology to IJV marketing performance was also noted, supporting Blodgett's (1991b) finding. Apart from host-country government reasons, the transfer of modern and innovative technology is one of the principal reasons why local firms and foreign partners enter into JV arrangements. In fact, access to modern and up-to-date technology is widely recognised as the principal reason why local firms in developing countries enter into JV arrangements with foreign corporations from developed countries (Beamish, 1988, 1993; Beamish and Delios, 1997a; Blodgett, 1991b; Inkpen and Beamish, 1997; Yan, 1998). Failure to deliver to the IJV the technology initially promised by the foreign partner(s) when entering into the IJV agreement could cause conflict between the foreign and local partners and this conflict together with the lack of the required technology could have a negative influence on the marketing performance of the IJV.

The importance of competitive pricing was also noted, supporting Christensen *et al.'s* (1987) finding. Christensen *et al.* found that successful exporters relied more on internationally competitive pricing strategies than asking for premiums for exchange and extraordinary risks. 'In general, however, successful exporters were more concerned with internal factors for pricing, that is, factors that are to some extent controllable by the firm. These internal pricing factors included production costs, the use or not of government incentives, the importance of taxes, including those on imports and exports, the setting of ROI hurdle rates, agent's margins and the premiums deemed necessary to compensate for extraordinary risks of foreign trade' (Christensen *et al.,* 1987, p. 69). The Julian (1998) study found support for their finding identifying the importance of intensity of price competition to market characteristics.

Finally, Beamish's (1988) finding that host-country government restrictions usually exist in some form and have a significant influence on IJV performance received support in this study. One of the principal market characteristics likely to influence the marketing performance of IJVs in developing countries is the policies of host-country governments (Beamish, 1988; Blodgett, 1991b; Griffith *et al.,* 2001; Makino and Delios, 1996; Yan, 1998). Changes in the power, roles and policies of host-country governments are the most crucial of all the uncontrollable forces affecting the future success of IJVs. Laws or pressure from the government can play a significant role in the marketing performance of the IJV. This study provided confirmation of this finding, identifying that Thai government intervention into the operation of the IJV was an important component of market characteristics.

The seven factors, namely, market characteristics, conflict, commitment, product characteristics, firm-specific characteristics, marketing orientation and organisational control, and the two independent statements relating to managerial control and adapting to foreign market needs, were then adopted for further analysis. Mean factor scores were obtained for the seven factors and the two independent statements and the results are reported in Table 4.3.

Table 4.3 Mean Factor Scores

Factor/Statement	Mean Score	Standard Deviation
(1) Market Characteristics	4.604	1.353
(2) Conflict	5.451	1.435
(3) Commitment	5.246	1.301
(4) Product Characteristics	4.316	0.839
(5) Firm-Specific Characteristics	5.627	1.019
(6) Marketing Orientation	5.398	1.178
(7) Organisational Control	4.609	1.763
(8) Managerial Control	4.727	1.827
(9) Adapting to Foreign Market Needs	4.957	1.818

In relation to market characteristics the mean score for the market characteristics factor was 4.604 with a standard deviation of 1.353. This indicated that generally respondents agreed with statements identifying certain market characteristics as either being unavailable, inaccessible or in short supply in Thailand e.g., a shortage of capital resources, a shortage of raw materials, inaccessibility to distribution channels, a lack of knowledge of Thai business practices, inadequate technology, Thai government intervention, and the intensity of price competition.

Further analysis was then conducted on the seven factors and two independent statements by conducting a multiple regression analysis to analyse the relationship between the dependent variable and a set of independent variables. In this study on IJV marketing performance in Thailand the dependent variable was IJV marketing performance. The independent variables were the seven factors, namely, market characteristics, conflict, commitment, product characteristics, firm-specific characteristics, marketing orientation, organisational control and the two independent statements relating to managerial control and adapting to foreign market needs. The results of the multiple regression analysis presented in Table 4.4 show that the factors of market characteristics, commitment and marketing orientation were clearly the most significant predictor variables and the only independent variables that could be used to explain the variation in the dependent variable of IJV marketing performance. All these key predictor variables were statistically significant at the 95 percent confidence interval.

Table 4.4 Multiple Regression Analysis

Variable	Coefficient	T-Statistic	Sig T	Sig at .05
Market Characteristics	-.225404	-2.999	.0031	Yes
Conflict	-.135348	-1.715	.0884	No
Commitment	.188456	2.329	.0212	Yes
Product Characteristics	-.086624	-0.953	.3421	No
Firm-Specific Characteristics	.118588	1.407	.1614	No
Marketing Orientation	.190572	2.336	.0208	Yes
Organisational Control	-.093877	-1.124	.2627	No
Managerial Control	-.007322	- .096	.9235	No
Adapting to Foreign Market Needs	.048608	.611	.5420	No

R^2: 0.14395; n: 161; df = 3

The R^2 statistic represents the proportion of variance in the dependent variable accounted for by the independent variables. In this study on IJVs in Thailand, that proportion being 14.395 percent of the explained variance in IJV marketing performance accounted for by the co-variation in the independent variables. The independent variables were identified as market characteristics, conflict, commitment, product characteristics, firm-specific characteristics, marketing orientation, organisational control, managerial control and adapting to foreign market needs. Thus, the model had modest predictive ability.

As the R^2 statistic that was achieved for the nominated independent and dependent variables was modest at 14.395 percent the data were taken for further analysis. Further analysis was undertaken to see if there was a significant relationship between some of the factors, the classification variables and demographic variables at different levels of IJV marketing performance. Therefore, a discriminant analysis was conducted on the classification variables of country of origin, equity structure, sales volume and industry classification, the demographic variable of age, the seven factors and two independent statements and IJV marketing performance with IJV marketing performance being categorised into low and high performers.

The objective of discriminant analysis was to distinguish statistically between the two groups. These groups were defined by the particular research situation. In the Julian (1998) study on IJV marketing performance in Thailand the interest was to classify the IJVs into low and high marketing performers to see if the discriminating variables would distinguish between the groups. Group 1 consisted of all those IJVs that were classified as low marketing performers (i.e. those IJVs that had a marketing performance score of 4 or less using the single-item measure of IJV marketing performance). Group 2 consisted of all those IJVs that were classified as high marketing performers (i.e. those IJVs that had a marketing performance score of 5, 6 or 7 using the single-item measure of IJV marketing performance).

Table 4.5 contains a summary of the results of the discriminant analysis that relates group membership to the same factors and independent statements that were used in the previously reported multiple regression analysis. The factors identified are market characteristics, conflict, commitment, product characteristics, firm-specific characteristics, marketing orientation and organisational control. The independent statements identified are related to managerial control and adapting to foreign market needs. In addition, the country of origin of the principal foreign partner (ORIGIN), the equity structure of the principal foreign partner (EQUITY), the industry the IJV operates in (INDUSTRY), the sales volume of the IJV (SALESVOL), and the age of the respondent (AGE) were also included as additional potentially discriminating variables.

Table 4.5 Summary of Univariate ANOVAs for the Discriminant Analysis

Variable	Wilk's Lambda	F	Significance
Age	.99171	1.0865	.2992
Equity	.99727	.3559	.5518
Market Characteristics	.97670	3.1009	.0806
Conflict	.93256	9.4010	.0026
Commitment	.94090	8.1655	.0050
Product Characteristics	.99638	.4726	.4930
Firm-Specific Characteristics	.99460	.7061	.4023
Marketing Orientation	.95794	5.7083	.0183
Organisational Control	.96838	4.2446	.0414
Managerial Control	.95132	6.6528	.0110
Adapting to Foreign Market Needs	.95916	5.5355	.0201
Industry	.95023	6.8089	.0101
Origin	.99662	.4415	.5076
Salesvol	.91434	12.1792	.0007

Table 4.5 shows the univariate ANOVAs of the discriminant analysis. The univariate ANOVAs indicate whether there is a statistically significant difference among the dependent variable means for each independent variable. From Table 4.5 it is apparent that the independent variables of the sales volume of the IJV (SALESVOL), conflict, commitment, the industry the IJV operates in (INDUSTRY), managerial control, marketing orientation, adapting to foreign market needs and organisational control are all significant at the 95 percent confidence interval ($p < .05$).

The discriminant analysis (see Table 4.6) shows that there were actually 44 IJVs in Group 1 (low marketing performers) and 88 IJVs in Group 2 (high marketing performers). Using the discriminant function, Table 4.6 provides an indication of the success rate for predictions of membership of the grouping variable's categories using the discriminant functions developed in the analysis and that the overall success rate is 72.2 percent.

From Table 4.6 it is also clear that the high marketing performers are the most accurately classified, with 75.0 percent of the cases correct. Low marketing performers are the least accurately classified with 72.7 percent of the cases correct. Notice that 27.3 percent of the incorrectly classified high marketing performers should be reclassified as low marketing performers and that 25.0 percent of the incorrectly classified low marketing performers should be reclassified as high marketing performers.

Table 4.6 Classification of Results using the Discriminant Function

Actual Group Membership	No. of Cases	Predicted	Group Membership
		Group 1 (Low Marketing Performers)	Group 2 (High Marketing Performers)
Group 1 (Low Marketing Performers)	44	32 (72.7%)	12 (27.3%)
Group2 (High Marketing Performers)	88	22 (25.0%)	66 (75.0%)

Percent of 'grouped' cases correctly classified: 72.2%

As is evident from the exploratory factor analysis, multiple regression analysis and discriminant analysis that were conducted market characteristics is a significant predictor of IJV marketing performance (see multiple regression analysis) yet a non-significant discriminator of high and low IJV marketing performance (see discriminant analysis). The reason for market characteristics being a non-significant discriminator of high and low IJV marketing performance could be explained partly by the relatively large number of high marketing performers versus the relatively small number of low marketing performers in the sample, yet it is approaching significance at .08. Furthermore, when 27.3 percent of the incorrectly classified high marketing performers are reclassified as low marketing performers and 25.0 percent of the incorrectly classified low marketing performers are reclassified as high marketing performers, market characteristics may then be a significant discriminator of high and low IJV marketing performance. Finally, when the IJV marketing performance categories were re-classified into low, medium and high marketing performers giving a more equal distribution between the different IJV marketing performance categories market characteristics was a significant discriminator between these groups. However, market characteristics was a significant predictor of IJV marketing performance using the multiple regression analysis. Regression has two advantages over discriminant analysis. First, it is more robust to violations of underlying assumptions, and second, the coefficient divided by its standard error is asymptotically interpretable as a T-statistic (Anderson and Coughlan, 1987). Therefore, market characteristics was a significant predictor of IJV marketing performance in the study on IJVs in Thailand (Julian, 1998).

It is important for the management of any company to be aware of these market characteristics when contemplating an IJV of any magnitude in a developing country of South East Asia. The Julian (1998) study clearly indicated that it was important for managers of IJVs to be aware of the market characteristics of a foreign market that could influence a firm's marketing performance. Availability of capital resources, raw materials and distribution channels; transfer of up-to-date technology; knowledge of local business practices; the level of government intervention; and knowledge of industry competition are very important for the successful marketing performance of IJVs in Thailand and South East Asia. Companies intending to enter into an IJV arrangement in Thailand and other South East Asian countries need to ensure the availability and existence of the above if they are to succeed in those markets.

5.   Conflict

5.1. Review of Conflict Literature

A review of early IJV research (Harrigan, 1985; Killing, 1983; Reynolds, 1984), suggests that the amount of conflict inversely affects IJV performance. More recently, some IJV scholars have provided empirical support (Fey and Beamish, 2000; Hebert, 1994; Johnson et al., 2001; Tillman, 1990). Based on a study of Japanese–Thai IJVs, Tillman (1990) showed that the amount of conflict significantly inversely affected IJV performance. Similarly, Hebert (1994) found a significant inverse relationship between conflict and performance when studying Canadian IJVs and Canadian domestic JVs. In addition, Habib (1987) developed a measure of conflict in the IJV context. Other IJV scholars have also provided anecdotal evidence relating to IJV conflict as part of larger studies.

Some of the best-known models for understanding managers actions have been based on the need for developing stable relations between social units (Barnard, 1948; March and Simon, 1958; Mayo, 1945). As a result, such models have often tried to downplay the importance of conflict. However, other scholars (Aldrich, 1979; Blau, 1964) have recognized that conflict must be dealt with since it is inherent in relationships. Interorganizational relationships like IJVs result in conflicting desires of parent firms for cooperation and autonomy. Parent firms form IJVs because they see benefits in cooperating with their IJV's other parent. However, at the same time, firms do not want to lose too much autonomy. As a result, in interorganizational relationships like IJVs, some level of conflict is likely since organizations normally strive to maintain their autonomy even in relationships where they desire cooperation (Fey and Beamish, 2000; Van de Ven and Walker, 1984).

Researchers have always had difficulty reaching a consensus about conflict. Several models of conflict have been developed (Evan and McDougall, 1967; Pondy, 1967; Schmidt and Kochan, 1972; Thomas, 1976; Walton and Dutton, 1969). In addition, there have been several attempts to experimentally test models of interorganizational conflict (Angelmar and Stern, 1978; Stern *et al.,* 1975; Walker, 1970). Models of interorganizational conflict have also been tested in the field (Brown and Day, 1981; Edgar, 1977; Lusch, 1976; Peterson and Schwind, 1977; Rosenberg and Stern, 1971).

Pondy (1967) provides probably the most widely accepted model of conflict (Fey and Beamish, 2000). His work tried to integrate scholars' views on the subject and was initially developed for the study of intraorganizational conflict. Others (Brown and Day, 1981; White, 1974) have argued that it is applicable to interorganizational conflict as well. Pondy's (1967) model of conflict viewed conflict as consisting of five stages: latent, perceived, affective, manifest and aftermath.

Latent conflict referred to conditions that are likely to be sources of conflict, such as differing goals in an IJV. Parent firms may have different goals, but the parents may not be aware that their goals actually differ. Unfortunately this is often the case in the early stages of an IJV if insufficient discussion took place between parent firms before the IJV was formed. Once parent firms recognize that their goals differ, perceived conflict exists (Pondy's second type of conflict). Perceived conflict refers to the participants' perception of the extent of conflict that exists. Affective conflict, in addition to the perception of conflict, includes feelings such as hostility, tension and stress which are necessary, but not sufficient, conditions for conflictual behaviour to exist. When one parent begins to feel angry that the other parent has goals that do not coincide with its goals, affective conflict exists. Manifest conflict is the action dimension of conflict characterized by overt conflictual behaviour when two or more parties express disagreement. In IJVs, manifest conflict occurs when parent firms argue about what the IJV should do as a result of their differing goals. Finally, aftermath is the dimension of conflict where conflicts are either resolved or suppressed. In the aftermath phase parent firms either come to a compromise about their differing goals, terminate the IJV, or suppress the disagreement for the short term (Fey and Beamish, 2000; Habib, 1987).

Like most of the past IJV conflict literature (Fey and Beamish, 2000; Habib, 1983, 1987; Hebert, 1994; Tillman, 1990), the study by Julian (1998) on the marketing performance of IJVs in Thailand focused on manifest conflict, that is, the action dimension of conflict (Fey and Beamish, 2000; Habib, 1987). Also, the Julian (1998) study defined conflict as 'overt behaviour arising out of a process in which one unit seeks the advancement of its own interests in its relationship with the others' (Schmidt and Kochan, 1972, p. 363). Support for this definition of conflict has been received from Fey and Beamish (2000), Habib (1987) and Hebert (1994).

Conflict among parties involved in an interorganizational relationship tends to cause frustration and unpleasantness which results in dissatisfaction (Anderson, 1990; Anderson and Narus, 1984; Robicheaux and El-Ansary, 1975). Since managers, like most people, wish their jobs to be enjoyable, this frustration, unpleasantness and dissatisfaction is likely to contribute to managers losing interest in, or in extreme cases even terminating, their IJVs. Also, conflict between parties involved in an IJV requires more parent-firm management time. This in turn requires, from the parent firm's point of view, the IJV to make a higher return (or perform better in some way) to justify the continuation of the IJV. Of course, conflict between parties involved in an IJV also limits IJV success by preventing the IJV from being able to accomplish much by blocking decision-making (Killing, 1983). Such circumstances may also limit an IJV's ability to respond to environmental changes and, thus, to be successful (Hebert, 1994). Conflict may also result in the unwillingness of parent firms to contribute resources that the IJV needs to achieve its goals (Friedman and Beguin, 1971; Friedman and Kalmanoff, 1961; Killing, 1983). Holding back such needed resources would obviously adversely affect IJV performance and survival. In conclusion, the existence of conflict requires managers to spend valuable time and effort in resolving or managing the conflict, preventing this time from being spent in more productive ways.

It is interesting to note, however, that a small amount of conflict may be healthy for the joint venture since it may force management to evaluate their decisions more carefully. Assael is a proponent of the potential benefits of a small amount of conflict as a result of his 1969 study (Assael, 1969) of conflict between General Motors and its dealers. Assael showed that a small amount of conflict can be constructive. Further, Cosier and Dalton (1990) suggest that a small amount of structured conflict enhances effectiveness of strategic decision-making. Thus, a small amount of conflict may be useful for a joint venture. For example, managers may find after some thought that the other party's plan is superior, or they may simply benefit from refining their plan in the process of thinking more carefully through their plan's logic.

The causes of interorganizational conflict have also been investigated in the general conflict literature. The most commonly cited causes of conflict are: (1) competition for scarce resources; (2) desire for autonomy; (3) goal divergence; and (4) perceptual incongruities (Kochan *et al.,* 1975; Perry and Levine, 1976; Pondy, 1967; Rosenberg and Stern, 1971). Many different causes of conflict in IJVs have also been suggested in the IJV-specific literature. For example, the need for scarce resources possessed by parent A has been shown to make parent B more careful about how it acts, and thus results in reduced conflict (Hebert, 1994; Hyder, 1988). Further, much IJV literature has discussed the fact that conflict often results from the IJV's desire to be more autonomous from its parents, depending on the need parent firms feel to control the IJV (Beamish, 1988; Fey, 1995; Gray and Yan, 1997; Hebert, 1994; Hyder, 1988; Killing, 1983). In addition, problems resulting from differences in parent goals have been frequently discussed in the IJV literature (Beamish, 1988; Geringer, 1986; Simiar, 1983). Finally, the fact that perceptual differences often result in conflict has been much discussed in the IJV literature dealing with cultural differences (Friedman and Beguin, 1971; Geringer, 1986; Hyder, 1988; Lane and Beamish, 1990; Lyles and Salk, 1997). In general, there is a high degree of overlap between the general conflict literature and the IJV-specific conflict literature (Fey and Beamish, 2000).

Perceptual incongruities are an important cause of conflict and often a manifestation of differing organizational climates. Building on this point, when firms have different organizational climates they often have different customs about how communication flows in the organization, the extent to which teams are used, the extent to which formal control is used, the degree the firm is willing to take risks, the level of formality present in an organization, and so forth. These and other differences stemming from differing organizational climates make conflict more likely to emerge in a joint venture where participating firms have different organizational climates (Fey and Beamish, 2000). Further, several authors have suggested that interfirm diversity can significantly impede firms' ability to work together effectively (Adler and Graham, 1989; Harrigan, 1988b; Parkhe, 1991; Perlmutter and Heenan, 1986). Evans (1963) went on to suggest that the more similar parties in a dyad are, the more likely a favourable outcome. Harrigan (1988b) argued that it is more important that cooperating firms have similar corporate cultures than similar national origins. Further, Whetten (1981) suggested that the costs of coordination increase as a function of the extent of differences between collaborating firms. One of the reasons that the costs of collaboration increase is because conflict increases.

The self-governance feature found in interfirm cooperative agreements like IJVs complicates such relationships since cooperation, whilst desirable, is not automatic. Each party's self-interest (Williamson, 1985) can lead to individually rational actions that produce a suboptimal outcome (Parkhe,

1993b). The drive of self-interest and the resulting suboptimal outcome often results in conflict between involved parties (Fey and Beamish, 2000).

The Fey and Beamish (2000) study provides evidence for the importance of monitoring and trying to minimize inter-party IJV conflict to ensure superior IJV performance (especially long-term success or IJV survival). In addition, the Fey and Beamish study indicated that conflict and performance are highly correlated. Given this high correlation it is understandable that conflict was an important outcome variable of IJV activity to monitor in and of itself. In fact, such a correlation should not be surprising since Beamish (1984) and Schaan (1988) previously observed that lack of conflict was one of the measures of success used by IJVGMs. Further, other IJV scholars (e.g. Hebert, 1994; Hyder, 1988; Lee and Beamish, 1995; Tillman, 1990) have also shown that there is a negative relationship between conflict and IJV performance (Fey and Beamish, 2000).

As was discussed previously, it seems reasonable to argue that a small amount of conflict can benefit IJV performance if properly managed. However, the empirical findings do not support that view. As is evident from the literature (Beamish, 1984; Fey and Beamish, 2000; Hebert, 1994; Hyder, 1988; Lee and Beamish, 1995; Schaan, 1988; Tillman, 1990) performance and conflict appear to have a strictly linear (inversely correlated) relationship. That is, high levels of conflict result in low levels of performance. Therefore, it may be as Pondy (1967, p. 310) concludes, 'in general, however, conflict can be expected to be negatively valued'.

As such, the key role of conflict in interorganisational relations has been acknowledged (e.g., Dant and Schul, 1992). Issues such as disagreement over obligations to the system, dissatisfaction over the allocation of scarce resources, incompatible goals from the relationship, and ineffective communication between partners can lead to conflict in interorganisational relationships (Stern and Gorman, 1969). Interorganisational conflict is episodic in nature and appears as a state of tension between two or more participants in the relationship. It can be present below the surface in latent forms or it can be present in overt confrontations, that is, in manifest forms (Pondy, 1967). Manifest conflict can range from passive resistance to open, overt confrontations (Habib, 1987).

Whilst some researchers have suggested that conflict may actually benefit relationships, the empirical findings are weak. While conflict inevitably occurs in any human relationship, the critical issue is its resolution and management. If kept to a functional level, conflict can serve as a problem-solving mechanism (Dant and Schul, 1992), as a spur innovation, and as a mechanism to 'clear the air' and keep the relationship healthy in general (Johnson *et al.*, 1993).

Unfortunately, managers have rarely been able to capitalise on any positive results of conflict (Johnson *et al.*, 1993). Research indicates, nearly without exception, that conflict has severe negative repercussions in international joint ventures (Beamish, 1984; Beamish and Banks, 1987; Connolly, 1984; Cullen *et al.*, 1995; Johnson *et al.*, 1993; Madhok, 1995). For example, Kaufman and Stern (1988) found that retained hostilities remaining from conflictual episodes inhibited the development of advantageous relational norms between firms. Conflict makes cooperation difficult. Without cooperation, the achievement of goals such as organisational learning and technology transfer would be nearly impossible. Conflict erodes satisfaction because participants in these relationships may be unable to keep up morale and function effectively on a day-to-day basis in such a dysfunctional situation.

Conflict erodes trust and cooperation in the relationship. Without trust, the potential for opportunism (described by Williamson, 1985, as self-interest seeking with guile and by John, 1984, as distortion or withholding of information to the advantage of the opportunistic party), shirking of obligations in the relationship, or failure to deliver on promises greatly increases. As conflict escalates and partners' feelings of retained hostility (Kaufman and Stern, 1988) dominate the relationship, opportunistic behaviour becomes standard operating procedure and the likelihood of poor IJV performance is further enhanced. Lane and Beamish (1990) and Kogut (1988) suggest that the problems and failures in IJVs are due to conflict between the partners. Moreover, even with adequate economic performance, empirical evidence suggests that conflict between the partners reduces satisfaction in the interorganisational relationship (Anderson and Narus, 1990; Dwyer, 1980) leading to lower perceived performance by the IJV partners.

Transaction cost theory also suggests that relationships, where conflict is evident between the parties, are economically less efficient (Beamish and Banks, 1987). Conflict erodes trust, increases the potential for opportunistic behaviour, and reduces the likelihood of partners dedicating the necessary idiosyncratic assets to the relationship. In addition, conflict management and the need to safeguard assets sap resources that might otherwise make the operation more efficient.

Therefore, greater conflict between the IJV partners creates both social and economic costs for the IJV relationship. These social and economic costs have been identified by previous researchers (Beamish, 1988; Habib, 1987; Lee and Beamish, 1995) as contributing significantly to poor overall IJV business performance. As marketing performance makes a significant contribution to overall business performance (Crocombe, 1991) these social and economic costs caused by conflict are also likely to impact upon IJV marketing performance in a negative manner.

Allocation of headquarters' administrative costs, royalties on licensing agreements, technical fees, and management fees in supplementary agreements negotiated by foreign corporations in JV arrangements can lead to serious conflicts with local partners and in some cases with host governments. Even though JV contracts may provide for such payments to the foreign corporation in supplementary agreements, the local partner may scrutinise such charges whilst the JV operates, in order to avoid excessive or unreasonable charges to the business. For example, the local partner or the host government may find royalties on licensing agreements excessive, when the foreign corporation contributes no new technology. Management fees may be considered unjustified, if local managers are not trained to take over managerial positions in the process. Particularly troublesome are allocations of a share of headquarters administrative costs by a foreign corporation to a JV affiliate. The local partner in a JV may want to revise licensing agreements, management contracts, and other supplementary agreements, when they perceive that foreign corporations are not providing the technological, managerial, technical, and training inputs to justify the continued payments of royalties, management and technical fees, and other charges. As a result, serious conflicts between the foreign and local partners erupt, which can lead to impasses and failures of IJVs (Blodgett, 1991b; Datta, 1988; Dymsza, 1988; Ganitsky *et al.,* 1991; Harrigan, 1988a; Schaan and Beamish, 1988).

The roles and functions to be performed by each partner are also likely to be important determinants of IJV marketing performance success. Harrigan (1985) argued that ventures are more likely to succeed when partners possess complementary missions, resource capabilities, managerial capabilities and other attributes that create a strategic fit in which the bargaining power of the venture's sponsors is evenly matched.

5.2. Conflict and Performance

From the Julian (1998) study that examined the factors influencing IJV marketing performance in Thailand, seven factors and two statements were identified from the initial exploratory factor analysis, conflict being one of those initial factors. All items loaded as intended. The data were considered suitable for factor analysis as the Bartlett Test of Sphericity was significant (2083.2278; 0.00000) and the Keyser-Meyer-Olkin (KMO) measure of sampling adequacy (0.75873) was greater than 0.60 (Coakes and Steed, 1997).

The results of the exploratory factor analysis are summarised in Table 4.1. The seven factors and two statements explained 64.7 percent of respondent variation on issues about IJV marketing performance in Thailand. The first four factors were the dominant factors, all with eigenvalues greater than 1.5, and explaining 46.3 percent of respondent variation on issues about IJV marketing performance in Thailand. The remaining three factors and two statements accounted for only 18.4 percent of respondent variation. Therefore, the first four factors were the dominant factors in this analysis, with the remaining three factors and two statements making a minimal contribution.

In this seven-factor model the factor of conflict (Factor 2) emerged as the second-strongest factor, explaining 14.2 percent of respondent variation on issues about IJV marketing performance in Thailand (see Table 4.2). Cronbach's Alpha for this measure of conflict was 0.87, indicating a strong level of reliability. The measures of manifest conflict used in this study were from Habib's (1987) study, and the findings of the Julian (1998) study support the findings of the Habib study that manifest conflict between the IJV partners can have a negative or disruptive influence on IJV marketing performance.

The mean score for the factor of conflict (see Table 4.3) in the Julian (1998) study was 5.451 with a standard deviation of 1.435 indicating that respondents often agreed with statements identifying that different types of conflict were prevalent in the Thai IJVs being studied. That is, respondents often agreed with statements that there were disagreements between the partners regarding interpreting the terms of the IJV contract, over a partner's attempt to make changes to the IJV contract, over the IJV's hiring policies, and regarding the roles and functions to be performed by each partner, and at least one partner considered the IJV arrangement unfair because of certain contractual provisions.

Further analysis was then conducted on the seven factors and two independent statements by conducting a multiple regression analysis to analyse the relationship between the dependent variable and a set of independent variables. In the Julian (1998) study on IJV marketing performance in Thailand the dependent variable was IJV marketing performance. The independent variables were the seven factors, namely, market characteristics, conflict, commitment, product characteristics, firm-specific characteristics, marketing orientation, organisational control and the two independent statements relating to managerial control and adapting to foreign market needs. The results of the multiple regression analysis presented in Table 4.4 show that the factors of market characteristics, commitment and marketing orientation were clearly the most significant predictor variables, and the only independent variables that could be used to explain the variation in the dependent variable of IJV marketing performance. All these key predictor variables were statistically significant at the 95 percent confidence interval. Therefore, the measure of conflict used in the Julian (1998) study adapted from Habib's (1987) study was not a significant predictor of IJV marketing performance.

As the R^2 statistic that was achieved for the nominated independent and dependent variables was modest at 14.395 percent and the regression model had modest predictive ability, the data were taken for further analysis. Further analysis was undertaken to see if there was a significant relationship between some of the factors, the classification variables and demographic variables at different levels of IJV marketing performance. Therefore, a discriminant analysis was conducted on the classification variables of country of origin, equity structure, sales volume and industry classification, the demographic variable of age, the seven factors and two independent statements, and IJV marketing performance with IJV marketing performance being categorised into low and high IJV marketing performers.

The objective of discriminant analysis was to statistically distinguish between the two groups. These groups were defined by the particular research situation. In the Julian (1998) study on IJV marketing performance in Thailand the interest was to classify the IJVs into low and high marketing performers to see if the discriminating variables would distinguish between the groups. Group 1 consisted of all those IJVs that were classified as low marketing performers (i.e. those IJVs that had a marketing performance score of 4 or less using the single-item measure of IJV marketing performance). Group 2 consisted of all those IJVs that were classified as high marketing performers (i.e. those IJVs that had a marketing performance score of 5, 6 or 7 using the single-item measure of IJV marketing performance).

Table 4.5 contained a summary of the results of the discriminant analysis that related group membership to the same factors and independent statements that were used in the previously reported multiple regression analysis. The factors identified were market characteristics, conflict, commitment, product characteristics, firm-specific characteristics, marketing orientation and organisational control. The independent statements identified were related to managerial control and adapting to foreign market needs. In addition, the country of origin of the principal foreign partner (ORIGIN), the equity structure of the principal foreign partner (EQUITY), the industry the IJV operates in (INDUSTRY), the sales volume of the IJV (SALESVOL), and the age of the respondent (AGE) were also included as additional potentially discriminating variables.

Table 4.5 showed the univariate ANOVAs of the discriminant analysis. The univariate ANOVAs indicate whether there is a statistically significant difference among the dependent variable means for each independent variable. From Table 4.5 it was apparent that the independent variables of the sales volume of the IJV (SALESVOL), conflict, commitment, the industry the IJV operates in (INDUSTRY), managerial control, marketing orientation, adapting to foreign market needs and organisational control were all significant at the 95 percent confidence interval ($p < .05$). Therefore, when using the discriminant analysis conflict was a significant predictor of group membership when the groups were classified as low and high IJV marketing performers.

Additionally, Tables 5.1, 5.2 and 5.3 provide the canonical discriminant function coefficients, the structure matrix and a summary table of the statistically significant variables that successfully discriminate between the low and high IJV marketing performance categories. The canonical discriminant function coefficients provided in Table 5.1, the structure matrix provided in Table 5.2 and a summary of the discriminant analysis provided in Table 5.3 suggest that SALESVOL, reflecting the gross dollar turnover of the IJV, was the most important variable in discriminating between the low and high IJV marketing performance categories. The next most important independent or predictor variable in predicting group membership to the low or high IJV marketing performance categories was the factor of conflict, reflecting the level of conflict between the IJV partners in the IJV arrangement. After the conflict factor, the next most important predictor variable in predicting group membership to the low or high IJV marketing performance categories was commitment, reflecting the level of commitment of the IJV partners to the IJV arrangement. After the commitment factor, the next most important predictor variable in predicting group membership to the high or low IJV marketing performance categories was the industry the IJV operates in. After the industry the IJV operates in, the next most important variable in predicting group membership to the high or low IJV marketing performance categories was managerial control, reflecting the level of effective managerial control over the IJV by at least one of the IJV partners. After managerial control, the next most important variable in predicting group membership to the high or low IJV marketing performance categories was marketing orientation, reflecting the level of knowledge of their customers by the IJV's senior management. After marketing orientation, the next most important variable in predicting group membership to the high or low IJV marketing performance categories was the willingness of the foreign parents to adapt their products/services to meet the needs of the local Thai market. Finally, the last important variable in predicting group membership to the high or low IJV marketing performance categories was organisational control, reflecting the level of control over the IJV entity one partner has in relation to the repatriation of profits and the sourcing of raw materials. However, all eight independent variables of sales volume, conflict, commitment, the industry the IJV operates in, managerial control, marketing orientation, adapting to foreign market needs, and organisational control were statistically significant at the 95 percent confidence interval ($p < .05$) in discriminating between the low and high IJV marketing performance categories.

Table 5.1 Canonical Discriminant Function Coefficients

Variable	Function 1 (coefficients)
Age	.11045
Equity	-.18150
Market Characteristics	-.22615
Conflict	-.27315
Commitment	.15300
Product Characteristics	.06820
Firm-Specific Characteristics	.18032
Marketing Orientation	.24438
Organisational Control	-.14544
Managerial Control	-.21458
Adapting to Foreign Market Needs	.20769
Industry	.43132
Origin	-.02169
Salesvol	.47073

Table 5.2 Structure Matrix: Pooled Within-Groups Correlations Between Discriminating Variables and Canonical Discriminating Functions

Variable	Function 1 (Coefficients)
Salesvol	.53750
Conflict	-.47224
Commitment	.44011
Industry	.40189
Managerial Control	-.39726
Marketing Orientation	.36798
Adapting to Foreign Market Needs	.36237
Organisational Control	-.31731
Market Characteristics	-.27122
Age	.16054
Firm-Specific Characteristics	.12942
Product Characteristics	-.10589
Origin	-.10234
Equity	.09189

Table 5.3 Summary Table of Discriminant Analysis

Variable	Wilks Lambda	Significance
Salesvol	.91434	.0007
Conflict	.93256	.0026
Commitment	.94090	.0050
Industry	.95023	.0101
Managerial Control	.95132	.0110
Marketing Orientation	.95794	.0183
Adapting to Foreign Market Needs	.95916	.0201
Organisational Control	.96838	.0414

The discriminant analysis (see Table 4.6) also showed that there were actually 44 IJVs in Group 1 (low marketing performers) and 88 IJVs in Group 2 (high marketing performers). Using the discriminant function, Table 4.6 provided an indication of the success rate for predictions of membership of the grouping variable's categories using the discriminant functions developed in the analysis and that the overall success rate was 74.2 percent which is quite acceptable (Crask and Perreault, 1977).

As is evident from the exploratory factor analysis, multiple regression analysis and discriminant analysis that were conducted, conflict is a non-significant predictor of IJV marketing performance (see multiple regression analysis) yet a significant discriminator of high and low IJV marketing performance (see disciminant analysis). That is, conflict between the partners over such issues as disagreements between the partners over the terms of the IJV contract, over a partner's attempt to make changes to the IJV contract, over the IJV's hiring policies, over the roles and functions to be performed by each partner and when at least one partner considers the IJV arrangement unfair, will determine whether the Thai IJV's marketing performance is low or high. Therefore, whilst conflict between the partners was a non-significant predictor of IJV marketing performance, if conflicts between the partners of the type just mentioned are prevalent within the IJV these conflicts increase the likelihood of low IJV marketing performance being achieved.

It is important for the management of any company to be aware of the possibility of these types of conflicts existing between the IJV partners when contemplating an IJV of any magnitude in a developing country of South East Asia. The Julian (1998) study clearly indicated that it was important for the managers of IJVs to minimise their interorganisational conflicts in order to improve the IJV's marketing performance. Companies intending to enter into an IJV arrangement with another company should be proactive by taking time to get to know their IJV partner in order to avoid any unnecessary misunderstandings and potential conflicts concerning the IJV contract and the roles and functions each partner is expected to fulfil for the successful marketing performance of IJVs in Thailand and South East Asia.

6.   Commitment and Performance

6.1. Review of Commitment Literature

Theories of exchange that emphasise the benefits of close, long-term relationships are receiving increasing emphasis in marketing (Achrol, 1991; Gundlach and Murphy, 1993). Researchers have examined various facets of these relationships, including the level of commitment (Achrol *et al.*, 1990; Anderson and Weitz, 1992; Dwyer *et al.*, 1987; Morgan and Hunt, 1994). Commitment is an essential ingredient for successful long-term relationships. It has been defined as 'an implicit or explicit pledge of relational continuity between exchange partners' (Dwyer *et al.*, 1987, p. 19). Commitment implies a willingness to make short-term sacrifices to realise longer-term benefits (Dwyer *et al.*, 1987). Commitment is believed to be associated with motivation and involvement (Mowday *et al.*, 1982), positive effect and loyalty (Kanter, 1972), and performance and obedience to organisational policies (Angle and Perry, 1981). It provides a foundation for the development of social norms of governance, which are considered important mechanisms for regulating long-term relational exchanges and reducing opportunism (Macneil, 1980; Gundlach *et al.*, 1995).

Committed partners are willing to invest in valuable assets specific to an exchange, indicating they can be relied upon to perform specific functions in the future (Anderson and Weitz, 1992). These self-interest stakes help stabilise associations, reducing the uncertainty and cost of continually seeking and consummating new exchanges. As such, commitments align incentive structures so as to deepen and strengthen involvement and lay the foundation for future exchange. Further, substantial commitments that are jointly pledged, cultivate shared trust and the development of social norms that help maintain the relationship and constrain opportunistic tendencies (Gundlach *et al.*, 1995).

The concept of commitment may well become the focal point in marketing as marketing moves from the transactional view of exchange to the relational view. This is the case regardless of whether or not it is consumer's relationships with companies or interorganisational commitment that is being investigated (Gundlach *et al.*, 1995).

Commitment is regarded as being closely related to mutuality, loyalty and forsaking of alternatives, variables that are at the core of relationship building. Furthermore, commitment has been quite clearly differentiated from the economic model of rationalism and discrete transactions. Cook and Emerson (1978) note that to the extent that forming commitments curtails the exploration of alternatives, it is irrational in the short-run sense of ignoring better alternatives in favour of old partners, although it might offer certain long-term utilities (Gundlach *et al.*, 1995).

The relationship approach to exchange also poses significant conditions for the conventional power-dependence interpretation of marketing channel relationships. The use of power as a coordinating mechanism makes more sense in organising exchanges that are loosely structured in the early stages of the relationship either for historical reasons, due to trade cultures or because of industry peculiarities (Gundlach *et al.*, 1995). It is expected that in more purposefully organised and socially developed exchange networks, power will be participative and subject to institutional checks and balances (Achrol, 1991). Cook and Emerson (1978) found some evidence that power use varies inversely with commitment in exchange networks (see also Provan and Gassenheimer, 1994). Influence strategies that are compatible with relational exchange are likely to rely on expert and referent bases of power rather than the instrumental kinds such as reward and coercion (Gundlach *et al.*, 1995).

As the marketing paradigm shifts to one in which social determinants of behaviour such as trust and commitment play an even more important role, researchers are going to be faced with the problem of dealing with very complex and often ambiguous constructs. As Morrow (1983, p. 486) points out, 'the growth of commitment-related concepts has not been accompanied by a careful segmentation of commitment's theoretical domain in terms of intended meaning of each concept or the concepts' relationships among each other'. It is the objective of this chapter to conceptualise the core components of commitment and study their relationship with IJV marketing performance.

6.2. Commitment and International Joint Ventures

Most commitment theory and research focuses on people within organisations (Mowday *et al.,* 1982). Commitment at this level of analysis consists of an individual's reaction to some group or organisation. Work by Beamish (Beamish, 1984; Beamish and Banks, 1987; Lee and Beamish, 1995) and Anderson and Weitz (1992), however, demonstrated that commitment also occurs at the organisational level of analysis. Research at the organisational level examines commitment primarily as part of the organisation-to-organisation relationship. Here, commitment reflects the actions and values of key decision-makers regarding continuation of the relationship, acceptance of the joint goals and values of the partnership, and the willingness to invest resources in the relationship (Beamish, 1984; Mowday *et al.,* 1982). Commitment at the organisational level plays an important role in a range of organisation-to-organisation relationships such as those between suppliers and manufacturers, manufacturers and distributors, and various forms of strategic alliances including the IJV.

Commitment at the organisational level, referred to as relationship commitment (Lin and Germain, 1999), exists when an IJV partner believes that 'an ongoing relationship with another is so important as to warrant maximum efforts at maintaining it' (Morgan and Hunt, 1994, p. 23). Commitment to a relationship by both parties demonstrates a willingness to forgo self-interest for mutual benefit (Florin, 1997; Gronroos, 1994; Gundlach *et al.,* 1995; Pruden, 1995). As such, opportunistic activity, that is, acting in self-interest to the detriment of the exchange partner, is minimized, which results in partners working together to rectify problems, coordinate activities and minimize conflict (Gundlach *et al.,* 1995; Morgan and Hunt, 1994). Enhanced social relations, coupled with a belief that the exchange partner will not act opportunistically, results in increased levels of satisfaction, where 'satisfaction' refers to an affective state that results from the appraisal of all aspects of a firm's working relationship with another firm, thus enhancing relationship efficiency, effectiveness and stability (Anderson and Narus, 1984, 1990; Griffith *et al.,* 2001).

Within the context of an IJV, the commitment of both parties to the IJV is necessary for the successful completion of the IJV's goals and its stability (Lin and Germain, 1999). As IJV partners increase their relative commitment to the relationship, coordination of activities allows the successful achievement of goals, which results in heightened satisfaction (Beamish and Banks, 1987).

Alternatively, a lack of commitment to the IJV by the partners will often lead to an ill-defined set of objectives and lack of overall direction (Hu and Chen, 1996; Killing, 1983). As a result, commitment by the joint venture partners will be reduced, which results in lower satisfaction with the relationship and possible eventual IJV dissolution.

As such, the establishment of relationship commitment is an important achievement in relationship development (Dwyer *et al.,* 1987). Until this point, cooperation is based largely on strategic considerations. When parties are committed to the relationship, cooperation evolves into 'commitment to cooperation in its own right' (Buckley and Casson, 1988b, p. 39). Committed parties tend to constrain their opportunistic inclination. As such, a committed relationship is likely to be more effective because the transaction costs associated with the relationship will be less (Lin and Germain, 1999). Specifically, though IJVs entail an ownership structure that may affect performance, commitment creates an alternative mechanism of influence through the engagement and support of relationships (Beamish, 1988; Lin and Germain, 1999). IJV partners deal with problems on a daily basis, problems that cannot be foreseen in written contracts. As far as this is concerned, commitment helps provide a foundation upon which problems can be addressed and solved, and adjustments made (Lane and Beamish, 1990). As such, relationship commitment will have a positive impact on IJV performance (Sarkar *et al.,* 1997; Lin and Germain, 1999).

The organisational behaviour literature recognises two types or components of commitment relevant to international cooperative relationships (Reichers, 1985). One is behavioural commitment, which focuses on the prime behaviours of continuing the relationship and compliance to organisational rules, largely in response to cost-benefit analyses (Becker, 1960; Coleman, 1990; Morris and Sherman, 1981). The other is attitudinal commitment, which focuses on the acceptance of organisational goals and values, a willingness to exert an effort for the organisation, and a strong desire to be a part of the organisation (Mowday *et al.,* 1982). Behavioural commitment represents the more instrumental side of the relationships. Attitudinal commitment represents the affective component (see Cullen *et al.,* 1995).

Attitudinal commitment has been described in terms of affective commitment, psychological attachment, identification, affiliation and value congruence (Allen and Meyer, 1990; O'Reilly and Chatman, 1986). As mentioned above, this type of commitment represents 'a partisan, affective attachment to the goals and values of an organisation, to one's role in relation to the goals and values, and to the organisation for its own sake, apart from its purely instrumental worth' (Buchanan, 1974, p. 533).

Organisations recognise the value of having members who are motivated to go beyond prescribed roles and perform above and beyond the call of duty. Relationships that are based on no more than the material benefits of the relationship are likely to require more costly and sophisticated control systems and are likely to suffer from higher turnover (O'Reilly and Chatman, 1986). Alternatively, where parties share goals, values and an affective attachment, they can be expected to act instinctively for the benefit of one another (Gundlach *et al.,* 1995).

The attitudinal component of commitment shares common domains of meaning with other prominent behavioural constructs, such as motivation, identification, loyalty, involvement and behavioural intention, and is most susceptible to Staw's (1977) criticism that the value of commitment as a separate and distinct construct remains to be demonstrated. That is why the Julian (1998) study on the marketing performance of international joint ventures (IJVs) in Thailand focused on the 'behavioural intentions' meaning of attitudinal commitment. Behavioural intentions can be operationalised in terms of future resource commitments and investments. An enduring level of commitment, as reflected in each party's long-term investment intentions, provides the basis for parties to develop confidence in the stability of their relationship. On the other hand, the absence of such expectations is likely to discourage future-oriented relationship investment. Thus, a behavioural intentions conceptualisation of attitudinal commitment complements the instrumental component (Gundlach *et al.,* 1995).

In joint ventures, the behaviours of remaining in a relationship and compliance with contractual stipulations indicate behavioural commitment. The relationship is based predominantly on cost-benefit analyses related to factors such as return on investment or profits, continued access to markets or technology, or compliance with government regulations regarding local participation.

Attitudinal commitment, however, requires that partners look beyond contractual requirements and their estimates of benefits to parent companies. The attitudinally committed partner feels obliged to, and pledged to the IJV entity itself, what it is, and what it represents (Cullen *et al.,* 1995). Attitudinal commitment implies that, at least in the short run, IJV partners may place parent profits and other benefits secondary to the goals of their JV organisations (Anderson, 1990; Cullen *et al.,* 1995; Lee, 1989; Lee and Beamish, 1995).

The investment of resources to initiate and to maintain the relationship is the main antecedent for commitment. Such resources may include equity contributions, organisational knowledge or technology, and human resources (Schaan and Beamish, 1988). Theory and research on behavioural commitment emphasises that resource investments must pay off to produce commitment (Coleman, 1990; Cullen *et al.,* 1995).

In addition, the behaviours associated with investment of resources in a relationship, including the initial act of entering the IJV relationship, also activate psychological processes that enhance the attachment of partners to the IJV and increase attitudinal commitment. Psychological theories that link behaviour and commitment focus on the need for consistency between behaviour and attitudes. Given an investment behaviour (e.g., equity contribution), attitudinal adjustment (e.g., commitment) occurs from the need to create consistency between behaviour and attitude and reduce any behaviour-attitude incompatibility (Festinger, 1959). Such attitude adjustments psychologically bind a partner to the IJV relationship and its organisational goals (Kiesler, 1971; Salancik, 1977). Indeed, research on organisational decision making shows that psychological pressures for commitment can become so strong that commitment continues even when success turns to failure (cf. Cullen *et al.,* 1995; Garland, 1990).

Research by Kiesler (1971) (cf. Beamish, 1984) suggests that certain characteristics of behaviours enhance commitment. These include behaviours that are volitional, public, important to the actor and difficult to revoke. Others note that responsibility for outcomes also affects commitment (Colon and Parks, 1987). Beamish's (1984) work suggests that many of these factors also affect attitudinal commitment to the IJV. That is, factors such as strategic importance of the relationship, public awareness of the IJV's creation, dominant managerial responsibility for the IJV's performance, and dominant economic investment in the IJV may affect partner commitment. Contractually stipulated behavioural investments in an IJV, however, may have two offsetting effects on commitment. On the one hand, the contract may retard later changes in commitment by limiting volitional control of investment behaviours once the contract is executed. On the other hand, starting levels of commitment may increase and remain high because acceptance of a contract is a volitional behaviour that makes many of the investments of human and capital resources difficult to revoke (Beamish, 1984; Cullen *et al.,* 1995).

One of several constructs found to be relevant to JV performance is commitment. Several researchers (Beamish, 1984, 1988; Cullen *et al.,* 1995; Devlin and Bleakley, 1988; Fey, 1995; Geringer, 1988; Raveed and Renforth, 1983; Schaan, 1983; Schaan and Beamish, 1988; Tomlinson and Willie, 1982) have emphasised the role of commitment to JV success. Beamish (1988) found a strong correlation between commitment and performance in JVs, noting that most of the commitment characteristics in the high-performing ventures were related to the multinational enterprise's (MNE's) willingness to do something: adapt products, increase employment of nationals, visit and offer assistance, or supply special skills. Lee (1989) also found in his work on JVs from Korea that mutual confidence and close business relationships between local partners and Korean investors significantly influenced the level of satisfaction that Korean management felt about the performance of their ventures. Fey (1995) also noted the importance of long-term commitment to IJV success in his study of the key success factors for Russian/foreign joint ventures. The Fey study indicated that it is beneficial to IJV success for both parents to be involved in the JV for the long term. It makes the JV easier to manage if one parent has more involvement than the other, but it is important that all parents make a real long-term commitment to the JV. Having parents that are committed to the JV for the long term decreases the risk of shirking and increases the likelihood of mutual forbearance (Beamish, 1988; Fey, 1995; Madhok, 1995; Sohn, 1994).

Therefore, commitment of the IJV partners is a factor having a significant influence on IJV performance. Given that marketing performance represents a substantial proportion of overall business performance, arguably the level of commitment by the IJV partners will also be a contributing factor to IJV marketing performance.

6.3. Commitment and Marketing Performance

From the Julian (1998) study that examined the factors influencing IJV marketing performance in Thailand, seven factors and two statements were identified from the initial exploratory factor analysis, commitment being one of those initial factors. All items loaded as intended. The data were considered suitable for factor analysis as the Bartlett Test of Sphericity was significant (2083.2278; 0.00000) and the Keyser-Meyer-Olkin (KMO) measure of sampling adequacy (0.75873) was greater than 0.60 (Coakes and Steed, 1997).

The results of the exploratory factor analysis were summarised in Table 4.1. The seven factors and two statements explained 64.7 percent of respondent variation on issues about IJV marketing performance in Thailand. The first four factors were the dominant factors, all with eigenvalues greater than 1.5, and explaining 46.3 percent of respondent variation on issues about IJV marketing performance in Thailand. The remaining three factors and two statements accounted for only 18.4 percent of respondent variation. Therefore, the first four factors were the dominant factors in this analysis, with the remaining three factors and two statements making a minimal contribution.

In this seven-factor model the factor of commitment (Factor 3) emerged as the third-strongest factor explaining 7.8 percent of respondent variation on issues about IJV marketing performance in Thailand (see Table 4.2). Cronbach's Alpha for this measure of commitment was 0.82 indicating a strong level of reliability. The measures of commitment used in this study were from Beamish (1988) and Lee and Beamish (1995) and the findings in this study support the findings of the Beamish study and the Lee and Beamish study that commitment of the IJV partners to the IJV will have a positive influence on IJV marketing performance.

Beamish (1988) found a strong correlation between commitment and performance in IJVs, noting that most of the commitment characteristics in the high-performing ventures were related to the MNE's willingness to do something: adapt products, increase employment of nationals, visit and offer assistance, or supply special skills and resources. Lee (1989) also found in his work on JVs from Korea that mutual confidence and close business relationships between local partners and Korean investors significantly influenced the level of satisfaction that Korean management felt about the performance of their ventures. Like the Beamish (1988) study the Julian (1998) study noted that most of the commitment characteristics in the high-performing ventures were related to the foreign partner's willingness to do something: commit key senior management people to the IJV, find special skills required by the venture in the foreign parent firm, regularly visit the IJV and offer assistance, furnish additional equity or loan capital when needed and make a general commitment to the IJV and the local Thai market. Therefore, the findings of the Julian (1998) study support the findings of Beamish (1988) and Lee (1989).

The seven factors, namely, market characteristics, conflict, commitment, product characteristics, firm-specific characteristics, marketing orientation, and organisational control and the two independent statements relating to managerial control and adapting to foreign market needs were then adopted for further analysis. Mean factor scores were obtained for the seven factors and the two independent statements and the results were reported in Table 4.3.

In relation to commitment, the mean score for the factor of commitment was 5.246 with a standard deviation of 1.301. This indicates that respondents often agreed with statements identifying that the IJV parents made a commitment to the IJV and the local Thai market that the IJV was operating in. That is, respondents often agreed with statements that the IJV parents were willing to commit key senior management people to the IJV, the foreign parents of the IJV were willing to find special skills required by the venture in the foreign parent firm, the foreign parents of the IJV were willing to regularly visit the IJV and offer assistance as and when required, the parents of the IJV were willing to furnish additional equity or loan capital as and when needed, and the foreign parents were committed to the IJV and the local Thai market.

Further analysis was then conducted on the seven factors and the two independent statements by conducting a multiple regression analysis to analyse the relationship between the dependent variable and a set of independent variables. In the Julian (1998) study on IJV marketing performance in Thailand the dependent variable was IJV marketing performance. The independent variables were the seven factors, namely, market characteristics, conflict, commitment, product characteristics, firm-specific characteristics, marketing orientation, organisational control and the two independent statements relating to managerial control and adapting to foreign market needs. The results of the multiple regression analysis presented in Table 4.4 show that the factors of market characteristics, commitment and marketing orientation were clearly the most significant predictor variables and the only independent variables that could be used to explain the variation in the dependent variable of IJV marketing performance. All these key predictor variables were statistically significant at the 95 percent confidence interval. Therefore, commitment of the IJV partners to the IJV and the local Thai market was a significant predictor of IJV marketing performance in Thailand and commitment of the IJV partners had a positive impact on IJV marketing performance in Thailand.

The R^2 statistic represents the proportion of variance in the dependent variable accounted for by the independent variables. In the Julian (1998) study on IJV marketing performance in Thailand, that proportion being 14.395 percent of the explained variance in IJV marketing performance accounted for by the covariation in the independent variables. The independent variables were identified as market characteristics, conflict, commitment, product characteristics, firm-specific characteristics, marketing orientation, organisational control, managerial control and adapting to foreign market needs. Thus, the model had modest predictive ability.

As the R^2 statistic that was achieved for the nominated independent and dependent variables was modest at 14.395 percent and because the regression model had modest predictive ability the data were taken for further analysis. Further analysis was undertaken to see if there was a significant relationship between some of the factors, the classification variables and demographic variables at different levels of IJV marketing performance. Therefore, a discriminant analysis was conducted on the classification variables of country of origin, equity structure, sales volume and industry classification, the demographic variable of age, the seven factors and two independent statements, and IJV marketing performance with IJV marketing performance being categorised into low and high performers.

The objective of discriminant analysis was to statistically distinguish between the two groups. These groups were defined by the particular research situation. In the Julian (1998) study on IJV marketing performance in Thailand the interest was to classify the IJVs into low and high marketing performers to see if the discriminating variables would distinguish between the groups. Group 1 consisted of all those IJVs that were classified as low marketing performers (i.e. those IJVs that had a marketing performance score of 4 or less using the single-item measure of IJV marketing performance). Group 2 consisted of all those IJVs that were classified as high marketing performers (i.e. those IJVs that had a marketing performance score of 5, 6 or 7 using the single-item measure of IJV marketing performance).

Table 4.5 contained a summary of the results of the discriminant analysis that related group membership to the same factors and independent statements that were used in the previously reported multiple regression analysis. The factors identified were market characteristics, conflict, commitment, product characteristics, firm-specific characteristics, marketing orientation and organisational control. The independent statements identified were related to managerial control and adapting to foreign market needs. In addition, the country of origin of the principal foreign partner (ORIGIN), the equity structure of the principal foreign partner (EQUITY), the industry the IJV operates in (INDUSTRY), the sales volume of the IJV (SALESVOL), and the age of the respondent (AGE) were also included as additional potentially discriminating variables.

Table 4.5 showed the univariate ANOVAs of the discriminant analysis. The univariate ANOVAs indicate whether there is a statistically significant difference among the dependent variable means for each independent variable. From Table 4.5 it is apparent that the independent variables of the sales volume of the IJV (SALESVOL), conflict, commitment, the industry the IJV operates in (INDUSTRY), managerial control, marketing orientation, adapting to foreign market needs and organisational control are all significant at the 95 percent confidence interval ($p < .05$). Therefore, when using the discriminant analysis commitment of the IJV partners to the IJV and the local Thai market was a significant predictor of group membership when the groups were classified as low and high marketing performers.

Additionally, Tables 5.1, 5.2 and 5.3 provided the canonical discriminant function coefficients, the structure matrix and a summary table of the statistically significant variables that successfully discriminate between the low and high IJV marketing performance categories.

The canonical discriminant function coefficients provided in Table 5.1, the structure matrix provided in Table 5.2 and a summary of the discriminant analysis provided in Table 5.3 suggest that SALESVOL, reflecting the gross dollar turnover of the IJV, was the most important variable in discriminating between the low and high IJV marketing performance categories. The next most important independent or predictor variable in predicting group membership to the low or high IJV marketing performance categories was the factor of conflict, reflecting the level of conflict between the IJV partners in the IJV arrangement.

After the conflict factor, the next most important predictor variable in predicting group membership to the low or high IJV marketing performance categories was commitment, reflecting the level of commitment of the IJV partners to the IJV arrangement. After the commitment factor, the next most important predictor variable in predicting group membership to the high or low IJV marketing performance categories was the industry the IJV operates in. After the industry the IJV operates in, the next most important variable in predicting group membership to the high or low IJV marketing performance categories was managerial control, reflecting the level of effective managerial control over the IJV by at least one of the IJV partners. After managerial control, the next most important variable in predicting group membership to the high or low IJV marketing performance categories was marketing orientation, reflecting the level of knowledge of their customers by the IJV's senior management. After marketing orientation, the next most important variable in predicting group membership to the high or low IJV marketing performance categories was the willingness of the foreign parents to adapt their products/services to meet the needs of the local Thai market.

Finally, the last important variable in predicting group membership to the high or low IJV marketing performance categories was organisational control, reflecting the level of control over the IJV entity one partner has in relation to the repatriation of profits and the sourcing of raw materials. However, all eight independent variables of sales volume, conflict, commitment, the industry the IJV operates in, managerial control, marketing orientation, adapting to foreign market needs and organisational control were statistically significant at the 95 percent confidence interval ($p < .05$) in discriminating between the low and high IJV marketing performance categories.

The discriminant analysis (see Table 4.6) also showed that there were actually 44 IJVs in Group 1 (low marketing performers) and 88 IJVs in Group 2 (high marketing performers). Using the discriminant function, Table 4.6 provided an indication of the success rate for predictions of membership of the grouping variable's categories using the discriminant functions developed in the analysis and that the overall success rate was 72.2 percent which is quite acceptable (Crask and Perreault, 1977).

As is evident from the exploratory factor analysis, multiple regression analysis and discriminant analysis that were conducted, commitment was a significant predictor of IJV marketing performance (see multiple regression analysis) and a significant discriminator of high and low IJV marketing performance (see disciminant analysis). That is, commitment of the IJV parents over such issues as the IJV parents being willing to commit senior management people to the IJV, the IJV's foreign parents being willing to find special skills required by the venture in the foreign parent firm, the IJV's foreign parents being willing to regularly visit the IJV and offer assistance as and when required, the IJV's parents being willing to furnish additional equity or loan capital as and when needed, and a general commitment to the IJV and the local Thai market by the IJV's foreign parents, all contributed significantly in being able to predict IJV marketing performance in Thailand. Furthermore, if the IJV's local and foreign parents were prepared to make commitments of the like identified above, these commitments increase the likelihood of high IJV marketing performance being achieved.

It is important for the management of any company to be aware of these measures of commitment when contemplating an IJV of any magnitude in a developing country of South East Asia. The Julian (1998) study clearly indicated that it was important for joint venture partners to make commitments to their joint venture by: providing key senior management people; supplying special skills; visiting and offering assistance; furnishing additional equity or loan capital when needed; and having a general commitment to the Thai market. The management of a company needs to be committed to the foreign market they are entering and to their IJV partner for successful marketing performance of their IJV.

7.   Product Characteristics

7.1. Review of Literature Surrounding the Marketing Programme Standardisation/Adaptation Controversy

Specific product characteristics can have a significant influence on the marketing strategy chosen for a specific venture in an international market (Cavusgil *et al.,* 1993; Cooper and Kleinschmidt, 1985; McGuiness and Little, 1981). Product attributes can affect the positional competitive advantage (Day and Wensley, 1988), which influences the choice of an offensive or defensive strategy (Cook, 1983). Arguably, the marketing performance of a specific venture in an international market is determined by the relevant marketing strategies and management's capability to implement them (Aaby and Slater, 1989; Cooper and Kleinschmidt, 1985). Therefore, specific product characteristics can have a significant influence on the marketing performance of a specific venture in an international market.

Some empirical evidence supports the relationship between specific product characteristics and marketing performance when applied to an export venture (Cavusgil and Zou, 1994). However, there appears to be no empirical evidence to support the relationship between marketing performance and specific product characteristics when applied to an IJV. The particular theoretical perspective adopted here is that the relationship between specific product characteristics and marketing performance could be applied to any form of market entry strategy, including an IJV. This perspective is adopted on the principle of strategy/environment coalignment (Aldrich, 1979; Porter, 1980; Venkatraman and Prescott, 1990), which states that the 'fit' between strategy and its context, whether it is the external environment (Anderson and Zeithaml, 1984; Hofer, 1975) or organisational characteristics (Chandler, 1962; Gupta and Govindarajan, 1984), has significant positive implications for firm performance (Cavusgil and Zou, 1994).

The influence of relevant product characteristics on marketing strategy and performance relates to the diverse perspectives of the product standardisation/adaptation controversy as applied to international marketing (Douglas and Craig, 1989; Jain, 1989; Levitt, 1983). The product standardisation/adaptation controversy looks at whether a product should be standardised to satisfy the requirements of the global market or whether it should be adapted to satisfy the requirements of individual country markets (Douglas and Craig, 1989; Jain, 1989; Levitt, 1983). Product standardisation is possible where a product meets universal needs. However, if a product meets only unique needs then some degree of product adaptation will be required to meet customers' product use conditions (Buzzell, 1968; Cavusgil *et al.*, 1993; Keegan, 1969), and to educate customers in using and maintaining the product. Product adaptation is the means by which a firm's offerings are adapted to or fit the idiosyncracies of foreign markets (Douglas and Craig, 1989; Douglas and Wind, 1987; Quelch and Hoff, 1986; Walters and Toyne, 1989).

Those researchers who support the product adaptation point of view tend to cite differences among nations in terms of culture, stages of economic development, political and legal systems and lifestyle values (Cavusgil *et al.*, 1993). Researchers adopting this perspective argue that the marketing programme is largely a local issue, and the best course of action for a product will vary from market to market (Buzzell, 1968; Hill and Still, 1984; Wind, 1986).

Strong critics of standardisation Wind (1986) and Douglas and Wind (1987) argue that the strategy of developing standardised world brands with common product features, names and advertising is, at best, a special case that can be inappropriate for some situations. These authors also argue that the introduction of new global brands can cannibalise existing brands. Hill and Still (1984) found that greater product adaptation is required in rural areas than in the urban areas of the developing world. Hill and Still further noted that product adaptation can strengthen the product's competitive position in the marketplace. Limited availability and cost of communication media, as well as media habits of consumers, further undermine the suitability of a standardised marketing programme. Walters (1986) also suggested that variations in company and product characteristics make a poor case for the argument that a universal approach to marketing will be successful. Boddewyn *et al.* (1986) found that whilst standardisation as a trend was on the rise, the number of firms adopting it other than for branding and advertising of consumer non-durables was very small. Simmonds (1985) also contended that for multinational firms to survive intense international competition they must be responsive to market segments that require unique treatment by virtue of customer or environmental characteristics. Significant differences in the attribute importance structures for consumer goods exists between nations. Therefore, advertising messages used in different nations should not contain the same appeal (Johansson, 2003). Green and Langeard (1975) also found that substantial differences in consumer habits and innovator characteristics exist between countries. Finally, Kotler (1986) and Kashani (1989) cautioned managers about blind implementation of standardised marketing programmes (see Cavusgil *et al.*, 1993).

In relation to standardisation, the supporters of standardisation emphasise the trend toward the homogenisation of world markets and the cost-saving benefits of standardisation. According to these researchers (Levitt, 1983; Ohmae, 1989b) technology has contributed towards homogenisation of demand patterns. To compete effectively in the global market, firms must achieve cost efficiencies by standardising their marketing programmes.

As early as 1972, Stopford and Wells (1972) recognised that global coordination calls for products to be standardised to some extent in world markets. Porter (1986) further argued that coordination among increasingly complex networks of activities dispersed worldwide is becoming a primary source of competitive advantage. Kotabe and Omura (1989) found that a high level of product adaptation cuts into a product's profitability and market share. They reason that product adaptation tends to be a reactive, rather than proactive, strategic response to the market. Therefore, a high level of product adaptation may make it difficult for multinational firms to reap economies of scale in production and marketing and to coordinate their networks of activities on a global scale (Kotabe, 1990). Arguably, as many multinationals seeking to penetrate developing country markets use the foreign market entry mode of the IJV (Ahn, 1980; Beamish, 1984, 1988, 1993; Connolly, 1984; Gullander, 1976; Wright and Russel, 1975) this inability to coordinate their networks of activities on a global scale is likely to have an influence on the marketing performance of their IJV.

One of the strongest supporters of standardisation was Levitt (1983) and he argued that advances in technology together with increased travel contribute to the globalisation of markets. As a result global customer groups have begun to emerge. In order to survive and be successful in the global market a firm must be able to deliver a high-quality product at a competitive price. Marketing programme standardisation is, therefore, the means by which a firm can achieve a low-cost competitive position in the global market since standardisation helps realise economies of scale in the value-added chain. Levitt also felt that this adaptation philosophy was mainly a result of a lack of vision by the multinational companies. As such, he argued that the multinational firms are likely to disappear and be replaced by truly 'global corporations' selling the same product in the same manner in every country they operate.

Another major supporter of standardisation was Kenichi Ohmae (1985). He argued that the Triad (US, Western Europe and Japan) constitute the major markets, accounting for most of the world's market potential. Customers in these markets have become fairly homogeneous, making standardisation possible. Ohmae (1989b) also suggested that successful firms are those that stress the commonalities among markets. Terpstra (1987) also felt that standardisation of marketing was facilitated by consumer mobility, media overflow and the global similarity of many industrial and consumer products. Terpstra (1987) further argued that a universal brand and position can be a powerful marketing tool in international markets, and that by being able to reduce costs through standardisation this would be an attractive option for exporters and multinational firms. However, as Douglas and Wind (1987) point out, the more internationally competent a firm is the more likely it is that standardisation alone will not lead to optimal results. A competent firm because of its international experience and resources, knows the differences in environmental conditions, market demand and the degree of competition and is more likely to select the most attractive market for the venture and adapt the marketing strategy (product, price, promotion and distribution) to accommodate the environmental conditions prevailing in the foreign market (Cavusgil *et al.,* 1993; Cavusgil and Zou, 1994; Douglas and Craig, 1989; Hill and Still, 1984). An inexperienced firm seeks the closest match between its current offerings and foreign market conditions so that minimal adaptation is necessary (Douglas and Craig, 1989).

Therefore, despite the fact that a number of articles have been published on the topic, there is little agreement on the conditions under which either standardisation or adaptation is appropriate in foreign markets. No conclusive guidelines are available for international marketing managers with respect to how much standardisation or adaptation is appropriate when a product is introduced into a foreign market. This is largely due to the lack of empirical studies in this area, and that company practice in this area has preceded academic research (Jain, 1989; Wind, 1985). The decision on standardisation is not a dichotomous one between complete standardisation or complete adaptation. Rather, researchers advocate a contingency perspective on the standardisation versus adaptation issue. According to this perspective, standardisation and adaptation should be viewed as two extremes of the same continuum where there can be degrees of standardisation and adaptation

(Jain, 1989; Quelch and Hoff, 1986; Walters, 1986). Furthermore, the degree of standardisation or adaptation is contingent upon a variety of internal and external factors (Jain, 1989). Building on a review of previous research, Jain presented a conceptual framework for determining the degree of marketing programme standardisation. According to Jain's framework, the degree of marketing programme standardisation is determined by factors such as target market, market position, nature of product, environment and organisational factors. Other researchers have also postulated correlates of the degree of standardisation (Buzzell, 1968; Sorensen and Wiechmann, 1975; Walters, 1986). These authors argued that differences in the cultural and legal environment, conditions of product use, company factors and competition are important barriers to standardisation. Samiee and Roth (1992) also found that product characteristics, market coverage and capacity utilisation all impact upon standardisation decisions.

Therefore, according to Cavusgil *et al.* (1993), when making standardisation/adaptation decisions managers are advised to adopt a contingency approach thereby providing support for Jain's (1989) framework. Blind standardisation of a firm's product and promotional strategy is likely to fail in foreign markets. As conditions in the firm, product, and foreign market dictate, managers should seek a certain degree of adaptation of their marketing programme and monitor that decision over time. Furthermore, managers of foreign ventures must realise that various aspects of the marketing programme may require varying degrees of modification over time. The answer is to find that combination which yields the maximum return in a particular foreign market (Cavusgil *et al.,* 1993). In the Cavusgil *et al.* study they concluded that managers may attempt to standardise their products and promotional programmes in foreign markets when the industry is technology intensive, the product is not culture specific, there is not intense competition in the foreign market, and when management lacks international experience and expertise to formulate and implement an adaptation strategy. Furthermore, managers may be able to avoid physical modification of a unique product through adaptation of positioning, packaging and labelling, and their promotional approach. Finally, upon entering a foreign market that calls for different legal and technical regulations, managers are only able to make those modifications to the product mandated by the regulations.

The marketing performance of an IJV is determined by the venture's marketing strategies and management's capabilities to implement them (Aaby and Slater, 1989; Cooper and Kleinschmidt, 1985). When an IJV's marketing strategies are coaligned with firm, industry, product and foreign market characteristics, positive performance for the venture can be expected (Anderson and Zeithaml, 1984; Cavusgil and Zou, 1994; Porter, 1980; Venktraman and Prescott, 1990). Product/service adaptation and promotion adaptation have been described as the means by which firm's offerings adapt to or fit the idiosyncracies of foreign markets (Douglas and Craig, 1989; Douglas and Wind, 1987; Quelch and Hoff, 1986; Walters and Toyne, 1989). Hence, these strategies can be interpreted as the means by which a firm achieves coalignment between the marketing strategies and the internal and external environmental factors affecting the venture. Therefore, it is expected that marketing performance will be influenced significantly by product adaptation and promotion adaptation. There is also empirical evidence to support a positive significant relationship between marketing performance and product adaptation (Cooper and Kleinschmidt, 1985; Hill and Still, 1984; Kirpalani and McKintosh, 1980) and promotion adaptation (Killough, 1978). Therefore, the objective of this chapter is to identify those IJVs where some degree of product adaptation has occurred and to then empirically test the influence of a number of product characteristics on IJV marketing performance in a South East Asian country market, that South East Asian country market being Thailand.

Some of the relevant product characteristics that have influenced marketing strategy and performance in an international venture where there is some degree of product adaptation include the following: product uniqueness, culture-specificity of the product, familiarity of consumers to the product/service, strength of the patent the product enjoys, age of the product (or the stage of the product life cycle the product is in), and service and maintenance requirements of the product (Cavusgil and Zou, 1994).

7.2. Product Uniqueness

Product uniqueness is defined as the degree to which the product is designed and made to satisfy unique needs or to be used for unique purposes. Cultural specificity of the product differs from product uniqueness in that culture-specificity is culture based, whilst product uniqueness is not. If a product meets universal needs, standardisation is facilitated (Levitt, 1983). However, if a product meets only unique needs, greater adaptation will be required to meet customers' product use conditions (Hill and Still, 1984) and to educate customers in using and maintaining the product.

7.3. Culture-Specificity of the Product

As far as culture-specificity of the product is concerned, this pertains to the extent to which the product caters to the needs of a specific culture or sub-culture. When a culture-specific product is being marketed in a foreign market, the cultural base on which the product is developed may not match the cultural base of the foreign market. In order to have viable growth opportunities, the product must be adapted to the conditions of the foreign market, and its relative positioning, packaging and labelling, and promotional approach must be customised to fit the cultural idiosyncracies (e.g., language and symbolism) in the foreign market (Buzzell, 1968; Cavusgil *et al.,* 1993; Cavusgil and Zou, 1994; Douglas and Wind, 1987; Jain, 1989).

7.4. Familiarity of Consumers to the Product/Service

As far as familiarity of consumers to the products/services of the IJV is concerned, a consumer's familiarity with a particular product or brand can ease the entry of the product or brand into the foreign market. Varying levels of awareness, knowledge, familiarity and experience with a product or brand may result in differential attitudes toward similar products. Therefore, a familiar product requires lower promotion and product adaptation in the foreign market than an unfamiliar one, because familiarity can translate into a favourable attitude (Parameswaran and Yaprak, 1987), which forms brand equity and can be exploited in the foreign market (Kashani and Quelch, 1990). A lesser known product or brand, on the other hand, may require reformulation in order to enhance consumer reception (Cavusgil *et al.,* 1993; Cavusgil and Zou, 1994).

7.5. Strength of the Patent

As for the strength of the patent the product enjoys, companies spend millions of dollars establishing brand names or trademarks to symbolise quality and a host of other product features designed to entice customers to buy their brands to the exclusion of others. Millions more are spent on research to develop new products, processes, designs and formulae that provide companies with advantages over their competitors. Such intellectual or industrial property rights are among the more valuable assets a company may possess. Names such as Kodak, Coca-Cola and Gucci, rights to processes such as xerography, and rights to computer software are invaluable. One financial group estimated that the Marlboro brand had a value of US$ 33 billion, Kellogg's US$ 9 billion, Microsoft a value of US$ 9.8 billion, and US$ 5 billion for Levi's. Estimates are that lost sales from unauthorised use of patents, trademarks, and copyrights from the US alone amount to about US$ 60 billion annually (Cateora, 1996). Therefore, the strength of the patent that an international organisation enjoys in a foreign market is likely to be a contributing factor to marketing performance success.

7.6. Stage of the Product Life Cycle

As for the age of a firm's products or the stage of the product life cycle the firm's products are in, even between markets with few cultural differences, substantial adaptation can be necessary if the product is in a different stage of its life cycle in each market. Product life cycle and the marketing mix are interrelated; a product in a mature stage of its life cycle in one market can have unwanted and/or unknown attributes in a market where the product is perceived as new and thus in its introductory stage. Marketing history is full of examples of mature products in one market being introduced in another and failing. After 20 years of success with the instant camera, Polaroid introduced the Swinger Land Camera to a mature US market. The Swinger was designed to place Polaroid in the mass market for inexpensive cameras. The Swinger capitalised on the reputation of Polaroid and was very successful. Polaroid then introduced the Swinger into the French market using its successful US marketing program. The Swinger was Polaroid's first product in France and it was a spectacular failure. To the French, the Swinger and its concept of instant photography were unknown. In France, the product was in the introductory stage of its life cycle, and the marketing effort required adaptation of the marketing programme that had been designed for the mature US market. Polaroid withdrew the product, changed the marketing approach, and successfully reintroduced it. What Polaroid failed to appreciate was the 20 years of development and use of instant photography that was lacking in France. Therefore, an important approach in analysing a product's performance and a firm's marketing performance in a foreign market is determining the stage of its product life cycle. All marketing plans must then include adaptations necessary to correspond to the stage of the product life cycle in the new market (Cateora, 1996).

For example, strategies for the introduction stage emphasise a buyer focus, building on advertising and increasing purchase frequency. Product development is seen as being important (Hofer, 1975). In the growth stage, there is movement toward strategic segmentation and building efficiencies in production and marketing. Performance of the product as it relates to customer needs is crucial, and product modification may be necessary. The capital investment and expenses associated with these strategies may be detrimental to short-term profits. Intense distribution is also emphasised. In the maturity stage, high-performance strategies are more complex than for the previous two stages because they centre on improving efficiencies in process, reducing overall costs in marketing and distribution with further differentiation of products and market segmentation being required. Relatively little work has been done regarding strategies leading to high performance in the decline stage; however, a piece of landmark research was conducted by Harrigan (1980) who developed a contingency model for strategies in declining businesses. Strategy in this stage depends on industry traits (e.g., the certainty with which demand will decline), whether some segments will have enduring demand, whether barriers impede the exit of firms, and the nature of competition. The other variable, competitive strength, includes average returns compared to competitors, relationships with customers, and vertical relationships. Depending on the mix of these factors, strategies range from an immediate exit to increasing investment in the declining business (Anderson and Zeithaml, 1984). As such, strategy researchers have concluded that strategy content should vary for each stage of the PLC.

7.7. Service and Maintenance Requirements of the Product

Finally, as far as the service and maintenance requirements of the product is concerned, when a product that is sold in a foreign market requires repairs, parts or service, then of obtaining, training and holding a sophisticated engineering or repair staff is not easy. If the product breaks down, and the repair arrangements are not up to standard, the image of the product and the firm will suffer. In some cases, products abroad may not even be used for their intended purpose and may thus require modifications not only in product configuration but also in service frequency. Therefore, the importance of the service and maintenance requirements of the firm's product offerings in a foreign market should not be underestimated as a factor influencing marketing performance.

As such, statements were included in the Julian (1998) study to assess the product/service's age, uniqueness, culture-specificity and, the level of product and promotion adaptation required for the local Thai market and their impact on IJV marketing performance.

7.8. Product Characteristics and IJV Marketing Performance

From the Julian (1998) study that examined the factors influencing IJV marketing performance in Thailand seven factors and two statements were identified from the initial exploratory factor analysis, product characteristics being one of those initial factors. All items loaded as intended. The data were considered suitable for factor analysis as the Bartlett Test of Sphericity was significant (2083.2278; 0.00000) and the Keyser-Meyer-Olkin (KMO) measure of sampling adequacy (0.75873) was greater than 0.60 (Coakes and Steed, 1997).

The results of the exploratory factor analysis were summarised in Table 4.1. The seven factors and two statements explained 64.7 percent of respondent variation on issues about IJV marketing performance in Thailand. The first four factors were the dominant factors, all with eigenvalues greater than 1.5, and explaining 46.3 percent of respondent variation on issues about IJV marketing performance in Thailand. The remaining three factors and two statements accounted for only 18.4 percent of respondent variation. Therefore, the first four factors were the dominant factors in this analysis, with the remaining three factors and two statements making a minimal contribution.

In this seven-factor model the factor of product characteristics (Factor 4) emerged as the fourth strongest factor explaining 5.1 percent of respondent variation on issues about IJV marketing performance in Thailand (see Table 4.2.). Cronbach's Alpha for this measure of product characteristics was 0.70, indicating a strong level of reliability. The measures of product characteristics used in this study were from Cavusgil and Zou (1994) and the findings in the Julian (1998) study provide partial support to the findings of the Cavusgil and Zou study of the importance of certain product characteristics.

Marketing performance is determined by a venture's marketing strategies and management's capabilities to implement them (Aaby and Slater, 1989; Cooper and Kleinschmidt, 1985). When an IJV's marketing strategies are coaligned with firm, industry, product and foreign market characteristics, positive performance for the venture can be expected (Anderson and Zeithaml, 1984; Cavusgil and Zou, 1994; Porter, 1980; Venkatraman and Prescott, 1990). Product/service adaptation and promotion adaptation have been described as the means by which firm's offerings adapt to or fit the idiosyncracies of foreign markets (Douglas and Craig, 1989; Douglas and Wind, 1987; Quelch and Hoff, 1986; Walters and Toyne, 1989). Hence, these strategies can be interpreted as the means by which a firm achieves coalignment between the marketing strategies and the internal and external environmental factors affecting the venture (e.g., culture-specificity of the product/service, familiarity of consumers to the product/service, and the stage of the product life cycle the product/service is currently in). Therefore, it is expected that marketing performance will be influenced significantly by product/service adaptation and promotion adaptation. There is also empirical evidence to support a significant relationship between marketing performance and product adaptation (Cooper and Kleinschmidt, 1985; Hill and Still, 1984; Kirpalani and McKintosh, 1980) and promotion adaptation (Killough, 1978). However, the Julian (1998) study examining IJV marketing performance in Thailand provided only partial support of the importance of product/service adaptation, promotion adaptation and environmental issues (such as culture-specificity of the IJV's products/services, familiarity of consumers with the IJV's products/services, and stage of the product life cycle the IJV's products/services are in) to IJV marketing performance. They were identified as important variables in the factor of product characteristics; however, the factor of product characteristics was a non-significant predictor of IJV marketing performance in the subsequent multiple regression and discriminant analyses that were conducted.

The seven factors of market characteristics, conflict, commitment, product characteristics, firm-specific characteristics, marketing orientation and organisational control, and the two independent statements relating to managerial control and adapting to foreign market needs, were taken for further analysis. Mean factor scores were obtained for the seven factors and the two independent statements and the results were reported in Table 4.3.

The mean factor score for the factor of product characteristics was 4.316 with a standard deviation of 0.839 indicating that the factor of product characteristics had the lowest mean score. This indicates that generally respondents agreed with statements identifying certain product characteristics of the Thai IJVs products/services as being in existence. For example, product/service adaptation being required for the Thai market, lack of familiarity by Thai consumers to the IJV's products/services, promotion adaptation of the IJV's products/services being required for the Thai market, the age of the IJV's products/services, and the IJV's products/services were culture-specific.

A multiple regression analysis was then conducted to analyse the relationship between the dependent variable and a set of independent variables. In the Julian (1998) study on IJV marketing performance in Thailand the dependent variable was IJV marketing performance. The independent variables were the seven factors. The results of the multiple regression analysis presented in Table 4.4 show that the factors of market characteristics, commitment and marketing orientation were clearly the most significant predictor variables and the only independent variables that could be used to explain the variation in the dependent variable of IJV marketing performance. Therefore, product characteristics was a non-significant predictor of IJV marketing performance in Thailand.

The R^2 statistic represents the proportion of variance in the dependent variable accounted for by the independent variables. In the Julian (1998) study on IJV marketing performance in Thailand, that proportion being 14.395 percent of the explained variance in IJV marketing performance accounted for by the covariation in the independent variables. Thus, the model had modest predictive ability.

As the R^2 statistic that was achieved for the nominated independent and dependent variables was modest at 14.395 percent and because the regression model had modest predictive ability the data were taken for further analysis. Further analysis was undertaken to see if there was a significant relationship between some of the factors, the classification variables and demographic variables at different levels of IJV marketing performance. Therefore, a discriminant analysis was conducted on the classification variables of country of origin, equity structure, sales volume, and industry classification, the demographic variable of age, the seven factors and two independent statements and IJV marketing performance with IJV marketing performance being categorised into low and high performers.

The objective of discriminant analysis was to statistically distinguish between the two groups. These groups were defined by the particular research situation. In the Julian (1998) study on IJV marketing performance in Thailand the interest was to classify the IJVs into low and high marketing performers to see if the discriminating variables would distinguish between the groups. Group 1 consisted of all those IJVs that were classified as low marketing performers (i.e. those IJVs that had a marketing performance score of 4 or less using the single-item measure of IJV marketing performance). Group 2 consisted of all those IJVs that were classified as high marketing performers (i.e. those IJVs that had a marketing performance score of 5, 6 or 7 using the single-item measure of IJV marketing performance).

Table 4.5 contains a summary of the results of the discriminant analysis that related group membership to the same factors and independent statements that were used in the previously reported multiple regression analysis. The univariate ANOVAs indicate whether there is a statistically significant difference among the dependent variable means for each independent variable. From Table 4.5 it is apparent that the independent variables of the sales volume of the IJV (SALESVOL), conflict, commitment, the industry the IJV operates in (INDUSTRY), managerial control, marketing orientation, adapting to foreign market needs and organisational control are all significant at the 95 percent confidence interval (p < .05). Therefore, when using the discriminant analysis product characteristics was a non-significant predictor of group membership when the groups were classified as low and high marketing performers.

As is evident from the exploratory factor analysis, multiple regression analysis and discriminant analysis that were conducted product characteristics was a non-significant predictor of IJV marketing performance (see multiple regression analysis) and a non-significant discriminator of high and low IJV marketing performance (see disciminant analysis). That is, product characteristics such as the level of product/service and promotion adaptation required for the local Thai market, familiarity of consumers to the IJV's products/services, culture-specificity of the IJVs products/services and the age of the IJVs products/services were not significant predictors of IJV marketing performance in Thailand. Furthermore, product characteristics such as these could not be used to distinguish between high and low IJV marketing performance in Thailand.

However, it is still important for the management of any company to be aware of these product characteristics when contemplating an IJV of any magnitude in a developing country of South East Asia. Whilst product characteristics was a non-significant predictor of IJV marketing performance in Thailand in the Julian (1998) study, the study clearly indicated that managers of IJVs should make efforts to adapt their products/services to meet the needs of the local Thai market for achieving success in the marketing performance of their IJV. Specifically: product/service adaptation, adapting the promotional campaign, familiarity of consumers to the product/service, the product's age and culture-specificity of the product/service require management's attention. IJV managers must be aware of the importance of adapting the IJV's products/services to meet the needs of the local Thai market and restrain from opting for a globally standardised product/service. The Julian (1998) study findings, therefore, provide partial support for the findings of Cavusgil *et al.* (1993) and Cavusgil and Zou (1994) studies.

8. Marketing Orientation

8.1. Introduction

The degree of marketing orientation enjoyed by a firm is a proven determinant of business performance success (Ahmed and Krohn, 1994; Ghosh *et al.*, 1994; Lu *et al.*, 1994; Pitt and Jeantrout, 1994; Wilson and McDonald, 1994). Marketing orientation being defined as 'the degree to which individuals are aware of the needs and wants of one's customers, and how the firm might best meet those needs and wants' (Ahmed and Krohn, 1994, p. 115). Focusing on immediate and long-term consumer contentment is the obvious manifestation of an organisation imbued with marketing orientation. Greater consumer satisfaction, eventual competitive advantage over competitors, and the resultant increase in profits are the likely results of an organisation whose employees have been thoroughly trained in marketing orientation (Ahmed and Krohn, 1994; Broom *et al.*, 1983). Determining the degree of marketing orientation within an organisation can be discerned by seeking information from employees.

Marketing-oriented firms are skilled at learning about the articulated and unarticulated needs of their customers, and at satisfying those needs in a way that is superior to how competitors satisfy those needs. Customers are the primary stakeholders for marketing-oriented businesses. Employees are treated well because they are the customer value creators. Shareholders benefit because a marketing orientation is valuable, rare and difficult to imitate, the necessary conditions for a sustainable competitive advantage (Porter, 1985). Thus, a marketing orientation benefits at least three stakeholder groups: customers, employees and shareholders.

8.2. Review of the Marketing Orientation Literature

The central element of marketing orientation is a customer focus. Whilst a customer focus involves obtaining information from customers about their needs and wants, it goes beyond customer research. Being customer oriented involves taking actions based on market intelligence, not on verbalised customer opinions alone. Market intelligence is a broader concept than customer focus in that it includes consideration of external market factors such as competition and regulations that affect customer needs and preferences and current as well as future needs of customers. These extensions do not challenge customer focus they reflect broader more strategic concerns related to customers (Kohli and Jaworski, 1990).

The idea that market intelligence pertains not just to current needs, but to future needs as well, echoes Houston's (1986) assertion and reflects a departure from conventional views (e.g., 'find a need and fill it') in that it urges organizations to anticipate the needs of customers and initiate steps to meet them. The notion that market intelligence includes anticipated customer needs is important because it often takes years for an organization to develop a new product offering (Kohli and Jaworski, 1990).

Though assessment of customer needs is the cornerstone of marketing orientation, defining customers may not be simple. In some cases, businesses may have consumers (i.e., end users of products and services) as well as clients (i.e., organizations that may dictate or influence the choices of end users). As such, it is critical for organisations to understand the needs and preferences of not just end customers but also retailers through whom their products are sold. This sentiment reflects the growing power of retailers over manufacturers and increased competition among manufacturers due to the proliferation of brands (Kohli and Jaworski, 1990).

The generation of market intelligence relies not just on customer surveys, but on a host of complementary mechanisms. Intelligence may be generated through a variety of formal as well as informal means (e.g., informal discussions with trade partners) and may involve collecting primary data or consulting secondary sources. The mechanisms include meetings and discussions with customers and trade partners (e.g., distributors), analysis of sales reports, analysis of worldwide customer databases, and formal market research such as customer attitude surveys, sales response in test markets, and so on (Kohli and Jaworski, 1990).

Importantly, intelligence generation is not the exclusive responsibility of a marketing department. For example, R&D engineers may obtain information at scientific conferences, senior executives might uncover trends reported in trade journals, and so on. Industrial products companies have indicated that it was routine for their R&D personnel to interact directly with customers to assess their needs and problems and develop new business targeted at satisfying those needs (Kohli and Jaworski, 1990).

The generation of market intelligence does not stop at obtaining customer opinions, but also involves careful analysis and subsequent interpretation of the forces that impinge on customer needs and preferences. Equally important, the field findings suggest that the generation of market intelligence is not and probably cannot be the exclusive responsibility of a marketing department (Kohli and Jaworski, 1990; Webster, 1988). Rather, market intelligence is generated collectively by individuals and departments throughout an organization. Mechanisms, therefore, must be in place for intelligence generated at one location to be disseminated effectively to other parts of an organization.

Intelligence dissemination requires the participation of virtually all departments in an organization. R&D to design and develop a new product, manufacturing to gear up and produce it, purchasing to develop vendors for new parts and materials, finance to fund activities, and so on. As such, market intelligence need not always be disseminated by the marketing department to other departments. Intelligence may flow in the opposite direction, depending on where it is generated. Effective dissemination of market intelligence is important because it provides a shared basis for concerted actions by different departments (Kohli and Jaworski, 1990).

A formal intelligence dissemination procedure is obviously important; however, despite sparse treatments of the effects of informal information dissemination in the literature, 'hall talk' is an extremely powerful tool for keeping employees tuned to customers and their needs (Kohli and Jaworski, 1990). The emphasis on intelligence dissemination parallels acknowledgement of the important role of 'horizontal communication' in service organizations (Zeithaml *et al.,* 1988). Horizontal communication is the flow of information that occurs both within and between departments (Daft and Steers, 1985) and coordinates people and departments to facilitate the attainment of overall organizational goals. Horizontal communication of market intelligence is one form of intelligence dissemination within an organization.

Another element of marketing orientation is responsiveness to market intelligence. An organization can generate intelligence and disseminate it internally; however, unless it responds to market needs, very little is achieved. Responsiveness is the action taken in response to intelligence that is generated and disseminated (Kohli and Jaworski, 1990).

The field findings indicate that responsiveness to market intelligence takes the form of selecting target markets, designing and offering products/services that cater to their current and anticipated needs, and producing, distributing and promoting the products in a way that elicits favourable customer response. Virtually all departments, not just marketing, participate in responding to market trends in a marketing-oriented company (Kohli and Jaworski, 1990).

For an organization to achieve consistently above normal market performance, it must create a sustainable competitive advantage (SCA) (Aaker, 1989, p. 91; Narver and Slater, 1990; Porter, 1985, p. xv). That is, it must create sustainable superior value for its customers. The logic of SCA is that for a buyer to purchase offering X, the buyer must perceive that the expected value to him of that offering (i.e., that proposed solution to his need) exceeds the expected value to him of any alternative solution (Narver and Slater, 1990).

The value of a seller's offering to a buyer is the difference between what the buyer perceives as the offering's expected benefits and what the buyer perceives as its expected total acquisition and use costs (Zeithaml, 1988). A seller, any seller, has numerous alternative opportunities for creating additional buyer value through increasing a buyer's benefits and/or decreasing a buyer's total acquisition and use costs (e.g., Forbis and Mehta, 1981; Narver and Slater, 1990).

The desire to create superior value for customers and attain a SCA drives a business to create and maintain the culture that will produce the necessary behaviours. Marketing orientation is the organization culture (i.e., culture and climate: see Deshpande and Webster, 1989) that most effectively and efficiently creates the necessary behaviours for the creation of superior value for buyers and, thus, continuous superior performance for the business (Aaker, 1988; Kohli and Jaworski, 1990; Kotler, 1984; Kotler and Andreasen, 1987; Narver and Slater, 1990; Peters and Austin, 1985; Peters and Waterman, 1982; Shapiro, 1988; Webster, 1988).

A marketing-oriented seller understands that, through the numerous means of creating additional benefits for buyers as well as the numerous types of reductions in the buyers' total acquisition and use costs, there are many potential sources of SCA (Aaker, 1988; Hall, 1980; Porter, 1985). Thus, a marketing-oriented business continuously examines these alternative sources of SCA to see how it can be most effective in creating sustainable superior value for its present and future target buyers. To maximize its long-run performance, the business knows it must build and maintain a long-run, mutually beneficial relationship with its buyers. Accordingly, a market-oriented seller decides how best to share with its buyers the superior value it creates for them (Forbis and Mehta, 1981; Hanan, 1985; Jackson, 1985; Narver and Slater, 1990).

Kotler (1991) presented a model of three types of strategic marketing orientation, external marketing, internal marketing and interactive marketing, and explained how they are applied in the marketplace. External marketing describes how a company's marketing mix strategy consisting of product, price, promotion and place (distribution) is used to create a beneficial exchange relationship between producer and consumer. The emphasis is on improving marketing relationships between the company and its customers by adopting and utilising effective marketing mix strategies. However, this traditional marketing approach is no longer sufficient to retain customers in today's rapidly changing global marketplace (Kotler, 1991; Waterschoot and Van Den Bulte, 1992). Rather, two other marketing orientations, internal marketing and interactive marketing, are needed in order to meet the needs of today's companies effectively (Lu *et al.*, 1994).

Internal marketing is a concept that emphasises team management. The company should encourage and motivate employees in non-marketing departments to work as a team, and support employees in marketing-related areas (e.g., sales, marketing and customer service) who have frequent contact with customers. The emphasis of internal marketing is on the management of relationships between marketing and non-marketing personnel. Systems marketing, which is a current practice within the broader context of internal marketing, involves the interaction between the company's management and employees, and its customers. Here, emphasis is placed on pre-selling, selling and post-selling activities (Caruso, 1992; Lu *et al.*, 1994).

Interactive marketing measures the level of efficiency of the marketing department in contacting and addressing customers' needs. Database marketing can be used to illustrate this concept. Here, information on customers such as personal and/or organisational interests, goals and objectives is maintained in a database. The premise is: 'the more information a company has about its customers, the better it interacts with them and, therefore, the better their needs are satisfied' (Lu *et al.*, 1994, p. 43). A typical example is a company that has a customer service department that maintains a database on customer complaints, needs and, perhaps, expectations. This information can be used to improve work processes.

These three types of strategic marketing orientation proposed by Kotler (1991) can be adapted and further developed to support a company's vision and long-term goals and objectives in the global marketplace. As a result a number of marketing effectiveness studies have been undertaken (e.g., Pitt and Jeantout, 1994). The studies were based on the rationale that one of the practical ways of advancing the regeneration and growth process in companies is to isolate the best marketing practices at the individual firm level and to analyse their components. The research objective of these studies gives the impression of being twofold: first to isolate better-performing companies and to examine the contribution that marketing has made to their performance; and, second, to identify the better marketing practices used by these companies. Four such studies were undertaken in Singapore (Ghosh *et al.*, 1993), Australia (Kwan and Yau, 1992), New Zealand (Taylor, 1993) and Taiwan (Lai *et al.*, 1992).

The importance of effective marketing in industrial competitiveness is well established (Kohli and Jaworski, 1990). In a report on the findings of a major survey of UK companies, Hooley and Lynch (1985) and Hooley *et al.* (1984), commented that the profile of the most successful organisations was effectively a summary of conventional wisdom on marketing excellence. Kiel *et al.* (1986) conducted a similar survey in Australia and came up with the same conclusion. The National Economic Development Organization's (NEDO) report (1982) on transferable factors in Japan's rapid growth indicated that Japan's economic success was largely due to the strong emphasis on marketing for worldwide sales. Numerous books on marketing expound the importance of the process. Kotler (1991) believed that stronger company marketing skills can potentially launch a new era of high economic growth and rising living standards. Closeness to the customer (Peters and Waterman, 1982); the customer as king (Rodgers, 1986); emphasis on the central importance of dedication of the business to sensing, serving and satisfying the customers in a well-understood target market (Kotler, 1991); and that it will be marketing skills that distinguish the amateur from the professional players in the global market (Kotler, 1991) are some of the themes which point to the recognition given to marketing in the literature (Ghosh *et al.*, 1994).

Yet, despite the recognition of the important role of marketing competitiveness in industrial success, there is strong evidence that marketing remains an area of significant weakness for companies. Doyle *et al.* (1985), in comparing Japanese and British strategies, observed that British companies were often finance or production oriented, rather than marketing focused. The NEDO (1981a) report stressed the constraining effects of the widespread lack of commitment to marketing. On this same theme, NEDO (1981b, 1982) reported evidence that a number of innovations have not met commercial expectations because they had been based excessively on 'technology push', deriving from technical departments, with insufficient assessment of market needs as a starting point for product development. Baker (1979) and Hooley and Newcombe (1983) also drew attention to the prevalence of production orientation and a lack of marketing perspective among many companies. Taylor (1993) observed that in New Zealand, until very recently, little was known about how New Zealand organisations actually went about marketing.

Therefore, the importance of marketing orientation to marketing performance success cannot be underestimated. Ghosh *et al.* (1994) compared the marketing practices among the better performers in Australia, New Zealand and Singapore, and the importance of marketing orientation to successful marketing performance was evident. In the three countries, better-performing companies claimed a much stronger marketing orientation than their less successful counterparts, with 89 percent of New Zealand's better performers identifying with this approach, followed by Singapore (88 percent) and Australia (79 percent). Additionally, the Ghosh *et al.* study identified that a higher proportion of the better performers in all three countries tended to have a stronger commitment to marketing's role within the organisation, by adopting marketing as a guiding philosophy for the whole organisation.

Further support for marketing orientation as a significant determinant of marketing performance was given by Pitt and Jeantrout (1994). They described the results of a study of customer expectations management practices of a sample of British firms. Their study related customer expectations management practices to some organisational success criteria and proposed a checklist for organisations to use in evaluating their own expectations management practices. The most significant conclusion to come from the Pitt and Jeantrout study was that marketing orientation was the only significant individual factor to come from the study. The authors were able to conclude that there was a significant relationship between marketing orientation with regard to expectations management practices and relative market share (an accepted economic and strategic indicator of marketing performance). Pitt and Jeantrout concluded that firms with a higher relative market share would appear to be those which understood the impact of pricing on customer expectations; who regularly contact customers to understand their needs; and who generally have a better understanding, gained through research, of what their customers expect; or put simply, those firms who had a higher relative market share had a greater marketing orientation than their competitors.

Therefore, empirical evidence has been provided in the literature that the level of marketing orientation evident in an organisation could have a significant influence on its marketing performance. Arguably, this could also be the case for the IJV form of organisation structure. That is why the Julian (1998) study on IJV marketing performance in Thailand included a measure of marketing orientation, adapted from the Pitt and Jeantrout (1994) study, to ascertain the significance of the impact of marketing orientation on IJV marketing performance success in Thailand and South East Asia. The measures of marketing orientation used in the Julian study assessed how regularly the IJV's senior management contacted its customers to determine their needs and to better understand their business. The measures of marketing orientation used in the Julian study also assessed how frequently the IJV's senior management conducts research among its customers in order to find out what they expect of its products/services and how regularly the IJV's senior management attempts to assess the impact that the prices of its products/services have on customer expectations.

8.3. Marketing Orientation and IJV Marketing Performance

From the Julian (1998) study that examined the factors influencing IJV marketing performance in Thailand, seven factors and two statements were identified from the initial exploratory factor analysis. Marketing orientation was one of those initial factors. All items loaded as intended. The data were considered suitable for factor analysis as the Bartlett Test of Sphericity was significant (2083.2278; 0.00000) and the Keyser-Meyer-Olkin (KMO) measure of sampling adequacy (0.75873) was greater than 0.60 (Coakes and Steed, 1997).

The results of the exploratory factor analysis are summarised in Table 4.1. The seven factors and two statements explained 64.7 percent of respondent variation on issues about IJV marketing performance in Thailand. The first four factors were the dominant factors, all with eigenvalues greater than 1.5, and explaining 46.3 percent of respondent variation on issues about IJV marketing performance in Thailand. The remaining three factors and two statements accounted for only 18.4 percent of respondent variation. Therefore, the first four factors were the dominant factors in this analysis, with the remaining three factors and two statements making a minimal contribution.

Factor 6 of the seven-factor model was identified as marketing orientation explaining a further 3.9 percent of respondent variation on issues about IJV marketing performance in Thailand (see Table 4.2) thereby making a minimal contribution to the seven-factor model. Cronbach's Alpha for this measure of marketing orientation was 0.62 indicating a modest level of reliability. Though 0.62 is acceptable for a three-item scale (Anderson and Coughlan, 1987; Nunnally, 1978), more statements relating to marketing orientation could improve the scale's reliability. The measures of marketing orientation used in this study were adapted from Pitt and Jeantrout (1994).

The Pitt and Jeantrout study provided strong support for marketing orientation as a significant factor influencing the marketing performance of British firms in a domestic context. Pitt and Jeantrout concluded that there was a significant relationship between the level of marketing orientation evident in a firm and the relative market share achieved by that same firm, market share being widely recognised as a marketing performance indicator

(Buzzell *et al.,* 1975; Venkatraman and Ramanujam, 1986). Therefore, given the importance of marketing orientation to marketing performance success in a domestic context it was decided to test the importance of marketing orientation to marketing performance success in an international context. The findings of the Julian (1998) study support the findings of the Pitt and Jeantrout (1994) study that marketing orientation is an important factor concerning issues about IJV marketing performance in Thailand.

The seven factors, namely, market characteristics, conflict, commitment, product characteristics, firm-specific characteristics, marketing orientation and organisational control, and the two independent statements relating to managerial control and adapting to foreign market needs, were then adopted for further analysis. Mean factor scores were obtained for the seven factors and two independent statements and the results are reported in Table 4.3.

The mean score for the factor of marketing orientation was 5.398 with a standard deviation of 1.178. This indicates that respondents often agreed with statements identifying that the IJV's senior management was aware of the needs and wants of its customers and the impact that the prices of its products/services have on customer expectations. That is, respondents often agreed with statements identifying that the IJV frequently conducts research among its customers in order to find out what they expect of its products/services, that the IJV regularly contacts customers to determine their needs and to better understand their business and that the IJV regularly attempts to assess the impact that the prices of its products/services have on customer expectations.

Further analysis was then conducted on the seven factors and the two independent statements by conducting a multiple regression analysis to analyse the relationship between the dependent variable and a set of independent variables. In the Julian (1998) study on IJV marketing performance in Thailand the dependent variable was IJV marketing performance. The independent variables were the seven factors, namely, market characteristics, conflict, commitment, product characteristics, firm-specific characteristics, marketing orientation, organisational control, and the two independent statements relating to managerial control and adapting to foreign market needs. The results of the multiple regression analysis presented in Table 4.4 show that the factors of market characteristics, commitment and marketing orientation were clearly the most significant predictor variables and the only independent variables that could be used to explain the variation in the dependent variable of IJV marketing performance. All these key predictor variables were statistically significant at the 95 percent confidence interval. Therefore, the marketing orientation of the IJV's senior management was a significant predictor of IJV marketing performance in Thailand and this marketing orientation had a positive impact on IJV marketing performance in Thailand.

The R^2 statistic represents the proportion of variance in the dependent variable accounted for by the independent variables. In the Julian (1998) study on IJV marketing performance in Thailand, that proportion was 14.395 percent of the explained variance in IJV marketing performance accounted for by the covariation in the independent variables. The independent variables were again identified as market characteristics, conflict, commitment, product characteristics, firm-specific characteristics, marketing orientation, organisational control, managerial control and adapting to foreign market needs. Thus, the model had modest predictive ability.

As the R^2 statistic that was achieved for the nominated independent and dependent variables was modest at 14.395 percent, and because the regression model had modest predictive ability the data were taken for further analysis. This was undertaken to see if there was a significant relationship between some of the factors, the classification variables and demographic variables at different levels of IJV marketing performance. Therefore, a discriminant analysis was conducted on the classification variables of the country of origin of the principal foreign partner, equity participation of the principal foreign partner, sales volume and industry classification, the demographic variable of age, the seven factors and two independent statements, and IJV marketing performance with IJV marketing performance being categorised into low and high performers.

The objective of discriminant analysis was to statistically distinguish between the two groups. These groups were defined by the particular research situation. In the Julian (1998) study on IJV marketing performance in Thailand the interest was to classify the IJVs into low and high marketing performers to see if the discriminating variables would distinguish between the groups. Group 1 consisted of all those IJVs that were classified as low marketing performers (i.e. those IJVs that had a marketing performance score of 4 or less using the single-item measure of IJV marketing performance). Group 2 consisted of all those IJVs that were classified as high marketing performers (i.e. those IJVs that had a marketing performance score of 5, 6 or 7 using the single-item measure of IJV marketing performance).

Table 4.5 contained a summary of the results of the discriminant analysis that related group membership to the same factors and independent statements that were used in the previously reported multiple regression analysis. Table 4.5 showed the univariate ANOVAs of the discriminant analysis. The univariate ANOVAs indicate whether there is a statistically significant difference among the dependent variable means for each independent variable. From Table 4.5 it is apparent that the independent variables of the sales volume of the IJV (SALESVOL), conflict, commitment, the industry the IJV operates in (INDUSTRY), managerial control, marketing orientation, adapting to foreign market needs and organisational control were all significant at the 95 percent confidence interval ($p < .05$). Therefore, when using the discriminant analysis the marketing orientation of the IJV's senior management was a significant predictor of group membership when the groups were classified as low and high marketing performers.

As is evident from the exploratory factor analysis, multiple regression analysis and discriminant analysis that were conducted, the marketing orientation of the IJV's senior management was a significant predictor of IJV marketing performance (see multiple regression analysis) and a significant discriminator of high and low IJV marketing performance (see discriminant analysis) in Thailand. That is, the marketing orientation of the IJV's senior management over such issues as the IJV frequently conducting research among its customers in order to find out what they expect of its products/services, by regularly contacting customers to determine their needs and to better understand their business and by regularly attempting to assess the impact that the prices of the IJV's products/services have on customer expectations, all contributed significantly to being able to predict IJV marketing performance success in Thailand. Furthermore, if the IJV's senior management were marketing oriented in relation to issues of the like identified above, this marketing orientation increases the likelihood of high IJV marketing performance being achieved.

It is important for the management of any company to be aware of these measures of marketing orientation when contemplating an IJV of any magnitude in a developing country of South East Asia. The Julian (1998) study clearly indicated that marketing orientation must be with reference to senior management's knowledge of its customers. That is, for senior management to understand what its customers expect from its products and services and for senior management to be in regular contact with its customers. The senior management of a company needs to be marketing oriented when operating in a South East Asian country market for successful marketing performance of their IJV.

9.   Control

9.1. Introduction

The conflict between a foreign corporation and a local partner to control major policies and decisions constitutes a major reason for the failure of certain IJVs (Blodgett, 1991b; Dymsza, 1988; Ganitsky *et al.,* 1991; Schaan and Beamish, 1988). The foreign corporation may try to control major policies of the venture through the appointment of a majority of the board of directors, including outside, allegedly neutral directors, who are favourable to it. The role of the board of directors of joint venture affiliates varies a great deal. Some boards determine major policies of the venture, select the chief and top executives, and monitor the overall management and operations of the enterprise, but many boards primarily grant advice to the chief executive and perform perfunctory responsibilities. Other boards assume a legal function to meet the requirements of the law, for example, in Thailand, the appointment of a Thai national to the board of directors to accommodate Thailand's foreign investment policy.

Foreign corporations control the management of joint venture affiliates in other ways. They obtain authority to appoint the chief executive and key managers; they establish the managerial and control processes and have the right to veto major decisions. The continuing control by foreign corporations of combinations of manufacturing, finance, marketing, reinvestments and expansion (e.g., the commitment of a large proportion of the IJV's outputs to a parent company), sourcing (e.g., the sourcing of much of the input needs of the IJV from either one or both of the parent companies), and other decisions in the venture often leads to major conflicts with the national partners and the host governments. These conflicts can lead to the failure of IJVs (Dymsza, 1988).

However, the effect of management control on JV performance has remained one of the controversial factors determining JV performance. While domination of one parent in the overall management of the JV was found

137

most effective in some studies (Killing, 1983; Al-Aali, 1987; Phatak and Chowdhury, 1991), shared management control was found effective in other studies (Beamish, 1984; Blodgett, 1992a). Similarly, greater autonomy of the JV over operating decisions was expected to contribute to better performance (Anderson, 1990; Killing, 1983; Blumenthal, 1988) but the empirical findings seem to be tentative. Cooperation seems to be a core condition for success of a cooperative venture (Awadzi, 1987; Awadzi *et al.,* 1988; Berg and Friedmann, 1980; Phatak and Chowdhury, 1991), but its relative impact on performance in a broader multivariate model has received limited attention in the past.

Major differences with respect to management processes and style of management between the foreign corporation and the national partner can lead to serious conflicts, which contribute to the failure of IJVs. For example, foreign corporations may try to impose their processes of strategic and operational planning, information and control, budgeting and accounting on the joint venture affiliate. The local partner may not have any experience with these processes and consider them unsuitable. A foreign corporation may emphasise a more participatory style of management, delegation of responsibility to subordinates, profit centres and periodic evaluation of performance. The local partner, which is often a family-owned and operated business in a developing country, may have a more authoritarian management, with no delegation of responsibility to subordinates and very little formal planning and control. Although such differences in management processes and style can sometimes be harmonised through a learning process in the IJV, they can often disrupt the venture, and make a significant contribution to poor IJV performance.

Therefore, the level of control exerted by one partner over the other partners in the IJV relationship and over the IJV itself in relation to specific marketing strategies and policies, such as the sourcing of components for the production process and transfer pricing policies, could be a contributing factor towards IJV marketing performance. Studies such as the Lee and Beamish (1995) study on the characteristics and performance of Korean joint ventures in less-developed countries and the Julian (1998) study on IJV marketing performance in Thailand investigated the significance of control in predicting IJV performance. The literature surrounding those two studies is now discussed together with using alternative means of control other than equity participation to enhance IJV performance. For example, the use of social knowledge as proposed by Sohn (1994).

9.2. Literature Review

Much of the joint venture research has a developed country orientation. However, some researchers (Artisien and Buckley, 1985; Beamish, 1988; Daniels *et al.*, 1985; Julian, 1998; Lecraw, 1983; Schaan, 1983; Simiar, 1983) focused their attention on joint venture performance in developing countries. The relationship between ownership, control and performance has been the focus of much previous research (Beamish, 1988; Dymsza, 1988; Julian, 1998; Lee and Beamish, 1995). Some studies have attempted to identify predictors of both satisfactory and unsatisfactory joint venture performance.

Much of the previous research on joint ventures has been from a developed-country perspective, particularly US, and more recently Japanese foreign partners (Delios and Beamish, 2004; Makino and Beamish, 1998; Sohn, 1994; Woodcock *et al.*, 1994). It has shown that certain characteristics of joint ventures differ when located in developed and developing countries. Specifically, joint ventures in developing countries are characterised by: (1) minority ownership of the foreign partner, as measured by equity participation, is the most common in developing country joint ventures; (2) a strong relationship between ownership and control in developing country joint ventures; and (3) an inconclusive relationship between joint venture performance and dominant management control in joint ventures in developing countries, with shared control showing more satisfactory performance in joint ventures in less-developed countries (Beamish, 1988; Killing, 1983; Franko, 1971).

The study by Lee and Beamish (1995) examined the characteristics of joint ventures from developed and developing countries with those from a newly industrialized country, Korea. The characteristics that Lee and Beamish examined included the reasons for creating the venture, stability, performance, frequency of government partners and ownership. Particular emphasis was placed on the relationship between ownership, control and performance because this had been the focus of much previous research (Beamish, 1988; Blodgett, 1991a; Julian, 1998; Killing, 1983; Phatak and Chowdhury, 1991).

There has been much debate and controversy surrounding the equity participation of foreign firms in developing country IJVs and its relationship with performance. For example, Killing (1983) found that equal ownership (50 percent) was the most common in developing-country joint ventures whilst the Julian (1998) study on IJVs in Thailand found that most foreign firms held a minority equity position. However, in the less-developed country samples of Blodgett (1991a), Higginbottom (1980), Reynolds (1984) and others, the findings are more consistent with most foreign firms holding a minority equity position. Most developing countries have aspirations for local dominance in the shareholdings of local joint ventures. They set up regulations on ownership or provide local tax advantages for foreign partners taking minority equity positions.

Managers of firms from developed countries assess their joint ventures in less-developed countries as unsatisfactory performers more frequently than those in developing countries (Beamish, 1985). However, Korean firms that first invested in South East Asia (i.e., Singapore, Indonesia and Thailand) found the cultural environment, traditions and behaviour patterns to be similar to Korea, about which Korean firms possessed information and understanding (Kumar and Kim, 1984; Lee and Beamish, 1995). The Korean firms entering less-developed countries also do not confront as large a foreign knowledge gap regarding the economic situation. They may not have the same level of hesitancy in entering such markets as has been observed elsewhere (Agarwal and Ramaswami, 1992) because they do not perceive the same level of risk as do foreign investors from other developed countries (Lee and Beamish, 1995). This could be due to the fact that many Korean managers felt the socio-economic conditions of South East Asian developing countries are similar to those that they had faced in Korea in earlier periods.

Researchers in the past have had mixed results on the relationship between ownership and control. Killing (1983) found that there were strong relationships between ownership and control in developed countries with 70 percent of the dominant-management control ventures majority owned. However, Sohn (1994) observed that with social knowledge, investing firms could reduce their dependency on ownership as a means of control over their subsidiaries.

While accepting the value of ownership or equity positions as an important means of control, several studies have suggested that alternative means of control to ownership are available to foreign firms, such as superior access to raw materials, distribution channels, managerial ability, contractual arrangements and diversification (Schaan, 1988; Geringer and Hebert, 1989; Sohn, 1993). These alternative means of control could allow foreign firms to reduce their need to resort to equity participation in order to control their international subsidiaries or JV partners. If control is defined as the foreign partner's ability to influence the local partner to behave in accordance with the foreign firm's ultimate purpose (Tannenbaum, 1968), equity participation is one way of securing sufficient control. For a given level of control, then, firms that have alternative means available to them would hold lower equity positions in their subsidiaries than would other foreign firms.

In recent years, social control systems as a valuable alternative to bureaucratic control systems have also received wide attention (Egelhoff, 1984; Jaeger, 1983; Ouchi, 1980; Sohn, 1994; Tolbert, 1988). Although these studies have mainly been interested either in the patterns of control or effects of cultural control on performance in wholly owned subsidiaries, there exists strong evidence that control through social and non-bureaucratic means is available for foreign firms engaged in IJVs (Sohn, 1994).

Expanding upon this body of literature, Sohn suggested that with social knowledge of their proposed partner(s), foreign multinationals could reduce their dependency on equity participation as a means of control over their subsidiaries and JV partners. In brief, Sohn suggested that social knowledge could allow foreign firms to selectively transact with certain local parties with desirable behavioural characteristics and to control them with a reduced need to resort to bureaucratic authority through ownership via equity participation.

Sohn defined social knowledge as one's ability to understand and predict the other's general patterns of behaviour (Tolbert, 1988). Through social knowledge over the behavioural patterns of the local parties, foreign firms could predict how the local parties would behave under different conditions, relate their behaviours to how they interpret the present situation, recognize their evaluation process within their environmental context (Frank, 1989) drawing inferences about their behavioural patterns, detecting and deciphering various 'signals' (Spence, 1974) that they convey (Sohn, 1994). The foreign firms, through their ability to identify the frames of reference and process the signals, may also distinguish what the local parties' desired future state of affairs are and how they would attempt to attain that desired state. Sohn further claimed that taking advantage of these benefits of social knowledge does not require the foreign firm to share the same behavioural patterns with the local parties; the foreign firms need only to possess the knowledge over the local parties' patterns of behaviour to exert some control over them.

The most important benefit that foreign joint venture partners could realize would be that they would be able to distinguish potential local JV partners with desirable behavioural patterns (such as low opportunistic tendency) in a relatively costless manner. If such local JV partners could be credibly identified, the need for bureaucratic control mechanisms is seriously reduced. As foreign JV partners understand through social knowledge how the local JV partner determines what constitutes appropriate behaviour for a given stimulus, the foreign JV partner may provide appropriate stimuli to the local partner to induce the desired behaviour. Furthermore, social knowledge would also enable the foreign JV partner to offer meaningful social rewards (such as titles or commendations), which may also encourage desirable behaviour. In other words, effective application of social and non-bureaucratic means may indeed provide effective means with which the local partner's incentives for opportunistic behaviour would decrease, thereby reducing or eliminating the need for formal control mechanisms (Sohn, 1994).

Sohn further emphasised that he was not suggesting that substantial social knowledge would always function as a direct substitute for bureaucratic or ownership means of control. Sohn suggested there could be circumstances in which even a substantial extent of social knowledge may not enable the foreign JV partners to take advantage of the social means of control. For example, a foreign JV partner's extensive social knowledge may reveal that none of the prospective local parties possessed desirable behavioural characteristics. Or the foreign JV partner may be unable or unwilling to provide the local party with meaningful social incentives to effectively discourage opportunism. The foreign JV partner, then, despite its extensive social knowledge, may be forced to resort to equity participation to be able to effectively control the local partner's behaviour (Sohn, 1994).

However, depending on the extent that an appropriate local JV partner can be found and/or meaningful social incentives can be provided, the foreign JV partners with social knowledge may find it less essential to resort to bureaucratic authority and, therefore, to hold substantial equity positions in their IJV as a means of control than their counterparts without such knowledge. Actually, foreign JV partners holding whole or majority equity positions as a control-securing means would become redundant and inefficient with majority local equity positions being encouraged (Beamish, 1988; Sohn, 1994).

Other foreign firms without social knowledge, on the other hand, may not be convinced that potential local JV partners could be controlled through social means. Thus, they would be more reluctant to allow significant local equity positions. Local JV partners with a majority of the equity in the JV could disagree with or opportunistically exploit the foreign JV partners more easily than those without this majority equity position. Thus, the foreign JV partners without social knowledge would attempt to minimize local equity positions whenever possible. In contrast, the foreign JV partners with social knowledge would be less limited by such restrictions. Moreover, they may even encourage local equity positions and be willing to take a minority ownership position, depending upon the extent of social knowledge. In other words, the foreign firms with social knowledge may be more willing to establish joint ventures with local parties than others without such knowledge (Beamish, 1988; Beamish and Wang, 1989; Sohn, 1994).

By being able to allow local equity participation, foreign firms may realize many benefits. The most noteworthy advantage would probably be that, under a given amount of financial resources, foreign firms could invest in a larger number of JVs without necessarily compromising their control ability. Alternatively, other foreign firms would only be able to invest in fewer JVs as they have to take larger equity positions in each JV to maintain control ability. As such, those foreign firms that are able to hold lower equity positions in each of their JV relationships would be able to reduce the risk associated with that investment (Killing, 1991; Sohn, 1994).

Furthermore, foreign JV partners could provide the local partner with more incentives by allowing higher local equity positions. As has been previously suggested, local management shirking could be a problem in the JV entity. By offering the local JV partner partial residual claimant status, the foreign JV partner may better address potential opportunism problems. The local partner's income stream will now be more dependent upon the performance of the JV. Obviously, they would consume less shirking than otherwise (Alchian and Demsetz, 1972), with their potential opportunistic attempts controlled through social or behavioural means (Egelhoff, 1984; Jaeger, 1983; Sohn, 1994).

Another advantage of being able to allow local equity participation comes from the foreign firms ability to better accommodate host-country governments' demands. Many host-country governments in developing countries consider local ownership an important objective (Fagre and Wells, 1982; Hennart, 1989; Lecraw, 1984). As a result, if a foreign firm needs to depend mainly upon bureaucratic authority, it will have to incur certain bargaining costs over the ownership distribution of the JV with the host-country government, especially if the local JV partner is a state-owned enterprise which is often the case in South East Asia (Beamish, 1993; Julian, 1998). On the other hand, foreign firms with social knowledge may save on costs associated with such bargaining processes. Furthermore, these foreign firms could obtain even more returns from their technology, because the host-country governments are often willing to provide the foreign firm with additional economic and political benefits, if the foreign firm allows local majority equity participation in the JV (Beamish, 1988; Blodgett, 1991b; Sohn, 1994).

As such, social knowledge is a valuable supplementary control mechanism with which foreign firms may reduce their equity position in IJVs. Foreign firms with social knowledge, therefore, could maintain sufficient control ability without holding as much equity position as the local JV partner, because social knowledge provides additional means of control of the JV. Their equity position in the JV, therefore, would subsequently be adjusted for an optimal level of control, to reflect their ability to resort to control through social knowledge (Sohn, 1994).

Thus, the Sohn (1994) argument on social knowledge as a means of control suggests that previous research on control ability being positively related with equity participation (Negandhi and Welge, 1990; Hill *et al.*, 1990) would not always hold true. Rather, with substantial social knowledge, control ability by the foreign firm over the JV entity and the local JV partner would not be directly related to their equity positions. However, the value of equity participation as a means of control should not be underestimated (Sohn, 1994). In the absence of substantial social knowledge, one of the primary means available to the foreign firm to achieve effective control over the JV entity and the local JV partner would be via equity participation. Thus, according to the social knowledge argument provided by Sohn, if foreign JV partners do not have a substantial amount of social knowledge about their local partner or potential local partner, they would increase their equity position in the IJV, dependent upon their control needs. In this case, their control ability would be directly and positively affected by their equity position in the IJV.

However, in research on JVs in developing countries, Beamish (1985), found no correlation between ownership and control. With most Korean joint venturers in developing countries in the Lee and Beamish (1995) study, goals included not only expansion into local markets but the increase of exports (average export/sales ratio of Korean joint ventures was almost 50 percent). Additionally, the average lifespan of those Korean joint ventures was somewhat short (Lee and Beamish, 1995).

9.3. Control and International Joint Venture Marketing Performance

In studies of JVs in developed countries, inconclusive results have been obtained in the relationship between control and performance (Geringer and Hebert, 1989). Some studies have found that dominant-parent ventures perform better, while others have shown more satisfactory performance with shared control ventures. However, Beamish (1985) and Tomlinson (1970) found a strong correlation between unsatisfactory performance and dominant foreign control in less-developed country JVs while shared-control ventures obtained higher performance levels.

In the Lee and Beamish (1995) study one important function of Korean JVs in developing countries, as with the Thai IJVs (Julian, 1998), was to export their products to third countries (Min, 1985). With the need to meet third-country market requirements most Korean managers favoured a strong decision-making role and felt more comfortable with the performance of dominant-control ventures than with shared-control ventures, where their roles were minor (Lee and Beamish, 1995).

In Beamish's (1985) sample of less-developed country JVs from developed countries, when the MNE owned less than 50 percent of the equity there was a greater likelihood of satisfactory performance. Also, when MNEs were a minority or equal partner JV, performance was better than in those cases where the MNE was the single largest shareholder. However, in Korean JVs in both developed and developing countries, Lee (1989) found no relationship between ownership and performance. As such, the findings are inconclusive on the relationship between ownership and performance.

Furthermore, in the Lee and Beamish (1995) study concerning the relationship between the levels of ownership and satisfaction with performance in the majority of cases, the Korean partner held a minority equity position. This is consistent with other investments in developing countries (Julian, 1998). For example, in the Julian study the sample of 161 Thai/foreign IJVs revealed a trend where 64.0 percent of the sample showed the principal foreign partner as having equity participation of 49 percent or less. Additionally, the findings in the Lee and Beamish (1995) study indicate that overall satisfaction with the Korean JVs was higher than that experienced by developed-country partners with JVs in less-developed countries.

As far as the relationship between ownership and control was concerned, in the Lee and Beamish study the results show a significant positive relationship between control and ownership. This contrasts with previous findings on JVs in developing countries.

As far as the control/performance relationship was concerned, there was a positive relationship on the basis of the total sample. Again, these findings were not consistent with previous findings on JVs from developed countries in developing countries (Lee and Beamish, 1995).

In the Lee and Beamish study, regarding the determinants of performance of JVs from Korea the dependent variable was overall satisfaction with JV performance and the independent variables were four of the characteristics of JVs, namely, ownership rates, control, partner's needs, and commitment. The findings of their study indicated that ownership and commitment had no relationship with performance. Instead, control and partner's needs were found to be the primary determinants of Korean JV performance.

Their study findings also showed that control was the most important factor in determining the performance of Korean JVs. This was not surprising given that for Korean JVs in less-developed countries one of the primary motivations was exporting output to developed countries (Lee and Beamish, 1995). Therefore, by having strong management control this will play an important role in raising overall satisfaction with the JV's performance. The finding that partners' needs were significantly related to Korean JVs' performance, but ownership rates or commitment were not, were consistent with the result of Lee's (1989) previous work on Korean JVs. Also, this finding coincides with those from JVs from developed countries in less-developed countries, where greater need between partners resulted in more satisfactory performance (Lee and Beamish, 1995).

Several significant findings emerged from the Lee and Beamish (1995) study that differed from previous findings on JVs from developed countries in less-developed countries, in particular, the relationship between control and performance and between ownership and control. The Lee and Beamish findings quite clearly indicated that the control that one JV partner has over the other JV partners and the IJV entity itself was a significant predictor of IJV performance. For the Korean JVs, the relationships between ownership and control, and control and performance, were direct ownership had a positive relationship with control and control had the same relationship with performance. The major implication of the Lee and Beamish study for future research was to suggest that the characteristics of JVs differ depending on the development stage of both the originating country and the host country. Based on those implications and the importance of control as a predictor of IJV performance in JVs from developed countries in less-developed countries or developing countries the Julian (1998) study examined the importance of both organisational control and managerial control as a predictor of IJV marketing performance for Thai IJVs.

In the Julian study two statements were included in the research instrument aimed at measuring the extent to which control by one partner over the other partners in the IJV organisation can have an influence on IJV marketing performance. The measures of organisational control used were adapted from Dymsza (1988). The statements were designed to assess the impact on IJV marketing performance of transferring a large proportion of the IJV's outputs (e.g., profits or components for a future production process) to a parent company, and the impact on IJV marketing performance of sourcing much of the input needs (e.g., raw materials or components to be used in the production process) of the IJV from a parent company.

Major conflicts can erupt between partners in IJVs with respect to purchases of materials, intermediates and components. Some foreign corporations strive to have the IJV affiliate purchase intermediate goods or components from it on the grounds that it assures required quality standards and that competitive alternative sources are not readily available. Local partners, on the other hand, want to explore alternative sources in order to obtain the materials from lowest-cost suppliers internationally or domestically. They may believe that the foreign corporation is charging excessive prices and aims to earn additional income from selling the intermediaries to the affiliate. If the foreign corporation presses aggressively for continued sales of these intermediates to the affiliate, despite the fact that the local partner finds other suppliers at competitive or lower prices, serious conflicts could arise between the partners to the venture, which can disrupt the relationship (Dymsza, 1988).

The reverse could also occur when the foreign corporation wants to repatriate much of the profits earned by the IJV back to its home country. The local partner, on the other hand, may want to retain most of the profits earned by the IJV in the IJV for reasons of capital expansion and investment. If the foreign corporation insists on repatriating most of the IJV's earnings back to its home country leaving the IJV cash-poor this could not only negatively affect the marketing performance of the IJV but worse, serious conflicts could arise between the partners leading to the ultimate demise of the venture (Dymsza, 1988). Therefore, the impact on IJV marketing performance of control by one partner over the other partners in the IJV organisation could be significant.

As far as managerial control was concerned, one statement was included in the research instrument aimed at measuring the extent to which a lack of effective managerial control over the IJV by any of its parents could have an influence on IJV marketing performance. This measure of managerial control was adapted from Dymsza (1988). The effect of managerial control on JV performance has remained one of the controversial factors determining JV performance. While domination of one parent in the overall management of the JV was found most effective in some studies (Killing, 1983; Al-Aali, 1987; Phatak and Chowdhury, 1991), shared management control was found effective in other studies (Beamish, 1984; Blodgett, 1992a). Similarly, greater autonomy of the JV over operating decisions was expected to contribute to better performance (Anderson, 1990; Killing, 1983; Blumenthal, 1988) but the empirical findings seem to be very tentative. Cooperation seems to be a core condition for success of a cooperative venture (Berg and Friedman, 1980; Awadzi, 1987; Awadzi *et al.*, 1988; Phatak and Chowdhury, 1991), but its relative impact on performance in a broader multivariate model has received limited attention in the past. Therefore, the Julian (1998) study examined the influence on IJV marketing performance of a lack of effective managerial control by any of the IJV parents.

From the Julian (1998) study that examined the factors influencing IJV marketing performance in Thailand, seven factors and two statements were identified from the initial exploratory factor analysis. Organisational control was one of the initial factors and managerial control was one of the two independent statements. All items loaded as intended. The data were considered suitable for factor analysis as the Bartlett Test of Sphericity was significant (2083.2278; 0.00000) and the Keyser-Meyer-Olkin (KMO) measure of sampling adequacy (0.75873) was greater than 0.60 (Coakes and Steed, 1997).

The results of the exploratory factor analysis are summarised in Table 4.1. The seven factors and two statements explained 64.7 percent of respondent variation on issues about IJV marketing performance in Thailand. The first four factors were the dominant factors, all with eigenvalues greater than 1.5, and explaining 46.3 percent of respondent variation on issues about IJV marketing performance in Thailand. The remaining three factors and two independent statements, which included organisational control and managerial control, accounted for only 18.4 percent of respondent variation. Therefore, the first four factors were the dominant factors in this analysis, with the remaining three factors and two independent statements making a minimal contribution.

In this seven-factor model the factor of organisational control (Factor 7) emerged as the weakest factor explaining 3.8 percent of respondent variation on issues about IJV marketing performance in Thailand (see Table 4.2.). Cronbach's Alpha for this measure of organisational control was 0.67 indicating a modest level of reliability. However, this is acceptable for a two-item scale (Anderson and Coughlan, 1987; Nunnally, 1978). More statements relating to organisational control would improve the scale's reliability. The measures of organisational control used in this study were adapted from Dymsza (1988).

The Julian (1998) study findings support the findings of Dymsza (1988) that major conflicts can erupt between the partners in an IJV with respect to the purchase of materials, intermediates and components. If the foreign corporation insists on the IJV purchasing raw materials from it, when the local partner finds other sources at competitive or lower prices serious conflicts could arise between the partners leading to the demise of the venture. The reverse could also occur when the foreign corporation wants to repatriate much of the profits earned by the IJV back to its home country. If the foreign corporation insists on repatriating most of the profits earned by the IJV back to its home country, serious conflicts could arise between the partners leading to the demise of the venture. Therefore, from the findings of the Julian study and the Dymsza study, organisational control by one partner over the others in the IJV arrangement, in relation to the purchase of raw materials and the repatriation of profits, can have an important influence on the marketing performance of the IJV.

The mean score for the factor of organisational control (see Table 4.3) in the Julian (1998) study was 4.609 with a standard deviation of 1.763. This indicates that respondents generally agreed with statements identifying that a large amount of the IJV's input needs were sourced from a parent company and a large proportion of the IJV's outputs were transferred to a parent company.

Of the two independent statements that emerged from the exploratory factor analysis, statement 1 was identified as relating to managerial control and identified the lack of effective managerial control over the IJV by any of its parents. The statement relating to managerial control had a mean score of 4.727 with a standard deviation of 1.827. This indicates that respondents generally agreed with the statement that there was a lack of effective managerial control over the IJV by any of its parents.

Further analysis was then conducted on the seven factors and two independent statements by conducting a multiple regression analysis to analyse the relationship between the dependent variable and a set of independent variables. In the Julian (1998) study on IJV marketing performance in Thailand the dependent variable was IJV marketing performance. The independent variables were the seven factors, namely, market characteristics, conflict, commitment, product characteristics, firm-specific characteristics, marketing orientation, organisational control, and the two independent statements relating to managerial control and adapting to foreign market needs. The results of the multiple regression analysis presented in Table 4.4 show that the factors of market characteristics, commitment and marketing orientation were clearly the most significant predictor variables and the only independent variables that could be used to explain the variation in the dependent variable of IJV marketing performance. All these key predictor variables were statistically significant at the 95 percent confidence interval. Therefore, the measures of organisational control and managerial control used in the Julian (1998) study were not significant predictors of IJV marketing performance.

As the R^2 statistic that was achieved for the nominated independent and dependent variables was modest at 14.395 percent and the regression model had modest predictive ability the data were taken for further analysis. Further analysis was undertaken to see if there was a significant relationship between some of the factors, the classification variables and demographic variables at different levels of IJV marketing performance. Therefore, a discriminant analysis was conducted on the classification variables of country of origin, equity structure, sales volume, industry classification, the demographic variable of age, the seven factors and two independent statements and IJV marketing performance with IJV marketing performance being categorised into low and high IJV marketing performers.

The objective of discriminant analysis was to statistically distinguish between the two groups. These groups were defined by the particular research situation. In the Julian (1998) study on IJV marketing performance in Thailand the interest was to classify the IJVs into low and high marketing performers to see if the discriminating variables would distinguish between the groups. Group 1 consisted of all those IJVs that were classified as low marketing performers (i.e. those IJVs that had a marketing performance score of 4 or less using the single-item measure of IJV marketing performance). Group 2 consisted of all those IJVs that were classified as high marketing performers (i.e. those IJVs that had a marketing performance score of 5, 6 or 7 using the single-item measure of IJV marketing performance).

Table 4.5 contains a summary of the results of the discriminant analysis that related group membership to the same factors and independent statements that were used in the previously reported multiple regression analysis. The factors identified were market characteristics, conflict, commitment, product characteristics, firm-specific characteristics, marketing orientation and organisational control. The independent statements identified were related to managerial control and adapting to foreign market needs. In addition, the country of origin of the principal foreign partner (ORIGIN), the equity structure of the principal foreign partner (EQUITY), the industry the IJV operates in (INDUSTRY), the sales volume of the IJV (SALESVOL), and the age of the respondent (AGE) were also included as additional potentially discriminating variables.

Table 4.5 showed the univariate ANOVAs of the discriminant analysis. The univariate ANOVAs indicate whether there is a statistically significant difference among the dependent variable means for each independent variable. From Table 4.5 it is apparent that the independent variables of the sales volume of the IJV (SALESVOL), conflict, commitment, the industry the IJV operates in (INDUSTRY), managerial control, marketing orientation, adapting to foreign market needs and organisational control were all significant at the 95 percent confidence interval ($p < .05$). Therefore, when using the discriminant analysis organisational control and managerial control were significant predictors of group membership when the groups were classified as low and high IJV marketing performers.

The canonical discriminant function coefficients provided in Table 5.1, the structure matrix provided in Table 5.2 and a summary of the discriminant analysis provided in Table 5.3 suggest that SALESVOL, reflecting the gross dollar turnover of the IJV, was the most important variable in discriminating between the low and high IJV marketing performance categories. The next most important independent or predictor variable in predicting group membership to the low or high IJV marketing performance categories was the factor of conflict, reflecting the level of conflict between the IJV partners in the IJV arrangement. After the conflict factor, the next most important predictor variable in predicting group membership to the low or high IJV marketing performance categories was commitment, reflecting the level of commitment of the IJV partners to the IJV arrangement. After the commitment factor, the next most important predictor variable in predicting group membership to the high or low IJV marketing performance categories was the industry the IJV operates in. After the industry the IJV operates in, the next most important variable in predicting group membership to the high or low IJV marketing performance categories was managerial control, reflecting the level of effective managerial control over the IJV by at least one of the IJV partners. After managerial control, the next most important variable in predicting group membership to the high or low IJV marketing performance categories was marketing orientation, reflecting the level of knowledge of their customers by the IJV's senior management. After marketing orientation, the next most important variable in predicting group membership to the high or low IJV marketing performance categories was the willingness of the foreign parents to adapt their products/services to meet the needs of the local Thai market. Finally, the least important variable in predicting group membership to the high or low IJV marketing performance categories was organisational control, reflecting the level of control over the IJV entity one partner has in relation to the repatriation of profits and the sourcing of raw materials or other input needs. However, all eight independent variables of sales volume, conflict, commitment, industry the IJV operates in, managerial control, marketing orientation, adapting to foreign market needs, and organisational control were statistically significant at the 95 percent confidence interval ($p < .05$) in discriminating between the low and high IJV marketing performance categories.

As is evident from the exploratory factor analysis, multiple regression analysis and discriminant analysis that were conducted, both organisational control and managerial control were non-significant predictors of IJV marketing performance (see multiple regression analysis) yet significant discriminators of high and low IJV marketing performance (see disciminant analysis). That is, organisational control by one partner over other partners in the IJV arrangement and over the IJV entity itself over such issues as the purchase of raw materials, intermediates and components and the repatriation of the profits earned by the IJV back to the foreign partners' home country will determine whether the Thai IJV's marketing performance is low or high. Furthermore, if there is a lack of effective managerial control over the IJV by any of its parents this will make a significant contribution to low IJV marketing performance in Thailand. This finding lends support to the Lee and Beamish (1995) finding whereby they suggest that by having strong management control this will play an important role in raising overall satisfaction with the performance of the venture. Therefore, from the findings of the Julian (1998) study, the Lee and Beamish (1995) study and the Dymsza (1988) study, organisational control by one partner over the others in the IJV arrangement, in relation to the purchase of raw materials and the repatriation of profits, and the lack of effective managerial control over the IJV by any of its parents can have a significant influence on the marketing performance of the IJV. Whilst organisational control by one partner together with a lack of effective managerial control by any of the IJV parents over the IJV were non-significant predictors of IJV marketing performance if organisational control and the lack of managerial control of the type just mentioned are prevalent within the IJV these control-related issues increase the likelihood of low IJV marketing performance being achieved.

It is important for the management of any company to be aware of the possibility of these types of control-related issues between IJV partners when contemplating an IJV of any magnitude in a developing country of South East Asia. The Julian (1998) study clearly indicated that it was important for the managers of IJVs to minimise the transference of the IJV's output to a parent company and to minimise the sourcing of the IJV's input needs from a parent company for marketing performance success. Companies intending to enter into an IJV arrangement should take the time to allow the IJV to operate as a stand-alone entity instead of using it as a means of generating additional revenue from out-of-date products or as a subsidiary to generate greater profits for head office. The study findings also show that at least one of the IJV parents needs to have effective control over the IJV for marketing performance success. Companies intending to enter into a JV arrangement should make sure that at least one of the parents is responsible for ensuring that the JV meets the expectations and objectives of its parents for marketing performance success.

10. Trust

10.1. Introduction

Partner commitment and compatibility is a critical issue in JV relationships. Friedman and Beguin (1971) argued that ownership arrangements are not as important for successful JV performance as the similarity of outlook and objectives, i.e., compatibility. Greater compatibility increases the probability of balance between inducements and contributions with temporary imbalances being smoothed by trust. Greater compatibility manifests itself in greater commitment to the JV, which enables broader 'bands of tolerance' and makes the partners more flexible with respect to the JV's operations. In such cases, they would be more willing to accept minority ownership, adapt products to local markets, accept the partner's personnel in important positions and adapt systems to accommodate the partner's needs (Beamish, 1985). Such ventures are characterised by a greater allocation of time and effort towards building trust and knowledge transfer, greater interaction through more regular meetings and visits, and an open communication system (Schaan, 1983), all of which results in clear mutual expectations and enables more efficient coordination and performance (Madhok, 1995).

Beamish's (1988) identification of a positive correlation between commitment and need for the partner, and a negative correlation between commitment and extent of control desired, reflects both dimensions of trust in a JV relationship. The former addresses the mutual complementarities that underlie the structural dimension of trust while the latter addresses the social aspects, where the existence of commitment mitigates the desire for formal control measures.

Many researchers have noted the importance of trust in IJV relationships for IJV success (Beamish, 1985; Hebert, 1994; Madhok, 1995; Parkhe, 1993a; Tomlinson, 1970). As Parkhe (1993a, p. 307) writes, trust is 'the behavioural lubricant that can improve a system's operating efficiencies'. The Fey (1995) study also confirmed that having trust between the Russian/foreign IJV and its parents is extremely important for IJV success.

As such, research over the past decades on IJVs and strategic alliances has repeatedly argued that trust in the IJV relationship is essential for successful IJVs (Currall and Inkpen, 2002; Inkpen and Beamish, 1997; Madhok, 1995; Yan and Gray, 1994). Child and Faulkner (1998) suggested that trust is particularly fragile in IJVs because the normal risk and uncertainty with JVs is increased because of the cross-national differences between partner firms with respect to culture, law, politics and trade policy. However, despite the attention given to trust in the IJV literature, 'trust remains an under-theorized, under-researched, and, therefore, poorly understood phenomenon' (Child, 2001, p. 274). Particularly, collaborative trust at the person, group and firm levels has received limited empirical attention in the IJV literature. Multilevel trust has, however, been studied in other related literatures. Doney and Cannon (1997), for example, studied buyer/seller relationships empirically and found that interfirm trust differed from interpersonal trust. Zaheer *et al.* (1998) examined interfirm and interpersonal trust, also in the buyer/supplier setting, and identified JVs as an area where their research should be extended. Jeffries and Reed (2000) focused on relational contracting and explored the interaction between interfirm and interpersonal trust for the success of interorganizational relationships. In the JV literature, Barney and Hansen (1994) suggested that discrepancies arise between interpersonal trust and interfirm trust because trust between partner firms' managers may be strong even though trust between partner firms is weak. Dyer and Chu's (2000) study of cross-border collaboration concluded that the issue of interpersonal and interfirm trust should be examined in greater detail. Doz (1996) examined how alliances evolve and how trust at one organizational level impacts upon the development of trust at another level. Thus, given the widespread agreement that trust is critical for IJV performance, the issue of IJV trust and organizational levels is both relevant and underexplored (Currall and Inkpen, 2002). As such, this chapter examines the role of trust at the group and firm level by examining trust in IJV top management teams (TMTs) and its impact on decision quality, decision implementation and goal attainment.

The literature supports the notion that because they have different experiences in organizational and national backgrounds, members of an IJV's TMT tend to be quite dissimilar from each other (Schneider and De Meyer, 1991). As a result, these teams tend to be highly diverse groups of managers who may have difficulty communicating with each other, developing trust and maintaining commitment amongst themselves, and working cohesively to achieve venture goals (Fey and Beamish, 2000, 2001; Ding, 1997). The literature also supports the notion that despite their inherent heterogeneity, members of IJV TMTs must communicate with each other and build trust and cohesion among themselves to enable managers to reach high-quality decisions (Goll *et al.,* 2001). Furthermore, frequent communication, trust and cohesion is required so decisions can be implemented in a timely fashion and so team members can continue to work together as a team to successfully run their organization (Smith *et al.,* 1994). If not, the IJV will ultimately fail.

10.2. Review of the Literature

A survey of the literature (e.g., Amason, 1996; Fey and Beamish, 2001; Katzenbach and Smith, 1993; Smith *et al.,* 1994; Wallace, 1992) suggests that team performance is highly dependent on team processes such as the level of cooperation, cohesiveness and mutual accountability, as well as individual responses to team processes such as trust and commitment to a team purpose or performance goals. Others suggest that performance is dependent on the quality of a team's output or decisions (Goll *et al.,* 2001). This implies that effective top management teams (TMTs) must pay attention to issues that relate to tasks as well as issues that relate to group maintenance (Amason and Schweiger, 1992).

The literature supports the notion that because they have different experiences in organizational and national backgrounds, members of an IJV's TMT tend to be quite dissimilar from each other (Schneider and De Meyer, 1991). As a result, these teams tend to be highly diverse groups of managers who may have difficulty communicating with each other, developing trust and maintaining commitment amongst themselves, and working cohesively to achieve venture goals (Fey and Beamish, 2000, 2001; Ding, 1997). The literature also supports the notion that despite their inherent heterogeneity, members of IJV TMTs must communicate with each other and build trust and cohesion among themselves to enable managers to reach high-quality decisions (Goll *et al.,* 2001). Furthermore, frequent communication, trust and cohesion is required so decisions can be implemented in a timely fashion and so team members can continue to work together as a team to run their organizations successfully (Smith *et al.,* 1994). If not, the IJV will ultimately fail.

10.2.1. Effects of Culture

National cultural differences among managers have been found to negatively affect the nature of managerial interactions and result in poor working relationships (Child *et al.,* 1992). As a result, some have argued that deeply rooted cultural differences at the top management level, because of their effect on managerial relationships and strategic decision-making, are likely to have a direct bearing on a TMT's ability to realise stated venture goals

(Barkema *et al.*, 1996). Shenkar and Zeira (1992) assert that tensions among top managers of IJVs are often high because actions or attitudes are often misinterpreted due to cultural differences. These tensions often result in mistrust by one parent of the objectives of the other parent firm(s) (Shenkar and Zeira, 1992) who often pass feelings of mistrust down to managers whom parents appoint to their IJV's TMT, ultimately affecting the working relationships of these managers.

When an IJV has been formed which links dissimilar cultures, there is always a risk the arrangement will fail because managers are too dissimilar and become unwilling or unable to compromise together to resolve such differences (Brown *et al.*, 1989; Lane and Beamish, 1990). Research suggests that this impasse is likely to occur when IJV executives are dissimilar with respect to their demographic characteristics, if they enjoy differing socio-economic roots, or if their concepts of the role of the venture differ from that of other managers (e.g., Kogut and Singh, 1988; Putnam and Poole, 1987; Schneider and De Meyer, 1991). Therefore, the theory that cultural differences negatively affect business organisations is well supported, and researchers have consistently linked management problems of IJVs to cultural differences (Barkema *et al.*, 1996). However, this is not always the case as Park and Ungson (1997) discovered. Park and Ungson concluded from their study that prior relationships between firms provide a powerful counterbalance to cross-cultural differences. The Park and Ungson findings were consistent with Harrigan's (1988b) findings, with Bleeke and Ernst's (1993) case study result that cross-border ventures can overcome early difficulties caused by cultural differences, and with Barkema *et al.'s* (1996) suggestions that learning between partners may offset cultural differences. Prior relationships between partners create trust and familiarity (Gulati, 1995; Kogut, 1989; Park and Russo, 1996). Trust attenuates opportunistic behaviour and can facilitate conflict resolution. Familiarity enhances a partner's transparency and can reduce the cost of monitoring its activities thereby enhancing performance (Park and Ungson, 1997).

10.2.2. Team Processes and their Effects

Empirical studies of IJVs have consistently identified several factors that are associated with successful versus unsuccessful ventures (Ding, 1997; Inkpen and Beamish, 1997; Madhok, 1995; Yan and Gray; 1994). Results of these studies suggest that effectively managing an IJV depends on top managers' abilities to develop trust (Madhok, 1995) and work cohesively as a team as well as displaying a willingness to communicate, cooperate and negotiate any disputes (Fey and Beamish, 2000; Mueller, 1994; Smith *et al.*, 1994; Wallace, 1992). That is, previous research on IJVs suggests that the difficulties and the effects of differences among IJV managers are significantly reduced when levels of communication, trust and cohesion are high (Amason, 1996; Fey and Beamish, 2001; Smith *et al.,* 1994).

To develop the coordination, cooperation and decision quality required to achieve IJV goals, then, IJV managers must overcome any negative effects of heterogeneity and become integrated as a team within a management culture that encourages frequent communication, trust and cohesion (Goll *et al.,* 2001). To do so, IJV managers must engage in the decision-making process in such a way that encourages quality decisions without facilitating dysfunctional conflict that would prevent the implementation of those decisions (Ding, 1997; Fey and Beamish, 2000).

10.2.3. Decision Quality, Decision Implementation, and Goal Attainment

When investigating the relationship between team heterogeneity and creative problem solving, most previous studies have considered processes of uninational teams whose members were committed to or held loyalties to a single organisation (Bantel and Jackson, 1989). However, managers who constitute an IJV TMT often come from separate or distinct cultures and have well-developed beliefs and methods for dealing with the complexities of corporate decision-making. Thus, while excessive levels of trust and cohesion may lead to inferior decisions, theory posits that this outcome is not likely within IJV TMTs due to the complex nature of the heterogeneity found in such teams (Goll *et al.,* 2001; Mueller, 1994).

As a consequence, managers with different backgrounds and organisational experiences are likely to have different attitudes and values and hold divergent points of view (Bantel and Jackson, 1989). Team member differences may encourage debate among managers to such an extent that communication problems and negative reactions by members to the team experience (Roberts and O'Reilly, 1979) inhibit the development of cohesion and trust. These problems would tend to limit interaction among team members and the exchange of valuable information. As a result of this decreased communication and increased conflict associated with team heterogeneity, it could negatively influence team decision-making processes and outcomes (Bantel and Jackson, 1989). Specifically, low levels of trust and cohesion and less frequent communication are likely to negatively affect the quality of decisions these teams generate (Knight *et al.,* 1999). However, as previously discussed, prior relationships between firms provide a powerful counterbalance to cross-cultural differences (Park and Ungson, 1997). Prior relationships between partners create trust and familiarity (Gulati, 1995; Kogut, 1989; Park and Russo; 1996). Trust attenuates opportunistic behaviours and facilitates conflict resolution. Thereby, enhancing the quality of decisions these teams generate (Park and Ungson, 1997) that ultimately leads to improved performance.

The relevance of cultural and demographic team heterogeneity to this chapter is based on their effects on the group processes of cohesion, trust and communication, and the resulting quality of decisions, effective implementation of decisions and, ultimately, on IJV goal attainment and performance (Kogut and Singh, 1988; Putnam and Poole, 1987; Schneider and De Meyer, 1991). Cultural and demographic heterogeneity have been found to negatively affect trust, cohesion and the frequency of communication within multicultural teams because managers are either disinclined or unable to overcome their differences easily in order to function as a team (Barkema *et al.,* 1996). Some studies suggest that team heterogeneity positively affects decision quality because member differences tend to encourage the consideration of a wider range of alternatives during decision-making (Goll *et al.,* 2001; Park and Ungson, 1997). At the same time, heterogeneity has been found to negatively affect implementing team decisions through its indirect influence on trust, cohesion and communication frequency (Knight *et al.,* 1999). As such, heterogeneity is expected to directly but negatively affect trust, cohesion and communication frequency, indirectly but negatively affect decision implementation, and indirectly but positively affect decision quality within TMTs.

Regarding the team process variables, research and theory on cohesion and its importance to team processes support the contention that frequent communication positively affects trust, trust positively affects cohesion, and that cohesion and communication frequency positively affect and reinforce each other (Fey and Beamish, 2000; Mueller, 1994; Smith *et al.,* 1994; Wallace, 1992). All process variables positively and directly affect decision quality and decision implementation. Finally, high-quality decisions and the implementation of those decisions have been found to positively affect the attainment of organization goals (Amason, 1996; Goll *et al.,* 2001; Michel and Hambrick, 1992). The Julian *et al.* (2004) study was designed to examine these relationships in multicultural top management teams of IJVs in Thailand.

10.3. Trust and the Performance of International Joint Venture Top Management Teams in Thailand

The Julian *et al.* (2004) study used a multi-item questionnaire to collect the data. The research instrument was designed to measure two independent (cultural and demographic heterogeneity), three process (cohesion, trust and communication frequency), and three dependent (decision quality, decision implementation and goal attainment) variables. Each construct in the research instrument is now discussed in some detail.

10.3.1. Heterogeneity

Both general demographic characteristics and culture-based demographic characteristics were measured. Items used to measure demographic heterogeneity were team member's age, level of education, functional specialisation and length of team tenure. Items measuring cultural heterogeneity included member nationality, primary language spoken, country of education and organizational culture background (parent organization affiliation, if any). Each of the eight items was a self-report measure.

10.3.2. Communication Frequency

Two measures were constructed to evaluate how frequently team members communicated with each other. Each measure used a seven-point Likert-type scale ranging from 1, 1-5 times a week, to 7, more than 30 times a week. The first measure was based on subjects' responses to how frequently they communicated with other team members via seven of the most common types of communication media used in a business context (Russ *et al.,* 1990) as well as in social situations. For the second measure, respondents were requested to indicate how frequently they communicated with their respective team mates who were affiliated with a parent organisation versus team mates with no such affiliation. Higher scores on these measures indicated more frequent communication among members. The coefficient alpha for communication frequency was .87, well above the .70 level suggested by Nunnally (1978).

10.3.3. Trust

Through a content analysis of managers' suggestions and two previous studies of managerial trust, Butler (1991) developed the Conditions of Trust Inventory which includes one general, overall measure of trust proven to be reliable in several different contexts (e.g., Mueller, 1994). Therefore, this measure of trust was included in the questionnaire and consisted of four response items, one that was reverse scored to provide scale continuity. Higher scores indicated the presence of trust and lower scores reflected its absence. Generally, the four items required respondents to indicate the degree to which other members of their respective teams could be trusted. The coefficient alpha for trust was .71, above the .70 level suggested by Nunnally (1978) and more than acceptable for a four-item scale (Anderson and Coughlan, 1987).

10.3.4. Cohesion

A four-item cohesiveness index developed by Seashore (1954) was used to assess this cohesion. Seashore's (1954) index defined cohesion into four dimensions: (1) how readily members defended other team members from outside criticism, (2) how well members helped each other on the job, (3) how well members got along with each other, and (4) how well members stuck together as a team. Because Seashore's index did not measure cohesion relative to the group task, a fifth measure was added to reflect the commitment of members to the group task: (5) how well members coordinated their work toward common objectives. The coefficient alpha for cohesion was .76, above the .70 level suggested by Nunnally (1978).

10.3.5. Decision Quality, Decision Implementation and Goal Attainment

As decision quality, decision implementation and goal attainment were related to effective group processes during decision-making, these measures were grouped together in the questionnaire following a statement that requested subjects to respond based on decisions that their TMT had made during the last six months. While keeping items measuring these three constructs together in a group, individual items were alternated in the questionnaire to reduce the effect of respondent bias. Again, seven-point Likert-type scales ranging from 1, 'strongly disagree' to 7, 'strongly agree' were provided for responses for all items measuring these variables.

For decision quality, each respondent was asked to rate the overall quality of decisions his team made, the quality of alternative decisions his team considered, as well as the quality of alternative decisions the team chose. The coefficient alpha for decision quality was .65 indicating modest reliability even though .60 is acceptable for a three-item scale (Anderson and Coughlan, 1987). For decision implementation, respondents were asked to assess how well they understood the decisions their team made, their degree of commitment and support for those decisions, and the degree of assistance each provided to implement their team decisions. The coefficient alpha for decision implementation was .87, well above the .70 level suggested by Nunnally (1978). Finally, for goal attainment, respondents were asked to indicate their perceived degree of consensus among their team members on venture goals, their level of understanding of which goals were more important, and their perception of whether their team successfully reached its goals. The coefficient alpha for goal attainment was .83, again well above the .70 level suggested by Nunnally (1978).

10.3.6. Data Analysis

A path model incorporating all of the possible relationships was developed and analysed. Path regression was used to test the model and all model linkages were tested. Because of the possible influence of organizational size and team size on both the antecedent and outcome variables, they were included in the analysis as control variables. In the Julian *et al.* (2004) study, demographic and cultural heterogeneity and the control variables of team size and IJV size were the exogenous variables. Communication frequency, trust, cohesion, decision quality, decision implementation and goal attainment were the source variables. Five regression equations were used to identify significant causal relationships or paths among the variables. The assumptions that underlie path analysis (linearity, additivity, interval level of measurement, uncorrelated residuals) were not an issue given the theoretical basis for the model and an inspection of the scatterplots of residuals. Path coefficients for the model are found in Table 10.1.

As expected, there were significant correlations between trust and cohesion, decision quality, decision implementation and goal attainment. Regressing trust on the control variables, cultural and demographic heterogeneity, and communication frequency produced a significant R^2 of .69 ($p < .01$). While not apparent in the correlation pattern, demographic heterogeneity is the only significant predictor of trust in the regression analysis. Unexpectedly, the more diverse a team was with regard to demographics, the higher the level of trust reported. Communication frequency and cultural heterogeneity do not contribute much to predicting levels of trust among members of these teams.

Neither measure of heterogeneity was significantly correlated with cohesion. However, trust, decision quality, decision implementation and goal attainment all had significant associations with cohesion. Team size was also significantly correlated with cohesion but negatively, as might be expected. Regressing the control variables, trust, and both types of heterogeneity on cohesion yielded a significant R^2 of .81 ($p < .01$). However, the only significant predictor of cohesion was trust. Increased levels of trust were positively associated with increased levels of cohesion, but neither the control variables nor the heterogeneity measures were significant predictors of cohesion.

Table 10.1 Path Regression Results

Dependent Variable	Explanatory Variable	Standardized Coefficients	R^2
Communication Frequency	Constant	2.33	.39
	IJV Size	-1.18	
	Team Size	.50	
	Cultural Hetero.	*-.89	
	Demographic Hetero.	1.21	
Trust	Constant	6.41	.69
	IJV Size	-.79	
	Team Size	-.75	
	Cultural Hetero.	.00	
	Demographic Hetero.	*1.59	
	Com_Freq	-.28	
Cohesion	Constant	4.81	.81
	IJV Size	-.39	
	Team Size	-.54	
	Demographic Hetero.	.43	
	Cultural Hetero.	-.08	
	Trust	*.53	
Decision Quality	Constant	1.98	.97
	IJV Size	-.32	
	Team Size	-.06	
	Trust	**-.65	
	Cohesion	**1.20	
	Com_Freq	**-.30	
	Cultural Hetero.	-.20	
	Demographic Hetero.	**1.17	
Decision Implementation	Constant	1.07	.98
	IJV Size	-.39	
	Team Size	-.03	
	Trust	**-.81	
	Cohesion	**1.45	
	Com_Freq	-.08	
	Demographic Hetero.	*.74	
	Cultural Hetero.	-.00	
Goal Attainment	Constant	-1.11	.98
	IJV Size	*.37	
	Team Size	-.11	
	Decision Implement.	**1.21	
	Decision Quality	-.20	

* $p < .05$
** $p < .01$

The control variables, trust, cohesion, communication frequency and the heterogeneity variables were further regressed against decision quality and yielded a significant R^2 of .97 ($p < .01$). For these IJV teams, trust, communication frequency, cohesion and demographic heterogeneity were significant predictors of decision quality. Higher levels of communication were associated with lower levels of perceived decision quality. Unexpectedly, trust was also associated negatively with decision quality. Cohesion, however, was positively associated with decision quality. Finally, greater demographic heterogeneity was associated with better decision quality.

The control variables plus trust, cohesion, communication frequency and heterogeneity were next regressed against decision implementation. The R^2 was .98 ($p < .01$). Results for decision implementation were similar to those found for decision quality. Trust was negatively associated with decision implementation, and cohesion and demographic heterogeneity were positively associated with decision implementation. Finally, regressing the control variables, decision implementation, and decision quality against goal attainment yielded a significant R^2 of .98 ($p < .01$). IJV size and decision implementation were positively related to goal attainment.

Interestingly, the level of communication activity did not necessarily increase levels of trust. The mean level of communication frequency was quite low (2.71, std = 1.46), lower than one might have expected given the likely necessity of increased communication for resolving ambiguities and conflicts of interest. This might signify that these managers believed that greater levels of communication were desirable. These results are somewhat different than those of Jackson *et al.* (1991), where reduced communication and increased conflict were associated with greater demographic diversity.

The building of trust, on the other hand, seemed to be more dependent on the size of the team and differences in age, education level, functional experience and parent organization affiliation. However, the results were not as expected. Differences in age, level of education, affiliation with a parent organization and type of functional experience were associated with greater levels of trust. Perhaps, these differences were perceived by respondents as strengths rather than as points of contention.

In this study, the development of cohesion was dependent only on trust. Neither cultural nor demographic heterogeneity was a direct, significant predictor of cohesion. Rather, these results suggest that the effects of heterogeneity manifest themselves primarily through other variables that mediate the relationship between heterogeneity and cohesion.

A common assumption in the management literature is that heterogeneous teams tend to yield higher-quality decisions than do homogeneous teams because members tend to bring unique contributions and perspectives to the decision-making process (Wiersema and Bantel, 1992). In this study, such an assumption was supported, at least for the effects of demographic heterogeneity. One might have expected that not only demographic but also cultural differences among a team's members might encourage argumentation and debate to such an extent that they inhibit managers from effectively defusing dysfunctional conflict (Barkema *et al.*, 1996). Apparently, the levels of mutual trust within these teams provided managers with a mechanism to translate their differences into effective decision-making. The same pattern of results was found for the effects of demographic heterogeneity on decision implementation. High levels of demographic heterogeneity lead to perceptions that decisions were implemented effectively. This is contrary to research that suggests that such a decision-making team may initially perform its task well and make high-quality decisions, yet 'burn itself up' in the process by generating so much divisiveness and conflict among members that they are unwilling or unable to communicate effectively and work together in the future (Barkema *et al.*, 1996).

In summary, the effects of heterogeneity were not always as expected. Instead of a negative influence on decision quality and implementation (Bantel and Jackson, 1989), demographic heterogeneity was associated with greater levels of trust and improved decision quality and implementation. It may be that different perspectives, brought about by experience, wisdom and different functional view points, helped increase the level of confidence managers had during their decision-making and implementation activities (Wiersema and Bantel, 1992). Levels of trust, perceived decision quality and decision implementation were all reasonably high. As such, it was concluded from the findings of the Julian *et al.* (2004) study that the level of trust evident in a top management team plays a significant yet indirect role in goal attainment and ultimately IJV performance in IJVs in Thailand.

11. Partners' Contributions

11.1 Introduction

The JV agreement specifies the JV's outputs and inputs. Outputs are generated by the activities of the JV whilst inputs come from two main sources, from purchases of components or skills in the marketplace and from contributions made by the firms that have formed the venture. Thus JV partners contribute certain resources in return for certain benefits. However, the contributions and expected benefits of the firms engaged in the JV must be perceived to be fair so that the partners remain satisfied with the venture (Robinson, 1969) otherwise the JV is likely to fail (Blodgett, 1991b; Dymsza, 1988). The JV contract issue revolves around valuating the contributions of the partners and their respective pay-offs and assuring that the partners' expectations of the agreement are compatible. One way of assessing the initial JV agreement is to see it as a single equilibrium point in an ongoing relationship where the relative bargaining power and responsibility of the partners is defined (Blodgett, 1991b).

In any JV or cooperative arrangement the agreement entails contributions from the participants i.e. asset contributions that the partner firms can exploit either in the marketplace or within the JV (Blodgett, 1991b). Furthermore, JVs would not exist if firms did not feel the lack of some important ingredient to exploit business opportunities alone. So, the JV agreement that is made between the partners must reflect the need for and the complementarity of the resources offered by the partners to the JV (Fagre and Wells, 1982). As such, resources supplied by the JV partners can be a source of bargaining power for the JV partners. However, they are not the only source of bargaining power. Other factors play a part in determining which partner, if any, will dominate the venture. Industry characteristics, for example, are particularly important in this regard, as the nature of competition in a firm's industry can have a crucial impact on its alternative courses of action (Blodgett, 1991b; Fagre and Wells, 1982; Gomes-Casseres, 1988a). The focus, however, in this chapter is on the contributions or resources supplied by each of the partners and their impact on JV performance together with the role the partners' contributions play in achieving bargaining power within the JV arrangement.

11.2. Review of Literature

Partners' contributions have been identified in previous research as significantly impacting upon JV performance (Beamish, 1988). The partners' contributions that have impacted upon JV performance in previous research that are focused on in this chapter relate to government pressure, competitive learning, technology, knowledge of the local environment and/or marketing expertise, control of intrasystem transfers and financial capital (Beamish, 1988; Blodgett, 1991b; Dymsza, 1988).

11.2.1. Government Pressure

The relationship between MNCs and host-country governments has been the focus of many studies (Beamish, 1984; Contractor, 1990; Fagre and Wells, 1982; Gomes-Casseres, 1988b, 1988c; Root, 1988b). Frequently when a less-developed country (LDC) is involved, government pressure may cause a foreign firm to take on a local partner in order to successfully enter a foreign market. The government also may exercise influence over the choice of suppliers and over marketing, once the venture is established. The government may also impose exchange controls that can have a significant impact on the venture's financing decisions including reinvesting in the operation and repatriation decisions. Furthermore, when developed countries are involved, tariffs, quotas or non-tariff barriers may make it imperative for a foreign firm to rely more on local production than on exporting. In these examples of LDCs and developed countries, laws or pressure from the government can play a significant role in the local firm's bargaining power (Blodgett, 1991b) that can in turn impact upon performance (Beamish, 1985; Killing, 1983).

Governments may not actually require JV participation by MNCs, but government pressure for local participation usually exists in some form. Government pressure is identified as the direct or indirect imposition of restrictions on foreign investors by a host-country government (Blodgett, 1991b). Beamish (1985) found that 57 percent of joint ventures between US MNCs and entities in developing countries were formed because of government pressure, while only 17 percent of the joint ventures of US MNCs and firms in other developed countries were formed for that reason. Third world indigenisation programmes, by injecting a political factor into the bargaining power of a local entity, have had an important impact on how the developed-world MNCs operate overseas, and MNCs have formed IJVs in order to maintain good relations with host country governments (Beamish, 1984; Blodgett, 1991b).

If the government is an active partner to the IJV, which is the case with many developing countries e.g., China and Thailand, it means an important diminution of bargaining power for the MNC, since the government that owns equity in the IJV also has the power to regulate the venture's activities. In addition, when import substitution policies are pursued, the host-country government can be expected to have strong motivation to increase control over the venture once operations are going smoothly. Even when the local partner is private enterprise, the host-country government can exert control as a shadow partner by imposing and enforcing regulations that interfere with the venture's operations e.g., the choice of suppliers, the choice of markets and the repatriation of profit (Blodgett, 1991b).

As a bargaining resource, the implicit or explicit role of host-country governments as a gatekeeper to the investment process resides in the country's right of sovereignty. Therefore, government pressure is an enduring asset and is not readily appropriated by international law. Current nationalistic feeling dictates that few countries will tolerate uncontrolled foreign investment by foreign enterprises and they often erect barriers against certain types of foreign investment. Beamish (1985), Contractor (1985), and Gomes-Casseres (1987) found that the most crucial factor in relative bargaining power is government-imposed restrictions. The IJV, especially where the host-country government is an active partner, is a means of reducing the effect of government-imposed restrictions and developing good relations with host-country governments, and is often used as a market entry mode for that reason. Even if the host-country government is not an active partner to the JV arrangement, if the foreign MNC selects a local partner firm as its JV partner that has good connections with the host-country government this could be a significant contribution to the JV arrangement and a major contribution to successful JV performance (Beamish, 1984, 1993; Blodgett, 1991b; Dymsza, 1988).

Furthermore, IJVs reduce the risks of expropriation and satisfy nationalistic demands. There are many considerations required of developing countries when viewing relations with a foreign firm, including the amount of local employment, the supply and price of goods, access to marketing systems and foreign exchange earnings potential. However, two considerations increasingly dominate: developing countries are determined to regain control of economic decisions in order to ensure that these decisions are compatible with national objectives; and they acknowledge the importance of acquiring a sufficient quantity and quality of high-level skills to make effective control possible. Developing countries seek to minimise the surrender of control to foreigners, while at the same time maximising skills acquisition (Wright and Russel, 1975).

In order to achieve these objectives, developing countries around the world are increasingly resorting to the IJV as the only form of foreign investment that will be permitted in certain industries and are increasingly insisting upon local capital participation in foreign corporate ventures. Discriminatory taxation, selective foreign exchange restrictions, selective bureaucratic delays and foreign employment restrictions are also being sought (Wright and Russel, 1975). Independence, national sovereignty and a more representative and sophisticated national leadership have made such measures feasible. Developing countries are increasingly in control of the natural resources and markets sought by MNCs. Therefore, IJVs have proliferated for the reason that they have been one of only a few ways for foreign corporations to satisfy host-country governments' requirements for local participation in ownership and management of enterprises within their boundaries (Beamish, 1984; Blodgett, 1991a; Higginbottom, 1980; Wright and Russel, 1975). As such, a JV with a local partner firm that has good connections with the host-country government is a significant contribution by the local firm to the JV arrangement, one that is likely to impact upon performance.

11.2.2. Competitive Learning

Apart from the direct or indirect activity of host-country governments the firm-specific assets contributed by JV partner firms are important contributions to the JV arrangement as well. Within a JV, the contributions of the partners have been recognised as important sources of competitive advantage in the ongoing relationship that results from the activities of the partner firms. Doz *et al.* (1986) viewed contributions within the context of the JV, where partner firms encroach upon one another. This took the form of one partner firm extracting skills from other partner firms in the JV arrangement, thereby reducing the partners' capability for autonomy outside the JV. What enables one partner to encroach upon the others lies in the nature of the assets that they bring to the venture. Some assets lose their value faster than others; some know-how can be learned easier than others. For example, what lends power to one partner in a JV thereby having control over the JV is its possession of assets or know-how that cannot be readily appropriated by a partner firm e.g., technology (Blodgett, 1991b).

Certain resources in the economy are not always available through free markets. Technology and distribution networks are not always available for sale, and in such cases the need for access to these resources can only be satisfied through a JV. A typical case occurs when one firm possesses a product which it wants to market abroad. A JV with a local partner can then offer access to an efficient distribution network together with knowledge of local business practices and institutions. In such a case there is a high degree of complementarity between the partners. Generally, complementarity is found in many JVs, encompassing not only functional complementarity, as in the case mentioned, but also technological complementarity. For example, the development of a new product that requires technical know-how not available in a single company (Beamish and Inkpen, 1995; Blodgett, 1991b; Calof and Beamish, 1995; Dymsza, 1988; Fey, 1995; Harrigan, 1987; Hladik, 1988).

The local partner, on the other hand, usually enters the JV with a different set of objectives. For example, such a venture might be attractive because it provides access to technology that would otherwise be difficult to develop or buy (Berlew, 1984). In fact, transfer of technology probably constitutes the single most important reason why firms in developing countries seek JVs with organisations in technologically advanced countries (Beamish, 1984; Blodgett, 1991b; Connolly, 1984; Datta, 1988; Dymsza, 1988; Wright and Russel, 1975).

JVs, therefore, offer a unique opportunity of combining the distinctive competences and the complementary resources of participating firms. Such combinations provide a wide range of benefits, benefits that neither participant might be able to attain on their own. These include, among others, economic benefits in the form of reductions in factor costs, transportation costs, overheads and taxes. Therefore, JVs can be a particularly desirable alternative in situations and industries where the 'critical mass' (the input activity level that has to be surpassed to obtain any significant output or result) is very high (Hall, 1984). Technology is far more difficult to appropriate by a partner firm than are distribution networks and local market knowledge. As such, in an atmosphere of competitive learning, one firm can become dominant through the resource it provides, e.g., technology (Blodgett, 1991b).

11.2.3. Technology

As far as technology transfer is concerned, apart from host-country government reasons, the transfer of modern and innovative technology is one of the principal reasons why local firms and foreign partners enter into JV arrangements (Beamish, 1988; Blodgett, 1991b; Hladik, 1988; Lecraw, 1984). In fact, access to modern and up-to-date technology is widely recognised as the principal reason why local firms in developing countries enter into JV arrangements with foreign corporations from developed countries (Beamish, 1984, 1993; Beamish and Inkpen, 1995; Blodgett, 1991b; Connolly, 1984; Gomes-Casseres, 1989; Hladik, 1988; Lee and

Beamish, 1995). Failure to deliver to the IJV the technology initially promised by the foreign partner(s) when entering into the IJV agreement could cause conflict between the foreign and local partners and this conflict together with the lack of the required technology could have a negative influence on the marketing performance of the IJV.

Apart from government pressure, technology is widely considered a most powerful proprietary asset to contribute to the IJV by one of the partners. When it has not had a chance to become standardised in widely available machinery, technical knowledge provides an IJV partner with strong bargaining power in its IJV contract negotiations. It resides predominantly in the firm's personnel rather than in the firm's equipment or machinery. Against such an asset, particularly if it is protected by continuous innovation and patent protection, it is difficult for competing firms to compete against, and those firms that have access to such technology have a significant competitive advantage over those that do not. Such a competitive advantage is likely to make a significant contribution to marketing performance, especially in developing countries, where access to the latest technology is one of the primary reasons firms in those countries enter into JVs with firms from developed countries. Kogut (1977) and Fagre and Wells (1982) placed it highest in importance among resources that might be provided by a JV partner. Reich and Mankin (1986) believed that the greatest competitive advantage that could be derived from a cooperative agreement was knowledge of the production processes. Lecraw (1984) ranked technology high because technology, as a proprietary asset that is being contributed by a partner in a JV arrangement, gives the JV partner control through possession of asymmetric information. Gomes-Casseres (1988b) demonstrated that a MNC that has new technology needed by host-country governments can draw considerable leverage in JV bargaining when it possesses that technology. This is because host-country governments usually seek technology transfer above all the other resources that a MNC can provide. Paliwoda and Liebrenz (1984) also pointed out that Western firms with zero-equity positions in JVs in Eastern Bloc countries still dominate a JV as long as they control advanced technology. When studies have demonstrated that access to the latest technology was a non-significant predictor of bargaining power the findings have generally been attributed to the proxy that was used, i.e. R&D intensity (Blodgett, 1991b; Fagre and Wells, 1982; Gomes-Casseres, 1987).

Therefore, technology transfer, particularly when it is characterised by rapid innovation, may be considered a highly dominant contribution to the JV by one of its partners. Technology transfer is what most local firms from developing countries seek when entering a JV agreement with a foreign firm from a developed country; failure of the foreign corporation to deliver the promised technology is likely to have a negative influence on IJV marketing performance (Beamish, 1984; Blodgett, 1987, 1991b; Gomes-Casseres, 1989).

11.2.4. Knowledge of the Local Environment and/or Marketing Expertise

Knowledge of the local business environment is an asset often sought by an international firm trying to establish a position in a foreign market for the first time. This knowledge is an asset that has real value and can take many different forms. It usually involves familiarity with economic, political and business conditions, e.g., marketing channel availability that managers of the international firm may be unaware of. The foreign market the international firm is entering may be characterised by inadequate infrastructure, a large public sector, a unique colonial history and ethnic hostilities. Political connections are important also. Having a local partner may ease relations between the international firm and an unfriendly host-country government, which may perceive a joint venture as less threatening than a wholly owned subsidiary of a foreign firm (Connolly, 1984). The public relations benefit extends to local labour relations and to worker morale as well. Furthermore, a local partner may help in obtaining contracts, provide access to favourable tax treatment, enable the international firm to avoid various non-tariff barriers, and provide a means of entry into relationships with local businesses and officials. Such connections with the local environment are often an essential prerequisite for a venture's success. Related areas of expertise that may be placed in this category are distribution channels and marketing skill (Blodgett, 1991b).

Foreign firms may find it difficult to penetrate international markets without local marketing expertise. A joint venture partner may provide the know-how or established local distribution channels through which to market the product that may have not been available without the local JV partner. The importance of access to suitable distribution channels as a motive for both international and domestic JVs is apparent from even a cursory reading of the literature (Blodgett, 1991b; Hamel *et al.*, 1989; Ganitsky *et al.*, 1991; Jacque, 1986; Kogut and Singh, 1985). Kogut and Singh's (1985) database shows that 42 percent of the JVs entered by foreigners in the US over the 1971-83 period were for marketing and distribution, while Jacque (1986) found that close to 60 percent of US joint ventures in Japan were of that type.

An international firm wanting to expand across national boundaries often finds itself in the position of entering new markets. Obtaining distribution can be a major obstacle to establishing a position in a new market (Keegan, 1995). This obstacle is often encountered when a company enters a competitive market where brands and supply relationships are already established. There is little incentive for an independent channel agent to take on a new product when established names are accepted in the market and are satisfying current demands (Keegan, 1995). The international firm seeking to enter such a market must either provide some incentive to channel agents, establish its own direct distribution system, or enter into a strategic alliance (e.g., an IJV) with a local firm that has a comprehensive distribution network.

The provision of incentives to independent channel agents and the establishment of a direct distribution system as channel strategies have several disadvantages. Firstly, the provision of special incentives to independent channel agents can be extremely expensive. The company might offer outright payments as either direct cash bonuses or contest awards for sales performance. In competitive markets with sufficiently high prices, incentives could take the form of gross margin guarantees. Both incentive payments and margin guarantees are expensive. The incentive payments are directly expensive. The margin guarantees can be indirectly expensive because they affect the price to the consumer and the price competitiveness of a manufacturer's product.

The other alternative of establishing a direct distribution system in a new market also has the disadvantage of being expensive. Sales representatives and sales managers must be hired and trained. The sales organisation will inevitably be a heavy loser in its early stage of operation in a new market because it will not have sufficient volume to cover its overhead costs. Therefore, any company contemplating the establishment of a direct sales force, even one assigned to distributors, should be prepared to underwrite losses for this sales force for a reasonable period of time.

As such, the alternative of entering into a strategic alliance or some form of IJV with a local firm with a comprehensive distribution network gives the international firm access to a suitable distribution network and knowledge of the local business environment. At the same time it reduces the risk associated with entering the new market and is less expensive than the other channel strategies. Therefore, the contribution of resources made by the local IJV partner firm of providing the IJV foreign partner firm with access to a suitable distribution network is a significant contribution to say the least, often impacting upon performance (Blodgett, 1991a; Jacque, 1986; Julian, 1998) and is often cited as one of the principal reasons why foreign firms enter into IJVs in developing countries (Connolly, 1984).

As industries evolve, their distribution and communication channels must improve to provide closer and more efficient contacts between suppliers and customers. This long-term imperative may require considerable short-term investments. Though foreign partners might favour such investments, the local partner(s) will oppose such an investment if the change in channel arrangements clashes with their traditional concepts, limited resources, bargaining power base, and/or short-term expectations. The greater the divergence in the IJV partner's objectives and time-frame to achieve those objectives, the greater the difficulty for an IJV to take advantage of opportunities and cope with challenges created by changes in its industry's channels, and the greater their need to compromise, given the local partner's reluctance to change, which is a short-term view. As a consequence, IJV partners need to address the eventual changes in the IJV's roles and relationships with the marketing channels as these changes and the availability of suitable marketing channels not controlled by one or several of its competitors can have a significant influence on the marketing performance of the IJV (Ahn, 1980; Datta, 1988; Ganitsky *et al.*, 1991; Killing, 1983). Therefore, the importance to IJV marketing performance of certain partner's contributions like government pressure, technology transfer and knowledge of the local business environment and marketing expertise should not be underestimated.

Furthermore, IJVs allow international firms to enter new and potentially profitable foreign markets with a local partner firm that may have been restricted or prohibited without it. Given the fixed costs of innovation, the larger the market the higher the JV's expected rate of return on investment. A number of studies have shown, in fact, that JV investment is positively influenced by the expected domestic and international sales of the product (Harrigan, 1988a; Higginbottom, 1980). Immediate access to a large market can be especially important in industries where product lifetimes are short. Expected sales are dependent on both market size and the length of time over which the product is sold in these markets. As the time factor grows shorter, market access can become critical to long term product viability. As such, the local JV partner firm provides quick and easy access to the local domestic market for the expanding international firm that otherwise may not be available without the local firm. This is a significant contribution provided by the local partner firm considering the size and the growth of the domestic markets in South East Asia, e.g., Singapore, Malaysia, Thailand and Indonesia (Julian and O'Cass, 2002a).

From the international firm's perspective, the IJV offers the opportunity of entering promising new markets where other forms of market entry (e.g., as a wholly owned subsidiary) may be barred. Some country markets may be characterised by less formal barriers to entry. Still, foreign firms may find it difficult to penetrate these markets without local marketing expertise. The local JV partner firm may provide this marketing expertise. The local JV partner firm may also have been of critical value in markets where important customers have been state-owned enterprises or governments that favour national suppliers. Whilst many international firms have looked to local JV partners as a means of entering the host-country market alone, it has become increasingly important to ensure access to international markets as well and local partners have been useful in this respect also. Therefore, the local JV partner firm is making a significant contribution to the international firm and the JV entity by agreeing to participate in the JV agreement and by contributing resources to the JV entity, in return for assets contributed by the international firm and the derived benefit of being involved in the JV entity. The ultimate benefit to the international firm is enhanced return on investment by enabling it to participate in a high-growth domestic market that may have not been available without the local partner firm and through economies of scale.

In relation to economies of scale, a decreasing unit cost is linked to an increasing level of activity per time period. Economies of scale pertain not only to manufacturing but to some other functions as well, notably R&D and sales (Ganitsky *et al.,* 1991; Hladik, 1988; Luo and Chen, 1995). A JV with a local firm allows the international firm to benefit from these economies of scale in a way not possible if it remained completely independent (Anazawa, 1994; Aswicahyono and Hill, 1995; Datta, 1988; Dunning, 1993; Dymsza, 1988; Franko, 1971; Gullander, 1976; Hladik, 1988; Stopford and Wells, 1972).

Through a JV international firms can also benefit from the 'experience curve' effect. The experience curve shows how the unit cost decreases as the total product volume produced by the firm over the product's entire existence increases (Jain, 1989, 1994a). The reason for this is to be found in the successive improvements in efficiency that normally takes place in firms as they gain more experience in the production of a particular product/service. Therefore, as international firms produce a larger volume of products to satisfy the needs of consumers in a larger number of markets, they become more efficient in producing these products leading to increased product quality and lower unit production costs, thereby making them more effective and profitable in their domestic market as well as in their international markets, leading to higher returns on investment. All because they were able to engage in a JV with a local partner firm that in relation to market entry and participation in that marketplace may have otherwise not been possible.

11.2.5. Control of Intra-system Transfers

The level of bargaining power enjoyed by the JV partners is affected by the benefits to each of them from being involved in the JV agreement (Hladik, 1985). A common benefit of being involved in the JV arrangement for a MNC occurs when the MNC is given the exclusive rights to supply inputs to the JV entity or to distribute the JV's output to other affiliates within the MNC's global network. These benefits are fundamental to the MNC's global strategy that tries to rationalise production on a global scale. Essentially, this provides the MNC with the ability to interrupt the flow of the JV's operations, and can be an important control device. LDCs may be in a weak position to deny control of intra-system transfers to a foreign MNC (Blodgett, 1991b; Fagre and Wells, 1982; Poynter, 1982).

Intra-system transfers may contribute to bargaining power in another way. In JVs contractual components are often added into the agreement based on shared equity. It is impossible for the contractual component to have prior claim to the venture's earnings. If the foreign MNC is able to draw returns from its dominance of intra-network transfers in addition to its dividend entitlement based on ownership share, it has achieved dominance in the bargaining relationship (Blodgett, 1991b).

Evaluating the importance of this contribution to the JV is not easy because it is not a company's primary asset. A MNC is able to gain leverage from its network of global production when its main asset is technology. Even though the MNC's global network requires some intangible technical knowledge, the power that the MNC's network provides resides predominantly in the contract that it has been able to develop and finalise. Therefore, there is the potential for the asset to be replaced by contracts with outside suppliers or by contracts with the other partner. This is especially so for products that are standardised within specific industries (Blodgett, 1991b).

Root (1988b) believed that control of sourcing and exports was an important way of keeping the local firm dependent on the MNC. Poynter (1982) found that the supply of components was an important source of bargaining power when dealing with LDC host-country governments. However, it didn't have the same effect in JVs with partners in industrialized countries. Franko (1971) identified network control and intra-system transfers as a source of JV instability. Gomes-Casseres (1988b) found that control of supply networks was not a significant factor in bargaining power. However, the control of supply networks had an impact on the firm's choice of wholly owned subsidiaries over JVs.

Furthermore, Dymsza (1988) suggested that major conflicts can erupt between partners in IJVs with respect to purchases of materials, intermediates and components. Some foreign MNCs strive to have the IJV affiliate purchase intermediate goods or components from it on the grounds that it assures required quality standards and that competitive alternative sources are not readily available. Local partners, on the other hand, want to explore alternative sources in order to obtain the materials from lowest-cost suppliers internationally or domestically. They may believe that the foreign MNC is charging excessive prices and aims to earn additional income from selling the intermediate goods or components to the affiliate. If the foreign MNC presses aggressively for continued sales of these intermediates to the affiliate, despite the fact that the local partner finds other suppliers at competitive or lower prices, serious conflicts could arise between the partners to the venture, which can disrupt the relationship.

The reverse could also occur when the foreign MNC wants to repatriate much of the profits earned by the IJV back to its home country. The local partner, on the other hand, may want to retain most of the profits earned by the IJV in the IJV for reasons of capital expansion and investment. If the foreign MNC insists on repatriating most of the IJV's earnings back to its home country leaving the IJV cash-poor this could not only negatively affect the marketing performance of the IJV, but worse, serious conflicts could arise between the partners leading to the ultimate demise of the venture (Dymsza, 1988).

The Julian (1998) study that examined the marketing performance of IJVs in Thailand provided support for these findings that major conflicts can erupt between the partners in an IJV with respect to the purchase of materials, intermediates and components. If the foreign corporation insists on the IJV purchasing raw materials from it, when the local partner finds other sources at competitive or lower prices serious conflicts could arise between the partners leading to the demise of the venture. The reverse could also occur when the foreign corporation wants to repatriate much of the profits earned by the IJV back to its home country. If the foreign corporation insists on repatriating most of the profits earned by the IJV back to its home country, serious conflicts could arise between the partners leading to the demise of the venture.

The obvious conclusion that was drawn from the Julian (1998) study in Thailand was that it is important for managers of IJVs to minimise the transference of the IJV's output to a parent company and to minimise the sourcing of the IJV's input needs from a parent company for marketing performance success. Companies intending to enter into an IJV arrangement in the countries of South East Asia should take the time to allow the IJV to operate as a stand-alone entity instead of using it as a means of generating additional revenue from out-of-date products or as a subsidiary to generate greater profits for head office.

11.2.6. Financial Capital

It is quite often the case that one partner in the JV is there primarily because of its ability to provide the necessary capital needs of the JV. This quite often occurs when one partner is from a developing country that has capital controls and a weak currency and the other partner is a large MNC from a developed country. Essentially, the MNC by possessing large capital resources and/or having access to a large financial borrowing capacity assumes the role of a financial intermediary to the JV entity and the local JV partner (Berg *et al.,* 1982; Blodgett, 1991b).

Access to low-cost capital has been mentioned as one of the MNC's potential contributions to the JV entity and the local partner firm (Lecraw, 1984). However, the low-cost capital provided by the MNC has been identified as not a crucial source of bargaining power for the MNC because the asset is explicit and undifferentiated (Blodgett, 1991b). For example, the Fagre and Wells (1982) study produced inconclusive findings for the effect of the variable 'capital access' on the likelihood of obtaining sole ownership of an investment. However, using size of the MNC as a proxy for capital access, Poynter (1982) obtained statistically significant results. In spite of the fact that the parent firm gains some leverage through loan guarantees and access to international capital markets, financing is the most basic, and least understood, of the assets contributed by the MNC as alternative sources of financing are possible (Blodgett, 1991b).

Nevertheless, the Julian (1998) study that examined the marketing performance of IJVs in Thailand identified the shortage of capital resources to develop the Thai market effectively as an important statement in the factor of market characteristics, and the statements comprising the factor of market characteristics produced a significant negative effect on the marketing performance of IJVs in Thailand. In fact, the market characteristics factor in the Julian (1998) study was the single most dominant factor in predicting IJV marketing performance in Thailand. So the importance of capital resources, whether provided by the IJV foreign partner or not, should not be underestimated as a predictor of IJV marketing performance. Furthermore, Beamish and Banks (1987) identified the importance to IJV performance of access to an adequate supply of capital resources and low-cost raw materials. The understanding that access to capital resources and low-cost raw materials is one of the major reasons the JV form of organisation structure has been used is built around the theory of internalisation (Beamish and Banks, 1987). The internalisation theory posits that due to the transaction costs that must be borne as a result of conducting business in imperfect markets it is more efficient (less expensive) for the firm to use internal structures rather than market intermediaries to serve a foreign market. The Julian (1998) study, therefore, provided support for the notion that a shortage of capital resources and raw materials had a significant negative influence on IJV marketing performance in a developing country of South East Asia.

11.3. Conclusions

Many researchers have identified the importance of a clear understanding of what each partner is bringing to the IJV relationship (Beamish, 1988; Dymsza, 1988; Fey, 1995; Blodgett, 1991a; Geringer, 1988; Harrigan, 1988a). Harrigan (1985) and Dymsza (1988) argue that IJVs are more likely to succeed when partners possess complementary missions, resource capabilities, managerial capabilities and other attributes that create a strategic fit in which the bargaining power of the venture's sponsors is evenly matched. A more successful JV creates synergies through the partners pooling their resources, capabilities and strengths. These synergies lead to the establishment of a manufacturing operation in which the total results are greater than the sum of the contributions of the partners. As a result of combining the modern production processes, the product know-how, technical training, management development and management systems of a foreign corporation with the local partner's local capital, management, existing plant, marketing expertise and knowledge of the country environment, the JV results in a more efficient and productive enterprise than the participants could achieve on their own. The synergies occur through the partners working closely together, reinforcing each other's strengths, the cross-pollenisation of ideas concerning management of the enterprise, responding to competition, and developing the potential of the business in the country environment.

However, a perception by the foreign or local partner that it is not obtaining sufficient benefits from the JV in return for its contribution of resources leads to the failure of some ventures (Dymsza, 1988). What counts is not only the actual contributions made by each party and the profits and other benefits obtained by each one, but even more what the partners perceive over the life of the operation. In some cases, the foreign corporation perceives that it is not obtaining an adequate return for its contribution of manufacturing and product technology, management, technical training, trademarks and business expertise. In other instances, the local partner believes that its contribution of existing factories and facilities, management, local capital, sales organisation and contacts with the government are excessive in relationship to its share of ownership, the responsibilities it has in the venture and the profits it earns. These perceptions of benefits obtained in relation to contributions made can change over the years. When one or both partners perceive an unsatisfactory ratio between benefits and costs from the venture, serious conflicts develop, leading either one or both partners to refuse to contribute any further resources to the venture until some of their demands are met; and if a stalemate develops it can likely lead to the failure of the whole venture (Beamish, 1988; Beamish and Inkpen, 1995; Dymsza, 1988; Gullander, 1976; Hladik, 1988; Wright and Russel, 1975). Therefore, it is concluded that the contributions or perceived contributions made by each of the IJV partners' will have an important and significant influence on IJV marketing performance.

12. Partners' Needs

12.1. Introduction

External environments that include, to name a few, industry structure, competitive intensity, technology and the policies of host-country governments differ between countries, and these country-related differences influence the structure of a joint venture (Harrigan, 1985; Lee and Beamish, 1995). Previous studies have shown that JVs are created for different reasons in developed and developing countries. For example, in a study on JVs from developed countries, Killing (1983) found that the major reasons for setting up a JV were the need for the other partner's skills, needs of the other partner's attributes or assets, and government pressure or legislation. The Fey (1995) study on IJVs in Russia identified that the Russian government had little option but to open up its market to JVs because an infusion of capital was needed, as was access to technology, foreign equipment and managerial expertise. Forming an IJV with Russian firms was attractive for the foreign partners as well, since forming a JV in Russia meant the possibility of access to one of the world's largest closed economies. Many foreign firms commenced IJVs in Russia to establish a presence there in order to be well positioned for access to the Russian market as the economy changed. Russia also possessed vast natural resources that were in high demand, as well as a well-educated labour force that was very attractive to many international firms (Fey, 1995). Furthermore, Beamish's (1985) sample of JVs from developing countries showed that government pressure or legislation was the primary reason for creating the venture.

As such, there are many reasons for establishing JVs in developed countries and in developing countries with the needs of the partners, whether they be private or state-owned enterprises, varying depending on whether they are from a developed country or from a developing country. Partners' needs are, therefore, the focus of this chapter.

12.2. Motivations for Foreign Direct Investment in Thailand

Taking Thailand as an example of a developing country in South East Asia, the major motivations for most foreign direct investment (FDI) in Thailand are the availability of cheap labour and raw materials, Thai government incentives and adequate local demand (Julian, 1998; Michener and Ramstetter, 1990; Sibunruang, 1986).

The firm-specific advantages of FDI firms in Thailand over local firms was analysed by Sibunruang (1986). Parent contributions to subsidiaries were observed and the characteristics and performances of the subsidiaries were compared with that of local firms. Using variables for finance, the different types of inputs, production technique, marketing know-how and management know-how, the results of the Sibunruang (1986) study show that important contributions were made in machinery, production techniques and international marketing. Less important contributions but nevertheless considerable were equity and management know-how. Contributions were shown to be similar when firms were distinguished by marketing orientation or by industry. Further, when tested across nationality of FDI, there were significant differences in the provision of financial resources, foreign marketing and management know-how between transnationals from developing countries and those from industrialised or developed countries (Economic and Social Commission for Asia and the Pacific, 1995; Julian, 1998).

Additionally, Michener and Ramstetter (1990) surveyed the FDI motives of US firms operating in Thailand. This study revealed the most important motives of US firms operating in Thailand were (1) access to factors of production, (2) market access, and (3) Thailand's general economic characteristics. Within these sets of motives, concern with access to the Thai market, and the size and growth of this market were most frequently mentioned. This indicates that most of the surveyed firms were heavily oriented towards the local market. The isolation of non-exporters indicated that a number of additional financial and input access variables were shown to be of secondary importance. In marked contrast to the non-exporting firms, exporting firms, whose numbers were few in the survey and which also were the larger firms studied, expressed exclusive concern with labour inputs, production for external markets, exchange rates and tax incentives. Of particular interest was the lack of negative influences in all samples and the related unimportance of Thai restrictions and requirements affecting transnationals (Economic and Social Commission for Asia and the Pacific, 1995; Julian, 1998).

Another survey of 105 US firms conducted in 1986 revealed that the major reasons for investing in Thailand were expansion of business activities, investment incentives and economic and political stability (Industrial Market Research Services, 1986). Major deterrents identified were excessive import duties, high company and income taxes, arbitrary or cumbersome customs and taxation procedures, lack of patent protection and restrictions on firm growth. The manufacturing firms in this survey continually cited 'labour quality' as an investment incentive, with other positive factors including 'the stabilising effect of the monarchy, the generally positive attitude of the Thai government, and the flair of the private sector' (Economic and Social Commission for Asia and the Pacific, 1995, p. 154).

On the other hand, high import duties and taxes, along with inconsistent and slow government administrative procedures were the main deterrents to investment. In the trade sector, the respondents frequently identified market or business expansion as the primary investment motive. Other important factors were the investment climate and incentives, replacement or upgrading of existing facilities, starting operations or adding facilities, and cost rationalisation or efficiency improvement. On the negative side, complaints were registered about growth restrictions and government interference, the lack of patent protection, high import or excise duties, monetary constraints or price controls, and import taxes (Economic and Social Commission for Asia and the Pacific, 1995; Julian, 1998).

The Japanese publishing company Toyo Keizai also surveyed the motives of Japanese investors in Thailand for a number of years. The surveys indicated that the most common motive of FDI in Thailand has been to increase sales of Japanese investors in local and third (i.e. non-local, non-Japanese) markets. The results for the 1993 survey indicated that expansion in sales in local markets is the dominant objective in this respect. The desire to benefit from Thai policies and protectionism was the second most important motive for Japanese investors investing in Thailand in 1981 and 1985. However, due to the gradual liberalisation of the Thai economy this motive has gradually declined in importance and in 1993 was only the fourth most important motive for Japanese investors investing in Thailand. The importance of these two motives reflects the import-substitution orientation of Japanese investment in Thailand, and in South East Asia in general, which is also highlighted in other studies such as Tambunlertchai (1977) and Yoshihara (1978). The import-substitution orientation is also reflected by Japanese affiliates selling the majority of their output in Thailand (Japanese Chamber of Commerce, 1978, 1981, 1984, 1990, 1994) and that most of the replying affiliates in the Toyo Keizai surveys indicated the local (Thai) market as their major market. In the Toyo Keizai surveys, reduction of labour costs as a motive of FDI by Japanese investors was the third most important motive in 1981 and 1985, the second most important in 1989, and the third most important in 1993. One of the reasons that all motives accounted for a lower share of all identified motives in 1993 than in previous years was that the 1993 survey included a much larger number of possible motives than previous surveys. Moreover, one of these motives, network forming, was apparently quite important, being the second most important motive in 1993 (Economic and Social Commission for Asia and the Pacific, 1995; Julian, 1998).

Unlike firms in developed countries, most Thai firms rarely have the monopolistic advantages derived from the access to advanced technology. As such, they are willing to form joint ventures to gain access to this technology and in return are willing to provide the foreign JV partner firm with local market knowledge and access to cheap labour and raw materials. Thus, it is believed that JVs in Thailand and other South East Asian country markets will be created primarily because of a need for the other partner's knowledge of the local market or local business practices, and for the foreign JV partner's access to advanced technology. When examining the factor of market characteristics in the Julian (1998) study (see Table 4.1), which was the dominant factor in predicting IJV marketing performance in Thailand, this is quite clearly evident where five of the dominant statements in the market characteristics factor related to a need for the local JV partner's knowledge of the local market and local business practices and for the foreign JV partner's technology and capital resources. The lack of or shortage of these resources in the market characteristics factor had a significant negative effect on the marketing performance of IJVs in Thailand.

12.3. Joint Venture Performance in the Developing Countries of South East Asia

One of the measures used in previous studies to predict JV performance has been instability within the JV, joint venture instability being defined as 'equity changes or major reorganizations that were unplanned from one or both partners' perspective' (Lee and Beamish, 1995, p. 640). Beamish's earlier work and other JV studies have demonstrated that for JV partners from developed countries, the joint venture instability rate is higher in less-developed countries than in developed countries (Beamish, 1985; Reynolds, 1979; Killing, 1983; Franko, 1971). This is primarily due to a lack of knowledge by the foreign JV partner of the local economy, politics and culture (Julian, 1998). Developing countries are a more uncertain environment to which the foreign JV partner must adjust.

Firms from developed countries assessed their JV performance in less-developed countries as unsatisfactory more frequently than those in developed countries (Beamish, 1985). However, in the Lee and Beamish (1995) study the Korean JVs with firms in South East Asia (i.e., Singapore, Indonesia and Thailand) that were investigated found the local business environmental patterns to be similar to Korea, about which the Korean firms had empathy and information (Kumar and Kim, 1984; Lee and Beamish, 1995). Furthermore, firms from developing countries or newly industrialised countries (NICs) do not confront as large a foreign knowledge gap regarding the economic situation when they enter less-developed countries and the developing countries of South East Asia (Lee and Beamish, 1995). As such, they may be less resistant to enter the developing country markets of South East Asia (Agarwal and Ramaswami, 1992) because they perceive less risk in doing so than do foreign investors from developed countries.

This can be due in part to the reason that many foreign JV partner firms from developing countries feel that the socio-economic conditions of the developing countries in South East Asia are similar to those that they had faced in their own domestic market in earlier periods. Thus, similar local business practices and a familiar economic environment lead to the conclusion that JVs between partner firms from developing countries or NICs are likely to achieve better JV performance than JVs from developed-country partners in less-developed countries or developing countries (Lee and Beamish, 1995).

12.4. Partners Needs' and Joint Venture Performance

Firms establishing joint ventures typically need partners for a variety of potential contributions. Several researchers have examined the effect of partner need on joint venture performance. Raveed and Renforth (1983) have shown that the two most important objectives of joint ventures were to obtain local market knowledge and local management. Beamish and Banks (1987), in a sample of 66 joint ventures in less-developed countries, found that greater need between partners resulted in more satisfactory performance. Later on the Lee and Beamish (1995) study demonstrated a pattern that managers in high-performing ventures looked to their local partners for greater contributions than did managers in low-performing ventures. Therefore, the Korean JVs in the Lee and Beamish study showed a positive relationship between the extent of desired partner need and satisfactory performance.

As regards the types of contributions that can be made by each JV partner firm to satisfy the other JV partners needs, the foreign JV partner firm can provide firm-specific knowledge regarding technology, management and capital markets whilst the local JV partner firm can provide location-specific knowledge regarding host-country markets, marketing infrastructure and political conditions. From the sharing of knowledge and the pooling of resources through the JV organisation form the foreign JV partner firm is able to reduce the uncertainty associated with market entry at a lower long-term average cost than through traditional hierarchical and market approaches. From the perspective that JV partner firms would have very little incentive to behave opportunistically, the derived condition of information matching due to uncertainty and opportunism would not arise (Beamish and Banks, 1987). Although bounded rationality would still be an issue, the hierarchical method of conducting transactions would not constitute the sole solution to this problem alone. The low costs associated with opportunism, the small numbers, uncertainty and information matching in JVs under these conditions would tend to indicate that this method of transacting is the most efficient means of entering a foreign market (Beamish and Banks, 1987).

Furthermore, the Beamish and Banks study observed a pattern of results and when the importance of the local partner's contributions to the foreign JV partner firm were compared in the successful and unsuccessful JVs the Beamish and Banks study findings provided support for the theory of internalisation. The theory of internalisation suggests that due to the transaction costs that must be borne as a result of conducting business in imperfect markets it is more efficient (less expensive) for the firm to use internal structures rather than market intermediaries to serve a foreign market (Beamish and Banks, 1987).

The Beamish and Banks study identified differences in the value attached to the importance of local partners' contributions between the successful and unsuccessful JVs in terms of human resource needs, government, political and knowledge needs. The findings of the Beamish and Banks study identified as significantly important to the foreign JV partner firms involved in successful JVs, their local JV partner firms' contributions of general managers, functional managers, general knowledge of the local economy, politics and customs, and knowledge of current business practices. Not only were none of these local JV partner firm contributions important to the foreign JV partner firms involved in unsuccessful JVs but these foreign JV partner firms went further and identified the local JV partner firms' contributions of general and functional managers as being unimportant (Beamish and Banks, 1987). Of significance in the Beamish and Banks study of 66 JVs in less-developed countries was the relationship between success and obtaining access to local knowledge, and the relationship between lack of success and not attaching importance to this local partner contribution.

Furthermore, in the Beamish and Banks study the only area in which the foreign JV partner firms in the unsuccessful JVs felt their local partner made an important contribution was in the area of satisfying existing or future government requirements for local ownership. In this case, any local partner would meet their requirements because it was only access to the local JV partner's nationality (as opposed to knowledge) that was required. As such, any national partner would do and there would be no small numbers constraint. However, when the local partner was chosen primarily because of its nationality, poor performance was the result (Beamish and Banks, 1987).

Beamish (1988) also found that partners' needs were good predictors of both satisfactory and unsatisfactory performance. For example, MNE executives from the low-performing JVs regarded their local partners' contributions as unimportant, whilst those from the high-performing ventures considered their partners' contributions as being important.

Furthermore, the finding that partners' needs were significantly related to Korean JV performance, but ownership rates or commitment were not, was consistent with the result of Lee's (1989) previous research on Korean JVs (Lee and Beamish, 1995). Also, this finding coincides with those from JVs from developed countries in less-developed countries, where greater need between partners resulted in more satisfactory performance (Beamish, 1988).

The Lee and Beamish (1995) study suggested that the characteristics of Korean JVs in less-developed countries were, firstly, the need for the partner's local knowledge was a more important reason for creating a venture than government regulation on ownership. Secondly, Korean JVs were more stable than developed-country JVs. Thirdly, the stability of Korean JVs was related to the type of local partner whether they be government or public shareholder or private firm. Fourthly, the most common ownership level of Korean partners in JVs in the developing countries of South East Asia was a minority one. These findings were very much consistent with the findings of the Julian (1998) study on the marketing performance of IJVs in Thailand. Fifthly, the overall satisfaction with the performance of Korean JVs was higher than that of developed-country JVs in less-developed countries (Lee and Beamish, 1995). The Lee and Beamish study findings tend to suggest that the characteristics of JVs differ depending on the development stage of both the originating country and the host country.

Choosing a partner when establishing an IJV is the most important decision a foreign corporation will ever make. If the wrong partner is chosen, the venture is simply doomed to fail. IJVs that select a partner that is only needed initially, often do not make it in the long run once that partner is no longer needed. It is very important that all partners in the IJV are truly necessary and that they will continue to be needed in the future. Of course, it is also very important that firms select partners they can trust, and that each partner to the IJV clearly understands each other's objectives for the IJV and that they determine whether all sets of goals are mutually obtainable and compatible (Fey, 1995).

Harrigan (1985) also argued that JVs are more likely to succeed when the partners possess complementary missions, resource capabilities, managerial capabilities and other attributes that create a strategic fit in which the bargaining power of the JV partner firms is evenly matched. Partners' needs to be engaged in a particular IJV are stabilising to the relationship, whilst a wide variety of asymmetries are destabilising to the IJV relationship. Partners' asymmetries can occur in relation to the size of their assets, national origin and experience in using the JV structure. Significant asymmetries among the JV partners can be stabilizing to the JV relationship (survival and duration) because partners each need what the other can supply, but harmful to venturing performance (success) because their heterogeneity can exacerbate the difference in how the JV partners value their JV's activities. Thus, JV partners will stay together as long as they need each other and their venture remains successful, unless the terms invoked by the bargaining agreement's 'divorce clause' are so restrictive that they constitute an exit barrier that perpetuates a partnership long after its usefulness, to at least one of the partners, has expired (Caves and Porter, 1976; Harrigan, 1980, 1988a; Porter, 1976).

Furthermore, the findings of the Harrigan (1988a) study suggest that JVs are more successful where partners are related in products, markets and/or technologies to their JVs or horizontally related to them than when they are vertically related or unrelated to their JVs. The Harrigan study findings also suggest that JVs last longer between partners of similar cultures, asset sizes and JV experience levels, and when the JV's activities are related in products, markets and/or technologies to both of its partners.

Fey (1995) in his study on the key success factors for Russian IJVs found the most common cause of IJV failure was a basic misunderstanding about the roles and objectives of the partners. In most cases these differences existed from the very beginning, but the parents were not aware of them because they did not spend enough time initially learning about each other's objectives for the IJV. In-depth discussions during the formation stage could have alerted the parents to most of these differences so that they could have been resolved early. Or it could have been determined that the differences could not be resolved, and thus concluded that the firms should search for other partners. Of course, everyone is eager to finalise the negotiation phase and get on with the work of the IJV. Nevertheless, data in the Fey study showed that spending extra time in the negotiation phase to understand the other partner's objectives for the IJV was a wise investment.

Other major problems with the foreign partners identified by the Russian/foreign JV general managers in the Fey study included a shortage of the necessary investment of resources and insufficient attention paid to the JV entity. Furthermore, the JV's general managers had two significant problems with the local partners. Firstly, the Russian parents did not invest enough money in the JV entity, thereby making it difficult for the JV to operate efficiently because it was under-resourced. Secondly, the Russian parents were far too bureaucratic, thereby slowing down their business transactions. According to the Fey study findings the conclusion that was drawn suggests that with many of the Russian/foreign JVs the problems developed because the partners and the JV's management did not understand each other's resources and interests well enough when forming the JV. Many of the problems would have been apparent if the JV partners had discussed more openly the level of involvement they wanted in the JV and the amount and type of resources they were prepared to commit (Fey, 1995).

Anderson (1990), Dymsza (1988), Harrigan (1988a) and Koot (1988) also provide support for this process by identifying that the foreign corporation and the local partner in an IJV that fails may have significant differences in their objectives and goals with respect to the business, depending upon the size and type of companies involved; their particular business, industry and products; and their international and other experience. For example, a foreign corporation may desire to enter into a viable and expanding manufacturing operation through a JV that will yield a target rate of return on investment in the medium to long term. Therefore, it strives to reinvest a substantial portion of earnings in the venture in order to expand the operation and increase its return over this time horizon. The local partner, on the other hand, enters into the JV to earn an immediate rate of return on its investment. Therefore, it strives for a maximum pay-out of dividends. The situation, of course, can be the reverse. The foreign corporation may have the goal of a quick payback on its investment of capital, technology and management, for example, three to five years. The local partner may strive to develop a growing, profitable manufacturing business yielding satisfactory profits over the medium to long term. These divergent business objectives and goals over significantly different time-frames will require different marketing strategies for them to be achieved. A delay or stalemate between the partners over the implementation of the appropriate marketing strategy could have a negative influence on the marketing performance of the IJV, or it could cause the IJV to fail altogether.

12.5. Conclusion

As such, a successful JV provides for complementary contribution of resources by the major parties involved. The contribution by the foreign JV partner firm depends on the industry in which it is involved, its product lines, its business orientation, i.e. market, production or sales orientation, and many other factors. In many manufacturing operations, the major contributions of the foreign JV partner firm and the needs of the local JV partner firm include the foreign JV partner firm's technology, technical product knowledge, patents, expertise, technical training and management development. The significant contributions of marketing-oriented firms include product differentiation, trademarks, brand names, effective marketing programmes and training. Although some foreign JV partner firms are not necessarily export oriented or prefer to export from their home country or wholly owned subsidiaries, some of them do make available their global marketing network to expand exports (Julian, 1998; Lee and Beamish, 1995). The local JV partner firm in a manufacturing IJV commonly contributes some combination of capital, management, knowledge of the country environment and the market, and contacts with the government, financial institutions, local suppliers and labour unions (Dymsza, 1988) which is what most foreign JV partner firms enter into IJV arrangements in developing countries to gain access to. These contributions from the local JV partner firm to the foreign JV partner firm are not insignificant to say the least.

A more successful JV creates synergies through the partners pooling their resources, capabilities and strengths. These synergies are likely to lead a manufacturing operation in which the outcome is greater than the sum of the individual partners' contributions. By combining the modern production processes, the product know-how, technical training, management development and the management systems of a foreign MNC with the local

JV partner's capital, management, existing plant, marketing expertise and knowledge of the local market environment, the JV results in a more efficient and productive enterprise than the participants could achieve on their own. The synergies occur through the partners working closely together, reinforcing each other's strengths, the cross-pollenization of ideas concerning management of the JV, responding to competition and developing the business potential of the JV in the local market environment (Dymsza, 1988).

Furthermore, JVs can provide a suitable means of entry into a manufacturing operation in a developing company for a smaller or medium-sized international company, with limited capital and international managerial experience, but no great breadth in such management. At the same time, it limits the exposure to risk by such an international company. The local partner in such a JV provides a combination of local financing, an existing plant and facilities, most of the management, its marketing expertise, and relationships with the government, financial institutions and other groups. The manufacturing technology, the product know-how, technical training and business expertise contributed by the international firm lead to a more efficient manufacturing and marketing operation, introducing new products and/or improving existing products. As such, partners' needs and contributions provided by the local and foreign JV partner firms that are complementary result in a more successful venture.

13. Top Management Teams of International Joint Ventures

Craig C. Julian (University of Adelaide)
Carolyn B. Mueller (Stetson University)
Renee Wachter (Montana University)
Cheryl Van Deusen (University of North Florida)

13.1. Introduction

There are several advantages to entering a foreign country through an international joint venture (IJV) versus through a wholly owned subsidiary. For example, an IJV allows firms to share costs and risks of foreign entry and use their local partner's knowledge of the local markets, consumer tastes and business practices (Agarwal and Ramaswami, 1992; Johnson *et al.*, 2001; Makino and Delios, 1996; Kogut and Singh, 1988). However, IJVs also entail unique risks because cultural differences among managers may create problems when running their operation that may lead to conflict and even dissolution of the venture (Chaterjee *et al.*, 1992; Geringer and Hebert, 1991; Johnson *et al.*, 2001; Shenkar and Zeira, 1992; Wallace, 1992).

In previous studies, differences in the cultural backgrounds of the top managers responsible for the day-to-day operations of an IJV have been perceived as a threat to the venture's survival (Chua and Kin-Man, 1993; Ding, 1997; Mueller, 1994; Wallace, 1992). Presumably, these differences have led to problems among managers, particularly during strategic decision-making activities where group processes are negatively affected. However, in other studies, differences in the cultural backgrounds of the top managers because of shared management control between the IJV partners have been viewed as a positive contribution towards IJV performance (Beamish, 1993; Fey and Beamish, 2001; Phatak and Chowdhury, 1991; Yan and Gray, 1994). If one looks at IJV performance in the developing countries of South East Asia, like Thailand, shared management control is by definition a situation where diversity and heterogeneity will be present in the top management team (TMT). Therefore, the main objective of this chapter is to better understand how the various elements of diversity in an IJV top management team most positively influence goal attainment in a developing-country context in one of the developing countries of South East Asia.

To date the majority of studies on IJV TMTs have been conducted in developed countries (Goll *et al.*, 2001; Park and Ungson, 1997) with very little attention given to developing countries, especially those in South East Asia. Given the growth in the literature on IJV TMTs one ponders the lack of interest in South East Asia given the economic growth rates of several South East Asian countries over the past two decades and the emphasis on Asia by many governments around the world for trading opportunities. Given the paucity of IJV TMT studies conducted in the South East Asian countries, a further objective of this chapter was to examine the relationship between top management team composition, group processes and the effects of those processes on goal attainment for IJV teams in Thailand to see if the findings support previous findings generally from studies conducted in a developed-country context.

IJVs have been described in a variety of ways with general agreement that equity IJVs involve two or more legally distinct organizations which are headquartered in different countries (the parents), each of which controls a percentage of ownership shares, actively participating in the decision-making activities of the jointly owned entity (the venture) (Beamish and Banks, 1987). As such, in this chapter the authors define an IJV as a separate legal organizational entity representing the partial holdings and joint control of two or more economically and legally independent parent firms, where both the venture operation and headquarters of one parent firm are located in Thailand and the headquarters of the other parent firms are located outside of Thailand.

The presence of two or more parent organizations from different cultures and geographic locations tends to make an IJV a complex form of organization structure that is often difficult to manage (Baysinger and Hoskinson, 1989; Child *et al.*, 1992; Collins and Doorley, 1991; Lane and Beamish, 1990). Parents can be competitors as well as collaborators and enter into a venture for different reasons, control unequal levels of resources, bring differing levels of commitment to the venture and receive unequal benefits (Brown *et al.*, 1989; Shenkar and Zeira, 1987; Wallace, 1992). Also, because parent organizations are legally separate entities, each has its own corporate culture and managerial way of doing things which further increases managerial complexity and complicates issues of coordination and joint problem-solving for managers (Harrigan, 1988a; Lane and Beamish, 1990; Parkhe, 1991; Schaan and Beamish, 1988).

As managers of IJVs tend to come from different organizational and national cultures, they often speak different primary languages and have different orientations to business and management practices (Collins and Doorley, 1991; Schneider and De Meyer, 1991). Different cultural and personal orientations have also been found to affect communication patterns and practices, and frequently to result in confusion, annoyance and misunderstandings among IJV managers (Camerer and Vepsalainen, 1988; Lane and Beamish, 1990; Wallace, 1992). Therefore, despite their increased frequency and strategic importance, it is not surprising that IJVs have often been unsuccessful due to cultural dissimilarities and management problems of communication, coordination, control and goal diversity between the parents (Barkema *et al.,* 1996; Blodgett, 1992; Geringer, 1991; Hall, 1991; Lane and Beamish, 1990).

Yet, other studies (e.g., Park and Ungson, 1997) have identified that IJV partners from culturally distant countries have longer durations and are less likely to end. Empirical tests suggest that prior relationships between firms may provide a powerful counterbalance to cross-cultural differences (Barkema *et al.,* 1996; Bleeke and Ernst, 1993; Park and Ungson, 1997). Prior relationships between partners create trust and familiarity (Gulati, 1995; Park and Russo, 1996). Trust attenuates opportunistic behaviours and facilitates conflict resolution. Familiarity enhances a partner's transparency and reduces the costs of monitoring its activities (Park and Ungson, 1997), thereby enhancing performance. As such, with so many different and sometimes conflicting findings it makes sense to understand better how the various elements of diversity most positively influence goal attainment. That is one of the primary objectives of this chapter.

13.2. Literature Review

13.2.1. Top Management Teams

Prior studies of IJVs support the belief that a venture's TMT is a critical component of venture success (Collins and Doorley, 1991; Goll *et al.,* 2001; Hambrick *et al.,* 1996). This belief is based on the notion that the involvement of top managers in the operation of their organization affects performance and goal attainment (Goll *et al.,* 2001; Hall, 1984; Harrigan, 1985).

The importance of TMTs is generally based on the belief that the effective management of complex organizations requires the participation of multiple individuals at an organization's top level because each contributes different kinds of knowledge and expertise (Amason, 1996; Goll *et al.,* 2001). Thompson (1967) suggested that the contributions of multiple top managers are necessary in situations that require significant, non-programmed decisions where the nature of the relationships is often not known. Since the complexity, dynamism and ambiguity of such decisions tends to overwhelm the knowledge of any one person (Mason and Mitroff, 1981), top managers often work in teams to address important problems within their organizations (Eisenhardt, 1989; Schweiger and Sandberg, 1991).

The nature and outcomes of TMT member interactions and team processes have been argued to influence and shape an organization (Eisenhardt, 1989). Therefore, an understanding of the context and nature of team processes that affect strategic decision-making within IJVs should strengthen the association of strategic management with organizational performance. This association is consistent with a number of studies conducted in non-venture contexts where a significant relationship was found between the nature of TMT processes and a firm's financial performance (e.g., Dennison, 1990).

13.2.2. Strategic Management and Decision-Making

Assessing environmental opportunities and threats and organizational strengths and weaknesses are basic activities of strategic management (Smircich, 1983). Although these assessments may be formed objectively, they are often influenced by the highly subjective perceptions and interpretations of managers (Dutton and Duncan, 1987). Therefore, different interpretations of events trigger different processes as well as different behaviours in individuals (Amason, 1996).

Organizational goals, strategies, managerial intentions and motivations are intangible and top managers must deal with economic, legal, political and social factors that are hard to define and analyse. Therefore, when disagreement about choices in organizations is high, political processes are often used to obtain desired outcomes (Pfeffer, 1981). For example, when members of an IJV TMT are similar with respect to cultural and more general demographic characteristics, they would tend to approach problem-solving similarly and, therefore, reach agreement more often during the strategic decision-making process (Hambrick and Mason, 1984). In contrast, heterogeneous teams, whose members are dissimilar on the same characteristics, would be more prone to political behaviour since their perceptions of problems would be more likely to differ (Lane and Beamish, 1990). Thus, while social interaction encourages the formation of a common reality among managers, the social interaction process itself may be significantly influenced by other pressures that commonly surround managers.

Despite these influences, team members must meet the simultaneous demands of parent organizations, of various employee groups in their organizations, as well as of other internal and external stakeholders in the host country and other countries in which an IJV conducts business. To do so, team members must translate their various expectations into workable strategies. Therefore, establishing and maintaining a cooperative work environment is often critical for effective team performance (Fey and Beamish, 2001; Smith *et al.,* 1994).

A survey of the literature (e.g., Amason, 1996; Fey and Beamish, 2001; Katzenbach and Smith, 1993; Smith *et al.,* 1994; Wallace, 1992) suggests that team performance is highly dependent on team processes such as the level of cooperation, cohesiveness and mutual accountability, as well as individual responses to team processes such as trust and commitment to a team purpose or performance goals. Others suggest that performance is dependent on the quality of a team's output or decisions (Goll *et al.,* 2001). This implies that effective TMTs must pay attention to issues that relate to tasks as well as issues that relate to group maintenance (Amason and Schweiger, 1992).

TMT members must interact with each other in order to reach high-quality decisions, implement those decisions, and to continue to work together to guide their organization. However, when member differences negatively affect or impede the processes and interaction that members need to function together as a team, organizational performance is impaired (Knight *et al.,* 1999).

Group heterogeneity, on the other hand, is related to greater creativity and innovation (Bantel and Jackson, 1989; Murray, 1989). Heterogeneity is expected to bring a diversity of viewpoints to the decision-making process as individual group members have different interpretations and perspectives (Wiersema and Bantel, 1992). In the Hambrick *et al.* (1996) study they found that TMTs that were diverse had an overall positive effect on performance. IJV TMTs tend to include managers who differ from each other in general demographic as well as cultural backgrounds. As is evidenced by the literature and the conflicting findings, some studies suggest that group decision-making is enhanced by considering various alternatives and solutions (Goll *et al.,* 2001) whilst others are suggesting that differences among venture managers tend to be complex and negatively affect team performance and the achievement of venture goals (Knight *et al.,* 1999). With such diametrically opposed views the only conclusion that can be drawn is that research on TMTs and IJV success factors is far from conclusive, requiring further research on TMT diversity that positively impacts upon performance.

The literature supports the notion that because they have different experiences in organizational and national backgrounds, members of an IJV's TMT tend to be quite dissimilar from each other (Schneider and De Meyer, 1991). As a result, these teams tend to be highly diverse groups of managers who may have difficulty communicating with each other, developing trust and maintaining commitment amongst themselves, and working cohesively to achieve venture goals (Fey and Beamish, 2000, 2001; Ding, 1997). The literature also supports the notion that despite their inherent heterogeneity, members of IJV TMTs must communicate with each other and build trust and cohesion among themselves to enable managers to reach high-quality decisions (Goll *et al.,* 2001). Furthermore, frequent communication, trust and cohesion is required so decisions can be implemented in a timely fashion and so team members can continue to work together as a team to successfully run their organization (Smith *et al.,* 1994). If not, the IJV will ultimately fail. This overview has placed the variables of interest within the context of this chapter. Each construct is discussed next.

13.2.3. Effects of Culture

National cultural differences among managers have been found to negatively affect the nature of managerial interactions and result in poor working relationships (Child *et al.,* 1992). As a result, some have argued that deeply rooted cultural differences at the top management level, because of their effect on managerial relationships and strategic decision-making, are likely to have a direct bearing on a TMT's ability to realise stated venture goals (Barkema *et al.,* 1996). Shenkar and Zeira (1992) assert that tensions among top managers of IJVs are often high because actions or attitudes are often misinterpreted due to cultural differences. These tensions often result in mistrust by one parent of the objectives of the other parent firm(s) (Shenkar and Zeira, 1992) who often pass feelings of mistrust down to managers whom parents appoint to their IJV's TMT, ultimately affecting the working relationships of these managers.

When an IJV has been formed which links dissimilar cultures, there is always a risk the arrangement will fail because managers are too dissimilar and become unwilling or unable to compromise together to resolve such differences (Brown *et al.,* 1989; Lane and Beamish, 1990). Research suggests that this impasse is likely to occur when IJV executives are dissimilar with respect to their demographic characteristics, if they enjoy differing socio-economic roots, or if their concepts of the role of the venture differ from that of other managers (e.g., Kogut and Singh, 1988; Putnam and Poole, 1987; Schneider and De Meyer, 1991). Therefore, the theory that cultural differences negatively affect business organizations is well supported, and researchers have consistently linked management problems of IJVs to cultural differences (Barkema *et al.,* 1996).

However, this is not always the case, as Park and Ungson (1997) discovered. Park and Ungson concluded from their study that prior relationships between firms provide a powerful counterbalance to cross-cultural differences. The Park and Ungson findings were consistent with Harrigan's (1988b) findings, with Bleeke and Ernst's (1993) case study result that cross-border ventures can overcome early difficulties caused by cultural differences, and with Barkema *et al.'s* (1996) suggestions that learning between partners may offset cultural differences. Prior relationships between partners create trust and familiarity (Gulati, 1995; Kogut, 1989; Park and Russo, 1996). Trust attenuates opportunistic behaviours and can facilitate conflict resolution. Familiarity enhances a partner's transparency and can reduce the cost of monitoring its activities, thereby enhancing performance (Park and Ungson, 1997).

Additionally, partners' compatibility on specific organizational attributes can also affect the dissolution and performance of joint ventures (Fey and Beamish, 2001; Gray and Yan, 1992; Lane and Beamish, 1990). Dissimilarities in organizational structures, processes and organizational climate (Fey and Beamish, 2001) can create problems that could lead to the dissolution of the joint venture. In contrast, similarity in partners' organizational structures, processes and organizational climate can facilitate mutual understanding and collaboration (Fey and Beamish, 2001; Park and Ungson, 1997). This view is consistent with that of Bleeke and Ernst (1993) who found that cross-border ventures are not as troublesome as joint ventures between companies with strong and weak cultures. Fey and Beamish (2001) argued that the compatibility of organizational processes and organizational climate may be more significant than the similarity of national cultures in explaining the dissolution, performance and duration of a joint venture. As dissimilar partners in a JV may spend more time and energy establishing managerial processes that facilitate communication, they may incur higher costs and mistrust than similar partners in a JV (Park and Ungson, 1997). It appears, then, that team composition and member interactions or processes affect strategic decision-making.

13.2.4. Importance of Team Composition

The composition of a TMT, defined by the amount of similarity (i.e., homogeneity) or difference (i.e., heterogeneity) among team member characteristics, is generally considered to be important because of its effects on decision-making processes within organizations (Hambrick and Mason, 1984). Similarly, research on social interaction indicates that the probability of conflict is high among managers with differing demographic attributes because they are not likely to share the same goals, attitudes and values (Putnam and Poole, 1987). As a result, researchers such as Michel and Hambrick (1992) have argued that the demographic composition of a TMT will affect the strategic decision-making process, and that differences in demographic attributes, by increasing the level of conflict among members, may influence social interaction in a potentially negative manner.

In their summary of research on team composition and performance, Filley *et al.* (1976) concluded that routine problem-solving is best handled by homogeneous teams, but solving ill-defined or strategic problems is best handled by heterogeneous teams. This chapter acknowledges that solving strategic problems is best handled by heterogeneous teams (Goll *et al.,* 2001), but differences among team members have been found to negatively affect member interactions, resulting in dysfunctional conflict (Putnam and Poole, 1987). While some level of conflict has been found to be beneficial during strategic decision-making, a dysfunctional level of conflict within TMTs is likely to impede the development of trust, cohesion and frequent communication among members (Fey and Beamish, 2000). Therefore, it appears that team composition and member interactions or processes affect strategic decision-making.

13.2.5. Team Processes and their Effects

Empirical studies of IJVs have consistently identified several factors that are associated with successful versus unsuccessful ventures (Ding, 1997; Inkpen and Beamish, 1997; Madhok, 1995; Yan and Gray, 1994). Results of these studies suggest that effectively managing an IJV depends on top managers' abilities to develop trust (Madhok, 1995) and work cohesively as a team as well as displaying a willingness to communicate, cooperate and negotiate any disputes (Fey and Beamish, 2000; Mueller, 1994; Smith *et al.,* 1994; Wallace, 1992). That is, previous research on IJVs suggests that the difficulties and the effects of differences among IJV managers are significantly reduced when levels of communication, trust and cohesion are high (Amason, 1996; Fey and Beamish, 2001; Smith *et al.,* 1994).

To develop the coordination, cooperation and decision quality required to achieve IJV goals, then, IJV managers must overcome any negative effects of heterogeneity and become integrated as a team within a management culture that encourages frequent communication, trust and cohesion (Goll *et al.,* 2001). To do so, IJV managers must engage in the decision-making process in such a way that encourages quality decisions without facilitating dysfunctional conflict that would prevent the implementation of those decisions (Ding, 1997; Fey and Beamish, 2000). Based on these conclusions, the effects of communication, trust and cohesion are included in this chapter.

13.2.6. Decision Quality, Decision Implementation and Goal Attainment

When investigating the relationship between team heterogeneity and creative problem solving, most previous studies have considered processes of uninational teams whose members were committed to or held loyalties to a single organization (Bantel and Jackson, 1989). However, managers who constitute an IJV TMT often come from separate or distinct cultures and have well-developed beliefs and methods for dealing with the complexities of corporate decision-making. Thus, while excessive levels of trust and cohesion may lead to inferior decisions, theory posits that this outcome is not likely within IJV TMTs due to the complex nature of heterogeneity found in such teams (Goll *et al.,* 2001; Mueller, 1994).

As a consequence, managers with different backgrounds and organizational experiences are likely to have different attitudes and values and hold divergent points of view (Bantel and Jackson, 1989). Team member differences may encourage debate among managers to such an extent that communication problems and negative reactions by members to the team experience (Roberts and O'Reilly, 1979) inhibit the development of cohesion and trust. These problems would tend to limit interaction among team members and the exchange of valuable information. As a result of this decreased communication and increased conflict associated with team heterogeneity, it could negatively influence team decision-making processes and outcomes (Bantel and Jackson, 1989). Specifically, low levels of trust and cohesion and less frequent communication are likely to negatively affect the quality of decisions these teams generate (Knight *et al.,* 1999).

However, as previously discussed, prior relationships between firms provide a powerful counterbalance to cross-cultural differences (Park and Ungson, 1997). Prior relationships between partners create trust and familiarity (Gulati, 1995; Kogut, 1989; Park and Russo, 1996). Trust attenuates opportunistic behaviours and facilitates conflict resolution. Thereby, enhancing the quality of decisions these teams generate (Park and Ungson, 1997).

Other studies suggest that decision implementation is also influenced by the nature of team member interactions (Schwenk, 1990). Findings regarding the positive relationship between team processes and decision quality are consistent with research on group problem-solving (Hambrick *et al.*, 1996), but do not support arguments from the information processing perspective which contend that team heterogeneity interferes with group communication and interaction processes and leads to dysfunctional conflict (Bantel and Jackson, 1989). Therefore, in addition to their effects on decision quality and team composition, team processes may also affect members' reactions to the team experience that may be critical to its continued success, the implementation of decisions and the achievement of organizational goals.

Based on the previous discussion, a model of the variables that affect IJV TMT member processes is shown in Figure 13.1. The relevance of cultural and demographic team heterogeneity to this research is based on their effects on the group processes of cohesion, trust and communication, and the resulting quality of decisions, effective implementation of decisions and, ultimately, on IJV goal attainment (Kogut and Singh, 1988; Putnam and Poole, 1987; Schneider and De Meyer, 1991). To review, both cultural and demographic heterogeneity have been found to negatively affect trust, cohesion and the frequency of communication within multicultural teams because managers are either disinclined or unable to overcome their differences easily in order to function as a team (Barkema *et al.*, 1996).

Other studies suggest that team heterogeneity positively affects decision quality because member differences tend to encourage the consideration of a wider range of alternatives during decision-making (Goll *et al.*, 2001; Park and Ungson, 1997). At the same time, heterogeneity has been found to negatively affect implementing team decisions through its indirect influence on trust, cohesion and communication frequency (Knight *et al.*, 1999). As such, heterogeneity is expected to directly but negatively affect trust, cohesion and communication frequency, indirectly but negatively affect decision implementation, and indirectly but positively affect decision quality within TMTs.

Figure 13.1 Path Model

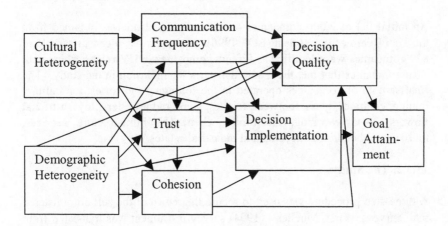

Regarding the team process variables, research and theory on cohesion and its importance to team processes support the contention that frequent communication positively affects trust, trust positively affects cohesion, and that cohesion and communication frequency positively affect and reinforce each other (Fey and Beamish, 2000; Mueller, 1994; Smith *et al.,* 1994; Wallace, 1992). All three process variables positively and directly affect decision quality and decision implementation. Finally, high-quality decisions and the implementation of those decisions have been found to positively affect the attainment of organization goals (Amason, 1996; Goll *et al.,* 2001; Michel and Hambrick, 1992). This chapter is designed to test these relationships on multicultural top management teams of IJVs in Thailand.

13.3. Research Methodology

13.3.1. The Sample

The relevant sample consisted of Thai companies that are in joint venture relationships with non-Thai firms. Two restrictions were used to identify the sample of IJV firms for this study. Firstly, no partner could have 95 percent or greater equity participation in the venture and, secondly, each partner must have greater than 5 percent equity participation. Although there is no consensus on a cut-off point to distinguish a joint venture from a wholly owned subsidiary (Horaguchi, 1992), the international business literature has used 95 percent or less equity as a cut-off point to differentiate a joint venture from a wholly owned subsidiary. Major studies that have used the 95 percent cut-off point include Anderson and Gatignon (1986), Gomes-Casseres (1989) and Hennart (1991). Therefore, this study followed the same convention.

An initial list of 2,000 companies operating in Thailand was obtained from the Thai Board of Investment (BOI, 1996). From this list, a census sample of 829 companies was identified as foreign companies in IJV relationships with Thai companies that met the required criteria for inclusion in the study. The final sample of companies operated in the following industries: agriculture, mining, ceramics, glass, footwear, textiles, gems and jewellery, toys, artificial flowers, metal working, electronics, chemicals, infrastructure services, tourism and hotels, and housing and industrial estates.

13.3.2. The Study

A three-step procedure was used to secure the return of the self-administered mail surveys. First, Mueller's (1994) survey instrument was translated from English into Thai and then back translated to ensure that the intended meaning of the statements was accurate. To reduce confusion and ambiguity, the survey was pre-tested through personal interviews with the managing directors of ten foreign/Thai IJVs in Thailand, and minor revisions were made.

Second, a covering letter and a copy of the revised survey were sent to all managing directors of companies identified as IJVs in Thailand. The covering letter as well as all instructions and statements had both English and Thai translations. In an effort to increase the response rate, a stamped self-addressed envelope addressed to a colleague at Bangkok University who had agreed to collect the completed questionnaires was included in the mailing.

Third, two weeks after the questionnaires were mailed, several attempts were made to contact each recipient via telephone to answer questions and encourage participation. Eighty eight (10.6 percent response rate) individual responses were received. It should also be acknowledged that this response rate is normal for most mail surveys (Groves, 1990; McDougall *et al.*, 1994) and similar response rates had been achieved in prior international marketing research by Kaynak and Kuan (1993) and Li and Ogunmokun (2000), and sample sizes of 53 have been reported in previous research (Mintu-Wimsatt and Calantone, 2000). It is acknowledged that, in general, the majority of US-based studies achieve a relatively higher response rate. However, considering the sample was drawn from a developing country where the first language was not English, and where many of the respondents' primary language was not English, the response rate was quite acceptable.

Given that the findings indicate a reasonable response rate, an extrapolation procedure was used to assess non-response bias to determine if respondents were similar to non-respondents (Armstrong and Overton, 1977). Frequencies and independent *t*-tests were used to determine whether significant differences existed between the sample of 88 respondents and the target population of Thai/foreign IJVs using the classification criteria of industry membership. It was determined that no significant differences existed between the sample and the target population for this classification variable. Therefore, the sample can be considered sufficient to draw conclusions about Thai/foreign IJVs for the issues under study.

13.3.3. The Research Instrument

A multi-item questionnaire was used to collect the data. The research instrument was designed to measure two independent (cultural and demographic heterogeneity), three process (cohesion, trust and communication frequency), and three dependent (decision quality, decision implementation and goal attainment) variables. Each construct in the research instrument is discussed below. Regarding data type, the use of open-ended response measures was considered. However, evidence suggests that structured scale measures similar to those used here are generally preferable to other methods for assessing attributions.

13.3.3.1. Heterogeneity

Both general demographic characteristics and culture-based demographic characteristics were measured. Items used to measure demographic heterogeneity were team member's age, level of education, functional specialisation and length of team tenure. Items measuring cultural heterogeneity included member nationality, primary language spoken, country of education and organizational culture background (parent organization affiliation, if any). Each of the eight items was a self-report measure.

13.3.3.2. Communication Frequency

Two measures were constructed to evaluate how frequently team members communicated with each other. Each measure used a seven-point Likert-type scale ranging from 1, 1-5 times a week, to 7, more than 30 times a week. The first measure was based on subjects' responses of how frequently they communicated with other team members via seven of the most common types of communication media used in a business context (Russ *et al.,* 1990) as well as in social situations. For the second measure, respondents were requested to indicate how frequently they communicated with their respective team mates who were affiliated with a parent organization versus team mates with no such affiliation. Higher scores on these measures indicated more frequent communication among members. The coefficient alpha for communication frequency was .87, well above the .70 level suggested by Nunnally (1978).

13.3.3.3. Trust

Through a content analysis of managers' suggestions and two previous studies of managerial trust, Butler (1991) developed the Conditions of Trust Inventory which includes one general, overall measure of trust proven to be reliable in several different contexts (e.g., Mueller, 1994). Therefore, this measure of trust was included in the questionnaire and consisted of four response items, one that is reverse scored to provide scale continuity. Higher scores indicated the presence of trust and lower scores reflected its absence. Generally, the four items required respondents to indicate the degree to which other members of their respective teams could be trusted. The coefficient alpha for trust was .71, above the .70 level suggested by Nunnally (1978).

13.3.3.4. Cohesion

A four-item cohesiveness index developed by Seashore (1954) was used to assess this construct. Seashore's (1954) index defined cohesion into four dimensions: (1) how readily members defended other team members from outside criticism, (2) how well members helped each other on the job, (3) how well members got along with each other, and (4) how well members stuck together as a team. Because Seashore's index did not measure cohesion relative to the group task, a fifth measure was added to reflect the commitment of members to the group task: (5) how well members coordinated their work toward common objectives. The coefficient alpha for cohesion was .76, above the .70 level suggested by Nunnally (1978).

13.3.3.5. Decision Quality, Decision Implementation and Goal Attainment

As decision quality, decision implementation and goal attainment were related to effective group processes during decision-making, these measures were grouped together in the questionnaire following a statement that requested subjects to respond based on decisions that their TMT had made during the last six months. While keeping items measuring these three constructs together in a group, individual items were alternated on the questionnaire to reduce the effect of respondent bias. Again, seven-point Likert-type scales ranging from 1, 'strongly disagree' to 7, 'strongly agree' were provided for responses for all items measuring these variables.

For decision quality, each respondent was asked to rate the overall quality of decisions his team made, the quality of alternative decisions his team considered, as well as the quality of alternative decisions the team chose. The coefficient alpha for decision quality was .65, indicating modest reliability even though .60 is acceptable for a three-item scale (Anderson and Coughlan, 1987). For decision implementation, respondents were asked to assess how well they understood the decisions their team made, their degree of commitment and support for those decisions, and the degree of assistance each provided to implement their team decisions. The coefficient alpha for decision implementation was .87, well above the .70 level suggested by Nunnally (1978). Finally, for goal attainment, respondents were asked to indicate their perceived degree of consensus among their team members on venture goals, their level of understanding of which goals were more important, and their perception of whether their team successfully reached its goals. The coefficient alpha for goal attainment was .83, again well above the .70 level suggested by Nunnally (1978).

13.4. Data Analysis

All of the items used to measure the two types of heterogeneity were categorical in nature. Therefore, Blau's (1977) index of heterogeneity (1-Σ pi^2) – where p is the proportion of group members in a category, and i is the number of different categories represented in a team – was used to construct the two separate measures of demographic and cultural heterogeneity. The means, standard deviations, reliability coefficients, and intercorrelations for the model variables are presented in Table 13.1.

Table 13.1 Correlations of Variables

	IJV Size	Team Size	Cult-Hetero	Demo-Hetero	Com Freq	Trust	Coh	Decis Qual	Decis Impl	Goal Attain
IJV Size										
Team Size	.701**									
Cult-Hetero	-.002	.384								
Demo-Hetero	.856**	.735**	.497*							
Com Freq	.206	.218	-.445	-.034						
Trust	-.010	-.196	.318	.273	-.190					
Coh	-.409	-.635**	.119	-.095	-.233	.730**				
Decis Qual	.240	-.074	.273	.517*	-.237	.619**	.698**			
Decis Impl	-.380	-.542*	.133	-.049	-.158	.489*	.913**	.771**		
Goal Attain	-.211	-.488*	-.007	.036	-.061	.439*	.864**	.820**	.972**	
Mean			.22	.28	2.71	4.274	4.925	4.906	5.444	5.329
Std.			.18	.15	1.46	.716	.886	.896	1.293	1.412
Alpha					.87	.71	.76	.65	.87	.83

* $p < .05$

** $p < .01$

*** $p < .001$

Next, a 'full effects' path model incorporating all of the possible relationships was analysed. Path regression was used to test the model and all model linkages were tested. Because of the possible influence of organizational size and team size on both the antecedent and outcome variables, they were included in the analysis as control variables. In this study, demographic and cultural heterogeneity and the control variables of team size and IJV size were the exogenous variables. Communication frequency, trust, cohesion, decision quality, decision implementation and goal attainment were the source variables. Five regression equations were used to identify significant causal relationships or paths among the variables. The assumptions that underlie path analysis (linearity, additivity, interval level of measurement, uncorrelated residuals) were not an issue given the theoretical basis for the model and an inspection of the scatterplots of residuals. Path coefficients for the model are found in Table 13.2.

Table 13.2 Path Regression Results

Dependent Variable	Explanatory Variable	Standardized Coefficients	R^2
Communication Frequency	Constant	2.33	.39
	IJV Size	-1.18	
	Team Size	.50	
	Cultural Hetero.	*-.89	
	Demographic Hetero.	1.21	
Trust	Constant	6.41	.69
	IJV Size	-.79	
	Team Size	-.75	
	Cultural Hetero.	.00	
	Demographic Hetero.	*1.59	
	Com_Freq	-.28	
Cohesion	Constant	4.81	.81
	IJV Size	-.39	
	Team Size	-.54	
	Demographic Hetero.	.43	
	Cultural Hetero.	-.08	
	Trust	*.53	
Decision Quality	Constant	1.98	.97
	IJV Size	-.32	
	Team Size	-.06	
	Trust	**-.65	
	Cohesion	**1.20	
	Com_Freq	**-.30	
	Cultural Hetero.	-.20	
	Demographic Hetero.	**1.17	
Decision Implementation	Constant	1.07	.98
	IJV Size	-.39	
	Team Size	-.03	
	Trust	**-.81	
	Cohesion	**1.45	
	Com_Freq	-.08	
	Demographic Hetero.	*.74	

Dependent Variable	Explanatory Variable	Standardized Coefficients	R^2
	Cultural Hetero.	-.00	
Goal Attainment	Constant	-1.11	.98
	IJV Size	*.37	
	Team Size	-.11	
	Decision Implement.	**1.21	
	Decision Quality	-.20	

* $p < .05$
** $p < .01$

13.4.1. Descriptive Statistics

In relation to the breakdown by nationality of the JV foreign partners, approximately 50.0 percent of the JV foreign partners came from Japan, 23.5 percent came from Western Europe, 11.8 percent of the JV foreign partners came from North America, the remainder of the sample of JV foreign partners came from Australia, ASEAN, India and Taiwan. This is very much consistent with the trends of foreign direct investment (FDI) in Thailand with Japan and the US being the principal contributors of FDI in Thailand since 1978 (Julian, 2001).

IJV teams ranged in size from two to nine members, and averaged five members per team (Mueller, 1994). The majority of respondents ranged from 40 to 49 years old, and had been at their organization an average of eight years. The majority (65.9 percent) of respondents had earned a four-year degree, 29.5 percent had Masters degrees and 2.3 percent held high school diplomas. Seven different countries of education were represented: 39.8 percent were primarily educated in Thailand, 10.2 percent in North America, 11.4 percent in Japan, 5.7 percent in the ASEAN[1] group of countries, and 4.5 percent each in India, Taiwan and Western European countries.

Seven different primary languages were represented: 53.4 percent spoke Thai, 17 percent English, 14.8 percent Japanese, 5.7 percent Mandarin, 2.3 percent Hindu, and 2.3 percent each spoke Taiwanese and French. Six different nationalities were represented: 67 percent were Thai, 14.8 percent

---

[1] The Association of Southeast Asian Nations includes Singapore, Thailand, Bruneii, The Philippines, Malaysia, Cambodia, Vietnam, Myanmar, Laos, and Indonesia.

Japanese, 4.5 percent Western European, 4.5 percent each were Indian and Taiwanese, and 2.3 percent Chinese.

Most respondents indicated they had some prior business experience: 23.9 percent in accounting/finance/economics, 21.6 percent in general business, 18.2 percent in production/operations, 17 percent in marketing/public relations, 9.1 percent in engineering, and 5.7 percent in research and development. Fifty-three percent were affiliated with a parent organization.

13.4.2. Top Management Team Characteristics and Group Processes

13.4.2.1. Communication Frequency

The correlation coefficients in Table 13.1 show that communication frequency was significantly correlated only with the degree of cultural heterogeneity in these teams. Regressing communication frequency on the full set of four explanatory variables yielded a significant R^2 of .39 ($p < .01$). Following the pattern of the correlations, only cultural heterogeneity was a significant predictor of communication frequency. Further, increased heterogeneity was negatively related to communication frequency.

13.4.2.2. Trust

As expected, there were significant correlations between trust and cohesion, decision quality, decision implementation and goal attainment. Regressing trust on the control variables, cultural and demographic heterogeneity, and communication frequency produced a significant R^2 of .69 ($p < .01$). While not apparent in the correlation pattern, demographic heterogeneity was the only significant predictor of trust in the regression analysis. Unexpectedly, the more diverse a team was with regard to demographics, the higher the level of trust reported. Communication frequency and cultural heterogeneity did not contribute much to predicting levels of trust among members of these teams.

13.4.2.3. Cohesion

Neither measure of heterogeneity was significantly correlated with cohesion. However, trust, decision quality, decision implementation and goal attainment all had significant associations with cohesion. Team size was also significantly correlated with cohesion but negatively, as might be expected. Regressing the control variables, trust, and both types of heterogeneity on cohesion yielded a significant R^2 of .81 ($p < .01$). However, the only significant predictor of cohesion was trust. Increased levels of trust were positively associated with increased levels of cohesion, but neither the control variables nor the heterogeneity measures were significant predictors of cohesion.

13.4.2.4. Decision Quality

The control variables, trust, cohesion, communication frequency and the heterogeneity variables were regressed against decision quality and yielded a significant R^2 of .97 ($p < .01$). For these IJV teams, trust, communication frequency, cohesion and demographic heterogeneity were significant predictors of decision quality. Higher levels of communication were associated with lower levels of perceived decision quality. Unexpectedly, trust was also associated negatively with decision quality. Cohesion, however, was positively associated with decision quality. Finally, greater demographic heterogeneity was associated with better decision quality.

13.4.2.5. Decision implementation

The control variables plus trust, cohesion, communication frequency and heterogeneity were regressed against decision implementation. The R^2 was .98 ($p < .01$). Results for decision implementation were similar to those found for decision quality. Trust was negatively associated with decision implementation, and cohesion and demographic heterogeneity were positively associated with decision implementation.

13.4.2.6. Goal attainment

Regressing the control variables, decision implementation and decision quality against goal attainment yielded a significant R^2 of .98 ($p < .01$). IJV size and decision implementation were positively related to goal attainment.

13.5. Discussion

The position taken in this research, that the effects of demographic and cultural heterogeneity in IJV TMTs are more complex than researchers have previously considered, was based on research that supports the conclusion that the rate of success for joint ventures is particularly poor for cross-cultural top teams (Knight *et al.,* 1999). The additional complexity of cultural influences on team member interactions increases the level of team heterogeneity and undermines the working relationships of venture managers unless they can become integrated to some degree and function as a team (Goll *et al.,* 2001).

One of the key findings of the study was the variable effect of heterogeneity. Apparently, cultural rather than demographic differences were more influential in determining the amount of communication that takes place in IJV teams. The closer team members were on cultural factors such as nationality, country of education and language, the more communication among them occurred. The lack of barriers for interpreting not only words themselves, but also context or frame of reference, greatly increased the level of communication that transpired. Interestingly, the level of communication activity did not necessarily increase levels of trust. The mean level of communication frequency was quite low (2.71, std = 1.46), lower than one might have expected given the likely necessity of increased communication for resolving ambiguities and conflicts of interest. This might signify that these managers believed that greater levels of communication were desirable. These results were somewhat different than those of Jackson *et al.* (1991), where reduced communication and increased conflict were associated with greater demographic diversity.

The building of trust, on the other hand, seemed to be more dependent on the size of the team and differences in age, education level, functional experience and parent organization affiliation. However, the results were not as expected. Differences in age, level of education, affiliation with a parent organization and type of functional experience were associated with greater levels of trust. Perhaps these differences were perceived by respondents as strengths rather than as points of contention.

In this study, the development of cohesion was dependent only on trust. Neither cultural nor demographic heterogeneity was a direct, significant predictor of cohesion. Rather, these results suggest that the effects of heterogeneity manifest themselves primarily through other variables that mediate the relationship between heterogeneity and cohesion.

A common assumption in the management literature is that heterogeneous teams tend to yield higher-quality decisions than do homogeneous teams because members tend to bring unique contributions and perspectives to the decision-making process (Wiersema and Bantel, 1992). In this study, such an assumption was supported, at least for the effects of demographic heterogeneity. One might have expected that not only demographic but cultural differences among a team's members might encourage argumentation and debate to such an extent that they inhibit managers from effectively defusing dysfunctional conflict (Barkema *et al.,* 1996). Apparently, the levels of mutual trust within these teams provided managers with a mechanism to translate their differences into effective decision-making.

The same pattern of results was found for the effects of demographic heterogeneity on decision implementation. High levels of demographic heterogeneity lead to perceptions that decisions were implemented effectively. This is contrary to research that suggests that such a decision-making team may initially perform its task well and make high-quality decisions, yet 'burn itself up' in the process by generating so much divisiveness and conflict among members that they are unwilling or unable to communicate effectively and work together in the future (Barkema *et al.,* 1996).

In summary, the effects of heterogeneity were not always as expected. Instead of a negative influence on decision quality and implementation (Bantel and Jackson, 1989), demographic heterogeneity was associated with greater levels of trust and improved decision quality and implementation. It may be that different perspectives, brought about by experience, wisdom and different functional viewpoints, helped increase the level of confidence managers had during their decision-making and implementation activities (Wiersema and Bantel, 1992). Levels of trust, perceived decision quality and decision implementation were all reasonably high.

13.6. Limitations

Some limitations of the study should be noted. Firstly, caution should be exercised in inferring causality from the model tested. The cross-sectional nature of the data makes this inference tenuous. Secondly, as in every research study investigating model interrelationships, model specification is a major concern. The process of selecting the variables and specifying their interrelationships was based on and guided by available theory, prior empirical findings, and the stated purpose of the study. Model misspecification was still possible, especially due to the omission of other antecedents of decision quality and implementation. Thirdly, from a methodological perspective, a potential concern may be that the measures were all self-reported. Consequently, the relationships tested may be susceptible to the influence of common method variance. Efforts were made to minimise the problem by pre-testing the instrument and selecting measures that minimise item overlap. While utmost care was taken with the translation of the instrument, items still may be interpreted differently by individuals with different cultural and organizational backgrounds. Fourthly, the findings can only be inferred to Thai/Japanese; Thai/Western European; and Thai/North American JVs as Japan, Western Europe and North America provided 85.3 percent of the principal foreign partners in the sample. Finally, the sample size was smaller than desired and the risk of misinterpreting the results due to sampling error increases with small sample sizes.

13.7. Implications for Future Research

The results and limitations of the study suggest several areas for future research on IJV teams and heterogeneity. Clearly, the study should be replicated with larger samples and IJVs from different cultures. The presence of heterogeneity in IJV top management teams and its relationship to the communication patterns and group processes which determine organizational performance (and other outcomes) is an under-researched topic and should be a fruitful area for further research. Moreover, the relationship between different types of heterogeneity and group outcomes requires more empirical work because some types of heterogeneity seem to cause different types of effects than others. Future research efforts could also investigate parent firm and IJV team contexts concurrently. Other competitive environments could be sampled, particularly high-growth, complex and unstable environments. In such environments, greater heterogeneity might have different effects on managers than those reported here. Finally, future empirical efforts could utilise longitudinal designs to overcome the cross-sectional nature of the current work.

14. Equity Joint Ventures and the Theory of the Multinational Enterprise

14.1. The Theory of Internalization

Internalization theory was developed to provide a basis for the development and proliferation of the multinational enterprise (MNE). Multinational enterprises are firms that establish operations in a foreign market as a means of serving that market rather than engaging in transactions with market intermediaries from a distance. The theory of internalization suggests that because of the transaction costs that occur as a result of doing business in imperfect markets it is more efficient (or less expensive) for the firm to use internal structures rather than market intermediaries to serve a foreign market (Beamish and Banks, 1987).

Williamson's (1975) conclusions suggest that these imperfect markets occur when two primary conditions are prevalent in the environment of the foreign market, these two primary environmental conditions being uncertainty and a small number of market agents. When these circumstances exist in a foreign market with two sets of human factors, opportunism and bounded rationality, Williamson suggested that the costs of conducting business with market intermediaries from a distance are greater than the costs of internalizing the market. That is, if a MNE faced a complex, uncertain marketing infrastructure and business environment that had few potential channel members to utilise it would be more profitable performing the distribution function itself if there was a strong likelihood that market agents would try to take advantage of the firm's lack of market knowledge and the MNE was unable to specify all possible future transaction contingencies (Beamish and Banks, 1987).

Researchers in international business have been very successful in providing a sound basis for the development and proliferation of an MNE as a way to participate in imperfect markets using the transaction cost theory (See

Beamish and Banks, 1987; Hennart, 1991; Park and Russo, 1996; Rugman 1981; Teece 1981). When extending this rationale to international markets, international business researchers have often evaluated separately the strategies of vertical integration and horizontal diversification because the cause of market failures is different in each case. The rationale behind the internalization of markets with vertical integration is about the failure of markets in intermediate goods. As far as horizontal diversification is concerned it is about the failure of markets in intangible assets for such things as management know-how, trade name or licensed technology. Although the completeness of the transaction cost framework has provided the theory of internalization with sound reasoning (Rugman, 1981, 1985), it is still inconclusive in relation to some aspects as a general theory for the MNE. The major limitation, as concluded by Beamish and Banks (1987), was that the theory up to 1987 only included one kind of organizational structure, that being the wholly owned subsidiary.

Prior to the Beamish and Banks paper the theory of internalization provided the MNE with only one solution to the problem of imperfect international markets, that being the establishment of a wholly owned subsidiary (WOS). However, as Beamish and Banks correctly identified there are a number of other market entry modes that firms can adopt to deal with imperfections in international markets including licensing, franchising, subcontracting and JVs. Furthermore, MNE's often use more than one market entry mode when entering a foreign market (Julian, 2004). As such, for the theory of internalization to be regarded as a general theory for the MNE it would need to provide a basis under which the other market entry modes could operate (Hennart, 1991) and identify the circumstances under which each different market entry mode would provide efficiency gains over wholly owned subsidiaries in the market. Therefore, the objective of this chapter is to use the Beamish and Banks framework to provide a sound basis for IJVs in the developing countries of South East Asia within the internalization framework (Beamish and Banks, 1987).

14.2. Joint Ventures and the Internalisation Theory

One of the major reasons for using the equity joint venture organisation form is a need for the attributes or assets of the other partner. Assets include such things as cash, capital resources and raw material sources (Beamish, 1993; Beamish and Banks, 1987; Julian, 1998). The understanding that access to capital resources and low-cost raw material access is one of the major reasons the JV form of organisational structure has been used is built around the theory of internalization (Beamish and Banks, 1987).

The theory of internalization, as already identified, suggests that because of the transaction costs associated with conducting business in imperfect markets it is less expensive for the MNE to use internal structures rather than market intermediaries to serve a foreign market. These imperfect markets occur when two primary conditions are prevalent in the environment of the foreign market, these two primary environmental conditions being uncertainty and a small number of market agents. When these circumstances exist in a foreign market with two sets of human factors, opportunism and bounded rationality, Williamson (1975) argued that the costs of conducting business with market intermediaries from a distance are greater than the costs of internalizing the market (Beamish and Banks, 1987). As such, if the theory of internalization was related to the JV market entry mode in the developing countries of South East Asia, it could be suggesting that it is more efficient or less expensive for the MNE to acquire the assets or resources needed (cash, capital or raw materials) from the local JV partner to conduct its business in a foreign market than from a market intermediary quite some distance away.

One of the most important issues confronting the management of an MNE considering engaging in a JV in one of the developing countries of South East Asia could be the problem of opportunism. However, even Williamson (1975, 1983) considered that opportunistic behavior is not always inevitable between firms engaging in some kind of JV. Furthermore, Beamish and Banks (1987) suggested that in situations where a JV is established in a spirit of mutual trust and commitment to its long-term benefit, opportunistic behaviour is unlikely to emerge. This is quite similar to the notion of mutual forbearance described by Buckley and Casson (1988b) where agents, on a reciprocal basis, deliberately pass up on short-term advantages for a long-term gain. With trust JV partners, especially where one JV partner is from a developing country of South East Asia, would be more willing to exercise tolerance and would continue with the JV long enough to see it through its difficult period. Problems like opportunism can be dealt with appropriately by the MNE without damaging the JV's long-run viability and the effectiveness of the arrangement between the JV partners. In circumstances such as these, overcoming the problem of opportunism would depend more on the approach adopted by management than on company lawyers manipulating the JV contract (Beamish and Banks, 1987).

If such a positive approach can be supported through inter-firm arrangements such as the manner in which profits will be divided in the JV arrangement, joint decision-making processes, and reward and control systems, the likelihood of JV partners engaging in opportunistic behaviour will be minimised (Beamish and Banks, 1987; Williamson, 1983). Under such an environment the problem of opportunism is unlikely to occur because each of the JV partners would be able to pursue and achieve their own objectives and goals for the JV without a need to resort to guile. The JV partners would be able to negotiate amongst themselves what each requires from the JV based on their respective contributions over time, and they should be able to establish an amicable division of profits and return on investment for each JV partner in an open and fair way (Berg and Friedmann, 1980). Being able to achieve this, the JV partners could then turn their attention towards long-term profit maximisation for the JV as there would be no need to make intermittent profit claims on the JV that could damage the JV's long-term performance. As such, the JV partners could take the long-term view for investment purposes whilst at the same time being able to adjust to changing market conditions, because of the mutual trust between the partners and a lack of opportunism demonstrated by each of the JV partners thereby enhancing the JV's overall performance (Beamish and Banks, 1987).

A small numbers situation, particularly when included with opportunism, can result in serious difficulties for the MNE (Williamson, 1975). In the case of JVs in the developing countries of South East Asia, even if initially there were many local firms from which to select a suitable JV partner, a small numbers condition could occur if the MNE wanted to change the JV contract at a later date and seek a new partner. Having had some experience with the MNE, the initial local JV partner would have cost advantages over the other local firms not originally selected. The decision to change JV partners is, therefore, not advantageous for the MNE. However, in the absence of opportunism by the local JV partner in a South East Asian developing country JV, this small numbers situation could be less of a transactional problem than normally might be expected. Furthermore, by creating those interfirm arrangements mentioned earlier, it is more than likely that the JV partners will be able to manage many of the types of difficulties associated with individual or joint maximisation of profits (Contractor, 1985). There will be much less of a need to secure individual benefits through strategic posturing, and the best interests of the joint venture can be promoted. Therefore, under the conditions already identified, the small numbers problem can quite easily be handled through a JV (Beamish and Banks, 1987).

The problem of uncertainty can also be handled quite well through some IJVs. Without opportunism and small numbers there are strong incentives for the partners to a JV to pool their respective resources. By pooling its resources through a JV arrangement it is possible for the MNE to economise on the information requirements of foreign direct investment (Beamish,

1984). Through an IJV the MNE can provide firm-specific knowledge regarding technology, management and capital markets whilst the local JV partner can provide location-specific knowledge regarding host-country markets, infrastructure, political trends and raw materials (Beamish and Banks, 1987). The MNE, by pooling and sharing information through the JV organizational structure, is able to reduce the uncertainty and risk associated with conducting transactions in foreign markets at a lower long-term average cost than it would be able to do through a traditional hierarchical approach or through market intermediaries.

In such a JV arrangement the environment between the parties would be such that the parties would have little incentive to behave opportunistically because the condition of information impairment due to uncertainty and opportunism would not occur. Although bounded rationality would still continue to be an issue, the traditional mode of conducting transactions in imperfect foreign markets would not represent a superior solution to this problem alone. The low costs associated with opportunism, small numbers, uncertainty and information impairment in JVs under the conditions outlined would tend to suggest that this mode of conducting transactions in foreign markets is the most efficient means of serving a foreign market (Beamish and Banks, 1987).

If the theory of internalization is applied to the JV market entry mode it could suggest that it is more efficient or less expensive for the MNE to acquire the assets or resources needed (cash, capital or raw materials) from a JV partner to conduct its business in a foreign market than from a market intermediary quite some distance away. From that premise Beamish and Banks (1987) identified the importance to IJV performance of access to an adequate supply of capital resources and low-cost raw materials.

As a result of the Beamish and Banks (1987) findings the Julian (1998) study on the marketing performance of IJVs in Thailand included under the factor of market characteristics two items measuring accessibility to low-cost raw materials and capital resources. The Julian (1998) study provided support for the Beamish and Banks (1987) study findings where access to capital resources and low-cost raw material access was confirmed as having a significant influence on IJV marketing performance in Thailand. Access to capital resources and low-cost raw material access were two dominant statements in the seven-statement factor of market characteristics. Market characteristics was the dominant factor in the Julian (1998) study explaining more than 19 percent of respondent variation on issues about the marketing performance of IJVs in Thailand. Furthermore, the market characteristics factor in the Julian study was the strongest predictor of IJV marketing performance in Thailand, thereby confirming the importance of access to capital resources and low-cost raw material access for IJV marketing performance success in Thailand. Finally, the Julian study and its findings in relation to the market characteristics factor provides support for the theory of internalization as a general theory of the MNE when using IJVs as the market entry mode for operating in Thailand.

14.3. Joint Ventures in Developing Countries

Prior to World War II, the main thrust of private international corporate activity in the developing nations was toward commodity trade and/or foreign direct investment involving full ownership. In the post-war years, three factors have been significant in modifying this concentration on export and foreign direct investment. The first has been the rising tide of nationalism with the most pervasive goal being that of rapid and sustained economic growth and development aimed at achieving economic independence. The foreign direct investment of MNEs has increasingly been perceived by less-developed countries (LDCs) as less than satisfactory contributions to this goal (Ahn, 1980; Ali and Sim, 1995; Beamish, 1984, 1993; Connolly, 1984; Wright and Russel, 1975; Zhao and Culpepper, 1995).

A second factor has been the explicit recognition that in order to achieve their ambitious growth and development goals, developing countries require a massive purposeful inflow of technical, managerial and entrepreneurial skills. The final factor affecting the emergence of new forms of corporate involvement has been the increasing technical complexity of much of the capital equipment exported to developing countries. Technology, telecommunications and basic production equipment are all required desperately by these nations as a development base (Wright and Russel, 1975).

Developing countries have responded to these factors by attempting to modify foreign corporations' involvement in their country. This has been achieved through more effective integration of economic activity under national development plans; maintaining full sovereignty and satisfying nationalistic sentiments; controlling the transfer of resources specifically required for development; minimising the time over which foreign exchange is spent on importing corporate skills; and minimising the time in which control of the operations lies with the foreign corporations (Wright and Russel, 1975).

There are many considerations required of developing countries when viewing relations with a foreign MNE, including the amount of local employment, the supply and price of goods, access to marketing systems and foreign exchange earnings. However, two considerations increasingly dominate: developing countries are determined to retain or regain control of economic decisions in order to ensure that these decisions are compatible with national objectives; and they acknowledge the importance of acquiring a sufficient quantity and quality of high-level skills to make effective control possible (Beamish, 1984; Blodgett, 1991a; Dymsza, 1988; Ganitsky *et al.,* 1991; Wright and Russel, 1975). Developing countries seek to minimise the surrender of control to foreigners, while at the same time maximising skills acquisition.

In order to achieve these objectives, developing countries are increasingly resorting to such measures as nationalisation of the foreign enterprise, exclusion of all foreign investment from certain fields, insistence on local capital participation in foreign corporate ventures, discriminatory taxation, selective foreign exchange restrictions, selective bureaucratic delays and foreign employment restrictions. Independence, national sovereignty and a more representative and sophisticated national leadership have made such measures feasible (Beamish, 1993; Wright and Russel, 1975).

Developing countries are increasingly in control of the natural resources and markets sought by foreign corporations, and the balance of power between the negotiating parties has swung towards the host nation. Previous researchers (Beamish, 1984, 1993; Fey, 1995; Koot, 1988; Lee and Beamish, 1995; Makino and Beamish, 1995; Wright and Russel, 1975) have identified additional factors that have contributed to the change in the relative bargaining power of foreign corporations and host-country governments. Some of these include, firstly, a new code of conduct toward the 'poor' countries has been imposed upon the industrial states and this has sharply limited the responsiveness of their foreign policy to private business interests. Secondly, the competition among the industrialised countries often permits the 'host' country to play one foreign investor off against another to secure terms most advantageous to itself. Finally, the growth in developing countries of local entrepreneurship, both public and private, in areas once the domain of capital, confronts the foreign investor with this dilemma: their very success in the host country promotes the growth of local capabilities that threaten the MNE's continued existence (Wright and Russel, 1975).

Basic factors such as return on investment and commercial risk are of fundamental concern to any firm. However, in the developing world, effective control of operations and the risk of compounding earnings or seizing assets command particular attention in the present environmental circumstances. In the international scene, there are as many differences in conception of faithfulness and moral duty as there are interpretations of profitability. Experience in developing countries reveals that both foreign and local JV partners grant themselves the authority as well as the moral right to alter contractual statements unilaterally without any consultation (Dymsza, 1988; Hodgetts and Luthans, 1994; Kogut and Singh, 1988; Koot, 1988).

Prior to 1980, maintaining effective control over the local JV partner by the MNE was seen as a fundamental prerequisite for ensuring overall corporate success (Anderson and Gatignon, 1986; Geringer and Hebert, 1989; Hill *et al.*, 1990; Jaeger, 1983; Sohn, 1994). Local JV partners in developing countries could have been doomed to become silent or even fake partners who after a few years had no effect on the performance or management of the venture's business (Connolly, 1984; Koot, 1988; Sethi *et al.*, 1990; Wright and Russel, 1975). Control in such an environment had many facets: profitability was controlled through operating decisions that ensured efficiency and effectiveness of the purchasing, production and marketing effort. Growth was controlled through investment and dividend policy and basic marketing strategy, including territory allocation for export marketing (Cavusgil and Zou, 1994). The MNE once could have achieved and maintained control of its overseas operation with relative ease. The operations of the parent company can be exported in a ready-made form in such a way that no adaptation in manufacture or sales methods is needed, keeping product quality and brand name intact. Many of the biggest multinationals, particularly in capital-intensive or high-precision product industries, try to transmit the exact design of managing the new operations to the newborn stepchild company (Wright and Russel, 1975).

If the venture is to keep the standards and procedures of the parents and negotiate on any adaptations, the parent can be said to mould the venture. In many developing-country ventures with a dominant partner, this seems to be the case as well (Koot, 1988). Today, control objectives set for the IJV by either one or both of its parents are often on a collision course with those of the host nation, and the accustomed degree of control becomes increasingly difficult to achieve. The risk element also traditionally has been a fundamental consideration of the firm. But in the past, risk was viewed primarily in terms of normal commercial risk. The new risk of impairment of earning power or seizure of assets is increasingly real and of prime concern for the foreign MNE. Based on these realities, the JV form of organisational structure has continued to gain acceptance in the developing countries of South East Asia (Julian, 1998).

Historically, the trend of foreign direct investment in developing countries has been marked by a continuous worldwide decline of 100 percent direct investment whilst the share of foreign minority holdings in JVs has been increasing at the expense of majority participation (Beamish, 1984, 1993; Gomes-Casseres, 1989; Higginbottom, 1980; Julian, 1998; Makino and Beamish, 1995; Millin, 1984). This trend is also evident in South East Asia where they pursue the 'indigenisation policy' with great consistency. Therefore, it can be predicted that in the future, foreign minority holdings will be the rule rather than the exception (Ahn, 1980; Baker and McKenzie, 1993; Higginbottom, 1980; Julian, 1998).

Apart from a few exceptions, foreign investors in most South East Asian countries are obligated to carry out their investment activities through the medium of JVs with indigenous partners. JVs between foreign and indigenous entrepreneurs are a special form of foreign direct investment and may occur through the establishment of a new enterprise in the legal form of a separate entity; through the participation of local partners in an existing foreign enterprise; or through the participation of foreign partners in an existing indigenous enterprise.

The governments of many South East Asian countries do not as a rule welcome the third variant and therefore sanction it only in rare cases (Ahn, 1980; Higginbottom, 1980). JVs are held to have positive importance as an instrument of investment policy that may be hoped to improve the effectiveness of foreign direct investments (Ahn, 1980; Higginbottom, 1980; Julian, 1998).

It is assumed that nationalistic feelings in developing countries may induce the state to keep foreign investments under strict control. The local public thinks of a foreign direct investment without indigenous participation as foreign, while a JV is frequently held to be a national firm. When it comes to the final decision a JV is less at risk than a direct investment. As several South East Asian countries tend to pursue a 'fading-out' strategy, involving the successive reduction of foreign interest in implemented projects, this can also be an added incentive for foreign investors to engage in JVs from the outset (Ahn, 1980; Beamish, 1993; Julian, 1998).

14.4. The Performance of Joint Ventures in Developing Countries

Research on JV performance has proliferated since the early 1970s and is one of the primary topics for IB researchers interested in JVs. Franko (1971) initiated research on JV performance, arguing that JVs can exhibit instability in ownership structure and in which ownership positions can change. Anderson (1990), Beamish (1985), Blodgett (1992a), Geringer and Hebert (1991), Gomes-Casseres (1987) and Hennart (1991) refined definitions and empirical evidence for JV performance, with Inkpen and Beamish (1997) providing the essential condition that if ownership changes were unplanned or unanticipated for the JV that it was to be considered unstable if ownership changes did eventually occur. Kogut (1988) supported the survival of a JV as the critical variable to be included when measuring its performance (Delios and Beamish, 2004).

Apart from research on what constitutes JV performance, another group of researchers have examined a broad variety of theoretical perspectives on this subject (Yan, 1998; Yan and Zeng, 1999; Das and Teng, 2000). At an industry or macro level, the matter of JV performance is likely to be included in entry mode and performance research that has also included many different theoretical approaches (Woodcock *et al.,* 1994). At a firm or micro level, the different theoretical approaches range from Parkhe's (1993b) game theory approach on JVs, to the network approach (Gulati 1995) to the learning, conflict and management-based approaches on JVs and JV performance (Inkpen and Beamish, 1997; Hambrick *et al.,* 2001). Included with the management-based approach are the design characteristics of the JV, for example, division of equity ownership, in order to promote the positive role of learning in the JV relationship over the destabilizing force of conflict (Beamish, 1985; Blodgett, 1992a). As suggested in the many reviews of JV performance, JV termination rates and changes in ownership structure are a product of destabilising and stabilising forces (Yan, 1998; Yan and Zeng, 1999), that occur in a series of internal inconsistencies, for example, cooperation versus competition and short-term versus long-term market orientations (Das and Teng, 2000; Delios and Beamish, 2004).

Yan (1998), Yan and Zeng (1999) and Das and Teng (2000) help integrate the diverse theoretical approaches into compelling frameworks with Julian (1998) and Yan and Zeng (1999) focusing on how a JV performs financially or in terms of satisfying partner objectives. The various indicators of JV performance can lead to different inferences about the success or failure of a JV that vary according to the different national settings the studies have been conducted in (Beamish and Delios, 1997b).

Studies using financial performance measures have shown that 100 percent foreign ownership by MNEs tends to have a higher perceived financial performance than IJVs for subsidiaries established in Western Europe (Nitsch *et al.*, 1996) and North America (Woodcock *et al.*, 1994). However, in South East Asia, JVs have a better perceived financial performance than 100 percent foreign ownership (Makino and Beamish, 1998) and higher success rates in developing economies (Delios and Beamish, 2004; Newman, 1992; Yan, 1993).

Much of the JV literature links the performance of foreign subsidiaries to national differences (Pennings *et al.*, 1994; Shenkar and Zeira, 1992). Even a cursory glace at the JV literature suggests that JVs formed in developed and developing countries demonstrate different performance outcomes, with JVs formed in developing countries exhibiting higher performance (Beamish and Delios, 1997b, p. 110). Other studies have suggested that firms with different national origins have different preferences about ownership because these firms do not all view equity ownership as a primary control mechanism (Delios and Beamish, 2004; Erramilli, 1996; Sohn, 1994).

Furthermore, Barkema *et al.* (1996) suggest that JVs are easier to manage in culturally close countries because JVs formed in culturally distant countries involve serious adjustments with respect to national culture and organizational culture. Additionally, management's capability to administer JVs in difficult cultural environments, the ease of management across different host countries, might also extend from the degree to which JVs are legitimate in the host country (Lu, 2002). JVs have been argued to have a greater alignment with institutional structures and historical norms when established in South East Asia than when established in North America and Europe (Yiu and Makino, 2002). Arguably, this research is suggesting that JVs formed in the developing countries of South East Asia are likely to have a higher overall performance than JVs formed in developed countries because the perceived legitimacy of the JV form is greater in the developing countries of South East Asia than in some developed countries and the cultural hurdles to be crossed are likely to be lower (Delios and Beamish, 2004).

14.5. Local knowledge and Joint Ventures Performance

Host country-specific knowledge is the driving force behind international expansion performance success because this kind of local knowledge is not easily acquired (Barkema and Vermeulen, 1997; Inkpen and Beamish, 1997). That is, MNEs that have spent a considerable amount of time in a host country may acquire a significant competitive advantage over firms that are not already in that country (Shaver *et al.*, 1997). Within the eclectic paradigm of international production, local host-country knowledge and experience is considered as an ownership-specific, intangible asset that generates economic rents (Dunning, 1988). Much previous research has found a positive correlation between ownership-specific assets and international expansion success (Beamish and Inkpen, 1995). As an overview, the longer MNEs operate in a foreign country, the more capable they become in that foreign market (Makino and Delios, 1996). As a result, the MNE's inherent disadvantage as a foreign invader can be substantially overcome (Luo and Peng, 1999).

Therefore, knowledge of the local business environment is an asset often avidly sought by an MNE that is trying to establish a position in a foreign market. This knowledge has economic value and can take several forms. It usually involves familiarity with economic, political and business conditions. The foreign market the MNE is trying to establish itself in may have an inadequate infrastructure, a large public sector and intransigent ethnic hostilities. Political connections play a part also. Having a local partner with good political connections may ease relations between the MNE and a suspicious host-country government, which may perceive a JV as less threatening than a wholly owned subsidiary of a foreign firm (Connolly, 1984). The public relations benefit often extends to local labour relations and to worker morale as well. In real terms, a local partner may provide advantages in obtaining contracts, access to favourable tax treatment, a chance to avoid various non-tariff barriers, and a means of entry into relationships with local businesses and officials. Such connections with the local environment are often an essential precondition to a venture's success. Related areas of expertise that may be placed in this category are distribution channels and marketing skill (Blodgett, 1991b).

Certain resources in an economy are not always available through free markets. Technology and distribution networks are not always available for sale, and in such cases the need for access to these resources can only be satisfied through a JV. A typical case occurs when one firm possesses a product which it wants to market abroad. A JV with local partners can then offer access to an efficient distribution network together with knowledge of local business practices and institutions. In such a case there is a high degree of complementarity between the partners. Generally, complementarity is found in many JVs, encompassing not only functional complementarity, as in the case mentioned, but also technological complementarity. For example, when new product development requires technical knowledge not available in a single company (Beamish and Inkpen, 1995; Blodgett, 1991b; Dymsza, 1988).

A foreign MNE may also find it difficult to penetrate international markets without local marketing expertise. A joint venture partner may provide the know-how or established local distribution channels through which to market the product that may not have been available without the local JV partner. As industries evolve, their distribution and communication channels must improve to provide closer and more efficient contacts between suppliers and customers. This long-term imperative may require considerable short-term investments. Though the foreign MNE might favour such investments, the local partner(s) will oppose such investments if the changes in channel arrangements clash with their traditional concepts, limited resources, bargaining power base, and/or short-term expectations. The greater the divergence in the IJV partner's objectives and time-frame to achieve those objectives, the greater the difficulty for an IJV to take advantage of opportunities and cope with challenges created by changes in its industry's channels, and the greater their need to compromise, given the local partner's reluctance to change, which is a short-term view. As a consequence, IJV partners need to address the eventual changes in the IJV's roles and relationships with the marketing channels as these changes and the availability of suitable marketing channels not controlled by one or several of its competitors can have a significant influence on the marketing performance of the IJV (Ahn, 1980; Datta, 1988; Ganitsky *et al.,* 1991; Killing, 1983).

Furthermore, knowledge of the local business environment also helps with determining what kind of marketing strategy the MNE will adopt when it enters a foreign market, especially in relation to the decision to standardise or adapt its marketing strategy. As Douglas and Wind (1987) point out, the more internationally competent a firm is, the more likely it is that standardisation will not lead to optimal results. A competent firm, because of its international experience and resources, knows the subtle differences in environmental conditions, market demand and the degree of competition, and is more likely to select the most attractive market for the venture and adapt the marketing strategy (e.g., product and promotion strategy) to meet the specific market needs (Cavusgil *et al.,* 1993; Douglas and Craig, 1989; Hill and Still, 1984). An inexperienced firm seeks the closest match between its current offerings and foreign market conditions so that minimal adaptation is required (Douglas and Craig, 1989).

When a product can meet universal needs, standardisation of product and promotion is facilitated (Levitt, 1983). However, if a product meets only unique needs, greater adaptation of product and promotion will be required to meet customers' product use conditions (Buzzell, 1968; Cavusgil *et al.,* 1993; Keegan, 1969), and to educate customers in using and maintaining the product. Similarly, when a culture-specific product is developed for a foreign market, the cultural base on which the product is developed may not match the cultural base in the foreign market (Terpstra, 1987). To be viable, the product must be adapted to the cultural idiosyncrasies of the foreign market (Douglas and Wind, 1987).

14.6. Conclusion

The theory of internalization was developed as a general theory for the existence of the MNE. However, to do so it would need to provide a basis under which other market entry modes, other than the wholly owned subsidiary, could operate (Hennart, 1991) and identify the circumstances under which each different market entry mode would provide efficiency gains over wholly owned subsidiaries in the market. This chapter has attempted to do this, drawing on the work of Beamish and Banks (1987) and linking it to the findings of the Julian (1998) study on IJV marketing performance in Thailand, making a case for the theory of internalization as a general theory for the existence of the MNE when using the JV as a market entry mode alternative.

The theory of internalization suggests that it would be less expensive for the MNE to develop these resources internally than to acquire them by establishing a JV. Due to the transaction difficulties associated with some JV arrangements, whatever the MNE gained in relation to local market knowledge, access to capital and raw materials it would apparently lose because of the costs associated with protecting these assets from exploitation by the local JV partner. Thus, according to the internalization theory, a MNE would be best using the wholly owned subsidiary as a market entry mode. However, this conclusion was arrived at on the basis that none of Williamson's (1975) transaction difficulties, opportunism, bounded rationality, uncertainty and small numbers condition can be solved through a JV.

This chapter has, primarily through the work of Beamish and Banks (1987) by linking it to Julian's (1998) study findings on IJV marketing performance in Thailand, hopefully demonstrated that this assumption need not hold true in all JV cases and has therefore provided a theoretical justification for JVs within the context of the theory of internalization. It is thereby concluded that in certain circumstances the associated threats to a MNE's assets incurred by opportunism and a small numbers condition can be ameliorated to a point where the JV market entry mode becomes an efficient means of dealing with foreign market uncertainty even where bounded rationality exists.

It is important for the management of any firm to be aware of these issues when using the JV market entry mode in a developing country of South East Asia. As far as IJV marketing performance in Thailand was concerned, the Julian (1998) study findings clearly indicated that it was important for managers of IJVs in Thailand to be aware of the market characteristics of the Thai market that could influence a firm's marketing performance. The market characteristics that were very important for the successful marketing performance of IJVs in Thailand included the availability of capital resources, raw materials and distribution channels; transfer of up-to-date technology; knowledge of local business practices; and knowledge of industry competition. Firms intending to enter into an IJV arrangement in Thailand needed to ensure the availability and existence of the above if they were to succeed in the Thai market.

As far as the firm's marketing strategy was concerned, the Julian (1998) study findings have shown that managers of IJVs in Thailand should make efforts to adapt their products/services to meet the needs of the local Thai market for achieving success in the marketing performance of their IJV. Specifically, product/service adaptation; adapting the promotional campaign; familiarity of consumers to the product; the stage of the product life cycle the product is in; and culture-specificity of the product/service require management's attention. IJV managers must be aware of the importance of adapting the IJV's products/services to meet the needs of the local Thai market and restrain from opting for a globally standardised product/service.

15. Investing in Thailand via Joint Ventures

15.1. Introduction

This chapter examines the role of the Thai Board of Investment (BOI) as the premier government institution promoting foreign direct investment (FDI) into Thailand together with the trends of international joint venture formation in Thailand since 1960. The BOI is the principal government agency responsible for providing investment incentives to stimulate FDI in Thailand. The BOI also conducts extensive investment promotion activities both in Thailand and overseas. Although investment promotion in Thailand stretches back more than three decades, the BOI is officially governed by the 1977 Investment Promotion Act. The agency is chaired by the Prime Minister, with economic ministers, senior civil servants, representatives of major private sector organisations, and academics serving as board members or advisers. The day-to-day investment promotion activities are carried out by the Office of the Board of Investment (OBOI) under the Office of the Prime Minister.

The BOI is empowered to grant a wide range of fiscal and non-fiscal incentives and guarantees to investment projects that meet national economic development goals. In addition to investment incentives, the BOI offers comprehensive business-related services to investors and potential investors. These services range from assistance in obtaining required licenses and permits to the identification of promising investment projects and joint venture partners. Recently, the BOI has begun to help Thai firms invest overseas, especially in Cambodia, Laos and the ASEAN countries. To sum up, the BOI provides unqualified support to both foreign and Thai businesses that are either planning to invest, or have already committed to invest in Thailand's rapidly growing and diversifying economy.

In relation to the trends of IJV formation in Thailand, the IJV is recognised as one of the primary sources of FDI in Thailand and the importance of FDI in

Thailand has drawn increasing attention since the late 1980s. Due to the dramatic increase in FDI inflows in Thailand after 1988, and the coincidence of these increased flows with an unprecedented economic boom between 1987 and 1990 when gross domestic product (GDP) growth reached highs of between 9.5 and 13.3 per cent (National Economic and Social Development Board 1988, 1992, 1993). FDI flows and GDP growth rates, however, declined somewhat in the 1990s. This chapter examines the nature of these FDI flows by analysing IJV formation in Thailand by industry classification, by country of origin of the principal foreign partner and by equity participation of the principal foreign partner. However, prior to outlining the major trends in IJV formation in Thailand, this chapter examines the key role of the Thai Board of Investment (BOI) in promoting FDI into Thailand.

15.2. Role of the Thai Board of Investment

The Thai Board of Investment (BOI) spearheads the Thai government's drive to attract FDI into Thailand, both by actively promoting the country at home and abroad as a premier investment destination, and by providing incentives to stimulate such investment. In tune with constantly changing global trends and demands, the BOI adopts a flexible and proactive approach to investment that enables them to adapt to the ever-changing global investment climate by providing a series of incentives that not only meet investor needs, but also are in line with national development objectives. The BOI is, therefore, chaired by the Prime Minister, with the Minister of Industry, economic ministers, senior civil servants, representatives of the private sector, and academics serving as members and advisors (BOI, 2004a).

The day-to-day investment promotion activities are carried out by the Office of the Board of Investment (OBOI). The BOI promotes projects that do the following:

- Strengthen Thailand's industrial and technological capability.
- Make use of domestic resources.
- Create employment opportunities.
- Develop basic and support industries.
- Earn foreign exchange.
- Contribute to the economic growth of regions outside of Bangkok.
- Develop infrastructure and conserve natural resources.
- Reduce environmental problems.

The BOI is empowered to grant a wide range of fiscal and non-fiscal incentives and guarantees to investment projects that meet national economic development goals. In addition to investment incentives, the BOI also offers comprehensive business-related services, ranging from working with investors to help them obtain licenses and permits to the identification of promising investment projects and joint venture partners (BOI, 2004a).

The OBOI comprises investment promotion divisions, non-sectoral divisions, and overseas and regional offices. The sectoral divisions look after a grouping of related industries and are responsible for all aspects of promoted projects, so that investors only need to deal with one division for most of their business with the BOI (BOI, 2004a).

The non-sectoral divisions take care of administrative functions, as well as public relations and international affairs. The BOI also maintains permanent offices in Frankfurt, New York, Paris, Shanghai and Tokyo, with more being planned, as well as six regional offices within Thailand. To sum up, the BOI provides extensive support to investors before, during and after the application process (BOI, 2004a).

15.2.1. Investment Services of the Thai Board of Investment (BOI)

The BOI offers a range of valuable business-related services to the international investment community. The office helps prospective investors and promoted firms in obtaining official permits and documents required for conducting business, including visas, work permits and permanent residency permits, and assists investors in gaining access to utilities (BOI, 2004a).

The Investment Services Center and the Marketing Division maintain comprehensive information on investment opportunities in Thailand, by both sector and region. Information and investment advice is available to all foreign investors at no charge (BOI, 2004a).

The BOI Unit for Industrial Linkage Development (BUILD) encourages growth in supporting industries in Thailand. BUILD provides information on subcontracting opportunities and offers its support to buyer firms seeking sourcing networks in Thailand. It helps small and medium-sized Thai suppliers achieve standards required to enter into productive subcontracting arrangements. BUILD's extensive database on subcontractors in Thailand provides matchmaking services for firms seeking specific components or raw materials. BUILD also operates the Vendors Meet Customers Programme, which promotes subcontracting by arranging factory visits to electronics and automotive assemblers (BOI, 2004a).

The BOI provides investment matchmaking services to both Thai and foreign investors seeking cooperation in the areas of technology, finance, management and marketing. In addition, the BOI offers a matchmaking service for investors in regional areas looking for joint venture partners from Bangkok and abroad, as well as for firms that want to invest in provincial areas (BOI, 2004a).

The Investor Club Association is a private membership organization within the BOI, serving the interests and needs of Thailand's investment community, and providing the most up-to-date information on Thailand's investment environment and rules and procedures concerning investment promotion. The Investor Club Association distributes information and serves as a networking organization for its members. Companies that belong to the BOI Investor Club Association are eligible to use its raw materials and machinery tracking system that facilitates the release of raw materials and machinery from the Customs Department within three hours (BOI, 2004a).

The BOI coordinated the establishment of a One-Stop Service Center for Visas and Work Permits. The center can process applications or renewals of visas and work permits within three hours, assuming all required documents are provided. In addition, the center handles many other transactions, including change of visa status, payment of fines, and processing of re-entry stamps, all within three hours or less. Investors or experts granted privileges under the Investment Promotion Act who are allowed to stay in Thailand on a temporary basis to undertake investment or business activities also have access to the services provided by the One-Stop Center (BOI, 2004a).

To provide information to global investors, the Investment Services Center of the BOI maintains five websites to permit investors to stay up to date about the investment climate in Thailand. As per the Thai Board of Investment (BOI, 2004a) these include the following.

The www.boi.th site is updated every business day with information pertaining to the business and investment climate in Thailand. The www.i-expertnet.com site is a part of the BOI's investment intelligence and 'e-strategy', which forms the key elements of the organization's drive to enhance the country's investment environment. The site enables the transfer of knowledge, know-how and expertise to strengthen the development of human resources for Thai industries.

The www.asidnet.org is the website for the ASEAN Supporting Industry Database (ASID), an extensive database that consolidates a full range of information and profiles of supporting industries and manufacturers of parts and components in the ten ASEAN member countries. The www.b-intelligence.net website aims to build a network of high-profile business executives. Here they can meet and exchange useful ideas, news, information and interests, and share personal viewpoints via surveys and seminars. Finally, the www.investmentthailand.com website has been introduced by the BOI to facilitate investment at the provincial level. The Thailand Provincial Gateway consolidates specific information of each province, including economic and commercial overviews, basic physical and social infrastructure, demographics and details of investment support policies.

To facilitate and solve problems experienced by promoted companies, the BOI has established an Investment Facilitation Division, whose responsibilities include working with other government organizations to trouble-shoot issues raised by investors, and to support investors in areas such as manpower, sourcing and subcontracting (BOI, 2004a). As such, the Thai Board of Investment (BOI) provides a substantial number of investment services to help facilitate FDI in Thailand including the location of suitable JV partners.

This chapter next reviews the trends of international joint venture (IJV) formation in Thailand, highlighting the significant contribution of Japan, Western Europe and Taiwan to FDI and IJV formation in Thailand which is arguably consistent with the main contributors of FDI for some of the other South East Asian countries (Julian, 1998).

15.3. Trends of International Joint Venture Formation in Thailand

From Table 15.1 it is possible to identify three periods during which IJV formation in Thailand exhibited distinctly different trends. (1) Between 1960 and 1980, out of a sample of 1047 companies (provided by the BOI, 1996), IJV formation was relatively low with only 152 IJVs formed during this period. At around 15 percent (14.5 percent) of the total number of IJVs being formed in the period 1960-95 this represents a very small percentage of the total. This is especially the case when you consider that this period (20 years) represents over half of the total period being examined. (2) Between 1981 and 1985, IJV formation was markedly higher, with a further 114 IJVs being formed during this period. This represents a twofold increase in IJV formation over previous five-year periods. However, IJV formation in the period 1960-85 is still relatively small, representing only 25.4 percent of the total number of IJVs formed between 1960 and 1995. (3) Between 1986 and 1995 the growth rate of IJV formation showed outstanding growth growing threefold over the previous 25-year period. A total number of 781 IJVs were formed during this ten-year period representing nearly 75 percent (74.6 percent) of the total number of IJVs formed during the period 1960-95. This is quite a remarkable achievement considering there was a slowing in economic growth during this period from 9.7 percent in 1986 to 8.6 percent in 1995 (Far Eastern Economic Review, August 17 1995); a slowing in total FDI (Economic and Social Commission for Asia and the Pacific, 1995); and three changes of government (Julian, 1998; Julian and Ramaseshan, 2001).

Table 15.1 Year of IJV Formation

Year	Frequency (number)	%	Cumulative %
Before 1960	1	0.1	0.1
1961-65	23	2.2	2.3
1966-70	32	3.0	5.3
1971-75	50	4.8	10.1
1976-80	46	4.4	14.5
1981-85	114	10.9	25.4
1986-90	484	46.2	71.6
1991-95	297	28.4	100.0
TOTAL	1047	100.0	

15.3.1. Industry Trends of IJV Formation

Agricultural and light industries (including gems, jewellery and textiles) have been the major industries involved in IJV formation, accounting for 38 percent of IJV formation prior to 1980 and over 40 percent (42 percent) of the total since 1981 (see Table 15.2). Therefore, the increase in FDI through the growth of IJV formation in agricultural and light industries is likely to be a contributing factor to the FDI boom of 1988. Metal working industries, that included machinery and transport equipment, were the next-largest industry sector to form IJVs, with a share of 21.7 percent between 1960 and 1980, and 14-15 percent between 1981 and 1995. Between 1960 and 1980, these industries were followed by chemical, mining, electronics and services. Between 1981 and 1985, chemical industries was the third-largest group to benefit from IJV formation followed by the metal working industries, which saw a large drop in its share. These industries were then followed by the services sector, which enjoyed a large increase in its share, electronics, which experienced a drop of 2.7 percent in its share and mining, which also experienced a large drop in its share. Between 1986 and 1995 the trend experienced between 1981 and 1985 continued, with chemical industries being the third-largest recipient of IJV formation behind agricultural and light industries. Chemical industries was followed again by metal working industries which saw a further drop of 0.4 percent in its share, electronics which saw a large increase in its share, and more distantly by mining and services, which both saw large drops in their share of IJV formation (Julian, 1998; Julian and Ramaseshan, 2001).

It is difficult to evaluate changes in the relative importance of IJV formation in Thailand at the sectoral level because there are no corresponding figures for equity investments by local firms. Moreover, even data on fixed investments are not available by sectors (Economic and Social Commission for Asia and the Pacific, 1995). Additionally, the spread of IJV formation across a number of industries is quite evenly spread. Between 1960 and 1995, 218 IJVs were formed in agricultural industries, 226 IJVs in light industries, 174 IJVs in chemical industries, and 164 IJVs in metal working industries. However, the interesting sectoral trend to note of IJV formation in Thailand is, firstly, the strong growth in IJV formation in agricultural, electronics, and chemical industries (Julian, 1998; Julian and Ramaseshan, 2001).

Secondly, IJV formation in light industries was relatively stable. Between 1960 and 1980 the share of IJV formation in light industries was 21.7 percent. Between 1981 and 1985 it was 22 percent and between 1986 and 1995 it was 21.4 percent (Julian, 1998; Julian and Ramaseshan, 2001).

Thirdly, IJV formation in the services industries was reasonably volatile. Between 1960 and 1980 the share of IJV formation in the services industries was 4 percent. Between 1981 and 1985 it was 11 percent and between 1986 and 1995 it was 5.2 percent. Finally, IJV formation in the mining and metal working industries was on the decline (see Table 15.2 for details of sectoral trends of IJV formation in Thailand) (Julian, 1998; Julian and Ramaseshan, 2001).

Table 15.2 Industry Classification of IJV Formation

Year	Agric	Min	Light	Metal	Elect	Chem	Serv	Total
Before 1960	0	0	1	0	0	0	0	1
1961-65	2	4	10	4	3	0	0	23
1966-70	4	4	8	7	5	4	0	32
1971-75	9	5	12	8	4	10	2	50
1976-80	10	4	3	14	4	7	4	46
1981-85	22	9	25	17	9	19	13	114
1986-90	104	21	113	68	74	87	17	484
1991-95	67	22	54	46	37	47	24	297
Totals	218	69	226	164	136	174	60	1,047
%	20.8	6.6	21.6	15.7	13.0	16.6	5.7	100

15.3.2. Country of Origin of the Principal Foreign Partner

Knowledge of where the foreign partners originate from helps to understand the nature and structure of IJVs in Thailand. In the Julian (1998) sample of Thai IJVs provided by the Thai Board of Investment (BOI, 1996), by far the three largest contributors of IJVs in Thailand were Japan, the newly industrialised economy (NIE) of Taiwan, and Western Europe. Japan, the newly industrialised economy (NIE) of Taiwan, and Western Europe provided 66 percent of the Julian (1998) sample of 1,047 IJVs in Thailand (a total of 692 IJVs were formed with the principal foreign partner coming from these countries). Japan was by far the largest contributor of IJVs in Thailand providing 33 percent of the total (or a total of 341 IJVs), double that of Taiwan and Western Europe (see Tables 15.3 and 15.4) (Julian, 1998; Julian and Ramaseshan, 2001).

Table 15.3 Country of Origin of the IJV's Principal Foreign Partner

Country	Frequency (number)	%	Cumulative %
US	50	4.8	4.8
Western Europe	170	16.2	21.0
Australia	14	1.3	22.3
ASEAN	69	6.6	28.9
Taiwan	181	17.3	46.2
China	54	5.2	51.4
Korea	25	2.4	53.8
Japan	341	32.6	86.4
Indochina	1	0.1	86.5
Hong Kong	78	7.4	93.9
Canada	4	0.4	94.3
India	21	2.0	96.3
Others	39	3.7	100.0
Total	1,047	100.0	

Table 15.4 A Summary of the IJV's Principal Foreign Partner by Country of Origin and by Year of Formation

Year	Japan	5-yr ave	Taiwan	5-yr ave	Europe	5-yr ave	Total
1960-80	70	17.5	10	2.5	32	8.0	112
1981-85	18	18.0	22	22.0	21	21.0	61
1986-95	253	126.5	149	74.5	117	53.5	519
Total	341		181		170		692

It is evident from Tables 15.3 and 15.4 that Japan is by far the single largest contributor of IJV activity in Thailand, nearly double that of Taiwan, the second-highest contributor (Julian, 1998; Julian and Ramaseshan, 2001). Japan's share of IJV activity in Thailand at 33 percent in 1995 closely mirrors its share of overall FDI in Thailand in 1993 which was also 33 percent (Economic and Social Commission for Asia and the Pacific, 1995).

From Table 15.4 it is evident that the growth of IJV formation in Thailand between Japanese and Thai companies remained relatively stable between

1960 and 1985. Between 1960 and 1985 around 17-18 IJVs were formed every five-year period, with 70 IJVs being formed between 1960 and 1980, and 18 IJVs being formed between 1981 and 1985. However, the growth in Japanese/Thai IJVs since 1985 can only be described as phenomenal. A total of 253 Japanese/Thai IJVs were formed in Thailand during the ten-year period between 1986 and 1995, representing an average of 126 IJVs being formed per five-year period since 1985. This is as compared to 18 per five-year period prior to 1985. Therefore, the Japanese have made a major contribution to the growth of IJVs in Thailand between 1986 and 1995 (Julian, 1998; Julian and Ramaseshan, 2001). This is very much consistent with the growth of Japanese FDI in Thailand, with the Japanese being the dominant foreign investment contributors into Thailand since 1986 (Economic and Social Commission for Asia and the Pacific, 1995).

The growth rate in IJV formation of Taiwanese and Western European companies with Thai companies demonstrates a similar pattern to that of Japanese/Thai IJVs; however, the growth rate is nowhere near as pronounced as with Japanese/Thai IJVs. In the case of Taiwanese/Thai IJVs, between 1960 and 1980 on average 2-3 IJVs were formed per five-year period. Between 1981 and 1985 this number grew to 22 and between 1986 and 1995 this number grew a further threefold to 74-75 IJVs being formed per five-year period (see Table 15.4) (Julian, 1998; Julian and Ramaseshan, 2001).

In the case of Western European/Thai IJVs, on average eight IJVs were formed per five-year period between 1960 and 1980. Between 1981 and 1985 the number of IJVs being formed grew to 21 and between 1986 and 1995 the number of IJVs being formed per five-year period grew more than a further twofold to 53-54 IJVs being formed per five-year period. These statistics indicate that the growth of IJV formation in Thailand between 1986 and 1995 is likely to come from the growth in IJV formation between Japanese, Taiwanese and Western European companies with Thai companies (Julian, 1998; Julian and Ramaseshan, 2001).

The United States accounted for only 4.8 percent of the total number of IJVs formed in Thailand during the period 1960-95 in the Julian (1998) sample provided by the Thai Board of Investment (BOI, 1996). This is in marked contrast to the total FDI flows into Thailand where the US was the largest investor in Thailand in 1978, accounting for 37 percent of all cumulative investment (based on data from the Bank of Thailand from 1970 onwards). As late as 1986, the US was still the largest investor with a share of 31 percent. However, by 1993 the US share of total FDI had dropped dramatically to only 17 percent (Economic and Social Commission for Asia and the Pacific, 1995). This is still much greater than the US contribution to total IJVs in Thailand per the Julian (1998) sample that, in 1995, stood at only 4.8 percent. Whilst these trends of US IJV activity in Thailand are surprising, it is important to note that these estimates that indicate US IJV activity in Thailand was rather low are based on Thai Board of Investment figures (BOI, 1996). However, since US firms often do not go through the BOI and BOI-promoted status is not a requirement to invest in Thailand, these figures are underestimates of total US IJV activity in Thailand (Julian, 1998; Julian and Ramaseshan, 2001).

15.3.3. Equity Percentage of the Principal Foreign Partner

Much has been written in the IJV literature on equity participation of foreign partners (Beamish, 1988; Beamish and Inkpen, 1995; Lee and Beamish, 1995; Sohn, 1994). Many authors claim that for an IJV to perform successfully, the foreign partner must maintain control over the relationship between the local partner and the IJV (Al-Aali, 1987; Killing, 1983; Phatak and Chowdhury, 1991). One of the best ways to achieve this is through majority equity participation in the IJV, which is difficult to achieve in the developing countries of South East Asia. Host governments, through government legislation, especially in the developing countries of South East Asia like Thailand, are restricting foreign companies to minority equity participation in industries which are not considered essential to national security and in industries where they already have access to the latest technology (Julian, 1998; Julian and Ramaseshan, 2001).

Some research indicates that there are better ways for a foreign corporation to control local partners other than through majority equity participation, e.g., through social knowledge (Sohn, 1994). Research has also shown that where foreign companies have been prepared to take a minority share in the IJV and make a commitment to a developing country market, minority equity participation has been a major factor of successful business performance (Beamish, 1988; Beamish and Inkpen, 1995; Cullen *et al.,* 1995; Lee and Beamish, 1995). Therefore, through changes in government legislation that restrict most foreign companies to minority equity participation in the developing countries of South East Asia, and the successful performance of many of these IJVs (see Beamish, 1984; Julian, 1998), this arguably indicates that minority equity participation will be the norm, not the exception.

In the Higginbottom (1980) study of IJVs in the ASEAN group of countries, minority equity participation by the foreign partner was commonplace in Malaysia, Thailand, Singapore, Indonesia and the Philippines. Higginbottom found that, on average, in more than 50 percent of the IJVs studied, the principal foreign partner had 49 percent or less equity in the IJV. In the case of Thailand, the number of IJVs where the principal foreign partner had 49 percent or less equity participation was above average (60 percent). Host-country government legislation was the reason cited by the foreign corporations, in most cases, for minority equity participation (Julian, 1998; Julian and Ramaseshan, 2001).

Knowledge of equity participation by foreign corporations in IJV relationships in South East Asia helps one to understand the climate and structure of IJVs in South East Asia. As was the case with the Higginbottom (1980) study, the Julian (1998) study of 1,047 BOI-promoted companies in IJV relationships in Thailand revealed that 74.8 percent of foreign corporations had minority equity participation in the IJV in which they were involved (see Table 15.5). In real terms, this represents 783 IJVs where the principal foreign partner had 49 percent or less equity participation. This is a significant number and cannot be overlooked in any analysis on the sectoral composition of FDI in Thailand (Julian, 1998; Julian and Ramaseshan, 2001).

Table 15.5 Equity Percentage of the Principal Foreign Partner

Equity	Frequency (number)	%	Cumulative %
5% to 9%	51	4.9	4.9
10% to 19%	101	9.6	14.5
20% to 29%	114	10.9	25.4
30% to 39%	151	14.4	39.8
40% to 49%	366	35.0	74.8
50% to 59%	48	4.6	79.4
60% to 69%	45	4.3	83.7
70% to 79%	62	5.9	89.6
80% to 89%	63	6.0	95.6
90% to 95%	46	4.4	100.0
TOTAL	1,047	100.0	

Government legislation preventing majority equity participation in many industries by foreign corporations came into effect in 1972 (the Alien Business Law) in Thailand (Baker and McKenzie, 1993). If this is taken into consideration, together with the knowledge that 75 percent of the IJVs being studied in the Julian (1998) sample were formed after 1980, the likely cause of this high minority equity participation is host-country government legislation. Another factor likely to contribute to the high minority equity participation by foreign corporations in the Julian sample was that they were all BOI-promoted companies. IJVs that are not BOI-promoted may have, on average, higher equity participation by the foreign partner but only specific industries qualify for promotion by the Thai BOI. Nevertheless, the Julian sample had a very high percentage of minority equity participation by foreign corporations and this is a significant finding on the sectoral composition of FDI and IJV formation in Thailand and could have a major effect on how the IJV's marketing performance is viewed by senior executives.

15.4. Conclusions

Thailand was selected as the country in which to examine IJV marketing performance, the sectoral composition of FDI and IJV formation for three principal reasons (see Julian, 1998). Firstly, Thailand's generally strong economic performance over the last 20 years resulted in strong economic growth rates during that period (Far Eastern Economic Review, 1995; Far Eastern Economic Review, 2001). This strong economic performance would indicate the likelihood of a significant amount of IJV activity in Thailand as the IJV is one of the principal forms of foreign investment available to foreign corporations wishing to invest in Thailand (Higginbottom, 1980; Millin, 1984; Tan, 1990). Secondly, a foreign investment climate that encourages the use of IJVs as a market entry mode and restricts nearly all other forms of FDI (Baker and McKenzie, 1993; Julian, 1998). Finally, the success of Australian IJVs in Thailand: examples of successful Thai/Australian IJVs include Concrete Constructions (Thailand) Pty. Ltd., The Thai Dairy Industry Authority Limited, Thai Industrial Gases, Thai Glass Industries, Kulthorn Kirby Limited, Snowy Mountains Engineering Corporation, Woodhead Firth Lee Corporation, Beta Clough Limited, and NIS Recruitment and Consulting Services Ltd., to name a few (Julian, 1998; Stier and Mills, 1994).

To summarise, in relation to the Thai Board of Investment (BOI), established in 1960, it is the government agency responsible for administering incentives to encourage private investment, both foreign and domestic, into priority areas. These priority areas have changed over time from import-substitution industries in the 1960s and 1970s to export-oriented industries during the 1980s to the present emphasis on more high value-added production to help deepen the country's industrialization (Stier and Mills, 1994). The BOI provides many services to foreign investors contemplating investing in Thailand, ranging from working with investors to help them obtain licenses and permits to the identification of promising investment projects and joint venture partners (BOI, 2004a).

As such, it would make sense if you were considering investing in Thailand to achieve BOI-promoted status. Yet many firms wishing to invest in Thailand do not seek BOI-promoted status. This is because some foreign firms may favour majority equity participation for one reason or another. Perhaps, because of a special arrangement they have been able to negotiate with the Thai government or perhaps they are contributing advanced technology that the country needs and is trademark or patent protected. IJVs that have BOI-promoted status tend to have minority equity participation and IJVs that are not BOI-promoted may have, on average, higher equity participation by the foreign partner. Furthermore, only specific industries qualify for promotion by the Thai BOI making BOI-promoted status not possible for some JVs in Thailand anyway. However, wherever possible BOI-promoted status should be desirable for firms considering investing in Thailand via a JV.

As far as the trends of IJV formation in Thailand was concerned there were three periods during which IJV formation exhibited distinctly different trends: (1) 1960-80, (2) 1981-85, and (3) 1986-95. Between 1986 and 1995, the growth rate of IJV formation expanded threefold over the previous 25-year period. The industries that attracted the most FDI in Thailand between 1960 and 1995 as far as IJV formation was concerned, were agriculture, light industries, chemical and metal working industries. Between 1960 and 1995, 218 IJVs were formed in agricultural industries, 226 IJVs were formed in light industries, 174 IJVs were formed in chemical industries and 164 IJVs were formed in metal working industries (Julian, 1998).

As far as the country of origin of the principal foreign partner was concerned, Japan, the newly industrialised economy (NIE) of Taiwan, and Western Europe provided 66 percent of the principal foreign partners for the Julian (1998) study on IJV marketing performance in Thailand. A total of 692 IJVs were formed with the principal foreign partner located in these countries. Japan was by far the largest contributor of IJVs in Thailand, providing 33 percent of the total (or a total of 341 IJVs), double that of Taiwan and Western Europe (see Table 15.3). Finally, with respect to equity participation, it was evident from the Julian study on IJV marketing performance in Thailand that a large majority of the foreign corporations had minority equity participation in the IJV in which they were involved, i.e. equity participation of 49 percent or less. This is not surprising since all JVs in the Julian sample had achieved BOI-promoted status.

16. Legal Implications of Investing in Thailand

16.1. Introduction

To set up a limited company in Thailand, the following procedures should be followed.

The corporate name to be reserved must not be the same or close to that of other companies. Certain names are not allowed and therefore the name reservation guidelines of the Commercial Registration Department in the Ministry of Commerce should be observed. The approved corporate name is valid for 30 days. No extension is allowed (BOI, 2004b).

A Memorandum of Association to be filed with the Commercial Registration Department must include the name of the company that has been successfully reserved, the province where the company will be located, its business objectives, the capital to be registered, and the names of seven promoters. The capital information must include the number of shares and their par value. At the formation stage, the authorised capital, although partly paid, must all be issued. Although there are no minimum capital requirements, the amount of capital should be respectable enough and adequate for the intended business operation. The Memorandum registration fee is 50 baht (or US$1.23) per 100,000 baht (or US$2,460.00) of registered capital. The minimum fee is 500 baht (or US$12.32); the maximum fee is 25,000 baht (or US$615.53) (BOI, 2004b).

Once the share structure has been defined, a statutory meeting is called during which the Articles of Incorporation and bylaws are approved, the board of directors is elected and an auditor appointed. A minimum of 25 percent of the par value of each subscribed share must be paid. Within three months of the date of the statutory meeting, the directors must submit the application to establish the company. Company registration fees are 500 baht (or US$12.30) per 100,000 baht (or US$2,460.00) of registered capital. The minimum fee is 5,000 baht (or US$123.00); the maximum fee is 250,000 baht (or US$6155.30) (BOI, 2004b).

Businesses liable for income tax must obtain a Tax ID card and number for the company from the Revenue Department within 60 days of incorporation or the start of operations. Business operators earning more than 600,000 baht (or US$14,756.30) per annum must register for value-added tax (VAT) within 30 days of the date they reach 600,000 baht (or US$14,756.30) in sales (BOI, 2004b).

Firms must keep books and follow accounting procedures specified in the Civil and Commercial Code, the Revenue Code and the Accounts Act. Documents may be prepared in any language, provided that a Thai translation is attached. All accounting entries should be written in ink, typewritten or printed. Specifically, Section 1206 of the Civil and Commercial Code provides rules on the accounts that should be maintained as follows (BOI, 2004b):

The directors must cause true accounts to be kept:

- Of the sums received and expended by the company and of the matters in respect of which each receipt or expenditure takes place.
- Of the assets and liabilities of the company.

Companies are required to withhold income tax from the salary of all regular employees. A value-added tax (VAT) of 7 percent is levied on the value-added at each stage of the production process, and is applicable to most firms. The VAT must be paid on a monthly basis. A specific business tax is levied on firms engaged in several categories of businesses not subject to VAT, based on gross receipts, at a variable rate ranging from 0.1 to 3.0 percent. Corporate income tax is 30 percent of net profits and is due twice each fiscal year. A mid-year profit forecast entails advance payment of corporate taxes (BOI, 2004b).

A newly established company or partnership should close accounts within 12 months from the date of its registration. Thereafter, the accounts should be closed every 12 months. The performance record is to be certified by the company auditor, approved by shareholders, and filed with the Commercial Registration Department, Ministry of Commerce, within five months of the end of the fiscal year, and with the Revenue Department, Ministry of Finance, within 150 days of the end of the fiscal year. If a company wishes to change its accounting period, it must obtain written approval from the Director-General of the Revenue Department (BOI, 2004b).

In general, the basic accounting principles practiced in the United States are accepted in Thailand, as are accounting methods and conventions as sanctioned by law. The Institute of Certified Accountants and Auditors of Thailand is the authoritative group promoting the application of generally accepted accounting principles. Any accounting method adopted by a company must be used consistently and may be changed only with the approval of the Revenue Department (BOI, 2004b).

The Revenue Code permits the use of varying depreciation rates according to the nature of the classes of assets which have the effect of depreciating the assets over periods that may be shorter than their estimated useful lives. These maximum depreciation rates are not mandatory; a company may use lower rates that approximate the estimated useful lives of the assets. But if a lower rate is used in the books of accounts, the same rate must be used in the income tax return (BOI, 2004b).

Contributions to a pension or provident fund are not deductible for tax purposes unless these are actually paid out to the employees, or the fund is approved as a qualified fund by the Revenue Department and is managed by a licensed fund manager (BOI, 2004b).

Local companies with either foreign or local subsidiaries are not required to consolidate their financial statements for tax and other government reporting purposes, except for listed companies which must submit consolidated financial statements to the Securities and Exchange Commission of Thailand (BOI, 2004b).

A statutory reserve of at least 5 percent of annual net profits arising from the business must be appropriated by the company at each distribution of dividends until the reserve reaches at least 10 percent of the company's authorised capital. Stock dividends are taxable as ordinary dividends and may be declared only if there is an approved increase in authorised capital. The law requires the authorised capital to be subscribed in full by the shareholders (BOI, 2004b).

Audited financial statements of juristic entities (that is, a limited company, a registered partnership, a branch, or representative office, or a regional office of a foreign corporation, or a joint venture) must be certified by an authorised auditor and submitted to the Revenue Department and (except for joint ventures) to the Commercial Registrar for each accounting year. Auditing standards conforming to international auditing standards are, to the greater extent, recognised and practiced by authorised auditors in Thailand (BOI, 2004b).

16.2. Types of Business Organisations

Thailand recognises three types of business organisations.

16.2.1. Partnership

Thai and Western concepts of partnerships are broadly similar. Thailand provides for three general types of partnerships (BOI, 2004b):

16.2.1.1. Unregistered Ordinary Partnerships

An Unregistered Ordinary Partnership is one in which all partners are jointly and wholly liable for all obligations of the partnership.

16.2.1.2. Registered Ordinary Partnerships

If registered, the partnership becomes a legal entity, separate and distinct from the individual partners.

16.2.1.3. Limited Partnerships

Limited Partnerships is where individual partner liability is restricted to the amount of capital contributed to the partnership. Limited partnerships must be registered.

16.2.2. Limited Companies

There are two types of limited companies, i.e. private or closely held companies, and public companies. The first is governed by the Civil and Commercial Code, the second by the Public Company Act (see BOI, 2004b).

16.2.2.1. Private Limited Companies

Private Limited Companies in Thailand have basic characteristics similar to those of Western corporations. A private limited company is formed through a process that leads to the registration of a Memorandum of Association (Articles of Incorporation) and Articles of Association (Bylaws), as its constitutive documents. Shareholders enjoy limited liability, i.e. limited to the remaining unpaid amount, if any, of the par values of their shares. The liability of the directors, however, may be unlimited if so provided in the company's Memorandum of Association or the Articles of Incorporation. A limited company is managed by a board of directors according to the company's charter and by-laws (BOI, 2004b).

All shares must be subscribed to, and at least 25 percent of the subscribed shares must be paid up. Both common and preferred shares of stock may be issued, but all shares must have voting rights. Thai law prohibits the issuance of shares with no par value. It also stipulates that only shares with par value of 5 baht or above may be issued. Treasury shares are prohibited (BOI, 2004b).

A minimum of seven shareholders is required at all times. A private limited company may be wholly owned by aliens. However, in those activities reserved for Thai nationals, aliens' participation is generally allowed up to a minimum of 49 percent. The registration fee for a private limited company is 5,500 baht (or US$135.25) per million baht (or US$24,590.10) of capital (BOI, 2004b).

16.2.2.2. Public Limited Companies

Public Limited Companies registered in Thailand may, subject to compliance with the prospectus, approval and other requirements, offer shares, debentures and warrants to the public and may apply to have their securities listed on the Stock Exchange of Thailand (SET) (BOI, 2004b).

A minimum of 15 promoters is required for the formation and registration of the Memorandum of Association of a public limited company, and the promoters must hold their shares for a minimum of two years before they can be transferred. The board of directors of a public limited company must have a minimum of five members, at least half of whom are Thai nationals. Shares must have a face value of at least 5 baht each and be fully paid up. Restrictions on share transfers are unlawful except those protecting the rights and benefits of the company allowed by law, and those maintaining a Thai/foreigner shareholder ratio. Debentures may only be issued with the approval of three-quarters of the voting shareholders. The registration fee is 2,000 baht (or US$49.15) per million baht (or US$24,590.10) of capital for a public limited company (BOI, 2004b).

16.2.3. Joint Venture

A joint venture may be described in accordance with general practice as a group of persons (natural and/or juristic) entering into an agreement in order to carry on a business together. It has not yet been recognised as a legal entity under the Civil and Commercial Code. However, income from the joint venture is subject to corporate taxation under the Revenue Code, which classifies it as a single entity (BOI, 2004b).

16.2.4. Other Forms of Corporate Presence

16.2.4.1. Branches of Foreign Companies

There is no special requirement for foreign companies to register their branches in order to do business in Thailand. However, most business activities fall within the scope of one or more laws or regulations that require special registration, either before or after the commencement of activities. Foreign business establishments must, therefore, follow generally accepted procedures. It is important to clarify beforehand what constitutes income subject to Thai tax because the Revenue Department may consider revenues directly earned by the foreign head office from sources within Thailand as subject to Thai taxes (BOI, 2004b).

As a condition for approval of a Foreign Business License to a branch of a foreign corporation, working capital amounting to a total of 5 million baht (or US$122,886.76) in foreign exchange must be brought into Thailand within certain intervals over a four-year period. The branch may be allowed to operate for a period of five years, unless a shorter period is indicated in the application. Extension of the original duration of the license to operate may be granted, provided the working capital required to be brought into Thailand is met (BOI, 2004b).

16.2.4.2. A Representative Office

A Representative Office of foreign corporations may also be established to engage in limited 'non-trading' activities, such as sourcing of goods or services in Thailand for its head office or inspecting and controlling quality of goods which its head office purchases in Thailand. Other activities can cover disseminating information about new products and services of its head office, and reporting to its head office on local business development and activities. Working capital contributions in respect to branches apply (BOI, 2004b).

16.2.5. Regional Operating Headquarters

On 16 August 2002, the Thai government introduced a new package to replace the one governing the establishment of regional Offices in Thailand. The package became effective following the announcement of Royal Decrees. The package on Regional Operating Headquarters (ROH) provides tax breaks and incentives to attract foreign companies to establish regional headquarters in Thailand (BOI, 2004b).

A ROH means a juristic company or partnership organised under Thai law that provides services to its domestic or overseas affiliated companies/or branches. Such services are with regard to administrative, technical, management and other supporting roles, including research and development and training. As per BOI (2004b) the requirements for a ROH are as follows:

* The ROH must have at least 10 million baht (or US$245,559.91) in paid-up capital on the closing date of any accounting period.
* The ROH must provide services to its overseas affiliated companies and/or branches in at least three countries.
* At least half of the revenue booked by the ROH must be derived from service provision to its overseas affiliated companies and/or branches, although this requirement will be reduced to not less than one-third of the ROH's revenue for the first three years.
* Any other requirements may be imposed by the Director-General of the Revenue Department.

Tax Privileges for an ROH include the following (see BOI, 2004b):

* A 10 percent corporate income tax, instead of the regular 30 percent rate, only for the service income provided to affiliated companies and/or branches.
* A 10 percent corporate income tax on interest income which the ROH receives as a result of re lending its borrowed funds to its affiliated companies and/or branches.
* A 10 percent corporate income tax on royalty income that is derived from its affiliated companies and/or branches, including its related companies and which is generated from its research and development work performed in Thailand.
* Exemption of corporate income tax on any dividends received from its domestic and overseas affiliated companies and/or branches.

- An accelerated depreciation of 25 percent on the acquisition of buildings and permanent construction that the ROH purchases for its own business use.

Personal income tax for the ROH include the following (see BOI, 2004b):

- A waiver on personal taxes to foreign employees of the ROH sent to work in other countries.
- Foreign employees of the ROH can choose to pay a 15 percent flat rate of their personal taxes if they forego withholding tax credit of their interest and dividend income.

When a permit to establish a regional office is issued, it may be subject to the following conditions (see BOI, 2004b):

- The total debt financing used in the business shall not exceed seven times the portion of the capital owned by shareholders or the owner of the business.
- Money used in the regional office shall be remitted from abroad and shall not be less than a total of 5 million baht (or US$122,886.76). During the first year period, at least 2 million baht (or US$49,159.13) of the total must be remitted, at least half of which must be remitted within the first six months. Then, no less than 1 million baht (or US$24,572.82) should be remitted each succeeding year until the full 5 million baht (or US$122,886.76) has been transferred. Documents verifying this transfer must be presented to the Department of Commercial Registration.
- At least one person who is responsible for operating the regional office must have their domicile in Thailand.

The Director-General of the Department of Business Development is also authorised to impose any conditions on a business permit granted under the rules.

16.2.6. Trade and Investment Support Offices

In April 1996, the Thai Board of Investment (BOI) announced the establishment of trade and investment support offices to be one of the activities eligible for investment promotion (see BOI, 2004b). Projects in this category are eligible for BOI non-tax incentives, including:

- Permission to own land for an office.

- Permission to bring in foreign nationals to undertake investment feasibility studies.
- Permission to bring in as many foreign technicians and experts as required.
- Permission to take or remit foreign currency abroad.
- No limit on number if shares owned by foreigners.

The range of activities eligible for promotion are (see BOI, 2004b):

- Controlling and advising affiliated companies.
- All types of consulting services, except those engaged in:
  - Buying and selling securities
  - Foreign currency exchange
  - Accounting
  - Advertising
  - Legal affairs
  - Architecture
  - Civil engineering.

Note: Exceptions may be granted by permission from the Department of Commercial Registration or concerned government agencies.

- Information services related to sourcing and procurement, but not brokerages or agencies.
- Engineering and technical services, except those related to architecture and civil engineering.
- Testifying and certifying standards of products, production and services standards.
- Exporting all types of products.
- Wholesaling of all types of products within the country, excluding local agricultural products, arts and crafts, antiques and natural resources.
- Wholesaling of imported machinery engines, tools and equipment.
- Provision of training on the use of machinery, engines, tools and equipment.
- Installation, maintenance and repairing of machinery, engines, tools and equipment.
- Calibration of machinery, engines, tools and equipment.
- Computer software design and development.

If there are any other activities deemed appropriate for investment promotion under the Establishment of Trade and Investment Support Offices, the Office of the Board of Investment (OBOI) will consider them on a case-by-case basis (BOI, 2004b).

16.2.6.1. Eligibility for Regional Trade and Investment Support Offices

Applicants must be either companies established under Thai law, or companies planning to establish under Thai law (BOI, 2004b).

16.2.6.2. Conditions for Regional Trade and Investment Support Offices (see BOI, 2004a)

- Operating licences must have been acquired from all relevant government agencies.
- Operating expenses must amount to no less than 10 million baht (or US$245,559.91) per year, which shall consist of sales and administrative expenses, as set forth in the Revenue Code.
- Operating plans must be approved by the BOI.
- Majority or total foreign ownership is allowed.
- Non-tax privileges, only, will be granted.

As part of the Thai government's effort to promote Regional Operating Headquarters the BOI has revised the list of activities eligible for promotion. While the tax benefits are being provided by the Ministry of Finance, the BOI offers an attractive package of non-tax incentives, including permission to bring in foreign nationals to conduct feasibility studies, permission to bring in foreign technicians and experts to work on promoted projects, and permission to own land, not only for factories, but also for residence of workers and foreign experts. BOI-promoted companies also receive a series of guarantees and protection measures (BOI, 2004b).

Under the Royal Decree, in order to receive BOI non-tax incentives, companies must supervise activities in at least three countries (down from five in the previous policy). Promoted projects are required to have a paid-up registered capital of at least 10 million baht (or US$245,559.91). The requirement that companies invest a minimum of 40 million baht (or US$982,239.64) in real estate has been eliminated, as has the requirement to have operating expenses of at least 50 million baht (or US$1,227,799.50) per year (BOI, 2004b).

16.3. The Implementing Regulations

16.3.1. Foreign Business Act

Foreigners in Thailand derive their legal rights primarily from the domestic laws of Thailand. In general, foreigners enjoy the same basic rights as Thai nationals. Restrictions on foreign ownership in commercial banks, insurance companies, commercial fishing, aviation business, commercial transportation, commodity export, mining and other enterprises exist under various laws. In addition, Thai participation will frequently be required in those activities seeking promotion from the BOI (BOI, 2004b).

The Foreign Business Act (the Act) has been in force since 3 March 2000. The Act repealed and replaced the 1972 Alien Business Law (BOI, 2004b).

While Thai law is silent on foreign participation limits, the Foreign Business Act (FBA) restricts the right of foreigners in the sense that they are required to have a licence prior to the operation or even before the establishment of a corporate vehicle in the country (BOI, 2004b).

The FBA defines a foreigner as (see BOI, 2004b):
* A natural person (as opposed to a corporate entity or juristic person) who does not have Thai nationality.
* Juristic persons not registered in Thailand.
* Juristic persons registered in Thailand with the following character:
  * Half or more than half of their capital shares is held by the person in 1 or 2 above.
  * Half or more than half of their capital fund is derived from the investment of the persons in 1 and 2 above.
  * Being limited partnerships or registered ordinary partnerships whose managing partner or manager is a person not of Thai nationality.
* Juristic persons registered in Thailand having half of their capital shares held by persons in I, 2, or 3 or a juristic person having the persons in 1, 2 or 3 above investing with a value of half or more of the total capital.

The shares of a limited company represented by bearer share certificates are treated as the shares of foreigners, unless the Ministry of Commerce provides otherwise in ministerial regulations. Where other laws regulate shareholding structure or restrict the rights of foreigners in certain businesses, the laws prevail and the shareholding provisions of the FBA do not apply (BOI, 2004b).

Foreign participation in three lists in the FBA are either totally prohibited or restricted by the FBA. The classification of the businesses in the lists must be made by a Royal Decree, except for those in List One and Group I of List Two, which have to be amended by an Act (BOI, 2004b).

The businesses falling outside the three lists may, subject to restrictions under other laws, be operated freely by foreigners provided the minimum capital at the start of the business operation is at least 2 million baht (or US$49,159.13). A committee set up under the FBA is assigned to review the lists once a year, and present its recommendations to the Commerce Minister (BOI, 2004b).

Foreigners operating businesses that are not in any of the three lists and which were in operation before the FBA took effect, but which subsequently require a licence, must inform the Director-General of the Commercial Registration Department, Ministry of Commerce, to receive a certificate to continue business within one year. While the request is being processed, the foreigner may continue operations (BOI, 2004b).

List One businesses are closed to foreigners for special reasons. List One businesses include newspaper, radio and television station undertakings; lowland and upland farming, or horticulture; raising animals; forestry and timber conversions from natural forests; fishing for aquatic animals in Thai waters and Thailand's Exclusive Economic Zone; extraction of Thai medical herbs; trade in and auctioning of Thai ancient objects or ancient objects of national historical value; making or casting Buddha images and making monk's bowls; and dealing in land. Foreigners may operate a business in List Two only when they have acquired permission from the Minister of Commerce, with the approval of the Cabinet. Foreigners may operate businesses in List Three only after obtaining permission from the Director-General of the Commercial Registration Department, with the approval of the Committee (BOI, 2004b).

List Two businesses include businesses concerning national security or safety that could have an adverse effect on art and culture, customs, or native manufacture or handicrafts, or with an impact on natural resources and the environment. List Three businesses include businesses where Thais are not ready to compete in undertakings with foreigners, such as, accounting, legal, architectural, engineering service undertakings, some construction businesses, some brokerage or agency undertakings, some auctioning functions, some domestic, retail and wholesale trade, advertising and hotel undertakings, guided tours, sale of food and/or beverages. For a complete list please see BOI (2004b).

In permitting foreigners to operate businesses under the FBA, the advantages and disadvantages to the nation's safety and security, economic and social development, public order and good morals, art, culture and traditions of the country, natural resource conservation, energy and environment, consumer protection, size of enterprise, employment, technology transfer and research and development opportunities are taken into account (BOI, 2004b).

A foreigner wishing to engage in any business in Lists Two and Three must submit an application to the Minister of Commerce (List Two) or the Director-General of the Commercial Registration Department (List Three). The Cabinet in the case of List Two and the Director-General in the case of List Three will review and make a decision within 60 days of the application filing date. The Cabinet may postpone a decision for another 60 days at the most (BOI, 2004b).

Once approved, a licence will be issued within 15 days. If a licence is not approved, written notification must be given within 30 days stating the reason in the case of List Two, and within 15 days in the case of List Three. In the latter case, an appeal can be made to the minister, who must respond within 30 days. His decision is then final (BOI, 2004b).

The licences have a perpetual life, but expire once the business no longer performs as licensed. The licence must be displayed in a prominent place on the business premises (BOI, 2004b).

Licences for both Lists Two and Three might be issued with ministerial regulations attached, such as total debt financing ratio to capital, technology transfer, minimum investment capital or the minimum number of foreign directors requested to reside in Thailand (BOI, 2004b).

A licence can be revoked if a business does not comply with its conditions, does not meet the Thai participation ratio requirement or engages in other businesses or assists other foreigners in doing business with a view to violating the FBA. Once issued with a warning letter, and if the violation persists, the licence can be revoked (BOI, 2004b).

Foreigners who were operating a business before the new law came into effect, and which consequently required a licence, must apply for a certificate from the Director-General of the Commercial Registration Department, Ministry of Commerce (BOI, 2004b).

Foreigners wishing to operate a business in any of the three lists with the specific permission of the Thai government or with national treatment under a bilateral treaty must inform the Director-General to obtain a business certificate (BOI, 2004b).

Foreigners who have obtained business promotion rights and privileges from the BOI or have written permission from the Industrial Estate Authority of Thailand to operate a business in List Two or List Three must inform the Director-General to obtain a business certificate. Foreigners who have BOI-promotion status are exempt from the FBA, except for the provisions relating to foreign business certificates, reporting requirements on changes of business premises, and the duty to respond to queries from registrars or competent officials (BOI, 2004b).

The FBA requires that the minimum capital to be used at the start of a foreign business must be in accordance with ministerial regulations but not less than 2 million baht (or US$49,159.13). The FBA introduces for the first time a minimum capital for foreigners. This, as opposed to the registered capital, is defined as the capital in foreign currencies that foreigners bring in or remit into Thailand for the business operation. Businesses within the lists must have a minimum capital as described in the ministerial regulations, but not less than 3 million baht (or US$73,667.97) (BOI, 2004b).

Foreigners may operate businesses in List Two only if at least 40 percent of the capital of the foreign corporate entity is held by Thai nationals or corporate entities and at least two-thirds of the directors must be Thai nationals. The Minister of Commerce with the approval of the Cabinet may reduce the percentage, but not lower than 25 percent (BOI, 2004b).

Foreigners may operate the following businesses without a foreign business license if the minimum capital exceeds the specified level (see BOI, 2004b):

- Construction of infrastructure with high technology and with minimum capital of at least 500 million baht (or US$12,277,995.00).
- Brokerages and agencies for selling or purchasing or marketing locally-produced goods or imported goods with minimum capital of at least 100 million baht (or US$2,455,599.00).

- Retailing of all categories of goods with total minimum capital of at least 100 million baht (or US$2,455,599.00) or where the minimum capital of each shop is at least 20 million baht (or US$491,119.80).
- Wholesale in all categories of goods with a total minimum capital of each shop of at least 100 million baht (or US$2,455,599.00).

The FBA allows for imprisonment for up to three years, in addition to fines, for violators of the Act (BOI, 2004b).

16.3.2. Work Permit

The Alien Occupation Law, adopted in 1973, requires all aliens working in Thailand to obtain a Work Permit prior to starting work in Thailand. An updated version of the Act, adopted in 1978, describes the procedures for issuance and maintenance of Work Permits and lists certain occupations from which foreigners may be excluded (BOI, 2004b).

The Act grants exemptions from the Work Permit requirement to persons occupying the following professions (see BOI, 2004b):

- Members of the diplomatic corps.
- Members of consular missions.
- Representatives of member countries and officials of the United Nations and its specialised agencies.
- Personal servants coming from abroad to work exclusively for persons listed under the above items.
- Persons who perform duties on missions in Thailand under an agreement between the government of Thailand and a foreign government or international organisation.
- Persons who enter Thailand for the performance of any duty or mission for the benefit of education, culture, arts, or sports.
- Persons who are specially permitted by the government of Thailand to enter and perform any duty or mission in Thailand.

While most foreigners must apply for a Work Permit, and may not begin work until the Permit is issued, the Alien Employment Act does provide special treatment in the following circumstances (see BOI, 2004b).

16.3.2.1. Urgent and Essential Work

Exemption from Work Permit requirements is granted to foreigners who enter Thailand temporarily, but in accordance with the immigration law, to perform any work of any 'urgent and essential nature' for a period not exceeding 15 days. However, such aliens may engage in work only after a written notification on a prescribed form, signed by the foreigner and endorsed by his employer, has been submitted to and accepted by the Director-General or his designee. Foreigners entitled to this treatment may enter Thailand with any kind of visa, including a transit visa. The term 'urgent and essential work' is not explicitly defined and consequently, the issuance of this sort of exemption is a matter of administrative discretion (BOI, 2004b).

16.3.2.2. Investment Promotion

An alien seeking permission to work in Thailand under the Investment Promotion Law must submit his application for a Work Permit within 30 days of notification by the BOI that his position has been approved. An alien in this category may engage in authorised work while the application is being processed (BOI, 2004b).

The Act requires that any alien working in Thailand must obtain a Work Permit before beginning work. A section of the Act stipulates that while a prospective employer may file an application on the alien's behalf in advance of his commencing work, the actual Work Permit will not be issued until the alien has entered Thailand in accordance with the immigration laws and has presented himself to receive his Work Permit (BOI, 2004b).

The permit initially will be valid only for the period of the alien's non-immigrant visa permits him to remain in Thailand under the immigration law. The Work Permit will be subject to renewal in accordance with the renewed or extended visa. For aliens who are holders of a Thai Certificate of Residence, the Work Permit can be renewed annually. The Labour Department, subject to subsequent renewal, will in principle grant an initial duration of one year for the Work Permit. A Work Permit must be renewed before its expiry date or it will automatically lapse (BOI, 2004b).

Applicants for Work Permits may not enter Thailand as tourists or transients. Thai law prohibits employers from allowing foreigners to perform any function other than that described in the foreigner's Work Permit. Employers must report changes in employment, transfers and termination of all foreigners in their organisation within 15 days of any such action. In cases of dismissal, foreigners must return their Work Permit to labour authorities in Bangkok at the Alien Occupation division or, if they are in a provincial area, to the province's Department of Employment. Failure to do so will result in a fine of up to 1,000 baht (or US$24.56) (BOI, 2004b).

Any foreigner who engages in work without a Work Permit, or in violation of the conditions of his work as stipulated in his permit, may be punished by a term of imprisonment not exceeding three months or a fine of up to 5,000 baht (or US$122.74), or both. Foreigners engaged in work prohibited to them by Royal Decree shall be liable to imprisonment for a term not exceeding five years or to a fine ranging from 2,000 (or US$49.10) to 100,000 baht (or US$2,454.15), or both (BOI, 2004b).

An employer who permits a foreigner to work in his organisation without a Work Permit or to act in violation of the nature of the work specified in the permit may be punished with imprisonment not exceeding three years or fined up to 60,000 baht (or US$1,472.49) or both (BOI, 2004b).

Permit holders must obtain prior permission to change their occupation and/or place of work. Change of employer location or the residential address of the permit holder must be properly endorsed in the Work Permit by the labour authorities. The Alien Employment Act does not prevent a foreigner from engaging in work in more than one field or for more than one employer (BOI, 2004b).

16.3.3. Visas and Immigration Law

All persons, other than those in transit and citizens of certain countries, are required to obtain a visa in order to enter Thailand. Foreign nationals who intend to remain in Thailand to work or conduct business must comply with visa requirements in addition to obtaining a work permit (BOI, 2004b).

The Immigration Act of 1979 as amended in 1980 establishes the following visa categories (see BOI, 2004b):

- Tourist
- Visitor transit
- Immigrant
- Non-quota immigrant
- Non-immigrant.

Nationals of most countries will, without applying for a visa from a Thai embassy or consulate in advance, be given a 30-day visa, except for those who are eligible for 90-day visas. Nationals of some countries who are entitled to a 30-day visa may be requested by the immigration officials to produce an onward ticket to establish that they will leave Thailand within 30 days. Tourist visas are initially valid for 60 days and are renewable at the discretion of the Immigration Department. Renewals are normally granted for periods of up to 30 days at a time (BOI, 2004b).

Foreigners who have obtained a transit visa from a Thai embassy or consulate will be granted a 30-day stay in Thailand. Extensions of stay are normally granted for periods of 7-l0 days. Transit, visitor transit and tourist visa holders are not authorised to work in Thailand (BOI, 2004b).

Non-quota immigrant visas include, inter alia, former residents who have lost their resident status but who have reapplied to resume their residency and who have been able to demonstrate a convincing reason to support the granting of this type of visa (BOI, 2004b).

Members of the diplomatic or consular corps, foreigners coming to perform their duties in Thailand with the approval of the Thai government, foreigners performing their duties in Thailand under an agreement between the Thai government and a foreign government, heads of international organisations or agencies operating in Thailand, and dependents of all the aforementioned persons, including private servants of members of the diplomatic corps, are exempted by the Act from the normal visa requirements (BOI, 2004b).

Foreigners seeking a prolonged stay, or those coming to work in Thailand, should obtain non-immigrant visas for all family members prior to entering Thailand. There are several categories of Non-Immigrant visas which include, among others, business visa category (B); dependent visa category (0); investment subject to the provision of the laws on investment promotion (BOI IB); diplomatic and consular visa category (D); performance of duties with the mass media (M); performance of skilled or expert work (EX); investment (with concurrence of ministries and departments concerned) (capital investment 1M); study or observation (ED) (see BOI, 2004b).

Advantages of a non-immigrant visa include the following (see BOI, 2004b):

- Entitlement of the holder to apply for a multiple re-entry visa to Thailand from the Immigration Division in Bangkok.
- Subject to the regulations of the Immigration Authorities, entitlement of the holder to apply for permanent residence in Thailand.
- Eligibility for issuance of a Work Permit to the holder.

- Eligibility for temporary visa renewal while processing issuance of a long-term annual visa.

Foreigners are advised to adhere strictly to the rules governing each visa category. They should report any changes of address or status to local police within 24 hours (BOI, 2004b).

In addition, foreigners residing in Thailand for more than 90 consecutive days are required to register their address with the Immigration Bureau every 90 days. This requirement applies to all foreigners, including holders of Work Permits and long-term visas. Failure to do so can result in substantial penalties (BOI, 2004b).

Transit, visitor transit, tourist and non-immigrant visas are issued only for the following purposes and duration (see BOI, 2004b):

- Diplomats or consular missions (duration as necessary).
- Official missions (duration as necessary).
- Tourism (90 days).
- Sports (30 days).
- Business purposes (one year).
- An investment that has received authorisation from the appropriate government authorities (two years).
- Investment or other business in connection with investment under the Investment Promotion Act (as determined by the BOI).
- Transit (30 days).
- The controller or crew of a conveyance entering a port or other locality in Thailand (30 days).
- Work as a skilled labourer or specialist (one year).

In response to feedback from investors, the BOI coordinated the establishment of a One-Stop Service centre for visas and Work Permits. Through joint cooperation with the Immigration Bureau and the Ministry of Labour, the centre can process applications or renewals of visas and Work Permits within three hours, upon receipt of proper and complete documentation. In addition, the centre handles other transactions, including the issuance of multiple re-entry stamps, changes in class of visa (to non-immigrant from tourist or transit), and payment of fines (BOI, 2004b).

Work Permits, which are valid for the period of the visa, have to be renewed every year. When an individual applies for a renewal of visa, he or she has to show that taxes for the previous year have been paid (BOI, 2004b).

Foreigners may also apply for permanent residence permits for Thailand under certain conditions, such as investment in a business, or a condominium. Application can either be made to the BOI or the Immigration Department (BOI, 2004b).

16.4. Conclusions

The legal requirements of investing in Thailand have been provided so the reader is able to understand the investment climate provided by the Thai government for FDI. As is quite clearly evident from the investment regulations in Thailand included in this chapter and provided by the Thai Board of Investment (BOI) that the Thai government is very supportive of firms wishing to invest in Thailand and does whatever it can to encourage FDI and to make the investment process for foreign firms wishing to invest in Thailand as transparent, as user friendly and as mutually beneficial as possible, thereby suggesting that the IJV form of FDI in Thailand is likely to proliferate under such an investment climate for a long time to come.

17. A Guide for Managers of International Joint Ventures

17.1. Introduction

Making an IJV successful is a universally shared goal of all parent firms. However, many IJVs do ultimately fail (Gomes-Casseres, 1987; Makino and Beamish, 1998). Therefore, what makes an IJV succeed or fail still remains an important yet somewhat elusive issue. Broadly viewed, the Julian (1998) study focused on the factors influencing the performance of IJVs in Thailand. However, instead of evaluating the broad-based issue of overall business performance, the Julian study specifically evaluated the marketing performance of IJVs in Thailand and developed an instrument for measuring IJV marketing performance. In particular, the Julian study focused on the following question: What are some of the primary factors that influence the marketing performance of IJVs in Thailand? Using the multivariate techniques of exploratory factor analysis, multiple regression analysis and discriminant analysis the Julian study identified those factors that have the most significant influence on the marketing performance of IJVs in Thailand, a centrally located country in South East Asia.

An international joint venture (IJV) is an interfirm organisation. It is a separate entity created by two or more other entities (parents or partners) and, essentially, represents a partnership arrangement between parenting firms. The IJV pursues its own goals and objectives but only within the constraints of the goals and strategies of its parents. It is simultaneously under two or more different management regimes. Composition of ownership, contractual arrangements, composition of the board of directors and senior management, and ongoing contributions of the parents are some of the elements that define the stake of the parents and the web of relationships between the IJV unit and each of its parents. For these reasons the IJV form of organizational structure represents a complex and unstable arrangement (Beamish, 1985; Killing, 1983; Makino and Beamish, 1998; Yan, 1998). It is often difficult to manage, control and integrate with the operations of the parent firms. In a sense, the instability of the arrangements between the parents manifests this complexity. It is often found that IJV failure is costly, frustrating and disruptive for both the foreign firm(s) and the domestic firm (Beamish, 1985; Cullen *et al.,* 1995; Dymsza, 1988; Killing, 1983; Yan, 1998).

Since the 1970s the IJV has become an important mode of overseas market entry (Franko, 1971) and in some countries, in specific industries, it is the only form of market entry available to the foreign firm (BOI, 2004a). This was further evident from the increasing number of IJVs formed each year in Thailand (BOI, 1996; Julian, 1998). This growth appeared to have come from a number of different sources: rising nationalism in Thailand; rising bargaining power due to sustained high levels of growth in GDP; resource limitations of foreign companies; increasing uncertainty in the economic and regulatory environments of both the foreign firm and the foreign market they are entering, in the Julian (1998) study that market being Thailand; and growing competition among foreign firms. In view of the increasing use of the IJV entry mode, on the one hand, and the high failure rate (see Makino and Beamish, 1998), on the other, the importance of identifying the factors influencing IJV marketing performance success can hardly be overstated.

17.2. The Joint Venture Process

The internationalisation process is referred to as the mode used to penetrate foreign markets (Calof and Beamish, 1995). Modes are the institutional arrangements that allow firms to use their products or services in a country. Mode forms include licensee or franchise agreements, indirect or direct export, sales subsidiary, joint venture, and wholly owned subsidiaries (Calof and Beamish, 1995; Padmanabhan and Cho, 1995).

Whilst there has been a diversity of studies undertaken to determine why firms use certain modes of market entry, one research approach has dominated the study of the appropriate market entry mode structure, that approach being stages research. Stages research is the main form of the pattern-oriented approach to analysing mode selection. It proposes that firms move sequentially through different stages as they develop their international activities (Burton and Schlegelmilch, 1987; Calof and Beamish, 1995; Cavusgil, 1984a; Cavusgil and Nevin, 1981; Johanson and Vahlne, 1977; Johanson and Wiedersheim-Paul, 1975).

Regardless of the stages process used or the element being institutionalised, each operates under the same basic philosophy. Each stage involves an increased commitment to international activities (Calof and Beamish, 1995; Jain, 1994a; Keegan, 1995; Terpstra and Sarathy, 1994).

Usually firms commence their international operations with some form of direct or indirect export. The internationalising firm can then move to establish a sales subsidiary in the foreign market of question. Once the sales subsidiary has produced satisfactory results, the internationalising firm may then get involved in some form of licensee or franchise agreement. Alternatively, the internationalising firm could move to establish some form of IJV with a suitable partner that has usually emerged from one of the earlier stages and is likely to have been a customer, consumer or user of the internationalising firm's products from one of the earlier stages. The final stage of the stages research process involves the internationalising firm establishing its own wholly owned subsidiary (Calof and Beamish, 1995).

Each stage the internationalising firm goes through involves an increased commitment to international activities, and this increased commitment is likely to be as a result of increased trust between the parties involved as each party goes through the internationalising process. Commitment increases as firms learn more, and therefore become less uncertain about foreign markets (Bilkey and Tesar, 1977; Calof and Beamish, 1995; Johanson and Vahlne, 1977; Cavusgil, 1984a; Kedia and Chhokar, 1986) and potential IJV partners.

As firms get to know potential partners better through the stages process there is an increased chance of them entering into IJV relationships with interested parties and of those IJVs being successful. The partners have been able to develop a clear understanding and trust of each other during the sometimes long negotiation process that is involved in moving from indirect or direct export to an IJV or wholly owned subsidiary. During the stages process the internationalising firm is able to acquire social knowledge of its potential partners and determine which of those firms best suits its requirements. Therefore, there is less chance for the IJV to fail.

Sohn (1994) identified the importance of social knowledge in the selection of a foreign partner for foreign market success, with social knowledge being defined as one's ability to understand and predict others' general patterns of behaviour (Tolbert, 1988). Sohn (1994) posited that social knowledge may allow a foreign corporation to (1) selectively transact with certain local parties with desirable behavioural characteristics, and (2) control them with a reduced need to resort to bureaucratic authority through ownership.

Through social knowledge of the behavioural patterns of the local parties, the foreign corporation would be able to (1) predict how the local parties would behave under different stimuli, (2) relate their behaviours to how they interpret the present state of affairs, and (3) detect and decipher various signals (Spence, 1974) that they may implicitly or explicitly convey. The foreign corporation, through its ability to correctly process the signals, may also distinguish (1) what the local parties' desired future state of affairs are, and (2) how they would attempt to attain the desired state (Sohn, 1994).

The most important benefit that the foreign corporation may realise in the selection of an IJV partner through social knowledge would perhaps be that they would be able to distinguish local parties with desirable behavioural patterns (such as low opportunistic tendencies) in a relatively costless manner and this could only enhance the ultimate performance of the IJV by selection of the right partner first time round (Sohn, 1994). This process is enhanced by the stages process in the internationalisation of the firm as each partner has good social knowledge of the other's behaviour before finalising the IJV agreement.

Koot (1988) provided support for this notion by concluding that a trustworthy relationship is logically a necessary condition for any capital investment risk to be taken, with the JV being a sort of a "marriage". The internationalisation process of stages research provides a safe process for the internationalising firm to have a competent look at potential IJV partners before getting involved in any IJV relationship. Having had a competent look at potential partners, the internationalising firm will only select those firms that it has had a strong and positive relationship with previously, those which it trusts, and that are likely to make a commitment to its products and services. These attributes can only be achieved after the internationalising firm has been dealing with a potential partner for a reasonable amount of time, thus offering support for the stages process of internationalisation.

17.3. Selecting a Partner

Choosing a partner when establishing an IJV is the most important decision a foreign corporation will ever make. If the wrong partner is chosen, the venture is simply doomed to fail. IJVs that select a partner that is only needed initially, often do not make it in the long run once that partner is no longer needed. It is very important that all partners in the IJV are truly necessary and that they will continue to be needed in the future. Of course, it is also very important that firms select partners they can trust, and that each partner to the IJV clearly understands each other's objectives for the IJV and that they determine whether all sets of goals are mutually obtainable and compatible (Fey, 1995).

Harrigan (1985) argued that JVs are more likely to succeed when the partners possess complementary missions, resource capabilities, managerial capabilities and other attributes that create a strategic fit in which the bargaining power of the venturers is evenly matched. Partners' needs to be engaged in a particular IJV are stabilising to the relationship, while a wide variety of dissimilarities are destabilising to the venturing relationship. Thus, partners will stay together as long as they need each other and their venture remains successful, unless the terms invoked by the bargaining agreement's 'divorce clause' are so egregious that they constitute an exit barrier that perpetuates a partnership long after its usefulness, to at least one of the partners, has expired (Caves and Porter, 1976; Harrigan, 1980; Porter, 1976).

Fey (1995) in his study on the key success factors for Russian IJVs found the most common cause of IJV failure was a basic misunderstanding about the roles and objectives of the partners. In most cases these differences existed from the very beginning, but the parents were not aware of them because they did not spend enough time initially learning about each other's objectives for the IJV. In-depth discussions during the formation stage could have alerted the parents to most of these differences so that they could have been resolved early. Or it could have been determined that the differences could not be resolved and thus concluded that the firms should search for other partners. Of course, everyone is eager to finalise the negotiation phase and get on with the work of the IJV. Nevertheless, data in the Fey (1995) study showed that spending extra time in the negotiation phase to understand the other partner's objectives for the IJV is a wise investment.

Anderson (1990), Dymsza (1988), Harrigan (1988a) and Koot (1988) also identify the importance of the partner selection process, suggesting that the foreign corporation and the local partner in an IJV that fails may have significant differences in their objectives and goals with respect to the business, depending upon the size and type of companies involved; their particular business, industry and products; and their international and other experience. For example, a foreign corporation may desire to enter into a viable and expanding manufacturing operation through a JV that will yield a target rate of return on investment in the medium to long term. Therefore, it strives to reinvest a substantial portion of earnings in the venture in order to expand the operation and increase its return over this time horizon. The local partner, on the other hand, enters into the JV to earn an immediate rate of return on its investment. Therefore, it strives for maximum pay-out of dividends (Dymsza, 1988).

The situation, of course, can be the reverse. The foreign corporation may have the goal of a quick payback on its investment of capital, technology and management, for example, three to five years. The local partner may strive to develop a growing, profitable manufacturing business yielding satisfactory profits over the medium to long term (Dymsza, 1988). These divergent business objectives and goals over significantly different time frames will require different marketing strategies for them to be achieved. A delay or stalemate between the partners over the implementation of the appropriate marketing strategy could have a negative influence on the marketing performance of the IJV or it could cause the IJV to fail altogether.

Many researchers have identified the importance of a clear understanding of what each partner is bringing to the IJV relationship (Beamish, 1988; Dymsza, 1988; Fey, 1995; Blodgett, 1991a; Geringer, 1988; Harrigan, 1988a). Harrigan (1985) and Dymsza (1988) argue that IJVs are more likely to succeed when partners possess complementary missions, resource capabilities, managerial capabilities and other attributes that create a strategic fit in which the bargaining power of the venture's sponsors is evenly matched. A more successful JV creates synergies through the partners pooling their resources, capabilities and strengths. These synergies lead to the establishment of a manufacturing operation in which the total results are greater than the sum of the contributions of the partners. As a result of combining the modern production processes, the product know-how, technical training, management development and management systems of a foreign corporation with the local partner's local capital, management, existing plant, marketing expertise and knowledge of the country environment, the JV results in a more efficient and productive enterprise than the participants could achieve on their own. The synergies occur through the partners working closely together, reinforcing each other's strengths, the cross-pollenisation of ideas concerning management of the enterprise, responding to competition, and developing the potential of the business in the country environment (Dymsza, 1988).

17.4. Mutual Need and Commitment

One of the major reasons for using the equity joint venture organisation form is a need for the attributes or assets of the other partner. Assets include such things as cash, capital resources and raw material sources (Beamish, 1993; Beamish and Banks, 1987). The understanding that access to capital resources and low-cost raw material access is one of the major reasons the JV form of organization structure has been used is built around the theory of internalization (Beamish and Banks, 1987). The internalization theory argues that due to the transaction costs that must be borne as a result of conducting business in imperfect markets it is more efficient (less expensive) for the firm to use internal structures rather than market intermediaries to serve a foreign market (Beamish and Banks, 1987).

Knowledge of the local business environment is an asset often avidly sought by a global company that is establishing a position in a foreign market, especially for the first time. This knowledge has economic value and can take several forms. It usually involves familiarity with economic, political and business conditions. The country may be burdened with inadequate infrastructure, a large public sector and intransigent ethnic hostilities. Political connections play a part also. Having a local partner may ease relations between the global company and a suspicious host-country government, which may perceive a JV as less threatening than a wholly owned subsidiary of a foreign firm (Connolly, 1984). The public relations benefit often extends to local labour relations and to worker morale as well. In concrete terms, a local partner may provide advantages in obtaining contracts, access to favourable tax treatment, a chance to avoid various non-tariff barriers, and a means of entry into relationships with local businesses and officials. Such connections with the local environment are often an essential precondition to a venture's success (Blodgett, 1991b).

Apart from host-country government reasons, the transfer of modern and innovative technology is one of the principal reasons why local firms and foreign partners enter into JV agreements. In fact, access to modern and up-to-date technology is widely recognised as the principal reason why local firms in developing countries enter into JV arrangements with foreign corporations from developed countries (Beamish, 1984, 1993; Blodgett, 1991b). Failure to deliver to the IJV the technology initially promised by the foreign partner(s) when entering into the IJV agreement could cause conflict between the foreign and local partners and this conflict together with the lack of the required technology could have a negative influence on the marketing performance of the IJV. This was certainly the case with Julian's (1998) study on IJV marketing performance in Thailand, with the lack of up-to-date technology being identified as one of the dominant statements in the factor of market characteristics that had a significant negative effect on IJV marketing performance in Thailand.

As such, firms establishing JVs typically need partners for a variety of potential contributions. Several researchers have examined the effect of partner need on JV performance. Raveed and Renforth (1983) have shown that the two most important objectives of joint ventures were to obtain local market knowledge and local management. Beamish and Banks (1987), in a sample of 66 JVs in less-developed countries, found that greater need between partners resulted in more satisfactory performance. The Beamish and Banks study demonstrated a pattern that managers in high-performing ventures looked to their local partners for greater contributions than did managers in low-performing ventures.

Finally, Fey (1995) noted the importance of long-term commitment for IJV success in his study of the key success factors for Russian/foreign joint ventures. The Fey study indicated that it is beneficial to IJV success for both parents to be involved in the JV for the long term. It makes the JV easier to manage if one parent has more involvement than the other, but it is important that all parents make a real long-term commitment to the JV. Having parents that are committed to the JV for the long term decreases the risk of shirking and increases the likelihood of mutual forbearance (Beamish, 1988; Fey, 1995; Madhok, 1995; Sohn, 1994).

17.5. Designing the Venture

A potential problem with IJVs involves the foreign corporation's global integration and the local partner's national orientation. A number of IJVs fail because the foreign corporation strives for global integration of their business, while the local partner is emphasising the operations within their country (Datta, 1988; Dymsza, 1988; Koot, 1988; Wright and Russel, 1975). Many foreign corporations aim to maximise their profits or earn a target rate of return on their investments globally, rather than maximise their business in a particular country, including those in which they have IJVs. Accordingly, foreign corporations strive to integrate their IJV affiliates with their system of enterprises around the world in production, finance, marketing and management. Furthermore, since IJV affiliates in developing countries are generally a small part of the total international business of most foreign corporations, they may not grant high priority to them in resource allocation, management and technological effort. On the other hand, an IJV involved in any sort of manufacturing commonly represents a major business involvement for the local partner. Thus, the national partner commits major capital and management effort to the IJV affiliate and expects comparable commitment from the foreign corporation in order to have a highly successful business. Serious conflicts can emerge when the local partner finds that the foreign corporation does not grant high priority to the IJV and does not commit sufficient resources and effort. These conflicts can become deeper and the IJV may fail (Datta, 1988; Dymsza, 1988).

A further area of concern that has led to the failure of some IJVs involves the joint venture agreement or contract. The long period between the first steps abroad and the rounding up of JV negotiations usually requires much attention of top managers and their staff (Berg and Friedmann, 1980; Calof and Beamish, 1995; Otterbeck, 1981; Schaan and Beamish, 1988). The composition and functioning of the JV's board and management, the informal and formal lines of communication, recruitment and compensation of key staff, and adaptation to political forces at hand all form potential built-in difficulties for the interacting companies (Cullen *et al.,* 1995; Geringer and Hebert, 1989, 1991; Johnson *et al.,* 1993; Killing, 1983; Madhok, 1995; Porter and Fuller, 1986). When the IJV agreement does not clearly specify the goals of each party, the resources contributed by the partners, their major responsibilities and obligations, their rights, the character of the business, their share of profits and mode of distribution, ways of resolving disputes, and other key aspects of the venture, disagreements can take place and disrupt the venture (Beamish, 1988; Dymsza, 1988; Geringer, 1988; Geringer and Hebert, 1989; Pan, 1996). These issues all require consideration when designing the JV.

17.6. Ongoing Management and Relationship

The next important area within the IJV organisation structure that requires attention involves possible conflicts over decision-making, managerial processes and style. The strife between a foreign corporation and a local partner to control major policies and decisions constitutes a major reason for the failure of many IJVs (Blodgett, 1991a; Dymsza, 1988; Ganitsky *et al.,* 1991; Geringer and Hebert, 1989; Schaan and Beamish, 1988). The foreign corporation may strive to control major policies of the venture through the appointment of a majority of the board of directors, including outside, allegedly neutral directors, who are favourable to it. The role of the board of directors of joint venture affiliates varies a great deal. Some boards determine major policies of the venture, select the chief and top executives, and monitor the overall management and operations of the enterprise, but many boards primarily grant advice to the Chief Executive and perform rather perfunctory responsibilities. Other boards assume a legal function to meet the requirements of law (Baker and McKenzie, 1993; Dymsza, 1988).

Foreign corporations control the management of joint venture affiliates in other ways. They obtain authority to appoint the Chief Executive and key managers; they establish the managerial and control processes and have the right to veto major decisions. The continuing control by the foreign corporation of combinations of manufacturing, marketing, finance and other decisions in the venture often leads to major conflicts with the national partners and the host governments. These conflicts can lead to the failure of IJVs (Dymsza, 1988).

Major differences with respect to management processes, style of management and corporate culture between the foreign corporation and the local partner can lead to serious conflicts which contribute to the failure of IJVs (Dymsza, 1988; Lane and Beamish, 1990; Schaan and Beamish, 1988; Zhu and Dowling, 1995). For example, a foreign corporation may seek to impose its process of strategic and operational planning, an information and control system, budgeting and accounting on the JV affiliate. The local partner may not have any experience with these processes and consider them inappropriate. A foreign corporation may emphasise a more participatory style of management, delegation of responsibility to subordinates, profit centres, and periodic evaluation of performance. The local partner that is often a family-owned business in the developing countries of South East Asia may have a more authoritarian style of management, with no delegation of responsibility to subordinates and very little formal planning and control. Although such differences in management processes and style can sometimes be harmonised through a learning process in the JV, they can often disrupt the venture causing it to fail (Dymsza, 1988; Schaan and Beamish, 1988).

Finally, major problems have been known to arise in IJVs over the payment of royalties, management fees and headquarters charges. Allocation of headquarters administrative costs, royalties on licensing agreements, technical fees and management fees in supplementary agreements negotiated by the foreign corporation in IJV agreements can lead to serious conflicts with the local partner and in some cases host governments. Even though IJV contracts may provide for such payments to the foreign partner, the local partner may scrutinise such charges in order to avoid excessive or unnecessary charges to the business. For example, the partner or the government may find royalties on licensing agreements excessive when the foreign partner contributes no new technology. Management fees may be considered unjustified, if national managers are not trained to take over management positions in the process. A specific grievance with many local firms in IJV relationships occurs when headquarters allocates a share of its administrative costs to a JV affiliate. The local partner in an IJV relationship often wants to revise licensing agreements, management contracts and other agreements when they perceive the foreign partner is not providing the technological, managerial, technical and training inputs to justify the continued payments of royalties, management and technical fees, and other charges. As a result, serious conflicts can arise between the foreign and local partner leading to the eventual failure of the IJV (Blodgett, 1991b; Contractor and Lorange, 1988c; Dymsza, 1988; Schaan and Beamish, 1988). All these issues require management's attention for a successful JV in the developing countries of South East Asia.

17.7. Managerial Implications for IJV Performance Success in South East Asia

The findings from the Julian (1998) study in Thailand indicated that several market-related, product-related and firm-related factors influence the marketing performance of IJVs in Thailand. Specifically, market characteristics, conflict, commitment, product characteristics, firm-specific characteristics, marketing orientation, organizational control, managerial control and adapting to foreign market needs were the factors that influenced the marketing performance of IJVs in Thailand. It is important for the management of any company to be aware of these factors when contemplating an IJV of any magnitude in a developing country of South East Asia.

As far as market characteristics were concerned, the Julian study clearly indicated that it was important for managers of IJVs to be aware of the market characteristics of a foreign market that can influence a firm's marketing performance. Availability of capital resources, raw materials and distribution channels; transfer of up-to-date technology; knowledge of local business practices; and knowledge of industry competition were very important for the successful marketing performance of IJVs in Thailand. Companies intending to enter into an IJV arrangement in Thailand and other South East Asian countries need to ensure the availability and existence of the above if they are to succeed in those markets.

The Julian (1998) study further indicated that it was important for the managers of IJVs in Thailand and other South East Asian countries to minimise their interorganizational conflicts in order to improve the IJV's marketing performance. Companies intending to enter into an IJV arrangement with another company should be proactive enough by taking time to get to know their IJV partner in order to avoid any unnecessary misunderstandings and potential conflicts concerning the IJV contract and the roles and functions each partner is expected to fulfil.

The Julian (1998) study also demonstrated that JV partners must make commitments of: providing key senior management people; supplying special skills; visiting and offering assistance; furnishing additional equity or loan capital when needed; and general commitment to the local market. The management of any company needs to be committed to the foreign market they are entering and to their IJV partner for successful marketing performance of their IJV.

In relation to product characteristics, the Julian study findings have shown that managers of IJVs should make efforts to adapt their products/services to meet the needs of the local market for achieving success in the marketing performance of their IJV. Specifically, product/service adaptation; adapting the promotional campaign; familiarity of consumers to the product; the stage of the product life cycle the product is in; and culture-specificity of the product/service require management's attention. IJV managers must be aware of the importance of adapting the IJV's products/services to meet the needs of the local market and restrain from opting for a globally standardised product/service.

With regard to firm-specific characteristics, the Julian study findings have shown the importance of product/service quality for marketing performance success. Specifically, the importance of firm-specific advantages such as product differentiation and customer knowledge for marketing performance success. IJV managers must be aware of the importance of differentiated products and knowledge of one's customers for marketing performance success and restrain from opting for undifferentiated products directed at the total market.

The Julian (1998) study findings also focused on the marketing orientation of senior management and concluded that marketing orientation must be with reference to senior management's knowledge of its customers. That is, for senior management to understand what its customers expect from its products and services and for senior management to be in regular contact with its customers. The senior management of a company needs to be marketing oriented when operating in a foreign market for successful marketing performance of their IJV.

In relation to organizational control, the Julian study clearly indicated that it was important for managers of IJVs to minimise the transference of the IJV's output to a parent company and to minimise the sourcing of the IJV's input needs from a parent company for marketing performance success. Companies intending to enter into an IJV arrangement should take the time to allow the IJV to operate as a stand-alone entity instead of using it as a means of generating additional revenue from out-of-date products or as a subsidiary to generate greater profits for head office.

The Julian study findings also concluded that at least one of the IJV parents must have effective control over the IJV for marketing performance success. Companies intending to enter into a JV arrangement should make sure that at least one of the parents is responsible for ensuring that the JV meets the expectations and objectives of its parents for marketing performance success.

Finally, the Julian study findings clearly demonstrated the importance of adapting the IJV's products/services to meet the needs of the local market for marketing performance success. Managers of companies intending to enter into a JV arrangement in Thailand and other countries in South East Asia must be prepared to adapt their products/services to meet the needs of the local market and restrain from opting for a globally standardised product/service.

17.8. Major Differences

Significant effort should be placed on ensuring that there is a clear agreement about each parent's contribution to and its role in the JV before the JV is started. A clear agreement about each parent's contribution to the IJV has been noted by previous researchers as vital for IJV success (Beamish, 1988; Blodgett, 1991a; Dymsza, 1988; Fey, 1995; Geringer, 1988; Harrigan, 1988a; Hladik, 1988; Killing, 1983; Lee and Beamish, 1995; Schaan and Beamish, 1988). Spending extra time up-front will save much time and trouble in the future.

Dymsza (1988) noted that a perception by the foreign corporation or the local partner that it is not obtaining sufficient benefits from the JV in return for its contribution of resources leads to the failure of some ventures. What counts is not only the actual contributions made by each party and the profits and other benefits obtained by each one, but even more what the partners perceive over the life of the operation. In some cases, the foreign corporation perceives that it is not obtaining an adequate return for its contribution of manufacturing and product technology, management, technical training, trademarks and business expertise. In other instances, the local partner believes that its contribution of existing factories and facilities, management, local capital, sales organization and contacts with the government are excessive in relationship to its share of ownership, the responsibilities it has in the venture and the profits it earns. These perceptions of benefits obtained in relation to contributions made can change over the years. When one or both partners perceive an unsatisfactory ratio between benefits and costs from the venture, serious conflicts develop leading either one or both partners to refuse to contribute any further resources to the venture until some of their demands are met and if a stalemate develops it can likely lead to the failure of the whole venture (Beamish, 1988; Beamish and Inkpen, 1995; Dymsza, 1988; Gullander, 1976; Hladik, 1988; Wright and Russel, 1975).

As such, managers of IJVs in the developing countries of South East Asia need to be aware of these issues. Wherever possible the JV contract should try and foresee these potential problems and provide a problem-solving mechanism that would enable certain problems to be solved before they damage the JV and the relationship between its parents.

18. Future Research Agenda for International Joint Ventures in South East Asia

18.1. Contributions to the Literature

The Julian (1998) study on IJV marketing performance in Thailand made major contributions to the IJV literature. Firstly, it evaluated the marketing performance of IJVs as opposed to general business performance. Secondly, it developed a quantitative measure of IJV marketing performance. Thirdly, it evaluated IJV marketing performance in a developing country context, more specifically a developing country of South East Asia, that country being Thailand. Finally, it considered marketing-related issues as well as management-related issues as antecedents of IJV marketing performance in Thailand. These four contributions to the IJV literature are significant contributions to say the least.

Firstly, the Julian study evaluated the marketing performance of IJVs in Thailand as opposed to their general business performance. There have been many studies conducted on IJV performance; however, nearly without exception all these studies focus on the general business performance of the IJV without looking specifically at the IJV's marketing performance. Marketing performance is arguably one of the most important components of general business performance to measure as it represents such a large percentage of total business performance (see Crocombe, 1991).

Previous studies have looked at narrow measures of business performance, principally the financial indicators, termination rates, duration and instability and have only considered factors or indicators that were likely to influence general business performance not marketing performance, e.g., conflict, control, trust and commitment. The Julian (1998) study attempted to overcome this void in the IJV literature and specifically examined the

277

marketing performance of IJVs in Thailand. The Julian study evaluated how specific marketing-related factors and management-related factors influenced the marketing performance of IJVs in Thailand, e.g., market characteristics, conflict, commitment, product characteristics, firm-specific characteristics, marketing orientation, organisational control, managerial control and adapting to foreign market needs, and developed a composite index to measure IJV marketing performance.

Secondly, the Julian study developed a composite index to measure IJV marketing performance. One of the most important issues identified from the IJV literature is how the performance of an IJV is to be evaluated. At first glance the answer seems quite obvious. Use the financial indicators: after all an IJV is a strategic business unit and should be assessed like any other strategic business unit and the financial indicators are the most appropriate performance indicators to use when evaluating performance.

The reason why the financial indicators should not be the sole indicator of performance lies in the setting of the IJV. An IJV is a hybrid with a minimum of two parents and it is likely each parent has different sets of objectives for the IJV and will assess IJV performance or marketing performance based on the achievement of those objectives. The financial indicators may not identify the extent to which the IJV has achieved its objectives as IJVs may be formed for a variety of objectives, e.g., technology transfer, reduction of risk, access to low-cost raw materials and labour force, economies of scale. As a consequence the financial indicators may not give a true indication of how the IJV is actually performing.

How should IJV performance or marketing performance be measured then? Previous studies have used a variety of different measures to measure IJV performance with the ultimate outcome being a lack of consensus on how an IJV's performance should be evaluated.

As such, the Julian (1998) study sought to overcome some of the limitations of previous studies on IJV performance and incorporated a number of different measures of marketing performance into a composite measure of marketing performance that could be used by other researchers. The objective of the measure of IJV marketing performance developed by Julian was to develop an objective and quantitative measure of IJV marketing performance that incorporated the majority of objectives for IJV formation.

Using the literature and the pre-tests of the research instrument, the Julian study pre-set 16 strategic objectives into the research instrument that corresponded with each of the measures of IJV marketing performance. Towards the end of the research instrument, respondents were asked to indicate the relative importance attached to each objective by allocating a constant-sum (100 points) to the individual objectives proportional to their importance. The composite index was computed as the extent to which the initial strategic objectives were achieved by multiplying the level of satisfaction associated with the achievement of each strategic objective by the points allocated to the importance of the same strategic objective. The combined scores for each of the 16 strategic objectives were then added together to give a composite index score for each IJV for measuring the marketing performance of IJVs in Thailand. The results of this measure of marketing performance were encouraging, if not conclusive, the implications being that this measure of marketing performance should be tested again on a larger sample before it is accepted as a reliable measure of IJV marketing performance.

Thirdly, the Julian study made a major contribution to the IJV literature by evaluating IJV marketing performance in South East Asia, and specifically Thailand. In the international business literature there are many studies that look at IJV performance in developing countries (e.g., Beamish, 1984, 1993; Lee and Beamish, 1995; Makino and Beamish, 1998; Schaan, 1983). There are also several studies that have examined IJV performance in South East Asia (e.g., Makino and Beamish, 1998). However, there have been very few conclusive empirical studies conducted on IJV marketing performance in the South East Asian economic region of the world. Given some of the cultural and religious factors unique to this economic region, arguably some of the factors likely to influence the marketing performance of IJVs in Thailand and other South East Asian countries could be unique to this economic region.

The Julian (1998) study tested the results of previous studies to see if proven factors of JV performance held true for a developing country of South East Asia and sought to identify whether or not market-related factors had a significant influence on IJV marketing performance. This proved to be the case in both instances with, firstly, commitment, conflict and organisational control proving to be some of the dominant factors influencing IJV marketing performance in Thailand. The factors of commitment, conflict and organisational control are proven determinants of IJV performance (Beamish, 1984; Dymsza, 1988; Habib, 1987; Lee and Beamish, 1995).

Secondly, when the factors of market characteristics and marketing orientation were identified as having a significant influence on IJV marketing performance, this indicated that certain market-related characteristics that were specifically related to Thailand had a significant influence on IJV marketing performance. Therefore, the Julian (1998) study makes a major contribution to the IJV literature by specifically studying IJV marketing performance in this economic region (South East Asia) and Thailand.

Finally, the Julian study made a major contribution to the IJV literature by considering marketing-related issues as well as management-related issues as factors influencing IJV marketing performance in Thailand. There have been many previous studies that have evaluated the factors influencing IJV performance (Beamish, 1984; Lee and Beamish, 1995; Cullen *et al.*, 1995; Madhok, 1995). Some of the factors identified in previous studies as having a significant influence on IJV performance have been identified as organisational control, conflict and commitment. The Julian study further tested the influence of these factors on IJV marketing performance.

Moreover, the Julian study added some marketing-related factors to the list of management-related factors (organisational control, conflict and commitment) likely to influence IJV marketing performance, and produced some statistically significant findings. The list of marketing-related factors added to the list of management-related factors likely to influence IJV marketing performance were identified as market characteristics, product characteristics, firm-specific characteristics and marketing orientation. The relationships between all four factors and the dependent variable of IJV marketing performance identified two of the four factors as having a significant influence on IJV marketing performance. Those two factors having a significant influence on IJV marketing performance were identified as market characteristics and marketing orientation.

Very few previous studies have considered these factors as influencing IJV performance or marketing performance. Therefore, the Julian (1998) study made a major contribution to the existing IJV literature by identifying additional factors that can significantly influence IJV marketing performance. These marketing-related factors of market characteristics and marketing orientation remain relatively unexplored by previous studies on IJV performance and by examining them in this context in a developing country of South East Asia new dimensions are added to the question of what the most salient factors influencing IJV performance in South East Asia are.

18.2. Study's Limitations

Whilst the Julian (1998) study made several major contributions to the JV literature there were several limitations with it that are important to discuss prior to identifying the directions for future research on IJVs in the developing countries of South East Asia. The major limitations of the study primarily involved the research instrument. They included the size of the sample, the composite measure of IJV marketing performance, the length of the questionnaire, and the use of single versus multiple respondents.

18.2.1. Sample Size

The response rate for the Julian (1998) sample was acceptable at 19.38 percent (161 useable responses were received from a target population of 831 IJVs) as a response rate of 10 percent or greater is acceptable for self-administered mail surveys (Groves, 1990). However, it was anticipated a much higher response rate would be achieved given the safeguards that were taken to ensure a higher response rate in the data collection process.

A three-stage data collection process was implemented. Firstly, a covering letter with the attached self-administered mail survey was sent to the respondent in Thailand. The covering letter together with each instruction and statement requesting information had both an English and Thai translation. Included with this first package was a stamped self-addressed envelope addressed to a Professor at Bangkok University. The respondents were required to forward the completed questionnaire to the Professor at Bangkok University who had agreed to coordinate the data collection. This procedure was adopted to ensure a maximum response rate was achieved. Secondly, after all the questionnaires had been received by the respondents for at least four weeks each company was followed up personally by a Thai national who was fluent in both English and Thai languages. This procedure was adopted because many of the respondents were Thai nationals who were not fluent in English and the conclusion that was drawn was that by using a Thai national to do the follow-up this may lead to a higher response rate. All of the IJVs in the sample were followed up by telephone by the Thai national fluent in English and Thai. Finally, the self-administered mail survey together with covering letter were sent out again, encouraging all those respondents who had not already responded to do so. The covering letter had both an English and Thai translation and the self-administered mail survey, once again, had both English and Thai translations for each instruction and statement requesting information.

After implementing this procedure and taking all the necessary precautions only a 19.38 percent response rate was achieved. The problem of a low response rate and a relatively small sample size of 161 respondents occurs when using multivariate data analysis techniques like factor analysis, multiple regression analysis and discriminant analysis to conduct the analyses. Coakes and Steed (1997) identify that for factor analysis, multiple regression analysis and discriminant analysis a minimum sample size of 100 respondents is satisfactory. However, it is desirable to have at least five cases per variable for complex analyses. In the Julian (1998) study as there were 45 independent statements the desirable sample size would have been 225. Having achieved a sample size of 161 this means the sample size is just less than desirable and this could have had an effect on some of the relationships between the independent and dependent variables. A much larger sample size may have generated different results between the independent and dependent variables. The implications here for future research would be to test this research instrument on a larger sample size to see if different results could be obtained.

18.2.2. Composite Measure of IJV Marketing Performance

The principal limitation with the composite measure of IJV marketing performance that Julian (1998) developed was very much related to sample size. The composite measure of IJV marketing performance used in the Julian study was developed from the literature. Using the literature and the pre-tests of the research instrument, Julian pre-set 16 strategic objectives into the research instrument that corresponded with each of the measures of IJV marketing performance. Towards the end of the research instrument, respondents were asked to indicate the relative importance attached to each objective by allocating a constant-sum (100 points) to the individual objectives proportional to their importance. The extent to which the initial strategic objectives were achieved was computed as the weighted sum of the importance of the initial strategic objectives. The two indicators were summed into a composite index for measuring IJV marketing performance in Thailand.

With such a complex measure of IJV marketing performance, 16 variables comprised this measure of IJV marketing performance, and a correspondingly small sample size it made it difficult for this measure of IJV marketing performance to differentiate between the high- and low-performing companies, i.e. between the high and low performance scores. This is because there was a large range of IJV marketing performance scores between 100 and 700 with only a small skew towards a specific score. This composite measure of IJV marketing performance, because of its complexity, the possible magnitude of total performance scores and the number of variables comprising the index, really required a larger sample to test its validity as a measure of IJV marketing performance. The larger sample was needed to enable the measure to differentiate between the high and the low performance scores. This is no doubt one of the implications for future research. The factor of a small sample size was further compounded when a significant number (15 percent) of respondents (all Thai in nationality) failed to respond to this section of the questionnaire altogether, indicating a lack of understanding of the measure. Therefore, to validate this measure of IJV marketing performance further it needs to be tested on a larger sample size.

Related to this possible lack of understanding by the respondents of the composite measure of IJV marketing performance developed by Julian (1998), from a methodological perspective, a potential concern may be that the measures are all self-reported. Consequently, the relationships tested may be susceptible to the influence of common method variance. Efforts were made to minimise the problem by pre-testing the instrument and selecting measures that minimise item overlap. Whilst utmost care was taken with the translation of the instrument, items still may be interpreted differently by individuals with different cultural and organizational backgrounds.

18.2.3. Questionnaire Length

The length of the questionnaire as a major study limitation was very much tied to the sample size. After four separate pre-tests of the research instrument a final list of 45 statements was included to potentially identify the factors influencing IJV marketing performance in Thailand. The list of 45 statements was reduced from an original list of approximately 90 statements. The length of the questionnaire was a critical issue in this respect. In order not to excessively burden the respondents, given that each statement, measure and instruction had both an English and Thai translation, it was decided that the questionnaire should not exceed ten pages. The number of statements and variables to be included in the research instrument was planned accordingly. Therefore, the number of statements and variables that were eventually included in the research instrument were constrained by the desired length of the research instrument. This meant that many measures of the various constructs were not included to accommodate the desired length of the questionnaire. This had the effect of reducing the reliability of the measures used for the various constructs and reducing the statistical significance of each of the constructs.

Additionally, the research instrument was designed so that the final list of 45 statements would potentially identify ten factors and two independent statements that could influence IJV marketing performance in Thailand. These factors and independent statements were identified as market characteristics, conflict, commitment, product characteristics, firm-specific characteristics, marketing orientation, organisational control, managerial control, adapting to foreign market needs, trust, partners' contributions and partners' needs. A research instrument of this complexity and size, i.e. with this many variables, really requires a sample of between 400 and 500 respondents to achieve its objectives and statistically significant results (Churchill, 1987).

The sample size that resulted of 161 respondents was approximately one-third of the size needed. This small sample size had the obvious impact of reducing the statistical significance of some of the constructs pre-set in the research instrument and the result may have been different with a larger sample. Therefore, the length of the research instrument in conjunction with the sample size was a major limitation of the study.

Ideally, if the sample was only going to be 161 respondents the research instrument should have been shorter in length with fewer constructs. Alternatively, a larger sample size should have been achieved to accurately determine the reliabilities for the various measures and to produce statistically significant results. The implications for future research are to amend the research instrument marginally and attract a larger sample using a larger population base. The length of the questionnaire in conjunction with the size of the sample also had negative implications for the composite measure of IJV marketing performance that was developed for the Julian (1998) study.

18.2.4. Single versus Multiple Respondents

The most basic issue in IJV performance evaluation is the question of whose performance to assess. Parents have their own objectives in creating IJVs, and obviously to measure a venture's performance against these objectives is relevant. But it is not the only basis for measuring results. Anderson (1990) argued IJVs should be measured primarily as stand-alone entities seeking to maximise their own performance, not the parents. Further, encouraging the IJV to stand alone promotes harmony among the parents. Most IJVs face a steep climb to begin with, as their high rates of dissolution show (Beamish, 1985; Gomes-Casseres, 1989; Makino and Beamish, 1998). Giving the IJV the opportunity to find its own way increases the chances of survival and prosperity. Additionally, giving the IJV autonomy facilitates learning and innovation, which are primary reasons to enter a venture.

Other researchers argue that using only the IJV entity to assess IJV performance represents an incomplete method for assessing IJV performance (Beamish, 1984; Schaan, 1983; Schaan and Beamish, 1988). Since IJVs are jointly owned, it is reasonable to examine whether both parties (local and foreign) are satisfied with performance. Because one partner is a local firm and one partner is a foreign firm, one could expect differences in how performance may be assessed (Beamish, 1984; Harrigan, 1988a; Schaan, 1983). A number of researchers also argue that more than one perspective on IJV performance is required to increase confidence in the findings, and for an IJV to be considered successful it needs to be rated as being successful by more than one partner (Schaan and Beamish, 1988). This is because IJV parents use different criteria to assess performance and the objectives of the parents can be significantly different.

Data collection from more than one respondent may enhance a measure's reliability, but may also confront a myriad of logistical and cost barriers. Researchers may have access to data from one of the parents, or even from the IJV Managing Director or General Manager, but seldom and often with great difficulty from each of the IJV's parents. The key research issue is thus whether data collected from one parent and/or the IJV Managing Director represents a reliable measure of IJV marketing performance and even a reliable estimate of the other partner's perception of this performance.

On this issue, Dess and Robinson (1984) found that multiple respondents evidenced a high degree of agreement in their assessments of their organization's performance. Similarly for IJVs, Geringer and Hebert (1991) found that evaluations of the venture's performance by the organization's members, i.e. the parent firms or the IJV Managing Director, will be consistent. Furthermore, since IJVs are organizations in which ownership and decision-making are shared, it is reasonable to suppose that one element (a parent firm or the IJV Managing Director) of the cooperative venture will evidence some degree of awareness or information regarding the other element's (parents or IJV Managing Director) satisfaction and assessment of performance. Therefore, one participant's evaluation of the other partner's satisfaction regarding the IJV's performance was expected to be correlated with the partner's actual reported satisfaction (Geringer and Hebert, 1991). It is for this reason, principally, that only the IJV Managing Director's or his/her appointed representative's satisfaction with IJV marketing performance was sought.

Additionally, the composite measure of IJV marketing performance developed for the Julian (1998) study incorporated all possible strategic objectives identified by the literature for IJV formation. Respondents had to identify their level of satisfaction with 16 independent strategic objectives that were designed to measure IJV marketing performance. The marketing performance of each venture was determined as the extent to which each of the predetermined strategic objectives was achieved. Therefore, as this measure of IJV marketing performance incorporated all possible strategic objectives for IJV formation as identified by the literature at the time, it went a long way towards eliminating the need for more than one partner's perception of IJV marketing performance. That is why the Julian (1998) measure of IJV marketing performance was developed.

It is also worthy to note that the single-item measure and composite measure of IJV marketing performance used in the Julian study produced similar results further validating the use of the single respondent versus multiple respondents.

18.3. Directions for Future Research

On the basis of the Julian (1998) study contributions to the JV literature and the study's limitations, several useful directions for future research can be suggested and are identified as follows:

- To develop scales of the statistically significant variables for predictive purposes.
- To test the stability of the constructs across time.
- To test the stability of the constructs across samples.
- To further test the Julian (1998) research instrument on a larger sample, including validating the composite measure of IJV marketing performance on a larger sample.
- To study a more comprehensive sample from the service sector.
- To study the foreign partners' perception of IJV marketing performance.

18.3.1. Developing Scales

The most logical extension of the Julian research would be to develop more comprehensive scales for each of the constructs and conduct a study taking the IJV as the unit of analysis. By reducing the number of constructs in the research instrument and at the same time increasing the number of statements used to measure each construct it is possible that the statistical significance of each construct and the reliability of each measure would be improved markedly. Additionally, by reducing the number of constructs in the study it is likely that the research instrument could be reduced in size, thus reducing respondent fatigue and therefore, increasing the overall sample size and response rate. The objective of the next study would be to test specific hypotheses regarding the relationship between the identified constructs and some criteria of effectiveness, e.g., reduction of risk, stability, longevity and marketing performance. A high level of association would suggest that the scales can be used in a predictive fashion to monitor IJV relationships on an ongoing basis.

18.3.2. Testing the Stability of the Constructs over Time

A second extension of the Julian (1998) study would be to test the stability of the constructs across time. For this purpose, the questionnaire used in the study would be smaller in length and have fewer constructs yet a larger number of statements to measure each construct. The proposed future study would involve administering a self-administered mail questionnaire to the same foreign/Thai IJVs at some later point in time. A similarity between the factor structures identified in the replication study and the factor structures obtained in the Julian (1998) study would indicate that the Julian factor structures are stable across time.

18.3.3. Testing the Stability of the Constructs Across other Samples

A third extension of the Julian (1998) research would be to test the stability of the constructs developed on the basis of a sample of IJVs based in other South East Asian countries, e.g., Indonesia, Malaysia, Singapore and the Philippines. The proposed future study would require intensive data collection efforts. The population of foreign-based IJVs in these countries will be quite large relative to the target population of foreign/Thai IJVs in Thailand. A much higher response rate would need to be achieved to further test the composite index of IJV marketing performance developed in the Julian study. If a study with a large sample size could be developed and the composite index of IJV marketing performance developed in the Julian study could be tested further so that it was accepted as a reliable measure of IJV marketing performance, it could be used for other studies on IJV marketing performance. Also a high similarity between the factor structures obtained from the replication study and those obtained from the Julian study in Thailand would indicate that the factor structures of the Julian study are stable across countries. Such a finding would provide support to the claim of generalisability of the factor structures identified in the Julian study.

18.3.4. Testing the Research Instrument on a Larger Thai Sample

It has been previously identified that one of the principal limitations of the Julian (1998) study was to do with sample size. The sample size of 161 respondents was described as being just adequate to conduct the multivariate data analysis techniques of factor analysis, multiple regression analysis and discriminant analysis, and a larger sample size would have been desirable. The small sample size may have had an influence on some of the relationships between the independent and dependent variables and a larger sample size may have generated different results.

Additionally, the composite index of IJV marketing performance needs to be further validated as a reliable measure of IJV marketing performance. To further validate the composite index of IJV marketing performance developed for the Julian (1998) study a much larger sample size is required. The reason is that the composite index of IJV marketing performance is quite a complex measure incorporating sixteen different measures of IJV marketing performance and required a larger sample size to validate its effectiveness.

The proposed future study would be to see if the composite index of IJV marketing performance developed for the Julian study could be further validated and to further test the relationships that were developed in the Julian study and perhaps add other constructs in order to explain a greater variation in the IJV marketing performance data. The results of the proposed future study could be reported on a longitudinal basis.

18.3.5. Studying a Sample from the Service Sector

The population of IJVs included in the Julian (1998) study consisted almost entirely of firms engaged in the agricultural, manufacturing, processing and extraction industries. Only 60 firms out of a total population of 1,047 firms were from the service sector and only seven firms out of a total of 161 firms in the sample were from the service sector. Therefore, the findings and conclusions developed from the Julian study can only be applied to firms engaged in the agricultural, manufacturing, processing and extraction industries. It would be a useful contribution to the IJV literature if a similar study were conducted on a sample of IJVs engaged only in the service sector across a number of different South East Asian countries, e.g., Indonesia, the Philippines, Singapore, Thailand and Malaysia. Service sector firms that enter into IJV agreements with some frequency in these countries are banks, insurance companies, finance companies, travel agencies, airlines, hotels and advertising agencies. For such a study the Julian research instrument could be used.

18.3.6. Studying the Foreign Partner's Perception of IJV Marketing Performance

The Julian (1998) study approached the issue of IJV marketing performance in Thailand from the IJV entity's point of view through the eyes of the IJV Managing Director. It can only be assumed and anticipated that the salient factors impacting upon IJV marketing performance in Thailand identified from the Julian study are versatile enough to remain valid (stable) if a similar study based on the responses from the foreign partners were conducted. Whether or not the factors are stable in this respect is an empirical question, and an important and interesting one. All of the items used in the Julian study questionnaire can be used in such a study, and it is important to validate that the foreign partner's perception of IJV marketing performance is similar to that of the IJV entity. Given the results of the Dess and Robinson (1984) study and the Geringer and Hebert (1991) study it is likely they are. However, it would be useful to validate the findings of the Julian (1998) study by studying the foreign partner's perception of IJV marketing performance of the same Thai IJVs.

References

Aaby, N-E. and Slater, S.F. (1989) 'Management Influences on Export Performance: A Review of the Empirical Literature 1978-1988', *International Marketing Review* **6**(4): 7-26.

Aaker, D.A. (1988) *Strategic Market Management,* 2nd Edition, New York: John Wiley and Sons.

Aaker, D.A. (1989) 'Managing Assets and Skills: The Key to Sustainable Competitive Advantage', *California Management Review* **31**(2): 91-106.

Abbeglen, J. (1982) 'US-Japanese Technological Exchange in Perspective, 1946-1981', *in C. Vehara (ed.) Technological Exchange: The US-Japanese Experience,* New York: University Press, pp 1-13.

Achrol, R.S. (1991) 'Evolution of the Marketing Organization: New Forms for Dynamic Environments', *Journal of Marketing* **55**(October): 77-93.

Achrol, R.S., Scheer, L.K. and Stern, L.W. (1990) *Designing Successful Transorganizational Marketing Alliances,* Report No. 90-118, Cambridge, MA: Marketing Science Institute.

Adler, N.J. (1983) 'Cross-Cultural Management Research: The Ostrich and the Trend', *Academy of Management Review* **8**: 226-232.

Adler, N. and Graham, J. (1989) 'Cross-Cultural Interaction: The International Comparison Fallacy?' *Journal of International Business Studies* **20**(Fall): 515-537.

Agarwal, R. and Weekly, J.K. (1982) 'Foreign Operations of Third World Multinationals: A Literature Review and Analysis of Indian Companies', *The Journal of Developing Areas* **17** (October): 13-30.

Agarwal, S. and Ramaswami, S.N. (1992) 'Choice of Foreign Market Entry Modes: Impact of Ownership, location and Internalization Factors', *Journal of International Business Studies* **23**(1): 1-27.

Ahmed, Z.U. and Krohn, F.B. (1994) 'Developing a Strategic Marketing Plan for a Small Tourism Firm', *Journal of Professional Services Marketing* **10**(2): 111-128.

Ahn, D-S. (1980) 'Joint Ventures in the ASEAN Countries', *Intereconomics* July-August: 193-198.

Ajami, R.A. and Khambata, D. (1991) 'Global Strategic Alliances: The New Transnationals', *Journal of Global Marketing* **5**(1/2): 55-69.

Al-Aali, A.Y. (1987) 'A Performance Model for American Manufacturing and Service Joint Ventures in Saudia Arabia', Unpublished PhD Dissertation, Georgia State University, Georgia, GA.

Al-Ali, A.Y. and Ali, A.J. (1991) 'US Corporate Assessment of Joint Ventures in a Non-Western Country', *Journal of Global Marketing* **5**(1/2): 125-144.

Alchian, A. and Demsetz, H. (1972) 'Production, Information Costs, and Economic Organizations', *American Economic Review* **62**: 777-795.

Aldrich, H. (1979) *Organizations and Environments,* Englewood Cliffs, NJ: Prentice Hall.

Ali, M.Y. and Sim, A.B. (1995) 'An Empirical Investigation of the Determinants of Success of International Joint Ventures in a Developing Country Context', in G. Tower (ed.) *Asia Pacific International Business Regional Integration and Global Competitiveness,* proceedings of the Academy of International Business South East Asia Regional Conference; 20-23 June 1995; Perth, Western Australia: Murdoch University Press, pp. 219-224.

Allen, N.J. and Meyer, J.P. (1990) 'The Measurement and Antecedents of Affective, Continuance, and Normative Commitment to the Organization', *Journal of Occupational Psychology* **63**: 1-18.

Amason, A.C. (1996) 'Distinguishing the Effects of Functional and Dysfunctional Conflict on Strategic Decision Making: Resolving a Paradox for Top Management Teams', *Academy of Management Journal* **39**(1): 123-148.

Amason, A.C. and Schweiger, D.M. (1992) 'Integrating Top Management Team Research: A Meta Theory', paper presented at the Academy of Management Annual Meeting, Las Vegas, NV.

AMC – Australian Manufacturing Council (1994) *Leading the Way, a Study of Best Manufacturing Practices in Australia and New Zealand.*

Anand, J.R., Ainuddin, A. and Makino, S. (1995) 'Multinational Strategy and Characteristics of Subsidiaries: Empirical Analysis of Japanese MNCs', paper presented at the Academy of International Business Meeting, Seoul, Korea.

Anazawa, M. (1994) 'Japanese Manufacturing Investment in Malaysia', in J.K. Sundaram (ed.) *Japan and Malaysian Development,* New York: Routledge.

Anderson, C.F. and Zeithaml, C.P. (1984) 'Stage of the Product Life Cycle, Business Strategy, and Business Performance', *Academy of Management Journal* 27(1): 5-24.

Anderson, E. (1990) 'Two Firms, One Frontier: On Assessing Joint Venture Performance', *Sloan Management Review* Winter: 19-30.

Anderson, E. and Coughlan, A.T. (1987) 'International Market Entry and Expansion via Independent or Integrated Channels of Distribution', *Journal of Marketing* 51(January): 71-82.

Anderson, E. and Gatignon, H. (1986) 'Modes of Foreign Entry: A Transaction Cost Analysis and Propositions', *Journal of International Business Studies* 17(Fall): 1-26.

Anderson, E. and Narus, J. (1984) 'A Model of the Distributors' Perspective of Distributor-Manufacturer Relationships', *Journal of Marketing* 48(Fall): 62-74.

Anderson, E. and Weitz, B. (1989) 'Determinants of Continuity in Conventional Industrial Channel Dyads', *Marketing Science* 8(4): 310-323.

Anderson, E. and Weitz, B. (1992) 'The Use of Pledges to Build and Sustain Commitment in Distribution Channels', *Journal of Marketing Research* 29(February): 18-34.

Anderson, J.C. and Gerbing, D.W. (1988) 'Structural Equation Modelling Practice: A Review and Recommended Two-Step Approach', *Psychological Bulletin* **103**(3): 411-423.

Anderson, J.C. and Narus, J.A. (1990) 'A Model of Distributor Firm and Manufacturer Firm Working Partnerships', *Journal of Marketing* **54** (January): 42-58.

Angelmar, R. and Stern, L. (1978) 'Development of a Content Analytic System for Analysis of Bargaining Communication in Marketing', *Journal of Marketing Research* **15**: 93-102.

Angle, H. and Perry, J. (1981) 'An Empirical Assessment of Organizational Commitment and Organizational Effectiveness', *Administrative Science Quarterly* **26**: 1-14.

Arbuckle, J.C. (1997) *Amos Users Guide Version 3.6,* Chicago, IL: Small Waters Corporation.

Armstrong, J.S. and Overton, T.S. (1977) 'Estimating Non-Response Bias in Mail Surveys', *Journal of Marketing Research* **14**(August): 396-402.

Arni, V.R.S. (1982) *Guidelines for the Establishment of Industrial Joint Ventures in Developing Countries,* New York: UNIDO.

Arnould, E.J. and Wallendorf, M. (1993) 'On Identical Methods in Cross-Cultural Research', paper presented at the 1993 American Marketing Association, Winter Educator's Meeting, 20-23 February 1993, Newport Beach, CA.

Artisien, P.F.R. and Buckley, P.J. (1985) 'Joint Ventures in Yugoslavia: Opportunities and Constraints', *Journal of International Business Studies* **16**(1): 111-135.

Assael, H. (1969) 'Constructive Role of Interorganizational Conflict', *Administrative Science Quarterly* **14**: 573-582.

Aswicahyono, H.H. and Hill, H. (1995) 'Determinants of Foreign Ownership in LDC Manufacturing: An Indonesian Case Study', *Journal of International Business Studies* **26**(1): 139-158.

Awadzi, W.K. (1987) 'Determinants of Joint Venture Performance: A Study of International Joint Ventures in the United States', Unpublished PhD Dissertation, Louisiana State University and Agricultural and Mechanical College, LA.

Awadzi, W.K., Kedia, B. and Chinta, R. (1988) 'Strategic Implications of Cooperation and Complementary Resources in International Joint Ventures', *Journal of International Management* **5**(2): 125-132.

Axinn, C.N. (1988) 'Export Performance: Do Managerial Perceptions Make a Difference'? *International Marketing Review* **5** (Summer): 61-71.

Ayal, I. (1981) 'International Product Life Cycle: A Reassessment, and Product Policy Implications', *Journal of Marketing* (Fall): 91-96.

Bagozzi, R.B. (1994) *Principles of Marketing Research,* Cambridge, MA: Blackwell Publishers.

Baker, M. (1979) 'Export Myopia', *Quarterly Review of Marketing* **4**(3): 25-35.

Baker and McKenzie (1993) *Thailand: A Legal Brief,* 4th Edition, Bangkok: Baker and McKenzie.

Banerji, K. and Sambharya, R.B. (1996) 'Vertical Keiretsu and International Market Entry: The Case of the Japanese Automobile Ancillary Industry', *Journal of International Business Studies* **27**(1): 89-113.

Bank of Thailand (1995) *Annual Report,* Bangkok: Bank of Thailand.

Bantel, K.A. and Jackson, S.E. (1989) 'Top Management and Innovations in Banking: Does the Composition of the Top Team Make a Difference?' *Strategic Management Journal* **10**: 107-124.

Baran, R., Pan, Y. and Kaynak, E. (1996) 'Research on International Joint Ventures in East Asia: A Critical Review and Future Directions', *Journal of Euromarketing* **4**(3): 7-21.

Barkema, H., Bell, J. and Pennings, J. (1996) 'Foreign Entry, Cultural Barriers, and Learning', *Strategic Management Journal* **17**: 151-166.

Barkema, H. and Vermeulen, F. (1997) 'What Differences in the Cultural Backgrounds of Partners are Detrimental for International Joint Ventures?' *Journal of International Business Studies* **28**(4): 845-864.

Barnard, A. (1948) *Organizations and Management*, Cambridge, MA: Harvard University Press.

Barney, J. and Hansen, M.H. (1994) 'Trustworthiness as a Source of Competitive Advantage', *Strategic Management Journal* **15**: 175-190.

Baumgarten, S.A. and Rivard, R.J. (1991) 'The Evolution for Joint Ventures in China', *Journal of Global Marketing* **5**(1/2): 183-200.

Baumgartner, H. and Homberg, C. (1996) 'Applications of Structural Equation Modelling in Marketing and Consumer Research: A Review', *International Journal of Research in Marketing* **13**: 139-161.

Baysinger, B. and Hoskinson, R.E. (1989) 'Diversification Strategy and R&D Intensity in Multiproduct Firms', *Academy of Management Journal* **32**: 310-332.

Beamish, P.W. (1984) 'Joint Venture Performance in Developing Countries', Unpublished PhD Dissertation, University of Western Ontario, Canada.

Beamish, P.W. (1985) 'The Characteristics of Joint Ventures in Developed and Developing Countries', *Columbia Journal of World Business* **20**(3): 13-19.

Beamish, P.W. (1988) *Multinational Joint Ventures in Developing Countries,* New York: Routledge.

Beamish, P.W. (1993) 'The Characteristics of Joint Ventures in The People's Republic of China', *Journal of International Marketing* **1**(2): 29-48.

Beamish, P.W. and Banks, J.C. (1987) 'Equity Joint Ventures and the Theory of the Multinational Enterprise', *Journal of International Business Studies* **18** (Summer): 1-16.

Beamish, P.W. and Delios, A. (1997a) 'Incidence and Propensity of Alliance Formation', in P.W. Beamish and J.P. Killing (eds.) *Cooperative Strategies: Asian Pacific Perspectives,* San Francisco, CA: The New Lexington Press, pp. 91-114.

Beamish, P.W. and Delios, A. (1997b) 'Improving Joint Venture Performance through Congruent Measures of Success', in P.W. Beamish and J.P. Killing (eds.) *Cooperative Strategies: European Perspectives,* San Francisco, CA: The New Lexington Press, pp. 103-127.

Beamish, P.W. and Inkpen, A.C. (1995), 'Keeping International Joint Ventures Stable and Profitable', *Long Range Planning* **28**(3): 26-36.

Beamish, P.W. and Wang, H.Y. (1989) 'Investing in China Via Joint Ventures', *Management International Review* **29**(1): 57-64.

Becker, H.S. (1960) 'Notes on the Concept of Commitment', *American Journal of Sociology* **66**: 32-40.

Bello, D.C. and Williamson, N.C. (1985) 'Contractual Arrangements and Marketing Practices in the Indirect Export Channel', *Journal of International Business Studies* **16** (Summer): 65-82.

Bentler, P.M. and Dudgeon, P. (1996) 'Covariance Structure Analaysis: Statistical Practice, Theory, and Directions', *Annual Review of Psychology* **47**: 563-592.

Berg, R.A. (1991) 'Cooperative Linkages: Selection Determinants and Performance in the Small Business Sector', *Journal of Global Marketing* **5**(1/2): 71-90.

Berg, S.V., Duncan, J. and Friedman. P. (1982) *Joint Venture Strategies and Corporate Innovation*, Cambridge, MA: Oegleschlager, Gunn and Hain.

Berg, S.V. and Friedmann, P. (1980) 'Corporate Courtship and Successful Joint Ventures', *California Management Review* **22**(2): 85-91.

Berlew, F.K. (1984) 'The Joint Venture: A Way into Foreign Markets', *Harvard Business Review* **62**(4): 48-52.

Bernstein, L. (1965) 'Joint Ventures in the Light of Recent Antitrust Developments: Anticompetitive Joint Ventures', *Antitrust Bulletin* **(10)**: 25-29.

Berry, L.L. (1983) 'Relationship Marketing', in L. Berry, L.G. Shostak and G.D. Upah (eds.) *Emerging Perspectives on Services Marketing,* Chicago, IL: American Marketing Association, pp. 25-28.

Berry, L.L. and Parasuraman, A. (1991) *Marketing Services: Competing through Quality,* New York: Free Press.

Bilkey, W.J. (1982) 'Variables Associated with Export Profitability', *Journal of International Business Studies* **13**(Fall): 39-55.

Bilkey, W.J. (1985) 'Development of Export Marketing Guidelines', *International Marketing Review* **2**(1): 31-40.

Bilkey, W.J. and Tesar, G. (1977) 'Export Behaviour of Smaller-Sized Wisconsin Manufacturing Firms', *Journal of International Business Studies* **8**: 93-98.

Bivens, K.K. and Lovell, E.B. (1966) *Joint Ventures with Foreign Partners,* New York: National Industrial Conference Board.

Bjorkman, I. and Kock, K. (1995) 'Social Relationships and Business Networks: The Case of Western Companies in China', *International Business Review* **4**(4): 519-535.

Blau, P. (1964) *Exchange and Power in Social Life*, New York: Wiley.

Blau, P.M. (1977) *Inequality and Heterogeneity*, New York: Free Press.

Bleeke, J. and Ernst, D. (1991) 'The Way to Win in Cross-Border Alliances', *Harvard Business Review* **69**(6): 127-135.

Bleeke, J. and Ernst, D. (1993) *Collaborating to Compete,* New York: John P. Wiley.

Blodgett, L.L. (1987) 'A Resource-based Study of Bargaining Power in US-Foreign Equity Joint Ventures', Unpublished PhD Dissertation, University of Michigan, MI.

Blodgett, L.L. (1991a) 'Partner Contributions as Predictors of Equity Share in International Joint Ventures', *Journal of International Business Studies* **22**(1): 63-78.

Blodgett, L.L. (1991b) 'Toward a Resource-Based Theory of Bargaining Power in International Joint Ventures', *Journal of Global Marketing* **5**(1/2): 35-54.

Blodgett, L.L. (1992a) 'Factors in the Instability of International Joint Ventures', *Strategic Management Journal* **13**(6): 475-481.

Blodgett, L.L. (1992b) 'Research Notes and Communications Factors in the Instability of International Joint Ventures: An Event History Analysis', *Strategic Management Journal* **13**(6): 475-481.

Blumenthal, J.F. (1988a) 'Strategic and Organizational Conditions for Joint Venture Formation and Success', Unpublished PhD Dissertation, University of Southern California.

Blumenthal, M.W. (1988b) 'The World Economy and Technological Change', *Foreign Affairs* **66**(3): 529-550.

Boddewyn, J.J., Soehl, R. and Picard, J. (1986) 'Standardization of International Marketing: Is Ted Levitt in Fact Right?' *Business Horizons* **29**(November-December): 69-75.

BOI (Thai Board of Investment) (1995) *Profile of BOI-Promoted Companies and Sectors,* Bangkok.

BOI (Thai Board of Investment) (1996) *Profile of BOI-Promoted Companies and Sectors,* Bangkok.

BOI (Thai Board of Investment) (2004a) *Thailand of Investment: A Guide to the Board of Investment,* Bangkok.

BOI (Thai Board of Investment) (2004b) *A Business Guide to Thailand,* Bangkok.

Bonoma, T.V. (1986) 'Marketing Subversives', *Harvard Business Review* November-December: 113-118.

Bower, L. (1986a) *When Markets Quake,* Boston, MA: Harvard Business School Press.

Bower, L. (1986b) 'Complementary Inputs and Market Power', *Anti Trust Bulletin* **31**(1): 51-90.

Boyd, H.W., Jr. and Westfall, R. (1972) *Marketing Research: Text and Cases,* 3rd Edition, Homewood, IL: Irwin.

Boyle, S.E. (1968) 'An Estimate of the Number and Size Distribution of Domestic Joint Subsidiaries', *Antitrust Law and Economics Review* **(1)**: 81-82.

Broom, H.N., Longnecker, J.G. and Moore, C.W. (1983) *Small Business Management,* 6th Edition, Cincinatti, OH: South-Western Publishing Co.

Brown, J.R. and Day, R.L. (1981) 'Measures of Manifest Conflict in Distribution Channels', *Journal of Marketing Research* **18**: 263-274.

Brown, L.T., Rugman, A.M. and Verbeke, A. (1989) 'Japanese Joint Ventures with Western Multinationals: Synthesizing the Economic and Cultural Explanations of Failure', *Asian Pacific Journal of Management* **6**(2): 225-242.

Brunner, J.A., Koh, A. and Lou, X. (1992) 'Chinese Perceptions of Issues and Obstacles Confronting Joint Ventures', *Journal of Global Marketing* **6**(1/2): 97-128.

Buchanan II, B. (1974) 'Building Organizational Commitment: The Socialization of Managers in Work Organizations', *Administrative Science Quarterly* **19**(December): 533-546.

Buckley, P.J. and Casson, M. (1985) *The Economic Theory of the Multinational Enterprise,* New York: St Martin's Press.

Buckley, P.J. and Casson, M. (1988a) 'A Theory of Co-Operation in International Business', *Management International Review* Special Issue: 19-38.

Buckley, P.J. and Casson, M. (1988b) 'A Theory of Cooperation in International Business', in F. Contractor and P. Lorange (eds.) *Cooperative Strategies in International Business*, Lexington, MA: Lexington Books, pp. 31-53.

Burton, F.N. and Schlegelmilch, B.B. (1987) 'Profile Analyses of Non-Exporters Versus Exporters Grouped by Export Involvement', *Management International Review* **27**(1): 38-49.

Butler, J.K.J. (1991) 'Toward Understanding and Measuring Conditions of Trust: Evolution of a Conditions of Trust Inventory', *Journal of Management* **17**(3): 643-663.

Buzzell, R.D. (1968) 'Can You Standardize Multinational Marketing?' *Harvard Business Review* **49**(November-December): 102-113.

Buzzell, R.D. and Gale, B.T. (1987) *The PIMS Principles: Linking Strategy to Performance,* New York: Free Press.

Buzzell, R.D., Gale, B.T. and Sultan, R.G.M. (1975) 'Market Share: A Key to Profitability', *Harvard Business Review* **53**(January-February): 97-106.

Byrne, N.J. (1978) 'Joint Ventures, Agreements, and Articles', *New Law Journal* **10**: 784-786.

Calof, J.L. and Beamish, P.W. (1995) 'Adapting to Foreign Markets: Explaining Internationalization', *International Business Review* **4**(2): 115-131.

Camerer, C. and Vepsalainen, A. (1988) 'The Economic Efficiency of Corporate Culture', *Strategic Management Journal* **9**: 115-126.

Cameron, K.S. (1986) 'Effectiveness as Paradox: Consensus and Conflict in Conceptions of Organizational Effectiveness', *Management Science* **32**: 539-553.

Campbell, N.C.G., Graham, J.L., Jolibert, A. and Meissner, H.G. (1988) 'Marketing Negotiations in France, Germany, The United Kingdom and The United States', *Journal of Marketing* **52**(April): 49-62.

Caruso, T.E. (1992) 'Kotler: Future Marketers Will Focus on Customer Database to Compete Globally', *Marketing News* **26**(12): 21.

Cateora, P. (1996) *International Marketing,* 9th Edition, Chicago, IL: Irwin Publishers.

Caves, R.E. and Porter, M.E. (1976) 'Barriers to Exit', in D.P. Qualls and R.T. Masson (eds.) *Essays in Industrial Organization in Honour of Joe. S. Bain,* Cambridge, MA: Ballinger.

Cavusgil, S.T. (1983) 'Success Factors in Export Marketing: An Empirical Analysis', *Journal of International Marketing and Marketing Research* **8**(2): 63-73.

Cavusgil, S.T. (1984a) 'Differences Among Exporting Firms Based on their Degree of Internationalization', *Journal of Business Science Research* **12**: 195-208.

Cavusgil, S.T. (1984b) 'Organizational Characteristics Associated with Export Activity', *Journal of Management Studies* **21**(1): 3-22.

Cavusgil, S.T. and Nevin, J.R. (1981) 'Internal Determinant of Export Marketing Behaviour: An Empirical Investigation', *Journal of Marketing Research* **23**(February): 114-119.

Cavusgil, S.T. and Zou, S. (1994) 'Marketing Strategy-Performance Relationship: An Investigation of the Empirical Link in Export Market Ventures', *Journal of Marketing* **58**: 1-21.

Cavusgil, S.T., Zou, S. and Naidu, G.M. (1993) 'Product and Promotion Adaptation in Export Ventures: An Empirical Investigation', *Journal of International Business Studies* **24**(3): 479-506.

Chakravarthy, B. (1986) 'Measuring Strategic Performance', *Strategic Management Journal* **7**(5): 437-458.

Chandler, A.D. (1962) *Strategy and Structure,* Cambridge, MA: MIT Press.

Chaterjee, S., Lubatkin, M., Schweiger, D. and Weber, Y. (1992) 'Cultural Differences and Shareholder Value in Related Mergers: Linking Equity and Human Capital', *Strategic Management Journal* **13**(5): 319-334.

Cherian, J. and Deshpande, R. (1985) 'The Impact of Organisational Culture on the Adoption of Industrial Innovations', in R.F. Lusch et al. (eds.) *AMA Educators' Proceedings, Series 51, Chicago: American Marketing Association,* pp. 30-34.

Chetty, S.K. and Hamilton, R.T. (1993) 'Firm-Level Determinants of Export Performance: A Meta Analysis', *International Marketing Review* **10**(3): 26-34.

Chi, T. and McGuire, D.T. (1996) 'Collaborative Ventures and Value of Learning: Integrating the Transaction Cost and Strategic Option Perspectives on the Choice of Market Entry Modes', *Journal of International Business Studies* **27**(2): 285-308.

Child, J. (2001) 'Trust: The Fundamental Bond in Global Collaboration', *Organizational Dynamics* **29**: 274-288.

Child, J. and Faulkner, D. (1998) *Strategies of Cooperation: Managing Alliances, Networks, and Joint Ventures*, New York: Oxford.

Child, J., Markoczy, L. and Cheung, T. (1992) 'Managerial Adaptation in Chinese and Hungarian Strategic Alliances with Culturally distinct Foreign Partners', Working Paper, Cambridge University.

Chowdhury, M.A.J. (1989) 'International Joint Ventures: Some Interfirm-Organization Specific Determinants of Successes and Failures: A Factor Analytic Exploration', Unpublished PhD Dissertation, Temple University, MI.

Chowdhury, M.A.J. (1992) 'Performance of International Joint Ventures and Wholly Owned Foreign Subsidiaries: A Comparative Perspective', *Management International Review* **32**(2): 115-133.

Christensen, C.H., da Rocha, A. and Gertner, R.K. (1987) 'An Empirical Investigation of the Factors Influencing Exporting Success of Brazilian Firms', *Journal of International Business Studies* **18**(Fall): 61-77.

Chua, B-L. and Kin-Man, G.L. (1993) 'Managing Joint Ventures in China: A Cross-Cultural Approach to Motivation and Quality', *International Journal of Management* **10**(3): 294-299.

Churchill, G.A., Jr. (1987) *Marketing Research: Methodological Foundations,* 4th Edition, Chicago, IL: Dryden Press.

Churchill, G.A., Jr. and Peter, J.P. (1984) 'Research Design Effects on the Reliability of Rating Scales: A Meta Analysis', *Journal of Marketing Research* **21**(November): 360-375.

Clad, J. (1990) 'Pepsi Canned: Opposition Intensifies against US Project in India', *Far Eastern Economic Review* **147**(March): 40-41.

Clark, K.B. (1989) 'What Strategy Can Do For Technology?' *Harvard Business Review* **67**(6): 94-98.

Clark, T. (1990) 'International Marketing and National Character: A Review and Proposal for an Integrative Theory', *Journal of Marketing* October: 66-79.

Coakes, S.J. and Steed, L.G. (1997) *SPSS: Analysis without Anguish,* Brisbane, Australia: John Wiley and Sons.

Coleman, J. (1990) *Foundations of Social Theory,* Cambridge, MA: Belnap.

Collins, T.M. and Doorley, T.L.I. (1991) *Teaming Up for the 90s: A Guide to International Joint Ventures and Strategic Alliances,* Homewood, IL: Business One Irwin.

Colon, E.J. and Parks, J.M. (1987) 'Information Requests in the Context of Escalation', *Journal of Applied Psychology* **72**: 344-350.

Connolly, S.G. (1984) 'Joint Ventures with Third World Multinationals: A New Form of Entry to International Markets', *Columbia Journal of World Business* **15**(Summer): 18-22.

Contractor, F.J. (1984) 'Strategies for Structuring Joint Ventures: A Negotiations Planning Paradigm', *Columbia Journal of World Business* Summer: 30-39.

Contractor, F.J. (1985) 'A Generalized Theorem for Joint Venture and Licensing Negotiation', *Journal of International Business Studies* **16**(2): 23-50.

Contractor, F.J. (1990) 'Ownership Patterns of U.S. Joint Ventures Abroad and the Liberalization of Foreign Government Regulations in the 1980s: Evidence from the Benchmark Surveys', *Journal of International Business Studies* **21**(1): 55-73.

Contractor, F.J. and Lorange, P. (1988a) *Cooperative Strategies in International Business,* Lexington, MA: Lexington Books.

Contractor, F.J. and Lorange, P. (1988b) 'Why Should Firms Cooperate? The Strategy and Economic Basis for Cooperative Ventures', in F. Contractor and P. Lorange (eds.) *Cooperative Strategies in International Business,* Lexington, MA: Lexington Books, pp. 3-30.

Contractor, F.J. and Lorange, P. (1988c) 'Competition v Cooperation: A Benefit Cost Framework for Choosing Between Fully-Owned Investments and Cooperative Relationships', *Management International Review* Special Issue: 5-18.

Cook, V. (1983) 'Marketing Strategy and Differential Advantage', *Journal of Marketing* (Spring): 68-75.

Cook, K.S. and Emerson, R.M. (1978) 'Power, Equity and Commitment in Exchange Networks', *American Sociological Review* **43**(October): 721-739.

Cooper, R.G. and Kleinschmidt, E.J. (1985) 'The Impact of Export Strategy on Export Sales Performance', *Journal of International Business Studies* **16**(Spring): 37-55.

Cosier, R. and Dalton, D. (1990) 'Positive Effects of Conflict: A Field Assessment', *International Journal of Conflict Management* January: 81-92.

Crask, M.R. and Perreault, W.D. (1977) 'Validation of Discriminant Analysis in Marketing Research', *Journal of Marketing Research* **14**: 60-68.

Crocombe, G. (1991) *Upgrading New Zealand's Competitive Advantage,* New Zealand: Oxford University Press.

Cronbach, L.J. (1951) 'Coefficient Alpha and the Internal Structure of Tests', *Psychometrika* **6**: 297-334.

Crosby, L.A. and Stephens, N. (1987) 'Effects of Relationship Marketing on Satisfaction, Retention, and Prices in the Life Insurance Industry', *Journal of Marketing Research* **24**(November): 404-411.

Crosby, L.A., Evans, K.R. and Cowles, D. (1990) 'Relationship Quality in Services Selling: An Interpersonal Influence Perspective', *Journal of Marketing* **54**(July): 68-81.

Cullen, J.B., Johnson, J.L. and Sakano, T. (1995) 'Japanese and Local Partner Commitment to IJVs: Psychological Consequences of Outcomes and Investments in the IJV Relationship', *Journal of International Business Studies* **26**(1): 91-115.

Curhan, J.P., Davidson, W.H. and Suri, R. (1977) *Tracing the Multinationals: A Sourcebook on U.S.-Based Enterprises,* Cambridge, MA: Ballinger.

Currall, S.C. and Inkpen, A.C. (2002) 'A Multilevel Approach to Trust in Joint Ventures', *Journal of International Business Studies* **33**(3): 479-495.

Dabholkar, P., Johnson, W.J. and Cathey, A.S. (1994) 'The Dynamics of Long-Term Business-to-Business Exchange Relationships', *Journal of the Academy of Marketing Science* **22**(2): 130-145.

Daft, R.L. and Steers, R. (1985) *Organizations: A Micro/Macro Approach*, Glenview, IL: Scott, Foresman and Company.

Dang, T.T. (1977) 'Ownership, Control and Performance of the Multinational Corporation: A Study of US Wholly Owned Subsidiaries and Joint Ventures in The Philippines and Taiwan', Unpublished PhD Dissertation, University of California and Los Angeles, CA.

Daniels, J.D., Krug, J. and Nigh, D. (1985) 'US Joint Ventures in China: Motivations and Management of Political Risk', *California Management Review* Summer: 46-58.

Dant, R.P. and Schul, P. (1992) 'Conflict Resolution Processes in Contractual Channels of Distribution', *Journal of Marketing* **56**(January): 38-54.

Das, T.K. and Teng, B.S. (2000) 'Instabilities of Strategic Alliances: An Internal Tensions Perspective', *Organization Science* **11**(1): 77-101.

Datta, D.K. (1988) 'International Joint Ventures: A Framework for Analysis', *Journal of General Management* **14**(2): 78-91.

Davidson, W.H. (1982) *Global Strategic Management,* New York: John Wiley and Sons.

Day, G.S. and Wensley, R. (1983) 'Marketing Theory with a Strategic Orientation', *Journal of Marketing* **47**(Fall): 79-89.

Day, G.S. and Wensley, R. (1988) 'Assessing Advantage: A Framework for Diagnosing Competitive Superiority', *Journal of Marketing* **52**(April): 1-20.

Deal, T. and Kennedy, A. (1982) *Corporate Cultures,* Reading, MA: Addison-Wesley.

Delios, A. and Beamish, P.W. (2004) 'Joint Venture Performance Revisited: Japanese Foreign Subsidiaries Worldwide', *Management International Review* **44**(1): 69-91.

Deloitte, Haskins and Sells International (1989) *Teaming up for The Nineties: Can you Survive Without a Partner,* New York: Deloitte, Haskins and Sells.

Deloitte, Touche and Tohmatsu (1994) *Stepping up Australia, Meeting the Global Manufacturing Challenge,* Sydney, Australia: Deloitte Touche and Tohmatsu.

Dennison, D. (1990) *Corporate Culture and Organizational Effectiveness,* New York: Free Press.

Deshpande, R. and Parasuraman, A. (1984) 'Organizational Culture and Marketing Effectiveness', in P.F. Anderson and M.J. Ryan (eds.) *Scientific Method in Marketing*, Chicago, IL: American Marketing Association, pp. 137-140.

Deshpande, R. and Webster, F.E. Jr. (1989) 'Organizational Culture and Marketing: Defining the Research Agenda', *Journal of Marketing* **53**(January): 3-15.

Dess, G.G. and Robinson, R.B. Jr. (1984) 'Measuring Organizational Performance in the Absence of Objective Measures: The Case of Privately Held Firms and Conglomerate Business Units', *Strategic Management Journal* **5**(3): 265-273.

Devlin, G. and Bleakley, M. (1988) 'Strategic Alliances-Guidelines for Success', *Long Range Planning* **21**:18-23.

Diamantopoulos, A. (1994) 'Modelling with Lisrel: A Guide for the Uninitiated', *Journal of Marketing Management* Special Issue **10**(1-3): 105-136.

Diamantopoulos, A. and Inglis, K. (1988) 'Identifying Differences Between High- and Low-Involvement Exporters', *International Marketing Review* **5**(Summer): 52-60.

Diamantopoulos, A. and Schlegelmilch, B. (1994) 'Linking Export Manpower to Export Performance: A Canonical Regression Analysis of European and US Data', in S.T. Cavusgil and C.N. Axinn (eds.) *Advances in International Marketing*, Vol. 6, Greenwich, CT: JAI Press.

Dillon, W.R. and Goldstein. M. (1984) *Multivariate Analysis: Methods and Applications,* New York: John Wiley and Sons.

Ding, D.Z. (1997) 'Control, Conflict and Performance: A Study of US-Chinese Joint Ventures', *Journal of International Marketing,* **5**(3): 31-45.

Dobkin, J.A., Burt, J.A., Spooner, M.J. and Krupsky, K.J. (1986) *International Joint Ventures,* Washington DC: Federal Publications.

Dobyns, L. and Crawford-Mason, C. (1991) *Quality or Else: The Revolution in World Business,* Boston, MA: Houghton-Mifflin.

Dominguez, L.V. and Sequeira, C.G. (1993) 'Determinants of LDC Exporters' Performance: A Cross-National Study', *Journal of International Business Studies* **24**(1): 19-40.

Donaton, S. and Mussey, D. (1995) 'Online's Next Battleground: Europe', *Advertising Age* March 6: 18.

Doney, P.M. and Cannon, J.P. (1997) 'An Examination of the Nature of Trust in Buyer-Seller Relationships', *Journal of Marketing* **61**(2): 35-51.

Douglas, S.F. and Craig, C.S. (1989) 'Evolution of Global Marketing Strategy', *Columbia Journal of World Business* Fall: 47-59.

Douglas, S.F. and Wind, Y. (1987) 'The Myth of Globalization', *Columbia Journal of World Business* Winter: 19-29.

Doyle, P., Saunders, J. and Wong, V. (1985) 'Comparative Investigation of Japanese Marketing Strategies in the British Market', *Report to the Economic and Scientific Research Council,* Ref: F20023203, January.

Doz, Y. (1996) 'The Evolution of Cooperation in Strategic Alliances: Initial Conditions or Learning Processes', *Strategic Management Journal* **17**(Summer Special Issue): 55-84.

Doz, Y., Hamel, G. and Prahalad, C. (1986) 'Strategic Partnerships: Success or Surrender? – The Challenge of Competitive Collaboration', *Working Paper,* University of Michigan.

Drucker, P. (1974) *Management Tasks, Responsibilities, Promise,* New York: Harper and Row.

Dunning, J.H. (1988) 'The Eclectic Paradigm of International Production: A Restatement and Some Possible Extensions', *Journal of International Business Studies* **19**: 1-31.

Dunning, J.H. (1993) *Multinational Enterprises and the Global Economy,* Reading, UK: Addison-Wesley.

Dussauge, P. and Garrette, B. (1995) 'Determinants of Success in International Strategic Alliances: Evidence from the Global Aerospace Industry', *Journal of International Business Studies* **26**(3): 505-530.

Dutton, J.E. and Duncan, R.B. (1987) 'The Creation of Momentum for Change Through the Process of Strategic Issue Diagnosis', *Strategic Management Journal* **8**: 279-295.

Dwyer, R.F. (1980) 'Channel-Member Satisfaction: Laboratory Insights', *Journal of Retailing* **56** (Summer): 45-65.

Dwyer, R.F., Schurr, P.H. and Oh, S. (1987) 'Developing Buyer-Seller Relationships', *Journal of Marketing* **51**(April): 11-27.

Dyer, J.H. and Chu, W. (2000) 'The Determinants of Trust in Supplier-Automaker Relationships in the US, Japan, and Korea', *Journal of International Business Studies* **31**: 259-286.

Dymsza, W.A. (1988) 'Successes and Failures of Joint Ventures in Developing Countries: Lessons from Experience', in F.J. Contractor and P. Lorange (eds.) *Cooperative Strategies in International Business,* Lexington MA: Lexington Books, pp. 403-424.

Economic and Social Commission for Asia and the Pacific (1995) 'Sectoral Flows of Foreign Direct Investment in Thailand', *ESCAP Studies in Trade and Investment* **(5)**: 149-182.

The Economist (1986) 21 June: 19.

The Economist (1995) 26 August.

Economist Intelligence Unit (1994) *Country Report,* Economist Intelligence Unit.

Edgar, M. (1977) 'Channel Environments and Channel Leadership', *Journal of Marketing Research* **14**(2): 69-76.

Egelhoff, W.G. (1984) 'Patterns of Control in US, UK, and European Multinational Corporations', *Journal of International Business Studies* **15**(2): 73-83.

Eisenhardt, K.M. (1989) 'Making Fast Strategic Decisions in High-Velocity Environments', *Academy of Management Journal* **32**: 543-576.

Eliashberg, J. and Michie, D.A. (1984) 'Multiple Business Goals Sets as Determinants of Marketing Channel Conflict: An Empirical Study', *Journal of Marketing Research* **21**(February): 75-88.

Encarnation, D.J. and Vachani, S. (1985) 'Foreign Ownership: When Hosts Changes the Rules', *Harvard Business Review* September-October: 152-160.

England, G.W. (1975) *The Manager and His Values: An International Perspective from the United States, Japan, Korea, India, and Australia,* Cambridge, MA: Ballinger Publishing Company.

Erramilli, M.K. (1996) 'Nationality and Subsidiary Ownership Patterns in Multinational Corporations,' *Journal of International Business Studies* **27**(2): 225-248.

Evan, W.M. (1978) 'The Organization-Set: Towards a Theory of Interorganizational Relations', in W.M. Evan (ed.) *Interorganizational Relations,* Philadelphia: University of Pennsylvania Press, pp. 78-90.

Evan, W. and MacDougall, J. (1967) 'Interorganizational Conflict: A Labor-Management Bargaining Experiment', *Journal of Conflict Resolution* **11**: 398-413.

Evangelista, F.U. (1995) 'Linking Business Relationships to Marketing Strategy and Export Performance: A Proposed Conceptual Framework', Proceedings of the *3rd Annual CIMAR Conference,* 30 May - 1 June 1995; Odense University, Denmark.

Evans, F. (1963) 'Selling as a Dyadic Relationship: A New Approach', *American Behavioral Scientist* 6(May): 76-79.

Fagre, N. and Wells, L.T. (1982) 'Bargaining Power of Multinationals and Host Governments,' *Journal of International Business Studies* 11(Fall): 9-23.

Far Eastern Economic Review (1995) 'Economic Monitor: Thailand', 17 August 1995.

Far Eastern Economic Review (1996) 'Economic Monitor: Thailand', 19 June 1996.

Far Eastern Economic Review (1997) 'Economic Monitor: Thailand', 21 August 1997.

Far Eastern Economic Review (2001) 'Economic Monitor: Thailand', 5 October 2001.

Festinger, L. (1959) *A Theory of Cognitive Dissonance,* Evanston, IL: Row Peterson.

Fey, C.F. (1995) 'Important Design Characteristics for Russian-Foreign JVs', *European Management Journal* 13(4): 405-415.

Fey, C.F. and Beamish, P.W. (2000) 'Joint Venture Conflict: The Case of Russian Joint Ventures,' *International Business Review* 9: 139-162.

Fey, C.F. and Beamish, P.W. (2001) 'Organizational Climate Similarity and Performance: International Joint Ventures in Russia', *Organization Studies* 22(5): 853-882.

Filley, A.C., House, R.J. and Kerr, S. (1976) *Managerial Processes and Organizational Behaviours,* Glenview, IL: Scott and Foresman.

Florin, J. (1997) 'Organizing for Efficiency and Innovation: The Case for Nonequity Interfirm Cooperative Arrangements', in P.W. Beamish and J.P. Killing (eds.) *Cooperative Strategies: North American Perspectives,* San Francisco, CA: The New Lexington Press, pp. 3-24.

Forbis, J.L. and Mehta, N.T. (1981) 'Value-Based Strategies for Industrial Products', *Business Horizons* **24**(3): 32-42.

Frank, R. (1989) 'Frames of Reference and Quality of Life', *American Economic Review* **79**: 80-85.

Franko, L.G. (1971) *Joint Venture Survival in Multinational Corporations,* New York: Praeger Publishers.

Franko, L.G. (1974) 'Joint Venture Divorce in the Multinational Company', *Columbia Journal of World Business* **6**(3): 13-22.

Franko, L.G. (1987) 'New Forms of Investment in Developing Countries by US Companies: A Five Industry Comparison', *Columbia Journal of World Business* Summer: 39-56.

Friedmann, W.G. and Beguin, J.P. (1971) *Joint International Business Ventures in Developing Countries,* New York: Columbia University Press.

Friedmann, W.G. and Kalmanoff, G. (1961) *Joint International Business Ventures,* New York: Columbia University Press.

Ganitsky, J.U., Rangan, S. and Watzke, G.E. (1991) 'Time Perspectives in International Joint Ventures: Implications for Marketing Management', *Journal of Global Marketing* **5**(1/2): 13-33.

Garland, H. (1990) 'Throwing Good Money After Bad: The Effect of Sunk Costs on the Decision to Escalate Commitment to an Ongoing Project', *Journal of Applied Psychology* **75**: 728-731.

Gaski, J.F. (1984) 'The Theory of Power and Conflict in Channels of Distribution', *Journal of Marketing* **48**: 9-29.

George, W.R. and Kelly, J.P. (1983) 'The Promotion and Selling of Services', *Business* July/September: 14-20.

Geringer, J.M. (1986) 'Criteria for Selecting Partners for Joint Ventures in Industrialized Market Economies', Unpublished PhD Dissertation, University of Washington.

Geringer, J.M. (1988) *Joint Venture Partner Selection: Strategies for Developed Countries,* Westport, CT: Quantum Books.

Geringer, J.M. (1991) 'Strategic Determinants of Partner Selection Criteria in International Joint Ventures', *Journal of International Business Studies* **22**(1): 41-62.

Geringer, J.M. and Hebert, L. (1989) 'Control and Performance of International Joint Ventures', *Journal of International Business Studies* **20**(2): 235-254.

Geringer, J.M. and Hebert, L. (1991) 'Measuring Performance of International Joint Ventures', *Journal of International Business Studies* **22**(2): 249-263.

Ghosh, B.C., Schoch, H.P., Kim, T.S. and Meng, L.A. (1993) 'A Study on Marketing Effectiveness of Singapore's Small and Medium-Sized Enterprises (MSEs)', a paper presented at the Enterprise Development Centre, *World Conference on Entrepreneurship,* July 1993, Singapore.

Ghosh, B.C., Schoch, H.P., Taylor, D.B., Kwan, W.W. and Kim, T.S. (1994) 'Top Performing Organisations of Australia, New Zealand and Singapore: A Comparative Study of Their Marketing Effectiveness', *Marketing Intelligence and Planning* **12**(7): 39-48.

Goldenberg, S. (1987) 'Joint Ventures in China', *Canadian Business Review* **14**(4): 31-33.

Goldstein, C. (1990) 'New Singer, Old Song: V.P. Singh Maintains India's Hardline on Foreign Investment', *Far Eastern Economic Review* **147**(January): 50-52.

Goll, I., Sambharya, R.B. and Tucci, L.A. (2001) 'Top Management Team Composition, Corporate Ideology, and Firm Performance', *Management International Review* **41**(2): 109-129.

Gomes-Casseres, B. (1985) 'Multinational Ownership Strategies', Unpublished PhD Dissertation, Graduate School of Business Administration, Harvard University, Boston, MA.

Gomes-Casseres, B. (1987) 'Ownership Structures of Foreign Subsidiaries: Theory and Evidence', Working Paper, Harvard Business School, Boston, MA.

Gomes-Casseres, B. (1988a) 'Joint Venture Cycles: The Evolution of Ownership Strategies of U.S. MNEs, 1945-75', in F. Contractor and P. Lorange (eds.) *Cooperative Strategies in International Business,* Lexington, MA: Lexington Books, pp. 111-127.

Gomes-Casseres, B. (1988b) 'Firm Ownership Preferences and Host Government Restrictions: An Integrated Approach', Harvard Business School Working Paper, Boston, MA.

Gomes-Casseres, B. (1988c) 'Joint Ventures in Global Competition', Harvard Business School Working Paper, Boston, MA.

Gomes-Casseres, B. (1989) 'Joint Ventures in the Face of Global Competition', *Sloan Management Review* 17(Spring): 17-26.

Good, L.L. (1972) 'United States Joint Ventures and National Manufacturing Firms in Monterrey, Mexico: Comparative Styles of Management', Unpublished PhD Dissertation, Cornell University, PN.

Gray, B. and Yan, A. (1992) 'A Negotiations Model of Joint Venture Formation, Structure and Performance', in S.D. Prasad, (ed.) *Advances in International Comparative Management*, Vol. 7, Greenwich, CT: JAI Press, pp. 1478-1517.

Gray, B. and Yan, A. (1997) 'Formation and Evolution of International Joint Ventures: Examples from US-Chinese Partnerships', in P.W. Beamish and J.P. Killing (eds.) *Cooperative Strategies: Asian Pacific Perspectives,* San Francisco, CA: The New Lexington Press, pp. 57-88.

Green, R.T. and Langeard, E. (1975) 'A Cross-National Comparison of Consumer Habits and Innovator Characteristics', *Journal of Marketing* 39(July): 34-41.

Gregory, K.L. (1983) 'Native-View Paradigms: Multiple Cultures and Culture Conflicts in Organizations', *Administrative Science Quarterly* 28: 359-376.

Griffeth, R.W., Hom, P.W., De Nisi, A. and Kirchner, W. (1980) 'A Multivariate Multinational Comparison of Managerial Attitudes', in R.C. Huseman (ed.) *Academy of Management Proceedings,* New York: Academy of Management, pp. 63-67.

Griffith, D.A., Zeybek, A.Y. and O'Brien, M. (2001) 'Knowledge Transfer as a Means for Relationship Development: A Kazakhstan-Foreign International Joint Venture Illustration', *Journal of International Marketing* **9**(2): 1-18.

Gronroos, C. (1990) 'Relationship Approach to Marketing in Service Contexts: The Marketing and Organizational Behaviour Interface', *Journal of Business Research* **20**: 3-11.

Gronroos, C. (1994) 'From Marketing Mix to Relationship Marketing: Towards a Paradigm Shift in Marketing', *Management Decision* **32**(2): 4-20.

Groves, R.M. (1990) *Survey Errors and Survey Costs,* New York: John P. Wiley.

Gulati, R. (1995) 'Does Familiarity Breed Trust? The Implications of Repeated Ties for Contractual Choice in Alliances', *Academy of Management Journal* **38**: 85-112.

Gullander, S. (1976) 'Joint Ventures and Corporate Strategy', *Columbia Journal of World Business* Spring: 104-114.

Gundlach, G.T., Achrol, R.S. and Mentzer, J.T. (1995) 'The Structure of Commitment in Exchange', *Journal of Marketing* **59**(January): 78-92.

Gundlach, G.T. and Murphy, P.E. (1993) 'Ethical and Legal Foundations of Relational Marketing Exchange', *Journal of Marketing* **57**(October): 35-46.

Gupta, A.K. and Govindarajan, V. (1984) 'Business Unit Strategy, Managerial Characteristics, and Business Unit Effectiveness at Strategy Implementation', *Academy of Management Journal* **27**(1): 25-41.

Habib, G.M. (1983) 'Conflict Measurement in the Distribution Channel of Joint Ventures: An Empirical Investigation', Unpublished PhD Dissertation, Texas Tech University, Lubbock, Texas.

Habib, G.M. (1987) 'Measures of Manifest Conflict in International Joint Ventures', *Academy of Management Journal* **30**(4): 808-816.

Hagedoorn, J. and Narula, R. (1996) 'Choosing Organisational Modes of Strategic Technology Partnering: International and Sectoral Differences', *Journal of International Business Studies* **27**(2): 265-284.

Hair, J.F. Jr., Anderson, R.E., Tatham, R.L. and Black, W.C. (1995) *Multivariate Data Analysis with Readings,* 4th Edition, Englewood Cliffs, NJ: Prentice-Hall Inc.

Hall, R.D. (1984) *The International Joint Venture,* New York: Praeger Publishers.

Hall, R.H. (1991) 'Communication', in R.H. Hall (ed.) *Organizations: Structures, Processes and Outcomes,* Englewood Cliffs, NJ: Prentice Hall, pp. 163-181.

Hall, W.K. (1980) 'Survival Strategies in a Hostile Environment', *Harvard Business Review* 58(5): 75-85.

Hallen, L. and Johanson, J. (1985) 'Industrial Marketing Strategies and Different National Environments', *Journal of Business Research* 13: 495-509.

Hambrick, D.C., Cho, T.S. and Chen, M.J. (1996) 'The Influence of Top Management Team Heterogeneity on Firms' Competitive Moves', *Administrative Science Quarterly* 41: 659-684.

Hambrick, D.C., Li, J.T., Xin, K. and Tsui, A. (2001) 'Compositional Gaps and Downward Spirals in International Joint Venture Management Groups', *Strategic Management Journal* 22(11): 1033-1053.

Hambrick, D.C. and Mason, P.A. (1984) 'Upper Echelons: The Organization as a Reflection of its Top Managers', *Academy of Management Journal* 9(2): 193-206.

Hamel, G. (1991) 'Competition for Competence and Inter-partner Learning within Strategic Alliances', *Strategic Management Journal* 12: 83-103.

Hamel, G., Doz, Y.L. and Prahalad, C.K. (1989) 'Collaborate With Your Competitors-and Win', *Harvard Business Review* March-April: 133-139.

Han, C.M (1989) 'Country Image: Halo or Summary Construct'? *Journal of Marketing Research* 26(May): 222-229.

Hanan, M. (1985) *Consultative Selling,* New York: American Management Association.

Harding, R.D. (1988) 'India: New Policies, New Opportunities', *Business America* 109(May): 32-33.

Harrigan, K.R. (1980) *Strategies for Declining Businesses,* Lexington, MA: Lexington Books.

Harrigan, K.R. (1985) *Strategies for Joint Ventures,* Lexington, MA: Lexington Books.

Harrigan, K.R. (1987) 'Strategic Alliances: Their New Role in Global Competition', *Columbia Journal of World Business* Summer: 67-69.

Harrigan, K.R. (1988a) 'Joint Ventures and Competitive Strategy', *Strategic Management Journal* **9**: 141-158.

Harrigan, K.R. (1988b) 'Strategic Alliances and Partner Asymmetries', *Management International Review* Special Issue: 53-72.

Harrison, N.J. (1994) 'The Use of Taxonomies to Assess Manufacturing Strategies', Working Paper, University of Technology, Sydney.

Hart, C.W.L. (1988) 'The Power of Unconditional Service Guarantees', *Harvard Business Review* July-August: 54-62.

Hart, C.W.L., Heskett, J. L. and Sasser Jr., W.E. (1990) 'The Profitable Art of Service Recovery', *Harvard Business Review* July-August: 148-156.

Harvey, M.G. and Lusch, R.F. (1995) 'A Systematic Assessment of Potential International Strategic Alliance Partners', *International Business Review* 4(2): 195-212.

Hattie, J.A. (1997) *Common Problems in Structural Equation Modelling,* SEMNET, 8 May: 1-83.

Hatton, J. (1995) 'Thailand Transit Projects on a Slow-Turning Wheel', *Asia Today,* February: 18, 20.

Hebert, L. (1994) 'Division of Control, Relationship Dynamics, and Joint Venture Performance', Unpublished PhD Dissertation, University of Western Ontario, Canada.

Hellman, P. (1996) 'The Internationalization of Finnish Firms', *International Business Review* 5(2): 191-208.

Hennart, J-F. (1988) 'A Transaction Costs Theory of Equity Joint Ventures', *Strategic Management Journal* **9**: 361-374.

Hennart, J-F. (1989) 'Can the 'New Forms of Investment' Substitute for the 'Old Forms'? A Transactions Cost Perspective,' *Journal of International Business Studies* **20**(Summer): 211-234.

Hennart, J-F. (1991) 'The Transaction Cost Theory of Joint Ventures: An Empirical Study of Japanese Subsidiaries in the United States', *Management Science* **37**(4): 483-497.

Hennart, J-F., Kim, D.J. and Zeng, M. (1998) 'The Impact of Joint Venture Status on the Longevity of Japanese Stakes in US Manufacturing Affiliates', *Organization Science* **9**(3): 382-395.

Hergert, M. and Morris, D. (1988) 'Trends in International Collaborative Agreements', in F. Contractor and P. Lorange (eds.) *Cooperative Strategies in International Business,* Lexington, MA: Lexington Books, pp. 99-109.

Hibner, D.T., Jr. (1982) 'Antitrust Considerations of Joint Ventures, Teaming Agreements, Co-production and Leader-Follower Agreements', *Antitrust Law Journal* **51**(4): 705-723.

Higginbottom, D. (1980) 'A Study of Australian Joint Ventures in South East Asia', *Australian Market Researcher* **4**(October): 21-38.

Hill, C.W.L., Hwang, P. and Kim, C.W. (1990) 'An Eclectic Theory of the Choice of International Entry Mode', *Strategic Management Journal* **11**(2): 117-128.

Hill, J.S. and Still, R.R. (1984) 'Adapting Products to LDC Tastes', *Harvard Business Review* **62**(March-April): 92-101.

Hladik, K.J. (1985) *International Joint Ventures: An Economic Analysis of U.S.-Foreign Business Partnerships,* Lexington, MA: Lexington Books.

Hladik, K.J. (1988) 'R&D and International Joint Ventures', in F. Contractor and P. Lorange (eds.) *Cooperative Strategies in International Business,* Lexington, MA: Lexington Books, pp. 187-203.

Hodgetts, R.M. and Luthans, F. (1994) *International Management,* 2nd Edition, New York: McGraw Hill.

Hofer, C.W. (1975) 'Toward a Contingency Theory of Business Strategy', *Academy of Management Journal* **18**: 784-810.

Hofer, C.W. (1980) 'Turnaround Strategies', *Journal of Business Strategy* **1**(1): 19-31.

Hofer, C.W. (1983) 'ROVA: A New Measure for Assessing Organizational Performance', in R. Lamb (ed.) *Advances in Strategic Management,* Vol. 2, Greenwich, CT: JAI Press, pp. 43-56.

Hofer, C.W. and Schendel, D. (1978) *Strategy Formulation: Analytical Concepts,* St. Paul, MI: West Publishing.

Hofstede, G. (1980) *Culture's Consequences: International Differences in Work-Related Values,* Beverly Hills, CA: Sage Publications.

Hofstede, G. (1986) 'Editorial: The Usefulness of the Organizational Culture' Concept', *Journal of Management Studies* **23**(3): 253-257.

Holton, R.H. (1981) 'Making International Joint Ventures Work', in L. Otterbeck (ed.) *The Management of Headquarters-Subsidiary Relationships in Multinational Corporations,* New York: Saint Martin's Press, pp 255-267.

Hooley, G.J. and Lynch, J.E. (1985) 'Marketing Lessons from the UK's High-Flying Companies', *Journal of Marketing Management* **1**(1): 1-16.

Hooley, G.J. and Newcomb, J.R. (1983) 'Ailing British Exports: Symptoms, Causes, and Cures', *Quarterly Review of Marketing* **8**(4): 12-25.

Hooley, G.J., West, C.J. and Lynch, J.E. (1984) *Marketing in the UK: A Survey of Current Practice and Performance,* London: Institute of Marketing.

Hoover, R.J., Green, R.T. and Saegert, J. (1978) 'A Cross-National Study of Perceived Risk', *Journal of Marketing* July: 102-108.

Horaguchi, H. (1992) *Nihon Kigyou no Kaigai Chokusetsu Toushi: Asia eno Shinshutsu tp Tettai,* (Foreign Direct Investment of Japanese Firms: Investment and Divestment in Asia), Tokyo, Japan: University of Tokyo Press.

Houston, F.S. (1986) 'The Marketing Concept: What It Is and What It Is Not', *Journal of Marketing* **50**(April): 81-87.

Hu, M.Y. and Chen, H. (1996) 'An Empirical Analysis of Factors Explaining Foreign Joint Venture Performance in China', *Journal of Business Research* **35**(2): 165-173.

Hulland, J., Chow, Y.H. and Lam, S. (1996) 'Use of Causal Models in Marketing Research: A Review', *International Journal of Research in Marketing* **13**: 181-197.

Hung, C.L. (1995) 'The Use of Strategic Business Alliances by Canadian Companies in Asia Pacific', *Journal of Asia-Pacific Business* **1**(1): 5-23.

Hunger, J.D. and Stern, L.W. (1976) 'An Assessment of the Functionality of the Superordinate Goal in Reducing Conflict', *Academy of Management Journal* **19**(4): 591-605.

Hunt, H.K. (1977) 'CS/D: Overview and Future Research Directions', in H.K. Hunt (ed.) *Conceptualization and Measurement of Consumer Satisfaction and Dissatisfaction,* Cambridge, MA: The Marketing Science Institute.

Hyder, S. (1988) 'The Development of International Joint Venture Relationships: A Longitudinal Study of Exchange of Resources, Control, and Conflict', Unpublished PhD Dissertation, Uppsala University, Sweden.

Industrial Market Research Services (1986) *Final Report: Survey of United States Investment in Thailand,* Mimeo.

Inkpen, A.C. (1992) 'Learning and Collaboration: An Examination of North American-Japanese Joint Ventures', Unpublished PhD Dissertation, University of Western Ontario.

Inkpen, AC. and Beamish, P.W. (1997) 'Knowledge, Bargaining Power, and the Instability of International Joint Ventures', *Academy of Management Review* **22**: 177-202.

Jackson, B.B. (1985) *Winning and Keeping Industrial Customers,* Lexington, MA: Lexington Books.

Jackson, S.E., Brett, J.F., Sessa, V.I., Cooper, D.M., Julin, J.A and Peyronnin, K. (1991) 'Some Differences make a Difference: Individual Dissimilarity and Group Heterogeneity as Correlates of Recruitment, Promotions, and Turnover', *Journal of Applied Psychology* **76**(5): 675-689.

Jacque, L.L. (1978) *Management of Foreign Exchange Risk,* Lexington, MA: Lexington Books.

Jacque, L.L. (1986) 'The Changing Personality of US-Japanese Joint Ventures: A Value-Added Chain Mapping Paradigm', Working Paper, Department of Management, Wharton Business School, Pennsylvania.

Jaeger, A.M. (1982) 'Contrasting Control Modes in the Multinational Corporation: Theory, Practice and Implications', *International Studies of Management and Organisation* **12**(1): 59-82.

Jaeger, A.M. (1983) 'The Transfer of Organizational Culture Overseas: An Approach to Control in the Multinational Corporation', *Journal of International Business Studies* **14**(3): 91-114.

Jain, S.C (1989) 'Standardization of International Marketing Strategy: Some Research Hypotheses', *Journal of Marketing* January: 70-79.

Jain, S.C. (1994a) *International Marketing Management,* 4th Edition, Belmont, CA: Wadsworth Publishing Company.

Jain, S.C. (1994b) *Marketing Planning and Strategy,* 4th Edition, Cincinnati, OH: South-Western Publishing Co.

Jain, S.C. and Tucker, L.R. (1995) 'The Influence of Culture on Strategic Constructs in the Process of Globalisation: An Empirical Study of North American and Japanese MNCs', *International Business Review* **4**(1): 19-37.

Janger, A.R. (1980) *Organization of International Joint Ventures,* New York: Conference Board.

Japanese Chamber of Commerce, Bangkok (1978) *Dai 7 Kai Nikkeikigyo (Seizogyo) no Tai Keizai ni Tai Suru Kokendo Chosa Kekka [The Seventh Survey on the Activities of Japanese Joint-Venture Manufacturing Companies in Thailand],* Bangkok: Japanese Chamber of Commerce.

Japanese Chamber of Commerce, Bangkok (1981) *Dai 8 Kai Nikkeikigyo Jittai Chosa (Kokendo Chosa) Kekka [The Results of the Eighth Survey (Survey of Contributions) of the State of Japanese Firms],* Bangkok: Japanese Chamber of Commerce.

Japanese Chamber of Commerce, Bangkok (1984) *Dai 9 Kai Nikkeikigyo no Jittai Chosa [The Ninth Survey of the State of Japanese Firms],* Bangkok: Japanese Chamber of Commerce.

Japanese Chamber of Commerce, Bangkok (1990) *Nikkeikigyo no Jittai (Kokendo) Chosa [A Survey of the State (contributions) of Japanese Firms],* Bangkok: Japanese Chamber of Commerce.

Japan Chamber of Commerce, Bangkok (1994) *Dai 12 Kai Nikkeikigyo no Jitta (Kokendo) Chosa [The Twelfth Survey of the State (Contributions) of Japanese Firms],* Bangkok: Japanese Chamber of Commerce.

Jeffries, F.L. and Reed, R. (2000) 'Trust and Adaptation in Relational Contracting', *Academy of Management Review* **25**: 873-882.

Joelson, M.R. and Griffin, P.J. (1975) 'Multinational Joint Ventures and the US Antitrust Laws', *Virginia Journal of International Law* **15**: 487-538.

Johanson, J. and Vahlne, J. (1977) 'The Internationalization Process of the Firm: A Model of Knowledge Development and Increasing Foreign Market Commitments', *Journal of International Business Studies* **8**: 23-32.

Johanson, J. and Weidersheim-Paul, F. (1975) 'The Internationalization of the Firm: Four Swedish Case Studies', *Journal of Management Studies* October: 305-322.

Johansson, J.K. (2003) *Global Marketing*, 3rd Edition, New York: McGraw-Hill/Irwin.

John, G. (1984) 'An Empirical Investigation of Some Antecedents of Opportunism in a Marketing Channel', *Journal of Marketing Research* **21**(August): 278-289.

Johnson, J.L., Black, G.S. and Sakano, T. (1993) 'The Consequences of Culture and Conflict in International Strategic Alliances', in R. Varadarajan and B. Jaworski (eds.) *Marketing Theory and Applications*, Proceedings of the American Marketing Association Conference; 20-23 February; Newport Beach, CA: American Marketing Association, pp. 32-37.

Johnson, J.L., Cullen, J.B., Sakano, T. and Bronson, J.W. (2001) 'Drivers and Outcomes of Parent Company Intervention in IJV Management: A Cross-Cultural Comparison', *Journal of Business Research* **52**: 35-49.

Johnson, J.L., Sakano, T. and Onzo, N. (1990) 'Behavioural Relations in Across-Culture Distribution Systems: Influence, Control and Conflict in US-Japanese Marketing Channels', *Journal of International Business Studies* **21**(4): 639-655.

Jones, G.R. (1983) 'Transaction Costs, Property Rights, and Organisational Culture: An Exchange Perspective', *Administrative Science Quarterly* **28**: 454-467.

Joreskog, K.G. and Sorbom, D. (1996) *Lisrel 8: Users Reference Guide,* Chicago, IL: Scientific Software International, Inc.

Julian, C.C. (1998) 'The Marketing Performance of International Joint Ventures (IJVs) in Thailand', Unpublished PhD Dissertation, School of Marketing, Curtin University of Technology, Perth, Western Australia.

Julian, C.C. (2001) 'Japanese Foreign Direct Investment (FDI) in Thailand', *Mid-Atlantic Journal of Business* **37**(1): 7-18.

Julian, C.C. (2003) 'Export Marketing Performance a Study of Thailand Firms', *Journal of Small Business Management* **41**(2): 213-221.

Julian, C.C. (2004) *International Marketing: A Strategic Approach*, Melbourne, Australia: Pearson Education.

Julian, C.C., Mueller, C.B., Wachter, R. and Van Deusen, C.A. (2004) 'Top Management Teams of International Joint Ventures in Thailand: The Effects of Heterogeneity on Group Processes and Goal Attainment', *Journal of International Business and Entrepreneurship Development* **1**(1): 104-117.

Julian, C.C. and O'Cass, A. (2002a) 'Examining the Internal-External Determinants of International Joint Venture (IJV) Marketing Performance in Thailand', *Australasian Marketing Journal* **10**(2): 55-71.

Julian, C.C. and O'Cass, A. (2002b) 'Drivers and Outcomes of Export Marketing Performance in a Developing Country Context', *Journal of Asia Pacific Marketing* **1**(2): 1-21.

Julian, C.C. and O'Cass, A. (2004a) 'The Impact of Firm and Environmental Characteristics on International Joint Venture (IJV) Marketing Performance in Thailand', *Thunderbird International Business Review* **46**(4): 359-380.

Julian, C.C. and O'Cass, A. (2004b) 'The Antecedents of Export Marketing Performance: An Australian Perspective', forthcoming in *Journal of Asia Pacific Marketing*, Special Issue on Advancing Export Marketing Theory in the Asia Pacific Region.

Julian, C.C. and Ramaseshan, B. (2001) 'International Joint Venture and Foreign Direct Investment (FDI) in Thailand', *Journal of International Marketing and Exporting* **6**(2): 96-111.

Julian, C.C. and Ramaseshan, B. (2004) 'Marketing Performance of International Joint Ventures: An Empirical Investigation', *Journal of Global Business Research* **1**(1): 84-93.

Kanter, R.M. (1972) *Commitment and Community*, Cambridge, MA: Harvard University Press.

Kashani, K. (1989) 'Beware the Pitfalls of Global Marketing', *Harvard Business Review* September-October: 91-98.

Kashani, K. and Quelch, J.A. (1990) 'Can Sales Promotion Go Global?' *Business Horizons* May-June: 37-43.

Katzenbach, J.R. and Smith, D.K. (1993) 'The Discipline of Teams', *Harvard Business Review* **71**(2): 111-120.

Kaufmann, P.J. and Stern, L.W. (1988) 'Relational Exchange Norms, Perceptions of Unfairness and Retained Hostility in Commercial Litigation', *Journal of Conflict Resolution* **32**(September): 534-552.

Kaye, L. (1988) 'Profits Without Performance: Suzuki's Indian Venture Comes Under Fire for Poor Quality Cars', *Far Eastern Economic Review* **141**(August): 74.

Kaynak, E. and Kuan, W. (1993) 'Environment, Strategy, Structure and Performance in the Context of Export Activity: An Empirical Study of Taiwanese Manufacturing Firms', *Journal of Business Research* **27**: 33-49.

Kedia, B.L. and Chhokar, J. (1986) 'Factors Inhibiting Export Performance of Firms: An Empirical Investigation', *Management International Review* **26**(4): 33-43.

Keegan, W.J. (1969) 'Multinational Product Planning: Strategic Alternatives', *Journal of Marketing* **33**(1): 58-62.

Keegan, W.J. (1995) *Global Marketing Management,* 5th Edition, Englewood Cliffs, NJ: Prentice-Hall.

Kerin, R.A., Mahajan, V. and Varadarajan, P.R. (1990) *Contemporary Perspectives on Strategic Market Planning,* Needham Heights, MA: Allyn and Bacon Publishers.

Kiel, G., McVey, V. and McColl-Kennedy, J.R. (1986) 'Marketing Planning-Practices in Australia', *Management Review No. 1,* Graduate School of Management, University of Queensland, Brisbane.

Kiesler, C.A. (1971) *The Psychology of Commitment: Experiments Linking Behaviour to Belief,* New York: Academic Press.

Killing, J.P. (1982) 'How to Make a Global Joint Venture Work', *Harvard Business Review* May-June: 120-127.

Killing, J.P. (1983) *Strategies for Joint Venture Success,* New York: Praeger Publishers.

Killing, J.P. (1988) 'Understanding Alliances: The Role of Task and Organizational Complexity', in F. Contractor and P. Lorange (eds.) *Cooperative Strategies in International Business*, Lexington, MA: Lexington Books, pp. 55-68.

Killing, J.P. (1991) 'The Design and Management of International Joint Ventures', in P.W. Beamish, J.P. Killing, D. Lecraw and H. Crookwell (eds.) *International Management: Text and Cases*, Homewood, IL: Irwin.

Killough, J. (1978) 'Improved Payoff from Transnational Advertising', *Harvard Business Review* July-August: 102-110.

Kim, W.C. (1988) 'The Effects of Competition and Corporate Political Responsiveness on Multinational Bargaining Power', *Strategic Management Journal* 9: 289-295.

Kim, K. (1995) 'An Integrative Model of Learning in the Context of International Joint Ventures (IJVs): Venture Learning and Partner Learning', Academy of International Business Meeting, October, Seoul.

King, H.T. Jr. (1969) 'Application of US Antitrust Laws to International Joint Ventures', Remarks before the Inter-American Bar Association, Caracas, Venezuela.

Kinnear, T.C., Taylor, J.R., Johnson, L. and Armstrong, R. (1993) *Australian Marketing Research,* Sydney: McGraw-Hill.

Kirpalani, V.H. and McKintosh, N.B. (1980) 'International Marketing Effectiveness of Technology Oriented Small Firms', *Journal of International Business Studies* **10**(Winter): 81-90.

Knight, D., Pearce, C.L., Smith, K.G., Olian, J.D., Sims, H.P., Smith, K.A. and Flood P. (1999) 'Top Management Team Diversity, Group Process, and Strategic Consensus', *Strategic Management Journal* **20**: 445-465.

Kobayashi, N. (1967a) 'Some Organizational Problems', in R.I. Ballon (ed.) *Joint Ventures and Japan,* Tokyo: Sophia University, pp. 99-118.

Kobayashi, N. (1967b) 'Human Aspects of Management', in R.I. Ballon (ed.) *Joint Ventures and Japan,* Tokyo: Sophia University, pp. 67-81.

Kobrin, S.J. (1980) 'Foreign Enterprise and Forced Divestment in LDCs', *International Organization* **34**(1): 65-88.

Kobrin, S.J. (1988) 'Trends in Ownership of American Manufacturing Subsidiaries in Developing Countries: An Inter-Industry Analysis', *Management International Review* Special Issue: 73-84.

Koch, M.J. and McGrath, R.G. (1996) 'Improving Labour Productivity: Human Resource Management Policies Do Matter', *Strategic Management Journal* **17**: 335-354.

Kochan, T., Hunter, P. and Cummings, L. (1975) 'Determinants of Interorganizational Conflict in Collective Bargaining in the Public Sector', *Administrative Science Quarterly* **20**(March): 10-23.

Kogut, B. (1977) 'FDI as a Sequential Process', in J. Bhagwati (ed.) *The New International Economic Order,* Cambridge, MA: MIT Press, pp. 38-56.

Kogut, B. (1985a) 'Designing Global Strategies: Comparative and Competitive Value Added Chains', *Sloan Management Review* Summer: 15-28.

Kogut, B. (1985b) 'Designing Global Strategies: Profiting from Operational Flexibility', *Sloan Management Review* Fall: 27-38.

Kogut, B. (1988) 'Joint Ventures: Theoretical and Empirical Perspectives', *Strategic Management Journal* **9**: 319-332.

Kogut, B. (1989) 'The Stability of Joint Ventures: Reciprocity and Competitive Rivalry', *Journal of Industrial* Economics **38**: 183-198.

Kogut, B. and Singh, H. (1985) 'Entering the United States by Acquisition or Joint Venture: Country Patterns and Cultural Characteristics', Working Paper, Reginald Jones Centre, Wharton School, Pennsylvania.

Kogut, B. and H. Singh (1988) 'The Effect of National Culture on the Choice of Entry Mode', *Journal of International Business Studies* **19**: 411-432.

Koh, A.C. (1991) 'Relationships Among Organisational Characteristics, Marketing Strategy and Export Performance', *International Marketing Review* **8**(3): 46-60.

Kohli, A.K. and Jaworski, B.J. (1990) 'Market Orientation: The Construct, Research Propositions, and Managerial Implications', *Journal of Marketing* **54**(April): 1-18.

Kohli, A.K., Jaworski, B.J. and Kuma, A. (1993) 'MARKOR: A Measure of Marketing Orientation', *Journal of Marketing Research* **30**(4): 467-477.

Koot, W.T.M. (1988) 'Underlying Dilemmas in the Management of International Joint Ventures', in F. Contractor and P. Lorange (eds.) *Cooperative Strategies in International Business*, Lexington, MA: Lexington Books, pp. 347-367.

Kotabe, M. (1990) 'Corporate Product Policy and Innovative Behaviour of European and Japanese Multinationals: An Empirical Investigation', *Journal of Marketing* **54**(April): 19-33.

Kotabe, M. and Murray, J.Y. (1996) 'Determinants of Intra-firm Sourcing and Market Performance', *International Business Review* **5**(2): 121-135.

Kotabe, M. and Omura, G.S. (1989) 'Sourcing Strategies of European and Japanese Multinationals: A Comparison', *Journal of International Business Studies* **20**(Spring): 113-130.

Kotler, P. (1984) *Marketing Management: Analysis, Planning and Control,* Englewood Cliffs, NJ: Prentice-Hall.

Kotler, P. (1986) 'Global Standardization: Courting Dangers', *Journal of Consumer Marketing* **3**(Spring): 13-15.

Kotler, P. (1991) *Marketing Management: Analysis, Planning, Implementation, and Control,* 7th Edition, Englewood Cliffs, NJ: Prentice-Hall.

Kotler, P. and Andreasen, A.R. (1987) *Strategic Marketing for Nonprofit Organizations,* Englewood Cliffs, NJ: Prentice-Hall.

KPMG (1993) *Manufacturing Survey Across Australia.*

Kumar, K. and Kim, K.Y. (1984) 'The Korean Manufacturing Multinationals', *Journal of International Business Studies* 15(1): 45-62.

Kumar, N. (1994) 'Determinants of Export Orientation of Foreign Production by U.S. Multinationals: An Inter-Country Analysis', *Journal of International Business Studies* 25(1): 141-156.

Kwan, W.W.H. and Yau, O.H.M. (1992) 'The Effectiveness of Australian Marketing: Profile of the Top Performers', *A Summary Report Submitted to the University Research Committee,* Edith Cowan University, Perth.

Lages, L.F. (2000) 'A Conceptual Framework of the Determinants of Export Performance: Reorganizing Key Variables and Shifting Contingencies in Export Marketing', *Journal of Global Marketing* 13(3): 29-51.

Lai, W.B., Hwang, J.Y., Hooley, G., Lynch, J. and Yau, O. (1992) 'Effective Marketing in Taiwan: Profits of Top Performers', *European Journal of Marketing* 26(3): 5-17

Lambkin, M. and Day, G.S. (1989) 'Evolutionary Processes in Competitive Markets: Beyond the Product Life Cycle', *Journal of Marketing* July: 4-20.

Lane, H. and Beamish, P.W. (1990) 'Cross-Cultural Cooperative Behaviour in Joint Ventures in LDCs', *Management International Review* Special Issue: 87-102.

Lecraw, D.J. (1983) 'Performance of Transnational Corporations in Less Developed Countries', *Journal of International Business Studies* 14(1): 15-34.

Lecraw, D.J. (1984) 'Bargaining Power, Ownership, and Profitability of Transnational Corporations in Developing Countries', *Journal of International Business Studies* 15(1): 27-43.

Lee, C. and Beamish, P.W. (1995) 'The Characteristics and Performance of Korean Joint Ventures in LDCs', *Journal of International Business Studies* 26(3): 637-654.

Lee, H., Kim, C. and Miller, J. (1992) 'The Relative Effects of Price, Warranty and Country of Origin on Consumer Product Evaluations', *Journal of Global Marketing* **6**(1/2): 55-80.

Lee, J. (1989) 'Study on Strategic Success of Korean Joint Ventures Overseas', *Song Kok Journal* **20**.

Lehmann, D.R. (1985) *Market Research and Analysis,* 2nd Edition, Homewood, IL: Irwin.

Levitt, T. (1983) 'The Globalization of Markets', *Harvard Business Review* **61**(May-June): 92-102.

Li, E. and Ogunmokun, G. (2000) 'The Effect of Flexibility on Export Venture Performance', *Journal of Global Marketing* **14**(3): 99-126.

Li, J. and Guisinger, S. (1991) 'Comparative Business Failures of Foreign-Controlled Firms in the United States', *Journal of International Business Studies* **22**(2): 209-224.

Li, J.T. (1995) 'Foreign Entry and Survival: Effects of Strategic Choices on Performance in International Markets', *Strategic Management Journal* **16**(5): 331-351.

Liebman, H.M. (1975) *US and Foreign Taxation of Joint Ventures,* Office of Tax Analysis, US Treasury Department.

Lin, X. and Germain, R. (1999) 'Predicting International Joint Venture Interaction Frequency in US-Chinese Ventures', *Journal of International Marketing* **7**(2): 5-23.

Lu, J.W. (2002) 'Intra- and Inter-organizational Imitative Behaviour: Institutional Influences on Japanese Firms' Entry Mode Choice', *Journal of International Business Studies* **33**(1): 19-38.

Lu, M.H., Madu, C.N., Kuei, C-H and Winokur, D. (1994) 'Integrating QFD, AHP and Benchmarking in Strategic Marketing', *Journal of Business and Industrial Marketing* **9**(1): 41-50.

Luo, Y. and Chen, M. (1995) 'An Empirical Analysis of Firm- and Industry-Specific Factors Affecting Performance of International Joint Ventures in The People's Republic of China', paper presented at the Academy of International Business Meeting, October, Seoul.

Luo, Y. and Peng, M.W. (1999) 'Learning to Compete in a Transition Economy: Experience, Environment, and Performance', *Journal of International Business Studies* **30**(2): 269-296.

Lusch, R.F. (1976) 'Sources of Power: Their Impact on Intrachannel Conflict', *Journal of Marketing Research* **13**: 382-390.

Lyles, M.A. (1991) 'A Study of the Interaction of Firm Business Area Relatedness and the Propensity to Joint Venture', *Journal of Global Marketing* **5**(1/2): 91-106.

Lyles, M. and Salk, J. (1997) 'Knowledge Acquisition from Foreign Parents in International Joint Ventures: An Empirical Examination in the Hungarian Context', in P.W. Beamish and J.P. Killing (eds.) *Cooperative Strategies: European Perspectives*, San Francisco: CA: The New Lexington Press, pp. 325-355.

Macneil, I.R. (1980) *The New Social Contract: An Inquiry Into Modern Contractual Relations*, New Haven, CT: Yale University Press.

Madhok, A. (1995) 'Revisiting Multinational Firms' Tolerance for Joint Ventures: A Trust-Based Approach', *Journal of International Business Studies* **26**(1): 117-137.

Madsen, T.K. (1987) 'Empirical Export Performance Studies: A Review of Conceptualizations and Findings', in S.T. Cavusgil (ed.) *Advances in International Marketing,* Vol. 2, Greenwich, CT: JAI Press, pp. 177-198.

Madsen, T.K. (1989) 'Successful Export Marketing Management: Some Empirical Evidence,' *International Marketing Review* **6**(4): 41-57.

Makino, S. (1995) 'Joint Venture Ownership Structure and Performance: Japanese Joint Ventures in Asia', Unpublished PhD Dissertation, University of Western Ontario, CA.

Makino, S. and Beamish, P.W. (1995) 'Joint Venture Ownership Characteristics and Performance: Japanese Joint Ventures in Asia', paper presented at the *Academy of International Business (A.I.B.) Meeting*, October, Seoul.

Makino, S. and Beamish, P.W. (1998) 'Performance and Survival of Joint Ventures with Non-Conventional Ownership Structures', *Journal of International Business Studies* **29**(4): 797-818.

Makino, S. and Delios, A. (1996) 'Local Knowledge Transfer and Performance: Implication for Alliance Formation in Asia', *Journal of International Business Studies* **27**(5): 905-927.

March, E. and Simon, H. (1958) *Organizations*, New York: Wiley.

Mascarenhas, B. (1995) 'International Industry Evolution Patterns', *International Business Review* **4**(2): 233-246.

Mason, R.O. and Mitroff, I.I. (1981) *Challenging Strategic Planning Assumptions,* New York: John Wiley and Sons.

Mayo, E. (1945) *The Social Problems of Industrial Civilization,* Cambridge, MA: Harvard University Press.

McDougall, P.P., Covin, J.G., Robinson, R.B. and Herron, L. (1994) 'The Effects of Industry Growth and Strategic Breadth on New Venture Performance and Strategy Content', *Strategic Management Journal* **15**: 537-554.

McGuinness, N.W. and Little, B. (1981) 'The Influence of Product Characteristics on the Export Performance of New Industrial Products', *Journal of Marketing* **45**(Spring): 110-122.

McNaughton, R.B. (1996) 'Foreign Market Channel Integration Decisions of Canadian Computer Software Firms', *International Business Review* **5**(1): 23-52.

McQueen, C. (1988) 'Liberal Economic Policies and Steady Growth are Luring more American Companies to India', *Business America* **109**(October): 14-18.

Metcalf, L.E., Frear, C.R. and Krishnan, R. (1992) 'Buyer-Seller Relationships: An Application of the IMP Interaction Model', *European Journal of Marketing* **26**(2): 27-46.

Michel, J.G. and Hambrick, D.C. (1992) 'Diversification Posture and Top Management Team Characteristics', *Academy of Management Journal* **35**(1): 9-37.

Michener, P. and Ramstetter, E.D. (1990) 'Motives for United States Direct Investment in Thailand: A Survey of Investors', *Asia-Pacific TNC Review, ESCAP/UNCTC Publication Series A* **7**: 1-21.

Miller, D. and Toulouse, J-M (1986) 'Chief Executive Personality and Corporate Strategy and Structure in Small Firms', *Management Science* **32**(November): 1389-1409.

Millin, L.J. (1984) 'Investment and Joint Ventures in ASEAN-Australia Business Relations', *The Practising Manager* **4**(2): 20-21.

Millington, A.I. and Bayliss, B.T. (1995) 'Transnational Joint Ventures Between UK and EU Manufacturing Companies and the Structure of Competition', *Journal of International Business Studies* **26**(2): 239-254.

Min, S.K. (1985) 'Korean Manufacturing FDIs', in B. Hwang (ed.) *Korean Business Management*, Seoul: Hanwool Books.

Mintu-Wimsatt, A. and Calantone, R. (2000) 'Crossing the Border: Testing a Negotiation Model Among Canadian Exporters', *Journal of Business & Industrial Marketing* **15**(5): 340-353.

Morgan, R.M. and Hunt, S.D. (1994) 'The Commitment-Trust Theory of Relationship Marketing', *Journal of Marketing* **58**(July): 20-38.

Morris, J. and Sherman, J.D. (1981) 'Generalizability of an Organizational Commitment Model', *Academy of Management Journal* **24**: 512-526.

Morrow, P. (1983) 'Concept Redundancy in Organizational Research: The Case of Work Commitment', *Academy of Management Review* **8**: 486-500.

Mowday, R.T., Porter, L.W. and Steers, R. (1982) *Employee-Organization Linkages: The Psychology of Commitment, Absenteeism, and Turnover*, New York: Academic Press.

Mueller, C.B. (1994) 'Top Management Teams of International Joint Ventures: The Effects of Heterogeneity on Group Process and Goal Attainment', Unpublished PhD Dissertation, University of South Carolina.

Muliak, S. (1996) 'SEMNET Discussion List', Accessed 10 September 1996.

Murray, A.I. (1989) 'Top Management Group Heterogeneity and Firm Performance', *Strategic Management Journal* **10**: 125-141.

Murray, J.Y., Kotabe, M. and Wildt, A.R. (1995) 'Strategic and Financial Performance Implications of Global Sourcing Strategy', *Journal of International Business Studies* **26**(1): 181-202.

Myers, S. (1984) 'Finance Theory and Financial Strategy', *Interfaces* January-February: 126-137.

Namiki, N. (1989) 'The Impact of Competitive Strategy on Export Sales Performance: An Exploratory Study', *Mid-Atlantic Journal of Business* **25**(6): 21-37.

Narver, J.C. and Slater, S.F. (1990) 'The Effect of a Market Orientation on Business Profitability', *Journal of Marketing* **54**(October): 20-35.

National Economic and Social Development Board (NESDB) (1988) *National Income of Thailand: New Series 1970-1987,* Bangkok: NESDB.

National Economic and Social Development Board (NESDB) (1992) *National Income of Thailand: Re-base Series 1980-1991,* Bangkok: NESDB.

National Economic and Social Development Board (NESDB) (1993) *National Income of Thailand 1992,* Bangkok: NESDB.

NEDO (1981a) *Industrial Performance: Trade Performance and Marketing.*

NEDO (1981b) *Industrial Performance: R&D and Innovations.*

NEDO (1982) *Innovation in the UK.*

Negandhi, A.R. and Donhowe, P.W. (1989) 'It's Time to Explore New Global Trade Options', *The Journal of Business Strategy* January/February: 27-31.

Negandhi, A.R. and Wedge, M. (1990) *Advances in International Comparative Management: Beyond Theory Z,* Greenwich: JAI Press.

Newman, W.H. (1992) 'Focused Joint Ventures in Transforming Economies', *Academy of Management Executive* **6**(1): 67-75.

Nielsen, R.P. (1988) 'Cooperative Strategy', *Strategic Management Journal* **9**: 475-492.

Nitsch, D., Beamish, P.W. and Makino, S. (1996) 'Entry Mode and Performance of Japanese FDI in Western Europe', *Management International Review* **36**(1): 27-43.

Nunnally, J.C. (1967) *Psychometric Theory,* 1st Edition, New York: McGraw Hill.

Nunnally, J.C. (1978) *Psychometric Theory,* 2nd Edition, New York: McGraw Hill.

Nunnally, J.C. and Bernstein, I.H. (1994) *Psychometric Theory,* 3rd Edition, New York: McGraw Hill.

O'Cass, A. and Julian, C.C. (2003a) 'Examining Firm and Environmental Influences on Export Marketing Mix Strategy and Export Performance of Australian Exporters', *European Journal of Marketing* **37**(3/4): 366-384.

O'Cass, A. and Julian, C.C. (2003b) 'Modelling the Effects of Firm-Specific and Environmental Characteristics on Export Marketing Performance', *Journal of Global Marketing* **16**(3): 53-74.

Ohmae, K. (1985) *Triad Power: The Coming Shape of Global Competition,* New York: Free Press.

Ohmae, K. (1989a) 'The Global Logic of Strategic Alliances', *Harvard Business Review* March-April: 143-154.

Ohmae, K. (1989b) 'Managing in a Borderless World', *Harvard Business Review* May-June: 152-161.

Oman, C.P. (1988) 'Cooperative Strategies in Developing Countries: The New Forms of Investment', in F. Contractor and P. Lorange (eds.) *Cooperative Strategies in International Business*, Lexington, MA: Lexington Books, pp. 383-401.

O'Reilly III, C. and Chatman, J. (1986) 'Organizational Commitment and Psychological Attachment: The Effects of Compliance, Identification and Internalization on Pro-social Behavior', *Journal of Applied Psychology* **71**(3): 492-499.

Otterbeck, L. (1981) *The Management of Headquarters Subsidiary Relations in Multinational Corporations,* London, UK: Gower.

Ouchi, W.C. (1979) 'A Conceptual Framework for the Design of Organisational Control Mechanisms', *Management Science* **25**(9): 833-848.

Ouchi, W.C. (1980) 'Markets, Bureaucracies, and Clans', *Administrative Science Quarterly* **25**: 129-141.

Ouchi, W.C. (1981) *Theory Z: How American Business can meet the Japanese Challenge,* Reading, MA: Addison-Wesley.

Ouchi, W.C. and Wilkins, A.L. (1985) 'Organizational Culture', *Annual Review of Sociology* **11**: 457-483.

Padmanabhan, P. and Cho, K.R. (1995) 'Methodological Issues in International Business Studies: The Case of Foreign Establishment Mode Decisions by Multinational Firms', *International Business Review* **4**(1): 55-73.

Paliwoda, S. and Liebrenz, M. (1984) 'Expectations and Results of Contractual Joint Ventures by US and UK MNCs in Eastern Europe', *European Journal of Marketing* **18**(3): 51-66.

Palmer, A. (1995) 'Relationship Marketing: Local Implementation of a Universal Concept', *International Business Review* **4**(4): 471-481.

Pan, Y. (1995) 'The Features of European Equity Joint Ventures in China: A Longitudinal Study', *Journal of Euromarketing* **4**(1): 5-21.

Pan, Y. (1996) 'Influences on Foreign Equity Ownership Level in Joint Ventures in China', *Journal of International Business Studies* **27**(1): 1-26.

Parameswaran, R. and Yaprak, A. (1987) 'A Cross-National Comparison of Consumer Research Measures', *Journal of International Business Studies* **18** (Spring): 35-50.

Park, H. (1991) 'Analysis of Joint Ventures Local Managers' Behaviour and its Impact on Joint Venture Cohesiveness: Korea Case', *Journal of Global Marketing* **5**(1/2): 201-224.

Park, S.H. and Russo, M.V. (1996) 'When Competition Eclipses Cooperation: An Event History Analysis of Alliance Failure', *Management Science* **42**: 875-890.

Park, S.H. and Ungson, G.R. (1997) 'The Effect of National Culture, Organizational Complementarity, and Economic Motivation on Joint Venture Dissolution', *Academy of Management Journal* **40**(2): 279-307.

Parke, H., Hwang, S.D. and Harrison, J.K. (1996) 'Sources and Consequences of Communication Problems in Foreign Subsidiaries: the Case of United States Firms in South Korea', *International Business Review* **5**(1): 79-98.

Parkhe, A. (1991) 'Interfirm Diversity, Organizational Learning, and Longevity in Global Strategic Alliances', *Journal of International Business Studies* **22**(4): 579-601.

Parkhe, A. (1993a) 'Partner Nationality and the Structure-Performance Relationship in Strategic Alliances', *Organization Science* **4**(2): 301-324.

Parkhe, A. (1993b) 'Strategic Alliance Structuring: A Game Theoretic and Transaction Cost Examination of Interfirm Cooperation', *Academy of Management Journal* **38**(4): 794-829.

Parsons, T. (1956) 'Suggestions for a Sociological Approach to the Theory of Organisations-I', *Administrative Science Quarterly* **1**(March): 63-85.

Pedersen, T. and Thomsen, S. (1995) 'European Models of Corporate Governance', competitive paper presented at the EIBA (European International Business Association Meeting), December, Urbino, Italy.

Pennings, J.M., Barkema, H.G. and Douma, S.G. (1994) 'Organisational Learning and Diversification', *Academy of Management Journal* **37**(3): 608-640.

Perlmutter, H. and Heenan, D. (1986) 'Cooperate to Compete Globally', *Harvard Business Review* March-April: 136-152.

Perry, J. and Levine, C. (1976) 'An Interorganizational Analysis of Power, Conflict, and Settlements in Public Sector Collective Bargaining', *American Political Science Review* **70**(4): 1185-1201.

Peters, T.J. and Austin, N. (1985) *A Passion for Excellence*, New York: Random House.

Peters, T.J. and Waterman, R.H. (1982) *In Search of Excellence,* New York, NY: Harper and Row.

Peterson, R. and Schwind, H. (1977) 'A Comparative Study of Personnel Problems in International Companies in Joint Ventures in Japan', *Journal of International Business Studies* **8**(1): 45-55.

Peterson, R.B. and Shimada, J. (1978) 'Sources of Management Problems in Japanese-American Joint Ventures', *Academy of Management Review* **3**: 796-804.

Pettigrew, A.M. (1979) 'On Studying Organisational Cultures', *Administrative Science Quarterly* **24**: 570-580.

Pfeffer, J. (1981) *Power in Organizations,* Cambridge, MA: Balinger.

Pfeffer, J. and Knowack, P. (1976) 'Joint Ventures and Interorganizational Interdependence', *Administrative Science Quarterly* **21**: 398-418.

Pfeffer, J. and Salancik, G.R. (1978) *The External Control of Organizations,* New York: Harper and Row.

Phatak, A.V. and Chowdhury, J. (1991) 'IJV Success in Developing Countries: An Empirical Testing of a Predictive Model Based on National Partners' Responses', paper presented at the Academy of International Business (AIB) Conference, Miami, Florida.

Phillips, L.W., Chang, D.R. and Buzzell, R.D. (1983) 'Product Quality, Cost Position and Business Performance: A Test of Some Key Hypotheses', *Journal of Marketing* **47**(Spring): 26-43.

Pilafidis, E.J. (1995a) 'On Structuring and Managing Non-Equity Strategic Alliances', paper presented at the Western Regional Conference of the Academy of International Business, May.

Pilafidis, E.J. (1995b) 'Managerial Operating Mechanisms in Non-Equity Strategic Alliances', paper presented at the Academy of International Business Meeting, October, Seoul.

Pitt, L.F. and Jeantrout, B. (1994) 'Management of Customer Expectations in Service Firms: A Study and a Checklist', *The Service Industries Journal* **14**(2): 170-189.

Pondy, L.R. (1967) 'Organizational Conflict: Concepts and Models', *Administrative Science Quarterly* **12**: 296-320.

Porter, M.E. (1976) 'Please Note Location of Nearest Exit: Exit Barriers and Strategic and Organizational Planning', *California Management Review* **19**(2): 21-33.

Porter, M.E. (1980) *Competitive Strategy,* New York: Free Press.

Porter, M.E. (1985) *Competitive Advantage,* New York: Free Press.

Porter, M.E. (1986) *Competition in Global Industries,* Boston, MA: Harvard Business School Press.

Porter, M.E. and Fuller, M.B. (1986) 'Coalitions and Global Strategy', in M.E. Porter (ed.) *Competition in Global Industries,* Boston, MA: Harvard Business School Press, pp. 315-342.

Poynter, T. (1982) 'Government Intervention in Less Developed Countries: The Experience of Multinational Companies', *Journal of International Business Studies* **13**(1): 9-25.

Prahalad, C.K. and Hamel, G. (1985) 'Do You Really have a Global Strategy?' *Harvard Business Review* **63**(4): 139-148.

Prahalad, C.K. and Hamel, G. (1989) 'Collaborate with your Competitors and Win', *Harvard Business Review* **67**(1): 133-139.

Provan, K.G. and Gassenheimer, J.B. (1994) 'Supplier Commitment in Relational Contract Exchange with Buyers: A Study of Interorganizational Dependence and Exercised Power', *Journal of Management Studies* **3**(January): 55-68.

Pruden, D.R. (1995) 'There's a Difference between Frequency Marketing and Relationship Marketing', *Direct Marketing* **58**(2): 30-31.

Pupphavesa, W., Anantanasuwong, D. and Chintakananda, K. (1992) 'Investment Trends and the Business Environment in Thailand', in *PITO Business Environment in ASEAN NO. 5.*, Honolulu, Hawaii: East-West Centre.

Putnam, L. and Poole, M. (1987) 'Conflict and Negotiation', in F.M. Jablin, L.L. Putnam, K.H. Roberts and L.W. Porter (eds.) *Handbook of Organizational Communication*, Newbury Park: Sage.

Quelch, J.A. and Hoff, E.J. (1986) 'Customizing Global Marketing', *Harvard Business Review* May-June: 59-68.

Quinn, R.E. and Rohrbaugh, J. (1983) 'A Spatial Model of Effectiveness Criteria: Towards a Competing Values Approach to Organisational Analysis', *Management Science* **29**(3): 363-377.

Ramstetter, E.D. (1993a) 'Macroeconomic Trends, Foreign Firms, and Economic Policy in Thailand', *Institute of Developing Economies*: 41-113.

Ramstetter, E.D. (1993b) 'Technology-Related Activities in Japanese and US Multinationals: Implications for Thai Manufacturing Industries', *Japan Centre for Economic Research* **3**: 11-57.

Ramstetter, E.D. (1994) 'Comparison of Japanese Multinationals and Other Firms in Thailand's Non-Oil Manufacturing Industries', *ASEAN Economic Bulletin* **11**(1): 36-58.

Ramstetter, E.D. (1995) 'Trends in Production in Foreign Multinational Firms in Asian Economies: A Note On An Economic Myth Related to Poor Measurement', *Kansai University Review of Economics and Business* **24**(1): 49-107.

Rao, A. and Hashimoto, K. (1996) 'Intercultural Influence: A Study of Japanese Expatriate Managers in Canada', *Journal of International Business Studies* **27**(3): 443-466.

Rao, B.P. and Reddy, S.K. (1995) 'A Dynamic Approach to the Analysis of Strategic Alliances', *International Business Review* **4**(4): 499-518.

Rao, C.P., Nwakanma, H.C. and Kurtz, D.L. (1995) 'The Relationships Between Imports and Marketing Skills Improvements in a Developing Country', *International Business Review* **4**(1): 1-17.

Rao, T.R. and Naidu, G.M. (1992) 'Are the Stages of Internationalization Empirically Supportable?' *Journal of Global Marketing* **6**(1/2): 147-170.

Raveed, S. (1976) 'Joint Ventures Between US Multinational Firms and Host Governments in Selected Developing Countries: A Case Study of Costa Rica, Trinidad and Venezuela', Unpublished PhD Dissertation, Indiana University.

Raveed, S.R. and Renforth, W. (1983) 'State Enterprise-Multinational Corporation Joint Ventures: How Well Do They Meet Both Partners' Needs?' *Management International Review* **23**(1): 47-57.

Reich, R. and Mankin, E. (1986), 'Joint Ventures with Japan Give Away our Future', *Harvard Business Review* **64**(2): 78-86.

Reicheld, F.F. and Sasser Jr., W.E. (1990) 'Zero Defections: Quality Comes to Services', *Harvard Business Review* **68**(September-October): 105-111.

Reichers, A.E. (1985) 'A Review and Reconceptualization of Organizational Commitment', *Academy of Management Review* **10**(3): 465-476.

Reid, S.D. (1982) 'The Impact of Size on Export Behaviour in Small Firms', in M.R. Czinkota and G. Tesar (eds.) *Export Management: An International Context,* New York: Praeger Publishers.

Reynolds, J.I. (1978) 'Developing Policy Responses to Cultural Differences', *Business Horizons* 21(August): 28-35.

Reynolds, J.I. (1979) *Indian-American Joint Ventures: Business Policy Relationships,* Washington DC: University Press of America.

Reynolds, J.I. (1984) 'The "Pinched Shoe" Effect of International Joint Ventures', *Columbia Journal of World Business* (Summer): 23-29.

Reynolds, P.D. (1986) 'Organizational Culture as Related to Industry, Position, and Performance: A Preliminary Report', *Journal of Management Studies* 23(3): 333-344.

Richardson, S.A. (1956) 'Organisational Contrasts on British and American Ships', *Administrative Science Quarterly* 1(September): 189-207.

Riley, P. (1983) 'A Structurationist Account of Political Culture', *Administrative Science Quarterly* 28: 414-437.

Rivoli, P. and Salorio, E. (1996) 'Foreign Direct Investment and Investment under Uncertainty', *Journal of International Business Studies* 27(2): 335-358.

Roberts, E.B. (1980) 'New Ventures for Corporate Growth', *Harvard Business Review* July: 134-142.

Roberts, K.H. and Boycagiller, N.A. (1984) 'Cross-National Organizational Research: The Grasp of Blind Men', in B.H. Staw and L.L. Cummings (eds.) *Research in Organizational Behaviour,* Vol. 6, Greenwich, CT: JAI Press, pp. 423-479.

Roberts, K.H. and O'Reilly, C.A. (1979) 'Some Correlates of Communication Roles in Organizations', *Academy of Management Journal* 22: 42-57.

Robey, D., Farrow, D.L. and Franz, C.R. (1989) 'Group Process and Conflict in System Development', *Management Science* 35(10): 1172-1191.

Robicheaux, R. and El-Ansary, A. (1975) 'A General Model for Understanding Channel Member Behavior', *Journal of Retailing* 52(Winter): 23-29.

Robin, S.S. (1965) 'A Procedure for Securing Returns to Mail Questionnaires', *Sociology and Social Research* **50**(October): 24-35.

Robinson, R. (1969) 'Ownership Across National Frontiers', *Industrial Management Review* Fall: 41-65.

Rodgers, F. (1986) *The IBM Way: Insights into the World's Most Successful Marketing Organization,* New York, NY: Harper and Row.

Root, F.R. (1988a) 'Some Taxonomies of International Cooperative Agreements', in F. Contractor and P. Lorange, (eds.) *Cooperative Strategies in International Business,* Lexington, MA: Lexington Books, pp. 69-80.

Root, F.R. (1988b) 'Environmental Risks and the Bargaining Power of Multinational Corporations', *The International Trade Journal* **3**(1): 111-124.

Rosenberg, L. and Stern, L. (1971) 'Conflict Measurement in the Distribution Channel', *Journal of Marketing Research* **8**(November): 437-442.

Rosson, Ph.J. and Ford, D.L. (1980) 'Stake, Conflict, and Performance in Export Marketing Channels', *Management International Review* **20**: 31-37.

Rosson, Ph.J. and Ford, D.L. (1982) 'Manufacturer-Overseas Distributor Relations and Export Performance', *Journal of International Business Studies* **13**(Fall): 57-72.

Ruekert, R.W. and Walker, O.C. (1987) 'Marketing's Interaction with Other Functional Units: A Conceptual Framework and Empirical Evidence', *Journal of Marketing,* **51**: 1-19.

Rugman, A.M. (1981) 'A New Theory of the Multinational Enterprise: Internationalization versus Internalization', *Columbia Journal of World Business* Spring: 23-29.

Rugman, A.M. (1985) 'Internalization is Still a General Theory of Foreign Direct Investment', *Welwirtschaftlicher Archiv* September.

Russ, G.S., Daft, R.L. and Lengel, R.H. (1990) 'Media Selection and Managerial Characteristics in Organizational Communications', *Management Communications Quarterly* **4**(2): 151-175.

Ryans, A.B. (1988) 'Strategic Market Entry Factors and Market Share Achievement in Japan', *Journal of International Business Studies* **19**(Fall): 389-409.

Salancik, G.R. (1977) 'Commitment and the Control of Organizational Behaviour and Belief', in B.M. Staw and G.R. Salancik (eds.) *New Directions in Organizational Behaviour,* Chicago, IL: St Clair Press.

Samiee, S. and Roth, K. (1992) 'The Influence of Global Marketing Standardization on Performance', *Journal of Marketing* **56**(April): 1-17.

Samonis, V. (1992) 'East-West Joint Ventures in the Soviet Union: Some Lessons from the East European Experience', *Journal of Global Marketing* **6**(1/2): 129-146.

Sarkar, M., Cavusgil, S.T. and Evirgen, C. (1997) 'A Commitment-Trust Mediated Framework of International Collaborative Venture Performance', in P.W. Beamish and J.P. Killing (eds.) *Cooperative Strategies: North American Perspectives*, San Francisco, CA: The New Lexington Press, pp. 255-285.

Schaan, J-L. (1983) 'Parent Control and Joint Venture Success: The Case of Mexico', Unpublished PhD Dissertation, University of Western Ontario, Canada.

Schaan, J-L. (1988) 'How to Control a Joint Venture Even as a Minority Partner?' *Journal of General Management* **14**(1): 4-16.

Schaan, J-L. and Beamish, P.W. (1988) 'Joint Venture General Managers in LDCs', in F. Contractor and P. Lorange (eds.) *Cooperative Strategies in International Business,* Lexington, MA: Lexington Books, pp. 279-299.

Scherer, F.M. and Ross, D. (1990*) Industrial Market Structure and Economic Performance,* 3rd Edition, Boston, MA: Houghton-Mifflin.

Schmidt, S.M. and Kochan, T.A. (1972) 'Conflict Toward Conceptual Clarity', *Administrative Science Quarterly* **19**: 359-370.

Schneider, S.C. (1988) 'National vs Corporate Culture: Implications for Human Resource Management', *Journal of Human Resource Management* **27**(2): 231-246.

Schneider, S.C. and De Meyer, A. (1991) 'Interpreting and Responding to Strategic Issues: The Impact of National Culture', *Strategic Management Journal* **12**: 307-320.

Schweiger, D.S. and Sandberg, W.R. (1991) 'A Team Approach to Top Management's Strategic Decisions', in H.E. Glass (ed.) *Handbook of Business Strategy*, New York: Warren, Gorham and Lamont.

Schwenk, C.R. (1990) 'Conflict in Organizational Decision Making: An Exploratory Study of its Effects in For-Profit and Not-for-Profit Organizations', *Management Science* 36: 436-448.

Seashore, S.E. (1954) *Group Cohesiveness in the Industrial Work Group*, Ann Arbor, MI: University of Michigan Press.

Sethi, V., Datta, L. and Wise, G. (1990) 'Passage to India: A Marketing Perspective', *International Marketing Review* 7(1): 48-67.

Shanks, D.C. (1985) 'Strategic Planning for Global Competition', *Journal of Business Strategy* 5(3): 80-89.

Shao, A.T. (1991) 'Joint Venture or Wholly-Own: Which Produces the Best Results in the Advertising Industry'? *Journal of Global Marketing* 5(1/2): 107-124.

Shapiro, B.P. (1988) 'What the Hell is Market Oriented?' *Harvard Business Review* 66(6): 119-125.

Shaver, J.M., Mitchell, W. and Yeung, B. (1997) 'The Effect of Own-Firm and Other-Firm Experience on Foreign Direct Investment Survival in the United States, 1987-92', *Strategic Management Journal* 18: 811-824.

Shenkar, O. and Zeira, Y. (1987) 'Human Resources Management in International Joint Ventures: Directions for Research', *Academy of Management Review* 12(3): 546-557.

Shenkar, O. and Zeira, Y. (1991) 'International Joint Ventures: The Case of Israel', *Journal of Global Marketing* 5(1/2): 145-162.

Shenkar, O. and Zeira, Y. (1992) 'Role Conflict and Role Ambiguity of Chief Executive Officers in International Joint Ventures', *Journal of International Business Studies* 23(1): 55-75.

Sibunruang, A. (1986) *Foreign Investment and Manufactured Exports in Thailand*, Bangkok: Chulalongkorn University Social Research Institute.

Simiar, F. (1983) 'Major Causes of Joint Venture Failure in the Middle East: The Case of Iran', *Management International Review* 23(1): 58-68.

Simmonds, K. (1985) 'Global Strategy: Achieving the Geocentric Ideal', *International Marketing Review* **2**(Spring): 8-17.

Simonin, B.L. (1999) 'Transfer of Marketing Know-How in International Strategic Alliances: An Empirical Investigation of the Role and Antecedents of Knowledge Ambiguity', *Journal of International Business Studies* **30**(3): 463-490.

Smircich, L. (1983) 'Concepts of Culture and Organisational Analysis', *Administrative Science Quarterly* **28**: 339-358.

Smith, K.G., Smith, K.A., Olian, J.D., Sims, H.P., O'Bannon, D.P. and Scully, J.A. (1994) 'Top Management Team Demography and Process: The Role of Social Integration and Communication', *Administrative Science Quarterly* **39**: 412-438.

Sohn, J.H.D. (1993) 'Diversification as a Supplementary Means of Control in International Joint Ventures: The Case of the Japanese MNCs in Korea', Best Paper Proceedings of the Association of Japanese Business Studies, pp. 47-53.

Sohn, J.H.D. (1994) 'Social Knowledge as a Control System: A Proposition and Evidence from the Japanese FDI Behaviour', *Journal of International Business Studies* **25**(2): 295-324.

Sood, J.H. and Adams, P. (1984) 'Model of Management Learning Styles as a Predictor of Export Behaviour and Performance', *Journal of Business Research* **12**(2): 169-182.

Sorenson, R.Z. and Weichmann, U.E. (1975) 'How Multinationals View Marketing Standardization', *Harvard Business Review* **53**(May-June): 38.

Spence, A. (1974) *Market Signalling: Informational Transfers in Hiring and Related Screening Processes,* Cambridge, MA: Harvard University.

Spinks, S.O. (1978) 'The Contemporary Antitrust Regulation of Joint Ventures in the European Economic Community', *Vanderbuilt Journal of Transnational Law* **11**: 373-420.

Staw, B.M. (1977) 'Two Sides of Commitment', paper presented at the Academy of Management Conference, Orlando, Florida.

Stern, L.W. and Gorman, R.H. (1969) 'Conflict in Distribution Channels: An Exploration', in L.W. Stern (ed.) *Distribution Channels: Behavioural Dimensions,* Boston, Massachusetts: Houghton-Mifflin Company, pp. 156-175.

Stern, L.W., Sternthal, B. and Craig, S. (1975) 'Strategies for Managing Interorganizational Conflict: A Laboratory Paradigm', *Journal of Applied Psychology* **60**: 472-482.

Stier, K. and Mills, S. (1994) 'Thailand', in S. Mills (ed.) *Asian Business Insight,* Sydney: John Fairfax Pty. Ltd., pp. 182-198.

Stopford, J.M. and Wells, Jr., L.T. (1972) *Managing the Multinational Enterprise: Organization of the Firm and Ownership of the Subsidiaries,* New York: Basic Books.

Stuckey, J.A. (1983) 'Vertical Integration and JVs in the International Aluminium Industry', Unpublished PhD Dissertation, Harvard Business School, Harvard University, Boston, MA.

Sullivan, J. and Peterson, R.B. (1982) 'Factors Associated with Trust in Japanese-American Joint Ventures', *Management International Review* **22**(2): 30-40.

Tabachnik, B. and Fidell, L (1996) *Using Multivariate Statistics,* 3rd Edition, New York: Harper Collins.

Tambunlertchai, S. (1977) *Japanese and American Investments in Thailand's Manufacturing Sector: An Assessment of the Relative Economic Contribution to the Host Country,* Tokyo, Japan: Institute of Developing Economies.

Tan, B. and Vertinsky, I. (1995) 'Strategic Advantages of Japanese Electronics Firms and the Scale of their Subsidiaries in the US and Canada', *International Business Review* **4**(3): 373-386.

Tan, C.H. (1990) 'Privatisation and Regional Joint Ventures in Southeast Asia', *Corporate Management* **42**(4): 136-139.

Tannenbaum, A.S. (1968) *Control in Organizations*, New York: McGraw-Hill.

Tayeb, M. (1995) 'Supervisory Styles and Cultural Contexts: A Comparative Study', *International Business Review* **4**(1): 75-89.

Taylor, D.B. (1993) 'New Zealand's Top Performing Organizations: What's Different About their Marketing?' Working Paper, University of Waikato, New Zealand.

Teas, K.R. (1993) 'Expectations, Performance Evaluation, and Consumers Perceptions of Quality', *Journal of Marketing* **57**(October): 18-34.

Teece, D.J. (1981) 'The Multinational Enterprise: Market Failure and Market Power Considerations', *Sloan Management Review* Spring: 3-17.

Terpstra, V.H. (1987) *International Marketing,* Hinsdale, IL: Dryden Press.

Terpstra, V.H. and Sarathy, R. (1994) *International Marketing,* 6th Edition, Fort Worth, TX: Dryden Press.

Thomas, K. (1976) 'Conflict and Conflict Management', in M. Dunnette (ed.) *Handbook of Industrial and Organizational Psychology,* Chicaogo, IL: Rand McNally.

Thompson, J.D. (1967) *Organizations in Action,* New York: McGraw-Hill.

Thomsen, S. and Pedersen, T. (1995) 'International Corporate Governance: Ownership Structures in Six European Nations', paper presented at the Academy of International Business Meeting, October, Seoul.

'Thriving Joint Ventures: Australian Investment in Thailand' (1980) *Business Review of Thailand* 8 June: 448-454.

Tillman, A. (1990) 'The Influence of Control and Conflict on Performance of Japanese-Thai Joint Ventures', Unpublished PhD Dissertation, Nova University, CA.

Tisdell, C. (1990) 'International Joint Ventures and Technology Transfer: Some Economic Issues', *Prometheus* **8**(1): 67-79.

Tolbert, P.S. (1988) 'Institutional Sources of Organizational Culture in Major Law Firms', in L. Zucker (ed.) *Institutional Patterns and Organizations,* Cambridge, MA: Ballinger Publishing Company.

Tomlinson, J.W.C. (1970) *The Joint Venture Process in International Business: India and Pakistan,* Cambridge, MA: MIT Press.

Tomlinson, J.W.C. and Willie, C.S.W. (1982) 'Modelling the Joint Venture Process in Latin America: Mexico', *Canadian Journal of Development Studies* 3(1): 30-50.

Toyo Keizai (1982, 1986, 1990, 1994) *Kaigai Shinshutsu Kigyo Soran (A Comprehensive Survey of Firms Operating Overseas),* Tokyo: Toyo Keizai (in Japanese).

Trevino, L.J. and Daniels, J.D. (1995) 'FDI Theory and Foreign Direct Investment in the United States: A Comparison of Investors and Non-Investors', *International Business Review* 4(2): 177-194.

Tse, D.K., Lee, K-H, Vertinsky, I. and Wehring, D.A. (1988) 'Does Culture Matter? A Cross Cultural Study of Executives' Choice, Decisiveness, and Risk Adjustment in International Marketing', *Journal of Marketing* 52(October): 81-95.

Tyebjee, T.T. (1988) 'Japan's Joint Ventures in the United States', in F. Contractor and P. Lorange (eds.) *Cooperative Strategies in International Business,* Lexington, MA: Lexington Books, pp. 457-471.

Van De Ven, A. and Walker, G. (1984) 'The Dynamics of Interorganizational Coordination', *Administrative Science Quarterly* 29(4): 598-621.

Vanhonacker, W. and Pan, Y. (1997) 'The Impact of National Culture, Business Scope, and Geographic Location on Joint Venture Operations in China', *Journal of International Marketing* 5(3): 11-30.

Vaupel, J.W. and Curhan, J.P. (1969) *The Making of the Multinational Enterprise,* Boston, MA: Harvard University Press.

Venkatraman, N. and Prescott, J.E. (1990) 'Environment-Strategy Coalignment: An Empirical Test of its Performance Implications', *Strategic Management Journal* 11: 1-23.

Venkatraman, N. and Ramanujam, V. (1986) 'Measurement of Business Performance in Strategy Research: A Comparison of Approaches', *Academy of Management Review* 11(4): 801-814.

Veugelers, R. (1995) 'Alliances and the Pattern of Comparative Advantages: A Sectoral Analysis', *International Business Review* 4(2): 213-231.

Walker, O. (1970) 'An Experimental Investigation of Conflict and Power in Marketing Channels', Unpublished PhD Dissertation, University of Wisconsin.

Walker, O.C. and Ruekert, R.W. (1987) 'Marketing's Role in the Implementation of Business Strategy', *Journal of Marketing* **51**: 15-33.

Wallace, A.W. (1992) 'Nationality and Organizational Culture as Influences on Japanese and American Managers' Criteria for Joint Venture Success in the United States', Unpublished PhD Dissertation, University of South Carolina.

Walters, P.G.P. (1986) 'International Marketing Policy: A Discussion of the Standardization Construct and its Relevance for Corporate Policy', *Journal of International Business Studies* **17**(Summer): 55-69.

Walters, P.G.P. and Toyne, B. (1989) 'Product Modification and Standardisation in International Markets: Strategic Options and Facilitating Policies', *Columbia Journal of World Business* (Winter): 37-44.

Walton, R. and Dutton, J. (1969) 'The Management of Interdepartmental Conflict: A Model and Review', *Administrative Science Quarterly* **14**(March): 73-84.

Waterschoot, W.V and Van Den Bulte, C. (1992) 'The 4P Classification of the Marketing Mix Revisited', *Journal of Marketing* **56**(October): 1-17.

Webster, Jr., F.E. (1988) 'Rediscovering the Marketing Concept', *Business Horizons* **31**(May-June): 29-39.

Wells, Jr. L.T. (1972) *The Product Life Cycle and International Trade,* Boston, MA: Harvard Business School Division of Research.

West, S.G., Finch, J.F. and Curran, P.J. (1995) 'Structural Equation Models with Normal Variables: Problems and Remedies', in R.H. Hoyle (ed.) *Structural Equation Modelling: Concepts, Issues, and Applications,* Thousand Oaks, CA: Sage, pp. 56-75.

Wharton, R., Baird, I.S. and Lyles, M.A. (1991) 'Conceptual Frameworks Among Chinese Managers: Joint Venture Management and Philosophy', *Journal of Global Marketing* **5**(1/2): 163-182.

Whetten, D. (1981) 'Interorganizational Relations: A Review of the Field', *Journal of Higher Education* **52**: 1-28.

White, P. (1974) 'Intra- and Organizational Studies: Do They Require Separate Conceptualizations?' *Administrative Science Quarterly* **19**: 107-152.

Wiersema, M.F. and Bantel, K.A. (1992) 'Top Management Team Demography and Corporate Strategic Change', *Academy of Management Journal* **35**: 91-121.

Wilkins, A.L. and Ouchi, W.G. (1983) 'Efficient Cultures: Exploring the Relationship Between Culture and Organisational Performance', *Administrative Science Quarterly* **28**: 468-481.

Williamson, O.E. (1975) *Markets and Hierarchies: Analysis and Antitrust Implications,* New York: Free Press.

Williamson, O.E. (1983) 'Credible Commitments: Using Hostages to Support Exchange', *American Economic Review* **73**(4): 519-540.

Williamson, O.E. (1985) *The Economic Institutions of Capitalism,* New York: Free Press.

Wilson, M. and McDonald, M. (1994) 'Marketing at the Crossroads', *Marketing Intelligence and Planning* **12**(1): 42-45.

Wind, Y. (1985) 'Agenda for Marketing', *Marketing News,* August 16.

Wind, Y. (1986) 'The Myth of Globalization', *Journal of Consumer Marketing* **3**(Spring): 23-26.

Wind, Y. and Robertson, T.S. (1983) 'Marketing Strategy: New Directions for Theory and Research', *Journal of Marketing* **47**(Spring): 12-25.

Woodcock, C.P., Beamish, P.W. and Makino, S. (1994) 'Ownership-Based Entry Mode Strategies and International Performance', *Journal of International Business Studies* **25**(2): 253-273.

Woodward, D.P. and Rolfe, R.J. (1993) 'The Location of Export-Oriented Foreign Direct Investment in the Caribbean Basin', *Journal of International Business Studies* **24**(1): 121-144.

Wright, R.W. and Russel, C.S. (1975) 'Joint Ventures in Developing Countries: Realities and Responses', *Columbia Journal of World Business* Summer: 74-80.

Xuejun, L. (1995) 'Cross-Cultural Management for Joint Ventures in the People's Republic of China', paper presented at the Academy of International Business Meeting, October, Seoul.

Yan. A. (1993) 'Bargaining Power, Management Control and Performance in International Joint Ventures: Development and Test of a Negotiations Model', Unpublished PhD Dissertation, Pennsylvania State University, PA.

Yan, A. (1998) 'Structural Stability and Reconfiguration of International Joint Ventures', *Journal of International Business Studies* **29**(4): 773-795.

Yan, A. and Gray, B. (1994) 'Bargaining Power, Management Control, and Performance in United States-China Joint Ventures: A Comparative Case Study', *Academy of Management Journal* **36**(7): 1478-1517.

Yan, A. and Zeng, M. (1999) 'International Joint Venture Stability: A Critique of Previous Research, a Reconceptualization and Directions for Future Research', *Journal of International Business Studies* **30**(2): 397-414.

Yip, G.S. (1989) 'Global Strategy....In a World of Nations', *Sloan Management Review* **31**(Fall): 29-41.

Yiu, D.W. and Makino, S. (2002) 'A Choice Between Joint Venture and Wholly-Owned Subsidiary: An Institutional Perspective', *Organization Science* **13**(6): 667-683.

Yosihara, K. (1978) *Japanese Investment in Southeast Asia,* Honolulu, Hawaii: University of Hawaii.

Young, R.G., and Bradford Jr., S. (1977) *Joint Ventures Planning and Action,* New York: Arthur D. Little Publications.

Zaheer, A., McEvily, W. and Perrone, V. (1998) 'Does Trust Matter? Exploring the Effects of Interorganizational and Interpersonal Trust on Performance', *Organizational Science* **9**: 141-159.

Zairi, M. and Sinclair, D. (1995) 'Business Process Re-Engineering and Process Management: A Survey of Current Practice and Future Trends in Integrated Management', *Business Process Re-Engineering and Management Journal* **1**(1): 8-30.

Zaphiriou, G.A. (1978) 'Methods of Cooperation between Independent Enterprises (Joint Ventures)', *American Journal of Comparative Law* **20**(Supplement): 245-264.

Zeithaml, V.A. (1988) 'Consumer Perceptions of Price, Quality and Value: A Means-End Model and Synthesis of Evidence', *Journal of Marketing* **52**(July): 2-22.

Zeithaml, V.A., Berry, L.I. and Parasuraman, A. (1988) 'Communication and Control Processes in the Delivering of Service Quality', *Journal of Marketing* **52**(April): 35-48.

Zhao, L. and Culpepper, R. (1995) 'Managerial Criteria for Joint Venture Performance: A Comparison of American and Chinese Managers', paper presented at the Academy of International Business Meeting, October, Seoul.

Zhu, C.J. and Dowling, P.J. (1995) 'An Unsuccessful Joint Venture in China: Case and Analysis', paper presented at the Academy of International Business Meeting, October, Seoul.

Williams, P. A. (1999) "Resource Management Outputs of the Conservation Estate", Science for Conservation and Synthesis of Research, Wellington: Department of Conservation.

Wilkinson, M., Cooper and Featherstone (1995) "Urbanisation and rural development in the distribution of ...", Journal of ..., 23(4) pp. 5-46.

Yukon, E. C. (genaur R. (1994) Managing Others' Behaviour at the Organisation: A Casebook in Organisation and Change Management, reproduced from Human International Business New York: ...

Index

Aaby, N-E. 58
accounting principles/procedures
    244–6
administrative factors, effects of 48
affective
    commitment 103–4
    conflict 88
agricultural industries 234–5, 242
Ahmed, Z.U. 126
Al-Aali, A.Y. 68
Alien Business Law, Thailand 41–2,
    240, 253
Alien Employment Act, Thailand 259
Alien Occupation Law (1973), Thailand
    257, 258
Anderson, E. 3, 6–7, 10, 22, 48, 53, 54,
    55, 67, 102, 188, 223, 267–8
antitrust regulations 31
Articles of Association 246
Articles of Incorporation 243, 247
ASEAN countries
    foreign investment in 22, 40–41, 208,
        209
    high market performers 68
    'indigenisation policy' 46–7
    Supporting Industry Database (ASID)
        232–3
Assael, H. 89
assets
    access to 70–71
    need for 215, 216, 268–9
    seizure of 45–6, 221–2
    see also; company-specific assets;
        ownership-specific assets
attitudinal commitment 103–5
Australia 131, 132, 208, 241
authoritarian management styles 138
autonomy 89–90, 138

Baker, M. 131
Bangkok University 12, 202, 281
Banks, J.C. 79, 102, 177, 184–6, 215,
    216, 217–18, 227–8, 270
bargaining power
    changes in 44–5, 72, 167, 220
    matching of 187
    of partners 22–3, 174–5
Barkema, H. 156, 224
Barney, J. 154
Bartlett Test of Sphericity 76, 94, 106,
    122, 133, 148
Beamish, P.W. 25–7, 30, 31, 49, 52, 54,
    64, 79, 81, 88, 89, 91, 92, 102, 105,
    106, 107, 138, 139, 144–5, 152,
    153, 167, 177, 180, 184–7, 197,
    215, 216, 217–18, 223, 227–8, 270
Beguin, J.P. 153
behaviour, social determinants of 101
behaviour-attitude incompatibility 105
behavioural
    characteristics 142
    commitment 103, 104, 105
    factors, effects of 47–8
    intentions 104
    patterns of local parties 141–2, 266
Bell, J. 156, 224
benefits, perceptions of 178–9, 275–6
Beta Clough Limited 241
Bivens, K.K. 5
Blau, P. 205
Bleeke, J. 156, 197
Blodgett, L.L. 22, 30, 79, 80, 139–40,
    223
boards of directors 137, 271
Boddewyn, J.J. 114
bounded rationality 185, 214, 216, 218
Bradford, Jr. J.S. 5, 24

brands
    cannibalisation of 114
    trademarks 119–20
    see also established brands; universal
        brands
Brett, J.F. 163, 211
Bronson, J.W. 53
Brown, J.R. 88
Buckley, P.J. 216
bureaucratic control systems 141, 142,
    143, 188
business
    culture 48
    foreign participation in 253–7
    strategies 57
    tax 244
    types, Thailand 246–52
Butler, J.K.J. 159, 204
buyer value 129

Cambodia 229
Canada 87
Cannon, J.P. 154
capital
    controls 177
    information 243
capital resources
    access to 70–71, 79–80, 86, 177,
        218–19
    foreign businessmen 256
    and risk 266
    shortage of 177
Casson, M. 216
Cavusgil, S.T. 57, 58, 117, 122, 125
Certificates of Residence, Thailand 258
chemical industries 234–5, 242
Child, J. 154
China 23, 30, 167
Chowdhury, M.A.J. 24, 68
Christiansen, C.A. 79, 80
Chu, W. 154
Civil and Commercial Code, Thailand
    246, 248
co-owned JVs see two-partner JVs
Coakes, S.J. 282
Coca-Cola 119
code of conduct, industrial states 44–5,
    220
cohesion 160, 161–4, 199, 200–213
collaborative trust 154

commercial risk 45, 220–21
commitment
    and international joint ventures
        102–6, 265
    and marketing performance 81–3,
        106–12, 123–5, 134–6, 149–52
    and mutual need 268–70
    nature of 274
    review of literature 100–101
communication
    channels 73–4, 75, 172–3, 226
    diverse groups 154–5, 196, 200, 201
    frequency 159, 161–4, 203–4,
        206–13
companies, prior relationships between
    193, 197, 200
company-related factors, effects on
    performance 273–5
company-specific
    advantages, internalisation of 57
    assets 168
    characteristics 60, 81–3, 95–9,
        107–12, 123–5, 134–6, 149–52
    knowledge 185, 218
competitive
    advantage 115, 170
    learning 168–9
    pricing 76, 80–81
complementarity
    effects of 93, 187
    resources 165–6, 189
    technology 225–6
complex organisations, management of
    194
composite measure, marketing
    performance 62–3
concentrated industries 31
Concrete Constructions (Thailand) Pty.
    Limited 241
Conditions of Trust Inventory 159, 204
conflict
    in decision-making, management
        processes and style 37–8, 198,
        271–3
    as independent variable 149–52
    of interest 49–50
    minimisation of 273–4
    and performance 81– 3, 94–9, 123–5,
        134–6
    review of literature 87–93

contingency perspective on
    standardisation/adaptation 116–17
continuous innovation 170
Contractor, F.J. 167
contracts
    'divorce clauses' in 187, 267
    terms of 36–7, 94, 175, 271
    unilateral alteration of 45
contractually stipulated behavioural
    investments 105
control 137–8, 274–5
    as cause for concern 35
    literature review 139–44
    of local partners 2, 21–2, 239
    and marketing performance 81–3,
        144–52
    objectives 45–6, 221–2
    of operations 271–2
Cook, K.S. 101
Cooper, D.M. 163, 211
cooperation
    commitment to 103
    erosion of 92
    importance of 147
cooperative work environments 195
core markets/technologies 22
corporate
    cultures 37–8, 90
    names 243
    tax 244, 248, 249
Cosier, R. 89
cost-benefit analyses 103, 104
cost-saving benefits of standardisation
    115
costs, allocation of 39–40, 93, 272–3
critical mass 32, 169
Cronbach's Alpha 79, 94, 107, 122,
    133, 148
cross-border expansion 25
cross-national differences, partner firms
    154
Cullen, J.B. 53
cultural heterogeneity 200, 206–13
culturally close/distant countries 224
culture
    differences/similarities 47, 156, 193
    effects of 47–8, 67, 155–6, 191,
        196–8
culture-specificity of products 117,
    119

customer
    characteristics 28
    expectations management 132–3
    focus 126–7, 132–3
    value 129
cycles, use of JVs 21

da Rocha, A. 79, 80
Dalton, D. 89
Das, T.K. 223
database marketing 130
Datta, D.K. 22
Day, R.L. 88
decision implementation and quality
    157–8, 160, 161–4, 199–201,
    204–5, 206–13
decision-making 37–8, 194–6
definitions 4–10
Delios, A. 25–7, 49, 52, 54, 64
demographic
    composition of management teams
        198
    team heterogeneity 200, 206–13
dependence 34, 141
depreciation rates 245
descriptive statistics 208–9
Dess, G.G. 10, 52–3, 56, 63–4, 285, 289
developed countries, characteristics of
    JVs 139–40
developing countries
    characteristics of JVs 139–40
    host government demands/restrictions
        22, 30, 71–2, 143
    joint venture performance 183–4,
        223–4
    joint ventures 219–22
    motivations for FDI 181–3
Ding, D.Z. 52, 64
direct
    distribution systems 74, 172
    export subsidiaries 264
    ownership 146
discounted cash flow (DCF) analysis
    50–51
discriminant analysis 83–6, 95–9,
    109–12, 124–5, 135–6, 149–52, 263
distribution
    channels 73–4, 75, 86, 171–3, 214
    networks 31–2, 168–9, 225–6
diversification 21, 24

divestment, ease of 26
'divorce clauses' 187, 267
domestic expansion 25
dominant
    management control 139, 140, 145
    parent control 144
Doney, P.M. 154
Douglas, S.F. 114, 116, 226
Doyle, P. 131
Doz, Y. 154
Drucker, P. 24
Dyer, J.H. 154
Dymsza, W.A. 146–7, 148, 152, 175,
    188, 267–8, 275–6

earning power, impairment of 221–2
East/West stalemate 44
Eastern Bloc countries 73, 170
    see also Russia
economic
    characteristics 181
    control 45–6, 220
    costs of conflict 93
    decisions 29–30, 167–8
    growth rates 192
    independence goals 43–4, 219
    measures of performance 58–62
    nationalism 29
    performance, Thailand 241
    risk 28–9
Economic and Social Commission for
    Asia and the Pacific 181, 182, 183,
    234, 235, 237, 238–9
economies of scale 31, 115, 174
electronics industries 234–5
Emerson, R.M. 101
equity
    participation 40–42, 139–42, 143–4,
        145, 192
    risk 32–3
    structure 68
    see also majority equity participation;
        minority equity participation
equity joint ventures
    advantages of 70–71, 215, 268–9
    developing countries 219–24
    local knowledge and performance
        224–7
    performance 26–7
Ernst, D. 156, 197

established brands 74
Europe 4, 23–4, 25, 68, 224
    see also Western Europe
Evan, W.M. 5
excellence, characteristics of 51–2
exchange theories 100–101
Exclusive Economic Zone, Thailand
    254
exclusive rights to distribute/supply
    174–5
'experience curve' effect 31, 174
exploratory factor analysis 57, 76–9, 85,
    95–9, 106–7, 122–5, 144–5, 151–2,
    175, 263
exporting companies 181
expropriation, risks of 28, 167
external marketing 130

factors of production, access to 181
'fading-out' strategy of foreign
    investment 222
Fagre, N. 73, 170, 177
failure rates 20, 24–7, 33
familiarity 156, 157–8, 197, 200
Far Eastern Economic Review 241
Faulkner, D 154
Fey, C.F. 88, 89, 91, 106, 153–4, 180,
    188, 197, 270
Filley, A.C. 198
financial
    capital 176–7
    performance indicators 25, 26, 49, 51,
        53–4, 224
    statements 245–6
Foreign Business Act (2000), Thailand
    253–7
Foreign Business License, Thailand
    248, 255–7
foreign companies
    branches of 248
    control of JVs 137, 271–2
    diversification of 21
    global integration of 35–6
foreign direct investment (FDI)
    Thailand 181–3, 208, 229–30, 237–8,
        241, 242
    trend of 222
foreign market needs, adapting to 81–3,
    95–9, 123–5, 134–6, 149–52
foreigners participation, Thailand 253–7

France 120
franchise agreements 264, 265
Frank, R. 141
Franko, L.G. 7, 24, 175, 223
Friedman, W.G. 153
functional complementarity 169,
    225–6

Gatignon, H. 7
General Motors 89
Geringer, J.M. 10, 22, 47–8, 51, 52, 54,
    56, 64, 67, 223, 285, 289
Gertner, R.K. 79, 80
Ghosh, B.C. 132
global
    business environment, changes in
        22–3
    integration 35–6, 270–71
    production networks 175
globalisation of markets 115–16
goals
    attainment 102, 157–8, 161–4,
        199–201, 204–13
    compatibility in 266–7
    differences in 34, 89–90, 188–9, 197,
        267–8
Gomes-Casseres, B. 6–7, 20, 22, 31, 73,
    167, 170, 175, 223
government
    as active partners 72
    suasion 30–31, 128
Green, R.T. 115
growth 20–24
Gucci 119

Habib, G.M. 87, 88, 89, 94, 95
'hall talk' 128
Hambrick, D.C. 198
Hansen, M.H. 154
Harrigan, K.R. 6, 93, 121, 156, 187,
    188, 197, 267–8
Harvard Multinational Enterprises
    (HMNE) 24
headquarters' charges, allocation of
    39–40, 93, 272–3
Hebert, L. 10, 22, 47–8, 51, 52, 54, 56,
    64, 67, 87, 88–9, 223, 289
Hennart, J-F. 7, 26, 223
heterogeneity 154–64, 194–6, 198, 199,
    200, 203, 205

Higginbottom, D. 15, 40–41, 139–40,
    239–40
high-growth markets 33
high-technology industries 35
Hill, J.S. 114
hiring policies 94
Hladik, K.J. 29
homogeneous teams 198
homogenisation of world markets
    115–16
Hooley, G.J. 131
'horizontal communication' 128
horizontal diversification 215
host country governments
    control objectives 45–6
    policies of 43–5, 71–2, 239, 241
    pressure from 166–8
    requirements 29–31, 143
    restrictions of 21–3, 81
House, R.J. 198
Houston, F.S. 127

immigrant visas, Thailand 259–61
immigration Act (1979), Thailand
    259–62
imperfect markets 214–15, 216, 218
implementing regulations, Thailand
    Foreign Business Act (2000) 253–7
    investment promotion 257–8
    visas and immigration law 259–62
    work permits 257
import substitution policies 30, 72,
    182–3
incentives 74, 100, 172, 250–51, 252
income tax 244, 250
independent channel agents 74, 172
India 22, 208
'indigenisation policy' 46–7, 166–7,
    222
indirect export subsidiaries 264
Indonesia 13, 40, 239
industrial
    competitiveness, importance of
        marketing 131–2
    sector 24
industries 234–5
industry
    characteristics 165
    competition 76
    factors affecting IJV formation 22

structure 68
trends of IJV formation 234–6
inequality, benefits and costs 36
information impairment 218
innovation 170–71
instability
    causes of 33–40
    rates of 183–4
Institute of Certified Accountants and
        Auditors of Thailand 245
intelligence dissemination 128
inter-firm
    arrangements 216–17
    conflict 88–92
    cooperation/diversity 90–91
    organisations, JVs as 263–4
    trust 154
interactive marketing 130
internal marketing 130
internationalisation process 264–6
internalization theory 70–71, 79–80,
        214–15, 227–8
    and joint ventures 215–19
international
    capital markets 177
    marketing research 58
    marketing strategy 60, 61
    markets, access to 173–4, 226
interpersonal trust 154
intra-system transfers, control of 174–6
investment
    promotion, Thailand 229–42, 258–9
    of resources 105
Investment Facilitation Division, Thai
        Board of Investment 233
Investment Promotion Act (1977),
        Thailand 229, 232, 258, 261
Investment Services Center, Thai Board
        of Investment 231
investment services, Thai Board of
        Investment 231–3
Investor Club Association, Thai Board
        of Investment 232
involvement, levels of 188
Iran 47

Jackson, S.E. 163, 211
Jacque, L.L. 73, 79, 80, 171
Jain, S.C. 117
Janger, A.R. 52, 64

Japan
    business culture 48, 67
    foreign investment 25, 26–7, 49
    joint ventures in 47, 73, 171
    marketing strength 131
Japanese Chamber of Commerce 182
Jaworski, B.J. 127–9
Jeantrout, B. 132, 133–4
Jeffries, F.L. 154
John, G. 92
Johnson, J.L. 53
joint venture process 264–6
Julian, C.C. 14, 15, 16, 17, 22, 52, 53,
        56, 58, 64, 80–81, 83, 86, 94, 95,
        99, 104, 106, 107, 108–9, 112,
        121–2, 123–4, 125, 132, 133,
        134–5, 138, 139, 147–9, 150, 152,
        158–9, 161, 164, 176, 177, 183,
        186, 218, 219, 223, 227–8, 236,
        239, 240–41, 263, 264, 269, 273–5,
        277–84
Julin, J.A. 163, 211

Kashani, K. 115
Kaufman, P.J. 92
Kaynak, E. 202
Kellogg's 119
Kerr, S. 198
key
    success factors 57, 267
    variables 4–10
Keyser-Meyer-Olkin (KMO) measure
        76, 94, 106, 122, 133, 148
Kiesler, C.A. 105
Killing, J.P. 52, 64, 68, 139, 140, 180
Kim, T.S. 132
knowledge
    of business practices 74–5
    of companies 23, 28
    of environment 140, 171–4, 269
    expectations of partners 34
    pooling of 28, 31
    of technology 73
    see also company-specific knowledge;
        local knowledge; tacit
        knowledge
Kodak 119
Kogut, B. 6, 73, 92, 170, 223
Kohli, A.K. 127–9
Koot, W.T.M. 6, 22, 188, 266, 267–8

Korea 106, 107, 139, 140, 144–6,
    184–5, 186–7
Kotabe, M. 115
Kotler, P. 115, 130, 131
Krohn, F.B. 126
Kuei, C-H. 130
Kulthorn Kirby Limited 241
Kwan, W.W.H. 132, 202

labour costs 183
Lages, L.F. 58
Lane, H. 92
Langeard, E. 115
Laos 229
latent conflict 88
Lecraw, D.J. 73, 79, 170
Lee, C. 102, 107, 138, 139, 144–5, 152,
    184–5
Lee, J. 106, 186
less developed countries (LDCs)
    control of intra-system transfers 175
    government pressure 166
    local knowledge 186
    partner needs 270
    perceptions of FDI 43, 219
Levi's 119
Levitt, T. 115
Li, E. 202
Li, J.T. 25
licensee agreements 264, 265
Liebrenz, M. 73, 170
life cycle stage of products 120–21
light industries 234–5, 242
limited
    companies 243–6
    partnerships 246
literature
    commitment 100–101
    control 139–44
    Julian (1998) study on marketing
        performance 277–84
    marketing orientation 126–33
    marketing programme
        standardisation/adaptation
        controversy 113–18
    partners' contributions 166–77
    research agenda 277–80
    Top Management Teams 193–201
    trust 155
loan guarantees 177

local
    business practices, knowledge of
        74–5
    communication/distribution channels
        171–3, 226
    entrepreneurship 220
    environment, knowledge of 171–4,
        225
    equity participation 142–3
    knowledge 184, 186, 224–7
    management 184
    networks, formation of 183
    participation, government pressure for
        166–7
local companies
    knowledge of 23, 28
    national orientation of 35–6
local markets
    expertise in 75
    sales expansion in 182–3
local partners
    behavioural patterns of 141–2, 266
    control over 221–2, 239
    identification of 141–2, 187
    nationality of 186
location-specific knowledge 185, 218
long-term
    commitment 106
    objectives 34
    profit maximisation 217
Lovell, E.B. 5
low-cost
    manufacturing 23
    raw materials, access to 70–71,
        79–80, 86, 177, 218–19, 269
Lu, M.H. 130
Lynch, J.E. 131

Madsen, T.K. 58
Madu, C.N. 130
majority equity participation 40–42,
    222, 239, 240–41, 242
Makino, S. 25
Malaysia 13, 40, 239
management
    capabilities 25–6
    control 81–3, 95–9, 108–12, 123–5,
        134–8, 147–9, 149–52
    cultures and personal orientations 193
    processes/style 37–8, 272

see also Top Management Teams
managers' guide, IJVs 263–4
  designing ventures 270–71
  joint venture process 264–6
  major differences 275–6
  managerial implications for successful
    performance 273–5
  mutual need and commitment 268–70
  ongoing management and
    relationships 271–3
  selecting partners 266–8
manifest conflict 88–9, 94
Mankin, E. 73, 170
manufacturing
  companies 24, 182, 189, 190, 270–71
  industries 36
margin guarantees, independent channel
    agents 74
market
  access 171–4, 181
  agents 214, 216
  intelligence 127–9
  segments 114–15
  share 132–4
market characteristics 81–3, 95–9,
    107–12, 134–6, 149–52, 183,
    218–19
  access to capital resources and raw
    materials 70–71
  distribution channels 73–4
  industry competition 76
  influence on performance 61
  knowledge of local business practices
    74–5
  and marketing performance 76–86,
    177
  policies of host country governments
    71–2
  technology transfer 72–3
market entry
  barriers to 28
  benefits of JVs 173–4, 190
  imperfect markets 215, 216, 228
  stages research in 264
  use of JVs 21–4
market-oriented companies 189
market-related factors, effects on
    performance 273–5
marketing
  channels 75, 226

expertise 131, 171–4
issues, conflicts on 38–9
mix 38
objectives 2–3
orientation 129, 274
Marketing Division, Thai Board of
    Investment 231
marketing effectiveness studies 130–31
  and marketing performance 81–3,
    95–9, 107–12, 123–5, 133–6,
    149–52
  review of literature 126–33
marketing performance 54–62, 76–86
  and commitment 106–12
  composite measure of 62–3, 282–3
  and control 144–52
  definition of 3
  Julian (1998) study 277–84
  and market orientation 133–6
  and product characteristics 121–5
  single-item measure of 63–9
  Thailand 269
marketing strategies
  adaptation/standardisation 226–7
  control of 138
  linkage with performance 57, 58, 62
marketing-intensive industries 22
marketing-related issues, conflict with
    38
markets, globalisation of 115–16
Marlboro 119
matchmaking services 232
mature products 120, 121
McEvily, W. 154
Memorandums of Association 243,
    246–7
metal working industries 234–5, 242
methodology 10–19
Mexico 2
Michel, J.G. 198
Michener, P. 181
Microsoft 119
mining industries 234–5
Ministry of Commerce, Thailand 243,
    244, 246, 250, 253–6
Ministry of Finance, Thailand 244,
    245–6, 248, 252
minority
  equity participation 40, 145, 239–40
  ownership 139, 142, 186, 222

mistrust 196
monitoring, importance of 91
Morrow, P. 101
motivation 104
Mueller, C.B. 202
multidimensional aspects of performance
    49
multilevel trust 154
multiple regression analysis 82, 85–6,
    95–9, 108–12, 123–5, 134–6,
    149–52, 263
mutual
    forbearance 216
    need 268–70

Naidu, G.M. 117
national
    backgrounds 196
    characteristics 197, 198
    culture 224
    orientation 35–6, 270–71
National Economic Development
    Organization (NEDO), Australia
    131, 230
nationalism, rising tide of 219, 222
nationalistic demands 28, 29, 167–8
nationality, principal foreign partner
    66–7, 236–9, 242
negotiation phase, IJV formation 167,
    188
New Zealand 131, 132
Newcombe, J.R. 131
newly industrialised countries (NICs)
    139, 184, 236, 242
NIS Recruitment and Consulting
    Services Limited 241
Nitsch, D. 25
non-exporting companies 181
non-immigrant visas, Thailand 259–61
non-quota immigrant visas, Thailand
    259–61
non-tariff barriers 75, 166
non-tax incentives 250–51, 252
non-trading activities 248
North America 4, 25, 67, 208, 213,
    224
    see also Canada; United States
Nunnally, J.C. 159, 160, 204, 205

O'Cass, A. 158–9, 161, 164

objective measures of performance 52–3
objectives of study 1–3
Office of the Board of Investment
    (OBOI), Thailand 230–31, 251–2
Ohmae, K. 116
Omura, G.S. 115
One-Stop Service Center, Thai Board of
    Investment 232
operating characteristics 51–2
operational performance indicators 53–4
operations, control of 221
opportunism 102–3, 142, 143, 214,
    216–17, 218
organisation-to-organisation
    relationships 102
organizational
    attributes 197–8
    backgrounds 196
    behaviour literature 103
    climates 90
    control 95–9, 107–12, 123–5, 134–6,
        149–52, 274–5
    culture 224
    politics 50
organizational structures 36–8, 271
    complex forms of 192–3
    importance of 48
    of JVs 263–4
Ouchi, W.C. 48, 67
ownership 40–42
    changes 223
    and control 139, 140, 142
    levels 186
    strategies 20–24
ownership-specific assets 225

package approach to performance
    evaluation 53
Paliwoda, S. 73, 170
parent companies
    contributions to subsidiaries 181
    moulding of JVs 221–2
    objectives 192–3
    size distribution of 21
parents' objectives and performance
    measurement 54–5, 67–8
Park, S.H. 156, 197
participatory
    management styles 138
    power 101

partner contributions 165–6, 178–9,
    185–6, 189
  literature review 166–77
partner needs 180, 189–90
  and joint venture performance in
      South East Asia 183–9
  motivations for FDI in Thailand
      181–3
partners'
  assets 215
  asymmetries 187
  change of 217
  commitment/compatibility 153,
      197–8
  dependence 34
  learning between 197
  need, effects of 270
  prior relationships between 156,
      157–8
  role and functions of 94, 188, 267
  satisfaction measures 52
  selection of 187, 232, 266–8
  social knowledge of 265–6
partnerships, Thailand 246
patent
  protection 170
  strength 119–20
path regression 161, 206
Pennings, J. 156, 224
pensions 245
perceived conflict 88
perceptual incongruities 89–90
performance 43–7
  and conflict 94–9
  in developing countries 183–4, 223–4
  evaluation 47–56
  and local knowledge 224–7
  managerial implications for success
      273–5
  managerial perceptions of 140
  multiple indicators of 25
  satisfaction with 186–7
  Top Management Teams 158–64
Perrone, V. 154
Peterson, R.B. 47
Peyronnin, K. 163, 211
Phatak, A.V. 68
Philippines 13, 40, 239
Picard, J. 114
Pitt, L.F. 132, 133–4

Polaroid 120
policies, host country governments
    71–2, 219–21, 239, 241
political
  connections 75, 171, 225, 269
  processes 194–5
  risk 28–9
Pondy, L.R. 88, 91
Porter, M.E. 115
power *see* bargaining power;
    participatory power
Poynter, T. 177
pricing strategies 76
principal foreign partner
  country of origin 66–7, 236–9, 242
  equity position 40–42, 68, 145,
      239–41
private limited companies 246–7
problem-solving mechanisms 92, 276
product
  development, starting point for 131
  standardisation/adaptation 113–18,
      122–5, 226–7, 228, 275
  viability 173
product characteristics
  culture-specificity 119
  life cycle stages 28, 120–21, 122–5,
      173
  influence on performance 61, 81–3
  and marketing performance 107–12,
      121–5, 134–6, 149–52
  patent strength 119–20
  review of literature 113–18
  service and maintenance 121
product-related factors, effects on
    performance 273–5
profitability indicators 50
profits
  compounding 221
  evaluation of 49
  expectations of partners 34, 268
  maximisation of 217
  repatriation of 147, 176
promotion adaptation 118, 122–5
property rights 119–20
proprietary technology 35
protectionism 182
provident funds 245
Public Company Act, Thailand 246
public limited companies 247

public relations benefits 75, 171, 225, 269

qualitative performance indicators 54
quotas 166

Ramanujam, V. 53, 54
Ramstetter, E.D. 181
rationales, venture creation 27–33
Raveed, S.R. 184
raw materials
    access to 70–71, 79–80, 86, 177, 218–19, 269
    purchasing of 146–7, 148–9, 175–6
Reed, R. 154
regional
    operating headquarters 249–50
    trade and investment support offices 252
registered ordinary partnerships 246
Reich, R. 73, 170
relationship approach to exchange 101–3
relationships 271–3
Renforth, W. 184
repatriation of profits 147, 176
representative offices 248
research agenda for IJVs
    composite measure of marketing performance 282–3
    contributions to the literature 277–80
    developing scales 286–7
    directions for future research 286
    limitations of study 280–81
    questionnaire length 283–4
    sample size 281–2
    single versus multiple respondents 284–6
    studying foreign partner's perception of marketing performance 289
    studying sample from service sector 288–9
    testing research instrument on larger sample 288
    testing stability of constructs 287
research and development (R&D)
    benefits of joint ventures 29
    collaboration in 58
    and economies of scale 24, 31, 174
    and intelligence generation 127, 128

intensity of 22
research methodology, Top Management Teams 201–5
residual claimant status 143
resources
    allocation of 270–71
    competition for 89–90
    contribution of 275–6
    investment in 105, 188
    pooling of 189–90, 217–18, 268
retailers, needs/preferences of 127
retained hostilities 92
return on investment (ROI)
    developing countries 220–21
    and market size 28, 173
    partners' expectations 34
    rates 80, 188–9
Reynolds, J.I. 139–40
Robinson, R.B. 10, 52–3, 56, 64, 285, 289
Root, F.R. 175
Roth, K. 117
Russia 106, 154, 180, 188, 270

Sakano, T. 53
sales
    subsidiaries 264, 265
    volume 69
Samiee, S. 117
satisfaction levels 106
Saunders, J. 131
Schaan, J-L. 2, 52, 64, 91
Schoch, H.P. 132
scope of study 3–4
Seashore, S.E. 160, 204
Securities and Exchange Commission of Thailand 245
senior executives perceptions 3
service
    industries 234–5
    requirements of products 121
services, adaptation of 228, 275
Sessa, V.I. 163, 211
shared
    control 144
    equity 175
    management control 138, 139, 145, 147, 191–2
shareholdings 243, 245, 247, 253
Shenkar, O. 5

Shimada, J. 47
short-term objectives 34
Sibunruang, A. 181
Simiar, F. 47
Simmonds, K. 114
Singapore 13, 40, 132, 239
Singh, H. 80
Single measure, marketing performance
    63–9
skills acquisition 29–30, 43–4, 168, 219,
    220
Slater, S.F. 58
small numbers problem 217–18
Snowy Mountains Engineering
    Corporation 241
social
    control systems 141–4
    costs of conflict 93
    interaction research 198
    knowledge 141–2, 239, 265–6
socio-economic differences 197
Soehl, R. 114
Sohn, J.H.D. 138, 140, 141, 142, 265–6
sourcing, control of 137, 175–6
South Korea 23
specialisation 32–3
Spence, A. 141
stages approach of internationalisation
    264–6
stand-alone entities, performance
    measurement 54, 55–6
standard operating procedure as
    performance measure 49–51
standardisation, cost-saving benefits of
    115
state-owned enterprises
    as customers 173–4
    as partners 30, 143
Staw, B.M. 104
Steed, L.G. 282
Stern, L.W. 92
Still, R.R. 114
Stock Exchange of Thailand 247
Stopford, J.M. 7, 115
strategic
    alliances 154
    management 194–6
    marketing 130–31
    measurement of performance 57–62
    weapons, JVs as 22

strategy/environment coalignment 113
structured conflict 89, 91–2
study
    key variables, definitions and terms
        4–10
    major objectives 1–3
    methodology 10–11
    scope 3–4
subjective measures of performance
    52–3
subsidiary survival rates as performance
    measurement 49
supply networks, control of 175
sustainable còmpetitive advantage (SCA)
    129
synergies 178, 189–90, 268
systems marketing 130

tacit knowledge 73
Taiwan
    culture 68
    as principal foreign partners 14, 208,
        236–8, 242
Tambunlertchai, S. 182
tariffs 166
tax 75, 244, 248, 249–51
Taylor, D.B. 131–2
team
    composition, importance of 198
    heterogeneity 157, 158, 195–6, 199,
        200
    processes 156–7, 194, 195, 198–9,
        200, 201
technical
    complementarity 169, 225–6
    complexity 43
    developments, objectives for 38–9
    knowledge 73
technology
    access to 183
    assets 175
    intensive industries 117
    need for 43–4, 219
    networks 31–2, 167–8, 225–6
    transfer 35, 72–3, 80, 86, 169–71,
        269
'technology push' 131
Teng, B.S. 223
terms 4–10
Terpstra, V.H. 116

Thai Board of Investment (BOI)
   investment services 231–3, 250–52,
     262
   promotion of IJVs 42, 241, 242
   research samples 10, 11, 13, 202, 236,
     239
Thai Glass Industries 241
Thai Industrial Gases 241
Thailand
   commitment 104, 106–9, 111–12
   conflict 88, 94, 99
   control 137–40, 144–6, 148–9, 152
   culture 67, 68
   equity joint ventures 218–19, 227–8
   foreign direct investment 181–3
   government partnerships 30
   government restrictions 23, 40
   IJVs in 22, 264
   influences of marketing performance
     94–9
   marketing orientation 132–3, 134–5,
     136
   marketing performance 56, 62, 67–8,
     76, 79, 82, 86, 263, 269, 273,
     275, 278, 282–3
   minority equity participation 40–41
   partners' contributions 167, 173,
     176–7
   product characteristics 118, 121–2,
     123–5
   research 8, 10–19, 287–9
   role of Thai Board of Investment
     230–31
   trends in 233–41
   trust 164
   see also Top Management Teams,
     Thailand
Thailand, legal implications of investing
   243–6
   implementing regulations 253–62
   investment services of Thai Board of
     Investment 231–3
   organisation types 246–52
Thailand Provincial Gateway, Thai
   Board of Investment 233
The Thai Dairy Industry Authority
   Limited 241
theoretical approaches to performance
   58–9, 223–4
Tomlinson, J.W.C. 144

Top Management Teams, IJVs 191–3
   data analysis 205–13
   literature review 193–201
   research methodology 201–5
Top Management Teams, Thailand
     59–66,154–8
   cohesion 160
   communication frequency 159
   data analysis 161–4
   decision quality, decision
     implementation and goal
     attainment 160
   heterogeneity 159
   trust 159
tourist visas, Thailand 259–61
Toyo Keizai 182, 183
trade and investment support offices
   250–52
transaction cost theory 92, 103, 214–15,
   216
transit visas, Thailand 259–61
Triad 116
   see also Japan; United States; Western
     Europe
trust 153–5
   decision quality, decision
     implementation and goal
     attainment 157–8
   development of 199, 200, 201
   effects of culture 155–6
   effects of team processes 156–7
   erosion of 92
   literature review 155
   and performance 158–64
   selection of partners 266–7
   Top Management Teams 204, 206–13
   see also mistrust
turnkey contracts 49
two-partner JVs 24–7
Tybejee, T.T. 47

uncertainty 214, 216, 217–18
Ungson, G.R. 156, 197
uninational teams 157
Unit for Industrial Linkage Development
   (BUILD), Thai Board of Investment
   231
United Kingdom 131, 133
United States
   business culture 48

investment in 73
objectives of IJV formation 30, 71–2,
    171, 181, 182, 238–9
participation in IJVs 24
patents 120
research 139, 202, 208
universal brands 116
unregistered ordinary partnerships 246
urgent and essential work, Thailand
    257–8

value-added tax (VAT) 244
Vendors Meets Customers Programme,
    Thai Board of Investment 231
Venkatraman, N. 53, 54
venture creation rationales 27–33
ventures, design of 270–71
vertical integration 215
visas, Thailand 232, 259–62

Walters, P.G.P. 114
websites 232–3
Weitz, B. 48, 67, 102
Wells, Jr. L.T. 7, 73, 115, 170, 177
West, C.J. 131
Western countries 170
Western Europe 14, 25, 208, 213, 224,
    236, 238, 242

see also France; United Kingdom
Whetten, D. 90
White, P. 88
wholly owned subsidiaries (WOSs)
    decline of 46, 222
    establishment of 215, 264, 265
    failure rates 26, 27
    performance of 24, 224
    performance evaluation 49–50
Williamson, O.E. 70, 92, 214, 227
Wind, Y. 114, 116, 226
Winokur, D. 130
Wong, V. 131
Woodcock, C.P. 25
Woodhead Firth Lee Corporation
    241
work permits, Thailand 232, 257, 258,
    259, 260, 261

Yan, A. 223
Yosihara, K. 182
Young, R.G. 5, 24

Zaheer, A. 154
Zeira, Y. 5
Zeng, M. 223
zero-equity 73, 170
Zou, S. 58, 117, 122, 125